Planning Industrial Development

Planning Industrial Development

Edited by
DAVID F. WALKER
*University of Waterloo,
Ontario, Canada*

JOHN WILEY & SONS
Chichester · New York · Brisbane · Toronto

British Library Cataloguing in Publication Data:

Planning industrial development.
1. Economic policy
I. Walker, David Frank
338.9 HD82 79-40519

ISBN 0 471 27621 9

Photosetting by Thomson Press (India) Limited, New Delhi and printed by The Pitman Press, Bath, Avon.

Contributors

CHRISTOPHER R. BRYANT — *University of Waterloo, Waterloo, Ontario, Canada*

WILLIAM P. BUCK — *Inducon Consultants of Canada Ltd, Willowdale, Ontario*

ROBERT C. CHRISTIE — *Manager, Planning and Urban Affairs Department, Board of Trade of Metropolitan Toronto, Canada*

CHRISTINE FLORES — *Coral Springs, Florida, USA*

HENRY L. HUNKER — *Professor, Department of Geography and Public Administration, The Ohio State University, Columbus, Ohio, USA*

PETER LIMQUECO — *Journal of Contemporary Asia, Stockholm, Sweden*

BRUCE MCFARLANE — *Department of Politics, University of Adelaide, South Australia*

GÖKHAN MENTES — *Secretary of Planning, Ministry of Rural Affairs, Ankara, Turkey*

MAURI PALOMÄKI — *Professor of Economic Geography, Vaasa School of Economics and Business Administration, Vaasa, Finland*

JEAN-MICHEL ROUX — *Co-Partner, AREA, Paris, France*

MORGAN SANT — *School of Geography, University of New South Wales, Sydney, Australia*

BARBARA M. D. SMITH — *Centre for Urban and Regional Studies, University of Birmingham, England*

ILHAN TEKELI — *Department of City and Regional Planning, Middle East Technical University, Ankara, Turkey*

Contents

Preface

In preparing a collection of original essays with contributors from all over the world, the editor is greatly indebted to each writer for his or her cooperation. I would like to thank all authors, and particularly those who came in at short notice. Two other people played an important role: Jackie Rugwell with typing and Diana Middleton with research and editorial assistance. The figures were drawn under the direction of Gary Brannon at Waterloo.

I hope that the book will appeal equally to academics and practitioners, stimulating innovative research and action. The need for such a collection arose from my involvement with students and industrial developers at the University of Waterloo, but I trust it will benefit readers in many places throughout the world.

DAVID F. WALKER
Waterloo
April 1979

List of Tables

List of Figures

Planning Industrial Development
Edited by David F. Walker

Chapter 1

Introduction

David F. Walker

Ever since the industrial revolution a healthy, dynamic manufacturing sector has been synonymous with progress and wealth, at least in the eyes of a substantial number of people. Manufacturing processes have transformed natural materials into an ever-increasing array of products which make life more comfortable and pleasurable. At the same time, establishment of this sector is the one way in which areas or countries with limited natural endowment can break out from the restrictions imposed on them and, by human ingenuity, create prosperity. Even if parts of the world are now in the 'post-industrial society' which places more emphasis on services than goods, even if industrialization has brought social and environmental problems and increased disparity between rich and poor, nevertheless most political authorities want it. Manufacturing remains at the core of development planning.

If industry is here to stay, how can it best serve the interests of the greatest number of people? Manufacturers concern themselves primarily with efficiency and returns to investment; workers look at wages and working conditions, but the development planner is responsible for a benefit/cost analysis concerning the community at large. Are there enough jobs to avoid out-migration from the community? Could rapid expansion lead to in-migration and, if so, what would be its consequences? How stable are the jobs? Do the tax returns attributable to manufacturing outweigh the costs imposed in terms of such things as road use, sewage treatment and the extension of water or electricity. Does a particular firm impose environmental degradation of one form or another? If so, can it be cleaned up and at whose cost? And what does industrial growth do to social structure? These are some of the complex questions facing an industrial development planner. He must know manufacturing trends intimately and in addition try to match them to the objectives of the authority for which he works.

The problem with industrialization is that it seems to be inextricably bound up with an increase in spatial disparity. The growth of industry in a particular place sets into motion a set of mechanisms which encourage a continuing development there (Pred, 1965). Multiplier effects create new demands in the retail and service sectors. Expansion of manufacturing may also help other firms and through these developments encourage a cumulative process to operate, a process that sends the point of initial expansion further ahead of its rivals. Admittedly the benefits may spread to other areas, but Pred (1977) has argued convincingly that the main beneficiaries are generally a few large metropolitan areas. Spread effects via the purchase of food or materials may bring prosperity to other regions but the latter tend to be slotted into a subsidiary role. In fact as new developments are put into practice, élite groups in a few core areas tend to assume more and more control of most of the space-economy, which forms the periphery (Friedmann, 1972).

Friedmann (1966, pp. 35–7) argues that the preindustrial period was characterized by a large number of relatively isolated, self-sufficient regions but that industrialization encouraged primacy, the condition of one city's domination of the space-economy of a nation. This city tends to drain the rest of the nation of its entrepreneurs, manpower and capital. Roux's essay (Chapter 4 in this volume) echoes this view; he argues that there is a fundamental conflict between industry and region. For Friedmann, however, primacy is a stage that may be passed. As development continues, various subcentres grow and expand their fields of influence, leaving less developed 'intermetropolitan peripheries' in-between. Gradually the whole national space-economy becomes functionally organized and all areas benefit to the full from economic development.

The extension of metropolitan influence depends on the attractiveness of the periphery to the city population (Friedmann and Miller, 1965). Peripheries have resources, space and beautiful landscapes and are, therefore, attractive for all kinds of recreational and cultural uses as well as certain types of economic activities including some manufacturing operations. This spread, which is certainly evident in the western world, depends, however, on increasing income, leisure and mobility. It is questionable if these three conditions can be met in sufficient degree across the world for the kind of spatial interdependence envisaged by Friedmann and Miller to be achieved in all countries. Further, it looks as though mobility could now begin to decline under the influence of high energy costs and we may revert to a higher degree of regional self-sufficiency.

Such a reversed trend would be in line with current political developments. In many parts of the world there is a reaction to increased centralization and a demand for greater regional autonomy. This is most evident in cases of cultural difference—Québecois, Scots, Welsh, Basques, Kurds, Somalis are but a few such minorities—but it is not solely a cry for cultural identity. It involves an attempt to fight alienation from the sources of political and economic power, a desire to control more of one's own life. On the economic front it involves fighting the multinationals and a branch plant economy with independent businesses and intermediate technology.

The 'small is beautiful' philosophy of E.F. Schumacher (1974) has made considerable inroads into popular attitudes and current policy. Schumacher questions a technology which has brought inhuman lifestyles, threatens the natural environment and makes demands upon non-renewable resources such that they could be exhausted in the foreseeable future. Twentieth-century industrial development seems to be creating problems faster than solutions. Modern technology, argues Schumacher, has replaced creative, interesting work by unenjoyable tasks and a high proportion of unproductive jobs. 'Mass production' should be replaced with 'production by the masses' and intermediate technology, 'making use of the best of modern knowledge and experience ... conducive to decentralisation, compatible with the laws of ecology, gentle in its use of scarce resources, and designed to serve the human person instead of making him the servant of machines', should be created (p. 128).

Schumacher's ideas imply smaller firms and local ownership. They, therefore, correspond well to cries for independence based on non-economic arguments. Small business encouragement has emerged as an important development strategy and there is no doubt that governments see it as a way of holding on to or regaining economic independence. In Canada, several provincial governments are also trying to encourage consumers to buy local products while the Federation of Independent Business has called for greater regional self-sufficiency. But can these sentiments and policies make inroads against the power of the giant corporations that have now emerged? Galbraith (1972, pp. 373–83) certainly argues that modern technology and the complex organization of these corporations has brought them into close co-operation with the state, that state planning is replacing the market for many of their products, and that technology has created trends which lead to increasing similarity of socialist and capitalist countries in terms of state/corporation relationships.

The desire and power of political spatial units to control their own destiny is of fundamental importance to development planning but this relevance does not only apply to one scale. At an international level, many analysts now see the poorer countries of the world as being the victims of the same kind of spatial imbalance that industrialization has brought within other, more developed countries. As long as there are developed countries with expanding economies, others will be cast in the role of suppliers of food and materials. Frank (1966) in fact argues that the process has been more pernicious, that systematic underdevelopment has been practised by the European and North American advanced capitalist nations. Many of today's poorer countries have had a very long history which has included in many cases stages of quite advanced civilization; their underdevelopment is a product of capitalist expansion in the core areas of the world (metropoles) with its consequent colonial penetration into peripheries (satellites). This structure drew capital, minerals, food and often slave labour from the satellite countries to support expansion in the metropoles. Eventually as industrialization proceeded, the satellites increasingly became the markets for manufactured products. Under colonial regimes, manufacturing was kept to a minimum in satellite countries.

Although most colonies have now attained independence, the historical legacy of colonialism is still with them, and it is difficult to break a whole economic structure in the matter of a few decades. In many cases the most powerful group in such countries benefits from close ties with advanced western countries and encourages the existing pattern to remain. Most formerly colonial countries have tried to industrialize but have found it difficult to do so because they are relatively poor and depend on world markets for one or a few materials or food items (prices fluctuate widely and have, apart from petroleum, tended to decline relative to manufactured goods). The most common strategy is one of import substitution, that is production of goods for which a national market exists but which was formerly supplied from outside. Apart from the general difficulties associated with embarking on industrialization (establishing infrastructure, skilled manpower, managers, etc.), the key problem involves relationships with companies that formerly supplied the market. Most countries have encouraged large multinationals to build factories within their territory instead of supplying from outside. While this creates jobs, dependence remains and there is little stimulus to local entrepreneurship, research or anything which will provide the basis for future industrial strength. Indeed the logical outcome, at its best, is probably an industrial structure such as Canada's with few strong national companies, low research and development, a high degree of foreign ownership and continuous threat of industrial decline in the absence of a high degree of protection (Britton and Gilmour, 1978).

The alternative is to make a break, to sever the ties and attempt to create a strong indigenous business sector. Japan did this through strong protectionism, other countries have nationalized certain industries and a few have opted for a socialist planned economy. It has not proved easy to carry through any of these options. The second and third in particular involve a fight with powerful national élites as well as multinational interests and the governments of their home countries. Implementation has frequently involved revolution, economic sanctions or very strained international relations. Cuba's break, for example, required a revolution, while Chile's attempt through democratic change was thwarted largely by multinational and United States' government action.

In many ways the less developed regions within a country are in the same situation, that is one of dependency which is difficult to break. Larger companies tend to have their offices in the core areas (Pred, 1977) and the peripheries find themselves unindustrialized and lacking economic or political power. In many cases their current situation has been brought about at least partly by closures, mergers and takeovers that broke an initial indigenous base (Acheson, 1972). As Leigh and North (1976) demonstrate, such movements tend to benefit core areas by transferring linkages (especially service linkages) to them. Thus poorer regions face the need to build up their own firms and to counteract the power of the large corporation in their economies. Only in cases of really rich resources and opportunities has this been relatively easy (for example, post-second World War California). The difficulty lies in the lack of any formal powers over most crucial economic areas. In federal states, however, provinces (or states) do possess a range of powers that give them the opportunity to behave more like national governments (see Chapter 6).

Roux in his essay (Chapter 4) argues that spatial imbalance has been carried down to even smaller miniregions, causing the life blood to be drawn out of rural areas and concentrated in urban centres where most industries locate. We have become too concerned in our planning with a few points (growth centres) and forgotten the spaces in between them. At a micro scale, as well, are the problems of balance between ageing city centres and fast-growing modern suburbs. At this scale, local municipalities in most countries do have some powers, but they are almost always small in comparison to the economic forces in operation.

If industry is inevitably intertwined with spatial imbalance, industrial development planning must be based on attitudes towards this imbalance. Do people have a right to live where they wish or should they move at the dictates of the location of manufacturing? Is imbalance all right at the micro scale but not at the macro scale? Should inefficient locational patterns be promoted to benefit the welfare of the majority? These are some of the questions which arise. But first it is important to know more about places and industry.

PLACES

Without a thorough knowledge of the area for which he is working, no industrial developer can hope to operate successfully. It is essential to know what is there; to know about food supplies, minerals, power resources, semifinished material components, services, labour supply, managers, entrepreneurs and local markets. It is vital to know about relative location, the time or cost of obtaining necessities and of reaching markets, and how these compare with the situation of competitors. Most important, however, is an appreciation of the current state of affairs in the light of past trends and future potential. Location decisions are generally long-run ones and, even if they are not, the resulting capital investments will remain for a long time. Thus an exclusively short-run perspective is completely inappropriate for an economic developer.

A consideration of spatial inequality and the development of cores and peripheries is quite instructive in categorizing regions. Friedmann (1966, pp. 66–101), in fact, set up such a schema along with corresponding policy prescriptions. Core regions are the loci of economic growth and development but can still suffer from adverse external conditions, so their businessmen and planners must be ready to adapt. In developed countries such areas often suffer from high costs, congestion and outdated facilities, while in less developed countries, rapid growth rates may cause tremendous social problems (housing shortages, inadequate services, congestion, health and sanitation difficulties, tension between different groups, political unrest, etc.). Core area problems primarily involve trying to order and plan the activities that are taking place naturally. Thus, a developer in these circumstances, while not neglecting existing firms, will be mainly concerned with efficient land-use planning. Industrial parks must be well located with respect to transport connections and labour supply, suitable infrastructure must be provided, sufficient industrial land should be available, etc. In particular, long-term projections are needed so that the authorities can keep ahead of demand and avoid inappropriate growth patterns.

Some important industrial regions, perhaps even core regions, eventually decline and become, in Friedmann's terms, downward-transitional areas. Friedmann himself, admittedly, is mainly concerned with rural areas that lack the ability to support existing population levels, but he also notes that the same cycle of increasing poverty can characterize old mining areas. Many older industrial areas, especially in Europe, are in much the same situation. Their initial rationale was usually based on coal and perhaps small iron deposits; now their heavier industries can no longer compete in the face of declining local materials, ageing plant and modern, efficient competitors, and their outdated infrastructure is not attractive to new business. In such situations, the development planner has a choice of planning for decline or beginning a mammoth task of new job creation in the face of a hostile environment. The task may well be compounded by the fact that major firms in the area are controlled from outside and lack any commitment to its stabilization or economic wellbeing.

In the opposite situation are upward-transitional areas, where significant growth impulses are already present. They have potential, which has previously not been recognized or, at least, not exploited. At the extreme are resource frontiers with little or no population but rich resources. In other cases, long-settled areas may be found to have resources that are in demand (Middle Eastern petroleum, for example) or locations which acquire new significance (for instance, superports such as Milford Haven or areas like Florida or California that have benefited from population movements to warmer climates). The nature of an industrial development strategy for these areas depends partly on their potential for permanent settlement; some resource areas, for example, are very harsh and probably will not attract many people. Given sizeable populations, however, the key element of strategy is likely to involve the question of ownership. The development impulse frequently comes from outside the area and firms based in a core area will wish to exploit the opportunity. In many cases, highly dependent economies have been built up. Where possible, it would appear to be much better for local people, either individually or through their authorities, to take a share in the action from the start. This would help to keep development more in line with regional needs and could well stimulate a more creative indigenous business sector.

The fact is, however, that many countries and even more regions already find themselves in highly dependent situations as a result of the events of the past few centuries. The relevant question then, is how to break out of a dependency situation. For nations, there is the option of nationalization, which can be used to great effect if the product concerned is in great demand in relation to supply, and if the country concerned is strong enough to face opposition from losing parties. It may also be possible to buy firms or, at least, to take a sizeable number of shares. A second strategy is to widen the industrial base. The most popular approach is by means of import substitution. This builds up the industrial sector and reduces dependency but its effects may be quite limited. If, for example, multinationals just build a branch plant in the country, dependency is not reduced very much and the materials for the plant will probably all be imported (Asiodu, 1977, pp. 338–339; Dos Santos, 1973). For long-term results it seems essential to build up an indigenous manufacturing sector, first to supply the local market but ultimately to compete in the rest of the country and the world. This involves emphases on technical and managerial training, encouragement of entrepreneurs and an effort to persuade the local wealthy to invest in business rather than spending their money on imported luxuries. It may also imply protective measures against outside competition at least for a while; the lack of ability of regions to protect themselves is one of the additional difficulties they face in comparison to nations.

The municipal industrial planner is less directly involved with these broad issues but, to appreciate the potential of his city, an understanding of the national and regional context is certainly essential. The general economic situation of the broader unit will govern the scale of potential activities of cities within it. The other main element is the relative status of each city. What kind of a city system is present (see Berry and Horton, 1970, pp. 1–249)? Is it highly primate, with one centre dominating the economy, or more akin to the rank-size rule? The municipal developer must know where his centre fits in and appreciate its internal and external linkages. The size of the city has relevance too. Norcliffe (1975, pp. 240–245) has shown the tendency of certain important location factors—infrastructure, specialized services, face-to-face communication—to be more readily available with increasing city size. Administrative, head office functions particularly concentrate in larger cities of core regions. Finally, the existing employment structure and current trends in employment play a major role in categorizing a place and suggesting its future potential. At least an analysis of employment indicates what has or has not worked in the past and it should provide some clues as to the reasons why.

INDUSTRIES

A tremendous number of studies have analysed location factors affecting manufacturing in numerous countries, regions and cities. Out of this some useful generalizations have arisen; for example, that transportation is a less important factor than it once was (Norcliffe, 1975; United Nations, 1967, pp. 1–15) and that access to market and labour supply are usually the most important elements in a location decision (Haggett, 1965, pp. 135–136, United Nations, 1967, pp. 1–5). Attempts to establish theories of industrial location with real predictive power, however, have not been very successful. Since the valuable work of Isard (1956), Greenhut (1956; 1963) and Smith (1971), it has become increasingly clear that the issues are very much more complex than they were originally thought to be.

One of the problems was that the theories had tended to follow economics in its assumption of 'economic man', implying economic optimization, perfect knowledge and complete ability to calculate a course of action even when the data were highly complex. Although Greenhut (1963) and Isard (1969) later used game-theoretic formulations to look at the difficulties posed by risk and uncertainty, their actors continued to be optimizers and to have incredible computing powers. From other sources, however, a different view of business behaviour was emerging. Simon (1957, p. 198; 1959) developed the concepts of 'satisficing', with decision-makers setting objectives and taking the first solution which satisfies them, and 'bounded rationality', the idea that decision-makers limit their field of considerations and then behave rationally with respect to this 'bounded' view. The work of Simon and his colleagues attracted considerable attention and Pred (1967) used it in his revision of location theory.

Most industrial location theory also implied perfect competition and small firms, conditions not appropriate to twentieth-century reality. In 1960, McNee called for recognition of the growing importance of large corporations in the economy and set off a spate of studies which looked at corporate spatial planning and the expansions and adaptations of firms over time (for example, Fleming and Krumme, 1968; Steed, 1968; Hayter, 1976). It is now clear that many branch plant decisions can only be fully explained in terms of corporate strategy rather than on the basis of objective economic facts. Moreover, conflicts within the firm may well influence that strategy. The outcome may depend on the strongest executive or on a compromise worked out between department heads (Cyert and March, 1963).

Locational choices depend ultimately on objectives, but objectives may differ. Perhaps the most important variation concerns the often unconscious limitation of areas within which the firm decides to look for a site. Political viewpoints may rule out certain countries for multinationals, while provinces or states may also have the 'wrong' government. There is also a very strong bias in favour of the known over the unknown so that small companies tend to locate near to the residence of the original entrepreneur and expand their horizons only with increasing size. Even quite large companies have an appreciable home bias and almost all favour their home country. A satisficing search procedure, which involves the acceptance of the first satisfactory solution, means that nearby locations will be chosen because they will be found first. Thus, small companies are located in unlikely places and a really major success could see a town build up around the entrepreneur. Add to this the complications of corporate strategy for multiplant firms, differences in security consciousness which lead to variations in reactions to risk and uncertainty (Bowman, 1958; Edwards, 1954; Simon, 1959), and variations in the desire for growth, it is hard to project a particular locational response to a specific economic situation. Perhaps there are some generalizations to be made, but little work has yet been done to discover them (Walker, 1975, pp. 145–147).

In terms of long-run beneficial economic development, it is probably more important to try to categorize firms on the basis of their day-to-day behaviour rather than on their choice of new locations. This could provide clues as to the most helpful industrial investment. Studies of goods linkages have not shown consistent patterns by firm size or ownership type. There is a tendency for multiplant companies to have a wider range of contacts than smaller ones, but many specialized small firms have surprisingly long links. Much seems to depend on the type of firm and the environment. Beyers (1974, pp. 107–111), for example, showed very restricted linkages for Boeing in the Pacific North West, while studies of metalworking in Hamilton, Ontario, show that American subsidiaries are highly linked into the industrialized southern Ontario economy (Bater and Walker, 1974, pp. 238–141).

On services linkages, however, the evidence is more clearcut. All firms buy a high proportion of services locally but it is clear that branch plants buy less per employee than locally owned companies (Bater and Walker, 1977). They consistently rely on head office for much legal and financial work, and for computer, technical and managerial services. In addition, machine repair and transportation are more likely to be bought from distant companies. Perhaps even more dangerous is the lack of research and innovation in most branches (Science Council of Canada, 1971; Thwaites, 1978, p. 457) because this cuts off the potential for future independent local expansion. It must be recognized, then, that reliance on branches reduces local multipliers and stifles the potential for change. It often also involves the best jobs being given to outsiders imported by the parent company from another part of the organization (Watt, 1977, pp. 131–136).

All this suggests a more active interest in local inventors, innovators and entrepreneurs, and perhaps a reorientation of policy away from incentive schemes for factory building and expansion by allcomers (Buck, Middleton, and Walker, 1979). In addition, much more attention should be paid to changes in ownership that allow local control of existing companies to slip away. If businesses are built up to a certain scale and then taken over or merged into larger enterprises controlled from elsewhere, they become branches with the attendant problems discussed above. On a national scale such loss of control has provoked considerable reaction in many countries, but on a regional or urban level its implications have not been fully appreciated. Many companies go through a crisis at a certain scale of production, find themselves short of cash and sell out. Careful support programmes may be able to prevent such a turn of events.

THE INDUSTRIAL DEVELOPMENT PLANNER

Those concerned with trying to plan for industrial development have an unenviable task, faced as they are with a dynamic and fluid situation in terms of economic circumstance, spatial imbalances, industrial behaviour, political reality and planning policies. The contention here is that this role depends primarily on a thorough appreciation of spatial relationships. In serving a municipality, region or country, a development planner must know where his area fits in spatially, the nature of its potential in terms of comparative advantage, and the way it is perceived by manufacturers. In devising strategies, the short and long-term spatial implications must be thought through carefully if self-sustained development is to be initiated or continued.

This viewpoint is based on the belief that, while interdependency between places is inevitable and indeed a major feature in specialization and efficiency, dependency and lack of control over one's affairs is unacceptable from a human point of view, impedes economic development, prevents self-sustained growth and is therefore detrimental to human welfare. Thus a knowledge of the flows of people, goods, services, technology and capital is important and an appreciation of the relationship between these and ownership patterns essential. Perhaps most fundamental of all is the flow of capital (see Chapter 4) and the recognition that outside investment has to be paid for. If it is direct rather than portfolio investment it will be paid in the form of profits forever. This is not to suggest that such investment may never be necessary, only to suggest that the cost has not always been counted.

From a knowledge of where a place stands and how it functions spatially, a development strategy can be built up. It will aim to satisfy the objectives set by the political authorities but all the traditional industrial development functions should fit into it. Detailed technical and marketing studies can be produced on sectors which have promise; the potential for import substitution can be investigated; promotional work will be necessary to translate opportunities into activities; support and advisory programmes can help existing companies to face problem situations, and public initiative may be taken to provide necessary infrastructure or to enter production in some sectors. All these, however, only make sense if they correspond to the needs of the particular country, region or city: they must be selective. The same applies to the character of more detailed industrial planning at the municipal level. The nature of zoning, industrial parks and environmental controls should correspond to the particular attributes of a community.

The proper appreciation of an area should lead to a recognition of its industrial limitations and, therefore, of the costs of certain policy initiatives. High hopes have often been held out for the rapid improvement of areas with very deep-seated problems, but the costs of maintaining downward-transitional areas in particular may be very high. Despite the resistance to out-migration and its deleterious social effects, policies of moving people out to jobs must at least be considered. Moreover, control policies may undermine the prosperity of other places, as has happened in London and the West Midlands (see Chapter 10). This points up the need for policy review and the recognition that development planners must be prepared to adapt to changing conditions.

This book cannot do justice to all themes related to industrial development planning and it does focus on development within countries rather than on national strategies. No essays on details of technical or managerial support programmes are provided. Rather the emphasis is on how these fit into planning strategies. Finally, despite reference to many countries, it is impossible to cover all, or even a fully representative sample. The objective has been to provide a selection useful to all except communist countries, where planning circumstances are completely different from elsewhere. The book, however, is not only designed for the industrial West and several essays reflect Marxist perspectives and Third World circumstances.

We start with a review of the evolution of industrial development as a distinct profession in North America. Henry Hunker (Chapter 2) shows how, particularly in the United States, development practice has been linked to the private sector; only recently, and especially in Canada, has governmental economic development been prominent. In contrast to many parts of the world, and in particular Europe, development planning has grown up as a separate entity from planning in general, and industrial commissioners in North America tend to feel an affinity for industrialists rather than civil servants or planners. In contrast to this chapter is a discussion of Marxist viewpoints on industrial development, with special emphasis on its applications to the Third World, provided by Peter Limqueco and Bruce McFarlane (Chapter 3). They examine Soviet experience for pointers to crucial planning issues in socialist states. The problem of the extent to which reliance should be placed on foreign technology is given extended treatment with reference to Vietnam.

Three essays then consider some particular issues in regional industrial development. Jean-Michel Roux (Chapter 4) notes the conflict between the kind of long-distance, impersonal linkages implied by industrialization and the natural local interrelationships found in small, traditional regions. He focuses on the harmful effects of industrial development and especially its tendency to concentrate attention on urban areas. To remedy the latter, the essay by Christopher Bryant (Chapter 5) deals with the scope for manufacturing in rural development. While Bryant notes the difficulties of remote areas, he shows potential for rural areas within range of metropolitan centres. Finally, my own contribution (Chapter 6) stresses the effect of the political organization of a country, especially the powers of various types of government, in increasing the complexity of development planning. Federal countries receive attention because of the interesting play between federal and provincial jurisdictions.

Two essays about large corporations then follow (Chapter 7 and 8). Both discuss the Third World and reflect deep concerns about the ability of corporations to thwart planning objective in those countries. As already noted, similar anxieties are found in the west as well. Ilhan Tekeli and Gökhan Mentes show how holding companies in Turkey have grown to control a wide range of financial, commercial and industrial activities all over the country. Christine Flores draws attention to difficulties faced by South-east Asian countries in setting up national development strategies and in coping with local planning situations. In many cases, local élites link with multinationals against the best interests of the citizens at large.

A group of four essays then examine industrial development planning at various scales. Mauri Palomäki (Chapter 9) discusses the role of industrial location in the broad scheme of dealing with regional disparity in Finland, noting the necessity of industry being considered as only one element in a total programme. Barbara Smith (Chapter 10) gives a very detailed account of metropolitan area development with reference to the West Midlands, a strongly industrial area in Britain. Redevelopment of central city manufacturing is the topic of Robert Christie's essay (Chapter 11), which is concerned with the considerable amount of research and policy implementation in Toronto, Canada. At the micro scale, William Buck outlines the current best practice for industrial park planning (Chapter 12).

In a concluding essay (Chapter 13), Morgan Sant draws our attention back to the primary focus of policy, the consideration of human welfare. He argues that, if economic activities are to be located with greater equality and improved environmental conditions in mind, more attention must be paid to political and institutional frameworks. This view echoes many of the essays in the book. Sant reminds us that in a welfare approach towards spatial patterns three elements—economic disparities, spatial accessibility to services and facilities, and negative externalities—are important. He then goes on to suggest some policy criteria: sensitivity to specific needs, direct action against conditions which lead to individual deprivation, long-term perspective, and an ultimate objective of removing impediments to progress. Sant discusses the planning process itself, covering issues concerning the way in which policies are formulated and implemented. Finally he reviews British regional policy in the light of his approach. Current dissatisfaction with the results of many years of British policy should serve as a timely reminder to those in the development planning profession that their task is not an easy one. In addition to the complexities already discussed, there is currently a very uncertain climate as to what society should be aiming for. Unless that is clear, it is hard to formulate policies and strategies. Adaptability is perhaps the key quality required of anyone in the field.

REFERENCES

Acheson, T. W. (1972). 'The National Policy and the industrialization of the Maritimes, 1880–1910'. *Acadiensis*, **1**, 3–28.

Asiodu, P. C. (1977). 'Planning for further industrial development in Nigeria'. In O. Teriba and M. O. Kayode (eds.), *Industrial Development in Nigeria*, Ibadan University Press, Ibadan, pp. 338–347.

Bater, J. H. and Walker, D. F. (1974). 'Aspects of industrial linkage: the example of the Hamilton metalworking complex'. *Révue de Géographie de Montréal*, **28**, 3, 233–243.

Bater, J. H. and Walker, D. F. (1977). 'Industrial services: literature and research prospects'. In D. F. Walker (ed.) *Industrial Services*, Department of Geography, University of Waterloo, Waterloo, pp. 1–24.

Berry, B. J. L. and Horton, F. E. (eds.) (1970). *Geographic Perspectives on Urban Systems*, Prentice-Hall, Englewood Cliffs, New Jersey.

Beyers, W. B. (1974). 'On the geographical properties of growth center linkage systems'. *Economic Geography*, **50**, 203–218.

Bowman, M. J. (ed.) (1958). *Expectations, Uncertainty, and Business Behavior*, Social Science Research Council, Committee on Business Enterprise Research, New York.

Britton, J. N. H. and Gilmour, J. M. (1978). *The Weakest Link: A Technological Perspective on Canadian Industrial Underdevelopment*, Science Council of Canada, Ottawa.

Buck, W. P., Middleton, D. J., and Walker, D. F. (1979). 'Encouraging innovative entrepreneurship: a neglected aspect of development policy'. In D. F. Walker (ed.), *The Human Dimension of Industrial Development*, Department of Geography, University of Waterloo, Waterloo.

Cyert, R. M. and March, J. G. (1963). *A Behavioral Theory of the Firm*, Prentice-Hall, Englewood Cliffs, New Jersey.

Dos Santos, T. (1973). 'The structure of dependence'. In C. K. Wilber (ed.) *The Political Economy of Development and Underdevelopment*, Random House, New York, pp. 109–117.

Edwards, W. (1954). 'The theory of decision making'. *Psychological Bulletin*, **51**, 380–417.

Fleming, D. K. and Krumme, G. (1968). 'The Royal Hoesch Union, case analysis of adjustment patterns in the European steel industry'. *Tijdschrift voor Economische en Sociale Geografie*, **59**, 177–199.

Frank, A. G. (1966). 'The development of underdevelopment'. *Monthly Review*, **18**, 17–31.

Friedmann, J. (1966). *Regional Development Policy: A Cass Study of Venezuela*, MIT Press, Cambridge, Mass.

Friedmann, J. (1972). 'A general theory of polarized development'. In N. M. Hansen (ed.), *Growth Centers in Regional Economic Development*, Free Press, New York, 82–107.

Friedmann, J. and Miller, J. (1965). 'The urban field'. *Journal, American Institute of Planners*, **31**, 312–320.

Galbraith, J. K. (1972). *The New Industrial State*, Revised edition, Mentor, New York.

Greenhut, M. (1956), *Plant Location in Theory and Practise*, The University of North Carolina Press, Chapel Hill.

Greenhut, M. (1963). *Microeconomics and the Space Economy*, Scott, Foresman and Co., Chicago.

Haggett, P. (1965). *Locational Analysis in Human Geography*, Edward Arnold, London.

Hayter, R. (1976). 'Corporate strategies and industrial change in the Canadian forest product industries'. *The Geographical Review*, **66**, 109–228.

Isard, W. (1956). *Location and Space-Economy*, MIT Press, Cambridge, Mass.

Isard, W. (1969). *General Theory: Social, Political, Economic and Regional*, MIT Press, Cambridge, Mass.

Leigh, R. and North, D. J. (1976). 'The spatial consequences of takeovers in some British industries and their implications for regional development' (mimeo), Industrial Research Project, Middlesex Polytechnic, England.

McNee, R. (1960). 'Towards a more humanistic economic geography: the geography of enterprise'. *Tijdschrift voor Economische en Sociale Geografie*, **51**, 201–206.

Norcliffe, G. B. (1975). 'A theory of manufacturing places'. In L. Collins and D. F. Walker (eds.) *Locational Dynamics of Manufacturing Activity*, John Wiley, London, 19–57.

Pred, A. R. (1965). 'Industrialization, initial advantage and American metropolitan growth'. *Geographical Review*, **55**, 158–185.

Pred, A. R. (1967). *Behavior and Location, Part 1*, C. W. K. Gleerup, Lund.

Pred, A. R. (1977). *City-Systems in Advanced Economies*, Hutchinson, London.

Schumacher, E. F. (1974). *Small is Beautiful*, Abacus, London.

Science Council of Canada (1971). *The Multinational Firm, Foreign Direct Investment, and Canadian Science Policy*, Ottawa.

Simon, H. A. (1957). *Models of Man: Social and Rational*, John Wiley, New York.

Simon, H. A. (1959). 'Theories of decision-making in economics and behavioral science'. *American Economic Review*, **49**, 153–283.

Smith, D. M. (1971). *Industrial Location: An Economic–Geographical Analysis*, John Wiley, New York.

Steed, G. P. F. (1968). 'The changing milieu of the firm: a case study of a shipbuilding concern'. *Annals, Association of American Geographers*, **58**, 506–525.

Thwaites, A. T. (1978). 'Technological change, mobile plants and regional development'. *Regional Studies*, **12**, 4, 445–461.

United Nations (1967). *Criteria for Location of Industrial Plants: Changes and Problems*, New York.

Walker, D. F. (1975). 'A behavioural approach to industrial location'. In L. Collins and D. F. Walker (eds.) *Locational Dynamics of Manufacturing Activity*, John Wiley, London, pp. 135–158.

Watt, J. A. (1977). 'The impact of a growth centre on labour migration: The Strait of Canso, Nova Scotia', unpublished MA thesis, University of Waterloo.

Planning Industrial Development
Edited by David F. Walker

Chapter 2

The Evolution of Industrial Development Planning in North America

Henry L. Hunker

INTRODUCTION

'... the attraction of manufacturing activity has been synonymous with industrial development. Almost to the exclusion of any other activity, North American industrial development was seen as smokestack-chasing and little else.' So states Richard Preston, President of the American Industrial Development Council's Educational Foundation, in the publication, *The Universe of Industrial Development* (1974, p. 8). Our purpose here is to examine the concept of industrial development and its place in the broader development spectrum, to review the evolution of industrial development practice in North America, to consider the forces that helped shape that evolution, and, finally, to assess the goals and objectives of North American industrial development.

Definitions

It is important to distinguish between the terms *economic development* and *industrial development*, and between the concepts that apply to each. Essentially, economic development is a generic term. It embraces all forms of economic activity that serve to further the development of a given political or spatial unit. Industrial development is more specific in its connotation and use. If, as Preston and other veterans of the industrial development profession express it, 'Industrial development means chasing smokestacks ... ' then it is a field distinct from the broad subject of economic development, in many ways, and yet a vital part of it.

Economic development whether with respect to a developed or an under-developed society, is concerned with the development and growth of the economy. Development and growth may be measured in terms of employment, increased per capita income, capital accumulation, improved socio-economic conditions, political stability, and in other ways. To achieve full fledged economic development requires attention to the entire set of productive sectors in the society and to the relationship of the society to other societies.

To a considerable degree, these same conditions do not apply to industrial development, at least in the traditional sense. And yet, effective industrial development may be essential to full fledged and successful economic development. Certainly, the mature and relatively stable modern nation has evolved with a highly sophisticated industrial economy basic to its development. Modern, underdeveloped nations—such as many of those in Latin America and Africa—currently attempting to improve the economic and social wellbeing of their peoples, as well as their political stability and national prestige, have observed this and, as a consequence, view industrial development (that is, manufacturing) as a primary goal. Gunnar Myrdal (1956, p. 226) in discussing these economies and in explaining their point of view, observes that '... the development of manufacturing industry has been concomitant with ... spectacular economic progress and rise in levels of living'. He notes that this is especially true in those societies with a high ratio of population to resources (land): '... the successful exploitation of a more favorable relation between population and natural resources requires mostly the growth of manufacturing industry'. Gill (1973, p. 28) apparently agrees, noting that in the underdeveloped society 'Economic development ... is regularly accompanied by an increase in the percentage importance of industry relative to agriculture'.

It is obvious, in reviewing the development history of the United States and Canada, that the return to be gained from the manufacturing enterprise was recognized in colonial North America even though manufacturing industry was in its infancy. It is just as obvious that present growth policies of the dynamic parts of the society as well as those policies aimed at aiding economically distressed or depressed areas are still focused upon the productive and generative character of the manufacturing enterprise.

The point is that the goals of industrial development have differed from the goals associated with economic development, although the results of the former serve to affect the latter in no small degree. Industrial development has, in effect, been concerned with one sector of the economy—manufacturing—and, as a professional field of activity, has kept narrowly to that concern. Only recently has the industrial development profession experienced several philosophical changes that have served to broaden the scope of the profession to include, on the one hand, interest in and attention to the non-manufacturing activities of a society—notably, the importance of the tertiary sector of the economy and the impact of tertiary sector locations and relocations upon society—and, on the other, to recognize that dedication to the narrowly prescribed field of industrial development is not enough. There is widespread understanding by industrial developers that the impact of any location decision must be measured not only in terms of the number of plants located, jobs created, and payrolls increased—noble as these achievements may be—but in terms of the impact of the industrial location upon the physical environment and upon the social and economic character of the community in which the development has taken place as well. The expression *total development* has become a part of the lexicon of the development profession as it recognizes its commitment to concerns for the total community as it is affected by any new development.

Background

The history of industrial development in the United States and Canada has antecedents in the initial efforts at political and economic development of the North American continent. Yet these early efforts cannot be construed as being part of an organized development effort nor did industrial development, as such, have a place in the scheme of things. There is, nonetheless, an obvious line of descent from precolonial and colonial times to the present with respect to philosophies of development, the means whereby development was achieved, and the factors affecting the development process.

A review of United States' and Canadian development history suggests that varied and inconsistent approaches to development have been the rule. No doubt this fact stems from several conditions:

1. The nature and intent of French and British colonial policy upon the continent.
2. The changing character of the political philosophies of the emerging two nations as reflected in development goals.
3. The changing nature of social and economic goals in the two societies which were, subsequently, reflected in the kind of development undertaken.
4. The changing governmental and business philosophies that prevailed in the two countries.

In both nations, there has been a significant drift in development philosophy, conscious or not, from positions in which government at several levels has served to stimulate development, to positions in which representatives of the private sector have been given a free hand, not necessarily always in a free market setting, in initiating and carrying out development.

Certainly, an important set of questions concerning the historical development process relates to public policy—that is, to what extent has there been a conscious policy either to encourage or retard development? To what extent has economic development policy served the purposes of the national governments in attaining their larger goals of national security and political stability? And finally, what has been the role of industrial development, *per se*, in the process?

There is evidence in colonial North America of some forms of 'planned' economic development, just as there is evidence of such planning today in the various regional commissions organized to foster development in areas described as lagging or depressed. In addition, there is abundant evidence of the role that the several governments—national, state or provincial, and town—played in rendering assistance to the industrial undertaking. At the same time, a concept of a free enterprise economic system was being moulded, a concept that has persisted to the present with modifications. Surely, the larger share of the development that has occurred and much of the initiative for development today has been generated by organizations and individuals identified with the private sector.[1]

THE HISTORICAL EXPERIENCE

By reviewing the historical experience, it is intended to show not only the nature of development policy, to the extent that it existed, but the kind of response to the policy as well. To this end, the following section documents examples both of policy and response to it.

Colonial Policy

The first evidence of an economic development policy in North America (if, indeed, it can be called that) was manifest in the colonial policies of the European powers, notably France and Great Britain. Their initial exploration and settlement of the continent led ultimately to political control and to the slow but steady economic development of the region. Cod fisheries were the first tangible evidence of development. Paquet (1968, p. 40), in discussing the concept of 'polarized space' in Canadian economic development, notes that these fisheries on the North Atlantic coast were '... the first pole to have an impact on the setting of the Canadian stage ...'. He argues further that '... the production function of cod was a major element in the determination of the pattern of settlement or further penetration of the continent'. The development of the fisheries was intended to satisfy home market demand in France and Great Britain; that this development was part of a conscious policy of economic development in North America is unlikely.

A change in the demand for cod in the late 1500s, again external to the affairs of the North American continent, led to the development by the French of the fur trade. Creighton has observed that 'They [the French] had fallen almost by accident upon the trade which was to dominate the history of their empire in North America for the next 150 years' (Paquet, 1968, p. 45). Clearly, the evolution of the fur trade was not part of a conscious development policy, but the development of this common property resource stimulated the process of capital accumulation and, later, the beginnings of the centralization of economic activity in Canada (that is, the transport system and series of forts essential to the fur trade, related production processes, etc.). As early as 1665, the French recognized the desirability of establishing manufacturing in New France, in part to meet the needs of its fur traders. According to Clark, 'The royal instructions to the intendant of New France, dated March 27, 1665, direct him to "observe that the establishment of manufactures and the attraction thither of fabricators of articles essential to the purposes of life constitute one of the great wants of Canada"'.[2] France's plans for development, initiated under Louis XIV, to create a stable if relatively docile society in New France built around the fur trade, is an example of a development policy directed towards the North American continent, but a policy that was destined to fail.

The British, while not uninvolved in Canada, had a freer hand in the development of the American colonies. Within the colonies, the nature and character of the industrial enterprise was determined by Great Britain. England's motives for founding the colonies have been summarized as follows (Clark, 1929, p. 9):

> The mercantile system governed the foreign-trade policy of Great Britain until the close of the eighteenth century. Its object was to produce at home what was consumed at home, and to increase exports but diminish imports, in order that the stock of coin within the country might be preserved and enlarged. The commercial motives for founding and maintaining colonies in America fell within the general lines of this policy.

The British policy was such that it used the colonies to increase the economic strength of England in several ways:

1. The colonies would provide the necessary goods (masts, naval stores, cordage) to free England of dependence upon foreign sources.
2. The colonies would produce 'luxuries' to replace those then being purchased by England from 'the East'.
3. The colonial forests were expected to provide a source of fuel for Britain's emerging industry.
4. Independent supplies of industrial raw materials could be obtained.
5. The colonies and their settlements would provide a market for English manufactures.

This was, in effect, a development policy for the American colonies, but one which would serve, essentially, to improve the financial condition of England.

British policy served both to encourage the development of certain colonial activities, particularly those associated with agriculture and resource production, and to restrict others—often manufacturing. To advance its goals, Britain introduced, for example, a 'Broad Arrow Policy' designed to give it control of all white pine timber 24 inches in diameter or larger (in Massachusetts) as well as a series of bounties for the production of naval stores and other commodities. While such programmes served England's purposes well, they had the effect of limiting the options of the colonists. To this end, it has been observed that 'As the system developed, the State put controls and regulations on more and more spheres of everyday life in the colonies. The residents soon understood that the purpose of these restrictions lay in transferring their wealth to England' (Petulla, 1977, p. 48). Here, indeed, was a development policy worthy of the name.

Manufacturing apparently existed in the Colonies as early as 1626 when the first flour mill was established at New Netherlands. But the expansion of manufacturing was limited due to inadequate capital and limited industrial experience. One important consequence of the former was that colonial legislatures and town councils alike authorized various forms of aid and support to fledgling industry. To the extent that industrial production was supported by the Crown, colonial legislatures enacted laws to encourage the establishment of manufacturing. Clark (1929, p. 31), commenting on these, states that '. . . most of these laws were based on British precedent, and aimed to encourage manufactures in the colonies by bounties and other forms of public aid, by providing abundant raw materials, and by maintaining standards of workmanship and quality'. Thus, at a very early date, public support of the industrial enterprise in America was established. Some legislation actually *required* that certain kinds of manufacturing be set up in an area. In Virginia, 'In 1661 the legislature ordered each county to set up one or more public tanneries and to provide tanners, curriers, and shoemakers. In 1666 each county was instructed to establish a loom and provide a weaver' (Shannon, 1940, p. 81). Other colonies followed this lead and required specific types of manufacture to be set up and maintained within individual townships or counties.

A variety of inducements were utilized by the colonies to stimulate the development of manufacturing activity, in general, and of specific commodites, in particular, where not restricted by the Crown. Bounties on raw materials were often given '. . . to encourage manufactures rather than agriculture . . . ' (Clark, 1929, p. 33). Massachusetts, for example, provided in 1640 a bounty on cloth made in the colony from wool, and Virginia, in 1662, offered a bounty of 5 lbs of tobacco for every yard of cloth made in that province. Public premiums, usually cash or tobacco, were also offered to encourage manufacturing, especially if taxpayers were reluctant to support additional taxes. Lotteries were used to raise funds to foster new industry and, more commonly, to assist manufacturers whose properties had been destroyed by fire. Tax incentives to the manufacturer and tax exemptions on his raw materials were provided to ease the financial burden of the industrial entrepreneur. Public lands were made available to prospective new industry, especially in the north (the southern colonies were less able to dispose of their land in this way), and individual communities offered assistance to mills, often in the form of land (Clark, 1929, p. 41):

> Town aid to mills was very common. As early as 1635 Watertown assigned a lot for a gristmill; in 1638 Portsmouth, Rhode Island, was negotiating with parties who were to receive ground for setting up a water mill; and five years later Boston granted 300 acres of land to the builders of a tide mill to grind corn.

When larger enterprises were forthcoming whose scope extended beyond the local community, colonial legislatures provided public loans. And not beyond consideration was the training of workers by the state to learn a manufacturing skill. Such activities, as noted, formed the heart of an aggressive economic development effort by the colonies. If it was not industrial development, *per se*, the effort had all of the symptoms of later ID programmes.

Why, one might ask, were such inducements offered to new manufacturing ventures? Very simply because the colonial legislatures recognized the additional wealth generated by the manufacturing process, wealth too frequently lost to the mother country, and because, realistically, they recognized the 'Lack of private capital and the inexperience of the colonists in collective capitalist undertakings . . . ' required to support the activity from the private sector alone (Clark, 1929, p. 42).

National Development

The colonial revolt against taxation by the English Crown following the passage of various revenue laws in 1764 and 1765 added ' . . . a political motive to earlier influences promoting colonial manufactures' (Clark, 1929, p. 215). Non-importation policies were instituted by the colonies against British goods in order to encourage domestic industry, but more important was the Revolution itself. The colonies perceived that industrial and trade relations would be altered by the Revolution and sought to expand industry at home to meet the consequences of the war and the loss of manufactured goods from Great Britain. Here, again, policies were established by the several colonies to assist in the development of new industries, to aid existing industry, and to protect industry against economic hardship. The effect was that the industry that survived the Revolution was, in fact, firmly entrenched and formed the basis for the ongoing industrial growth of the young nation.

Following the Revolution, a fundamental conflict that was to affect the strategy for development in the United States centred upon differing philosophies of government concerning the establishment of a national economy as opposed to a sectional one. In the end, those efforts supportive of a national identity succeeded, but with respect to manufacturing, 'Only gradually did the States relinquish to the National Government the function which they had exercised as colonies of encouraging local manufacturers (Clark, 1929, p. 263).

The elements necessary to the formation and stability of a national government were slowly achieved: a national bank, national bankruptcy laws, establishment of the post office and post roads, federal regulation of patents and copyrights, the federal judiciary system, etc. Alexander Hamilton, who '... unabashedly sought to create a strong central government which would protect American industries, build a merchant marine, and maintain public credit ...' was involved at the time in two related efforts affecting industrial development that are of particular interest to those involved with the industrial development process (Petulla, 1977, p. 109).

In 1790, Hamilton undertook a survey of American industry—'... the first attempt ever made to survey the industrial resources and activities of the United States ...'—that resulted in his *Report on Manufactures* being submitted to the House of Representatives in 1791 (Cole, 1968, p. xvi). The *Report*, based upon a survey carried out by means of correspondence between Hamilton and various manufacturers in the nation,[3] presented Hamilton's arguments for the support of industry by the national government by means of protective tariffs, financial bounties to manufacturing enterprises that the nation wanted to promote, and patent protection, among other provisions. Hamilton believed that the nation must take an active role in support of manufacturing '... for national independence and safety ...', and to compete effectively with European nations (Kirkland, 1969, p. 24).

He was convinced, in his support of manufacturing as opposed to agriculture, that the former was constant, uniform, and more ingenious than agriculture and, therefore, more productive. These observations were derived from arguments that he advanced in the *Report* and that were the foundations for his policies. The arguments are, in brief, that (Cole, 1968, pp. 236–237):

1. Manufactures promote a greater division of labor than agriculture and, thereby, '... an increase of productivity is assured ...'.
2. Manufactures lead to an extension in the use of machinery and thus lead to increased human productivity.
3. Productivity is increased by extending employment opportunities to '... classes of the community not originally engaged in the particular business ...'.
4. Manufactures encourage immigration of foreign workers.
5. Manufactures furnish '... greater scope for the diversity of talents ...'.
6. Manufactures offer '... a more ample and various field for enterprise ...', and serve to stimulate human productivity.
7. Manufactures contribute to the '... augmentation of the produce or revenue of the nation ...', and provide a market for the produce of the soil.

Many of the same arguments are advanced today, although the wording may be different, to justify or explain the rationale for industrial development.

Hamilton sought, in addition, to create a practical example of industrial development through the establishment by the New Jersey legislature in 1790 of the Society for Establishing Useful Manufactures. This was, arguably, the nation's first planned industrial development. With projected capital outlays of $1 million, facilities were established at the Great Falls of the Passaic River to manufacture products ranging from paper to brass wire. Although Paterson, New Jersey, was to evolve at the power site as an important industrial centre by 1807 (when it had '... 12 cotton mills, 3 woolen factories, 3 machine-shops, and several foundries and minor industries ...'), Hamilton's plan for industry failed (Clark, 1929, p. 404). In commenting on this failure, Kirkland (1969, p. 219) offers these judgements:

> The Paterson experiment represented a reversal of hopes. It was a premature enterprise. Hamilton in his report had foreseen the handicaps upon the growth of American manufacturing and had speculated upon the means to overcome them. Actually, problems of markets, technology, government aid, the supply of capital and of workers, all intermingled to frustrate the Paterson experiment.

It is clear that, despite his vision and initiative, 'Hamilton's argument for encouraging manufactures made no marked impression at this time' (Morris, 1953, p. 124).

The same fate appeared to influence Hamilton's efforts to obtain tariff protection for industry, although in the first quarter of the nineteenth century protective tariffs would emerge. Many of Hamilton's views relative to development reflected the philosophy of Adam Smith. Smith viewed tariffs as an anathema to the free flow of trade and to the free enterprise system. While Hamilton agreed philosophically, he determined that some form of protection must be provided to 'young industries' and, consequently, favoured a protective tariff (Cole, 1968, pp. 237–238). The 'infant industries doctrine' that evolved, argued, in effect, that certain industries have potential to be self-sustaining because all necessary conditions exist to allow them to compete with imports; that, for the time being, artificial constraints were restraining growth (that is, inexperience of labour, shortages of capital); and that, with protection, the industry would overcome the constraints and survive (Shannon, 1940, p. 189).

In the nation's first tariff law of 1789—essentially a revenue measure—Hamilton argued for protection for the 'infant industries' but met resistance, particularly from the agrarian South. Succeeding tariffs remained revenue measures, but showed '... intent to protect'.[4] These laws were, in effect, of little consequence to manufacturing enterprise.

On the other hand, self-imposed isolation by the United States that began with the Embargo Act of 1808 and extended throughout the War of 1812 stimulated industrial development in the early nineteenth century more than did the mildly protective tariffs. The Embargo Acts limited foreign trade with

England and provided an impetus to manufacturing. New factories were started up in the period from 1807–15 protected, at least in part, by the Embargos and stimulated by the demands of the United States' market during the War.

With the War's end and the fear of inundation of the American market by British manufactures, the Tariff of 1816 was enacted. It was, at its heart, a protective tariff intended to forestall Britain's efforts to regain its markets by protecting home industry. Even the agrarian South, then experiencing a mild industrial boom, supported it. From 1816 to 1833, '... the protective system secured its greatest popular support' (Kirkland, 1969, p. 179). The cause of protectionism found new supporters. Henry Clay, in a speech defending the protective features of the Tariff of 1824, introduced the concept of 'the American System' when he asserted that the nation should '... create a home market, to give further scope to the consumption of the produce of American industry ...' and, in addition, urged measures to encourage internal improvements (Billington, 1949, p. 351). The quarrels among sectional interests led, finally, to the Tariff of 1828, often called 'the Tariff of Abominations' because it sought to provide protection to almost every activity and geographical section of the nation. With respect to manufacturing and industrial development, John Randolph of Virginia observed of the Tariff that 'The bill referred to manufactures of no sort or kind, except the manufacture of a President of the United States ...', a reference to the political manoeuvrings associated with the passage of the bill (Kirkland, 1969, p. 180).

The concept of internal improvements embodied in the 'American System' of Clay was '... the first step in a system of internal improvements that should make the United States more prosperous and mobile' (Paxson, 1924, p. 241). But prior to the advocacy of national government involvement in internal improvements, the several individual states had embarked on projects aimed at improving transportation and commerce within and between states, and supported measures destined to benefit agriculture and industry alike. For example, the Enabling Act of 1802, which created the State of Ohio, had a provision authorizing funds to be set aside from federal land sales to support road construction. In 1806, construction of the Cumberland Road (later the National Road) was authorized by the federal government. 'There was no opposition of consequence against the undertaking of the Cumberland Road as a national work ...', but neither maintenance nor upkeep was to be forthcoming for fear the national government would intrude on state independence. While the Road was '... a symbol of Federal power, and a bond of union ...', it was clear that federal influence was weak (Paxson, 1924, p. 153).

The inability of the national government to provide forceful leadership—a result of strong philosophical differences regarding the role of government—led individual states as well as private investors (the latter particularly in turnpike construction) to undertake projects on their own. It was widely believed at the time that 'The State was not in business' and should not be. But, 'Chief among the influences that drove the American State into business was the American System . . . (and) with the building of the Erie Canal there began a new period both in the use of capital and the activities of the State' (Paxson, 1924, p. 312). New York State had sought federal aid in the construction of the Erie Canal, but aid was not forthcoming; the State went ahead with the project on its own. Slightly later, Ohio would embark on an extensive canal-building programme, again without federal support, but convinced that the canals would stimulate the economy of the State by opening eastern markets to crops and by improving its solvency.

By 1824, when the Road Survey Bill was passed, it could be argued that the United States had leadership finally committed to support of internal improvements. As Hamilton had suggested earlier, so it was recognized now, that national support of internal improvements could speed industrialization. Thus, while internal improvements, as such, were not directly linked to any industrial development scheme, the industrial enterprise of the nation stood to benefit from any project that increased its access to raw materials and markets, provided more flexible transportation, and lowered transport costs.

Canada also embarked on a programme aimed at improving access to the interior, especially via the St Lawrence route. As one writer has observed, '. . . the Canadian politico-entrepreneur had a certain magnificent dream to make the St Lawrence the commercial artery of North America' (Paquet, 1968, p. 51). As early as the 1820s, commercial groups, lacking adequate capital, petitioned the government (Great Britain) for aid in building the Rideau Canal (completed in 1832), in large measure to be able to meet the expected competition resulting from the opening of the Erie Canal in New York, but also '. . . to strengthen colonial policy and military control on the St Lawrence . . . ' (Glazebrook, 1956, p. 223).

The Welland Canal, completed in 1833, was begun as a private enterprise, but, again, inadequate capital necessitated purchase by the government. Involvement by the government in these water improvement projects led not only to government fiscal policy that responded to transportation improvement '. . . but also in developing manufactures, trade and traffic' (Innis, 1933, p. 11). This is not to say that government policy was directed to industrial development, as such; rather, the improvement in transportation was seen as necessary and desirable in several ways, not the least of which was promoting the development of the Canadian economy (Currie, 1967, p. 3).

Summary

To this point in time, the goals of the national governments were focused primarily upon the establishment of political stability, both in terms of international relations and between sectional interests within the nations, based upon an independent and expanding economy, of which manufacturing activity was but a part. As we have seen, individual states were often more active in the support of manufacturing industry than was the national government, although early supporters of the United States' Constitution anticipated that a national government would promote the cause of manufacturers (Beard, 1944, pp. 40–49). Hamilton's advocacy of support for industry and his ill-fated plan for industrial development at Paterson marked the principal tangible evidence of a policy directed towards industrial development as such. Beyond the efforts and concerns of private industrial entrepreneurs, with whatever support they could obtain from either state or national government, there was little to suggest that industrial development was a goal of the society. Industrial development was encouraged for reasons already noted, but in the main, the expansion of the industrial sector of the society was viewed as a necessary corollary to the economic and political development of the nations.

EVOLUTION OF THE DEVELOPMENT PROCESS

If government did not have a conscious policy of economic or industrial development, and if it did not always take a direct hand in implementing programmes of development, it did engage in actions that had the effect of stimulating, even promoting, the development principle in the mid- to late-nineteenth century. In particular, the federal policy in both the United States and Canada with respect to two separate but related actions provided a dynamic stimulus to development, in general, and to economic development, especially. Reference here is made to the land policies of the two governments and to their policies, as well as those of individual states and provinces, with respect to railroad expansion.

United States' Land Policy

The land policy of the United States has undergone change with the passage of time. Jefferson believed that the land of the west should be opened to settlement to provide for the development of the nation. To this end, he sponsored the Ordinance of 1784 which established a plan for the organization of the west—that is, the area known as the Old Northwest Territory—including provision for government and statehood. In the famous Land Ordinance of 1785, provisions were made for the introduction of the rectangular system of land survey and for the disposition of the land (to be available in tracts of 640 acres priced at $1 an acre). Jefferson believed that the domain should yield revenue to help support the depleted national treasury and to pay the obligations due to soldiers of the Revolution. The sale of public lands was at odds, however, with colonial experience wherein a settler frequently acquired land as a 'reward' for settling it (Paxson, 1924, p. 46). Opponents of the sale of land for revenue feared the role of the speculator and large landholder; they believed that the government's purpose in disposing of the domain should be the development of the country, not revenue. In response, the Land Law of 1800, as well as later adjustments in the law, reduced the minimum size requirements for purchase and attempted to make land more readily available for purchase at fair cost.

Believers in free land were not accommodated until 1862 when the Homestead Law was passed. The gist of the law, which was to open an increased amount of western land to settlement, largely by agricultural interests, was that an individual could acquire a quarter section of land (160 acre) and, after living on it for five years and improving it, receive full title free of charge. The Homestead Act, along with the beginnings of the mechanized revolution of agriculture, spurred development. Hedges has summarized this experience as well as that of Canada: 'Both governments rejected the revenue point of view in administering their public domains and, through the adoption of the homestead idea, committed themselves to the use of the land as an *instrument of national development*'.[5]

Both the United States' and Canadian governments gave land in the form of subsidies to newly formed railway companies as well. While it would appear that the two actions—the granting of free land to settlers and the provision of subsidized land to the railways—were at cross-purposes and served two entirely different groups, it was argued that the construction of the railways would increase the value of the settlers' acres and thus justify the subsidization programme (Hedges, 1934, p. 3). Despite these arguments, considerable hostility developed between advocates of the settlers' rights and those supporting land subsidies to railroads in the United States, so much so that its railroad subsidy programme was terminated in 1871.

Canadian Policy

It was in that same year that the Canadian government entered into its subsidy programme, a time-lag reflecting the different patterns of westward movement and expansion in the two countries. A Canadian government act in 1872 specified that a grant of land not to exceed 50 million acres be made to aid railway construction. The grant, made to the Canadian Pacific Railway, a national undertaking, was not intended to commit the Dominion government to an extended policy of grants. But, the government, '... with a firm faith in the efficacy of the railway as an agent of colonization ... gave generous aid ... ' in the form of land grants to numerous railway companies, companies that were called 'colonization railways' (Hedges, 1934, p. 68). Some of them appeared to incorporate only to obtain land so that, in many ways, the subsidy policy was severely abused.

As early as the Municipal Act of 1849, *municipalities* were empowered to lend money to railways. A Municipal Loan Fund Act (1852) broadened the role of municipalities in capitalizing railways in lieu of foreign investment. There was, as well, support of provincial railways, few of which were really successful. On the whole, though, support for railways by municipal, provincial, and the Dominion governments was important in terms of its impact upon Canadian economic development relative to establishing national economic unity and a competitive position *vis-à-vis* the United States (Easterbrook and Aitken, 1958, pp. 314–19).

In order to stimulate the colonization of the Canadian west, the government made public lands available in 1881 '... to companies organized purely for the purpose of colonization (and thus) created a new agency for promotion of settlement' (Hedges, 1934, p. 75). But, in fact, after five years in which twenty-six companies were organized to obtain over 2.8 million acres of land, fewer than 1250 settlers were brought to the land (Hedges, 1934, p. 78). Colonization in the Canadian west simply did not develop as it had in the United States; many experts felt that it would not, in fact, until good farm land to the south was no longer available.[6] In the final analysis, the railway land subsidy programmes, so enthusiastically supported at first both in Canada and the United States, met with public disapproval and were stopped.[7]

In Canada, the railways, and especially the Canadian Pacific, took a leadership role in the development of their regions. The Canadian Pacific, as early as 1881, promulgated a policy of land sale to settlers with special inducements (that is, rebate of purchase price) to those who actually occupied the land. The railway engaged in advertising the wonders of the Canadian west and joined in the recruitment of potential settlers from Great Britain, continental Europe, and, later, the United States. The railway often provided settlers with free transportation to their lands as part of its promotional scheme. It was a prime force in the colonization and development of the Canadian west.[8] As Glazebrook (1938, p. 195) stresses, 'The mutual interdependence of railways and general economic development is a theme which runs through the history of the Dominion, and one which played no small part in its creation ... '. And Innis (1933, p. 30) notes that 'Strong government support was essential in throwing a bridge from retarded development to an advanced state of industrialization as represented by the railroad ... '. He regards the railroad, and the Canadian Pacific in particular, as being essential to national unity.

Railroads and Industrial Development in the United States

In the United States millions of acres of public land had been given to railroads as early as the 1850s. While early railroad companies were financed by private capital through the issuance of common stock, government subsidization accounted for about half the capital to finance new lines by 1860 (Petulla, 1977, p. 127). Up to this point, federal aid had been limited, but 'The States were more generous ... and less conservative; and in the excitement of the new movement they passed laws authorizing the minor governmental districts, like towns or counties, to bond themselves and invest the proceeds in railroad stocks (Paxson, 1924, p. 415). Congress was persuaded, largely by western interests, to provide aid which it did mainly in the form of subsidies.

Railroads, supported by government assistance, engaged actively in schemes created to encourage settlement. It has been observed that a new geographical entity came into being at this time—the railroad town. Railroads often created towns out of nothing—laid out streets, donated lots for public buildings, and stimulated economic activity. They engaged extensively in advertising and promotional campaigns that were to mark what many view as the beginnings of organized development efforts.

Gill (1973, p. 61) in reviewing economic development in the United States, observes that '... we often find other industries, and particularly the railroads, playing a dominant role in the early stages of industrialization ... They were almost certainly the "key" industry in the case of the United States'. It is a consensus among industrial development professionals, that the *practice* of industrial development, as distinctive from the broader contexts of economic development, can be traced back to competition among the railroad companies. In more than one case, railroads which had established Departments of Immigration to encourage settlement and development along their rights-of-way, changed their focus and, by the later 1800s, had established Departments of Manufactories recognizing in manufacturing an opportunity to generate their own traffic (Preston, 1974, p. 8). Collison (1977, p. iv) offers this explanation:

> In order to develop revenue freight, the companies began assisting industries with their locational problems. Support was offered to local civic organizations as they endeavored to lure business and industry to their communities. As early as the first decade of this century, railroad agents were involved in industrial development programs.

Two illustrations suggest the nature of the industrial development effort 75 years ago by the railroads and the perception of those involved with respect to their goals.

> In 1912, the General Freight Agent of the Erie Railroad, headquartered at Cleveland, sent a letter to each Board of Trade, Chamber of Commerce, and other development groups situated along the Erie lines in Ohio. In that communication, the railroad official offered the 'full services' of the Erie in efforts to locate new industrial enterprises along the railway in any community served by his line.

> The Pennsylvania Railroad, which did not establish its industrial development department until many years later, was offering similar assistance to local community associations. The P.R.R. noted that the railroad company owned considerable property along its rights-of-way which 'might be made available at reasonable cost' to 'qualified' industries . . . the Pennsy pointed out, that whether or not an industry located on its lines, its representatives were available to assist in the location of industrial operations in any community served by the railroad. The philosophy of the railroad management . . . was that any solid growth that occurred in a town served by the railroad would be of general benefit to the railroad company (Collison, 1977, p. 9).

Despite the railroad industry's early and active role in land development, its recognition of the industrial sector as a prime revenue source, and its consequent involvement in industrial development, it was not until 1914 that the American Railway Developers Association was formed as '. . . the first organization of Industrial Development practitioners in this country' (Cohick, 1976, p. 3).

If the railroads were the first organizations to engage in industrial development, and in this sense 'pioneered the profession', they were not alone for long. For example, boards of trade were operating in several Ohio cities by 1880, and, in 1893, the Ohio State Board of Commerce, the forerunner of the Ohio Chamber of Commerce, was organized in Cleveland with the purpose of making '. . . its views (concerning development and business related topics) known to the legislative bodies . . . ' of the state (Collison, 1977, p. 7). Ohio, at the time, was not unlike most other states; it had no programme for attracting new industry or business to the state. But local boards of trade and/or chambers of commerce were organized, among which some of the larger offered services designed to attract business and industry to locate in their communities. These groups actively promoted their territory as a place to live and as a location for industrial activity. Brochures and advertisements were used to publicize a community's 'attractions' and some effort at co-operation between development groups began. By 1912, the United States Chamber of Commerce had been formed as an extension of the local chambers of commerce. The national chamber was not involved directly in industrial development, but represented the points of view of business and commercial interests nationally.

Public and Private Sector Development

To this point, an attempt has been made to illustrate the variety of broad approaches taken to the concept of development. It is important to distinguish between goals of the public sector and those of the private, and the role of the two sectors in the development process. It seems quite clear that the funda-

railroads, public utilities, and some financial institutions (although industrial development professionals in 1930 noted the difficulty of securing co-operation from the financial industry in obtaining loans for industry). There were no representatives from state or federal governments; those practising industrial development were identified essentially with the private sector. A possible hint of things to come, however, was a discussion at the 1930 meeting of the services to industry of a *regional council*—the New England Council—which was based on internal (that is, New England States) co-operation used to promote the region, to undertake industrial surveys in the region, and to encourage and assist industrial development of the region.

It should not be surprising that government at all levels was missing from the organization. The previous several decades had witnessed the rapid growth and expansion of the private sector of the society operating in what has been popularly perceived to be a *laissez-faire* economy. It was in such an environment that the field evolved: 'Its early years coincided with a period of population growth, the expansion of the nation's physical frontiers, a time of discovery and development of seemingly unlimited natural resources, and an economy in which manufacturing was the dominant force' (Hunker, 1974, p. 2).

Government's Increasing Role

Fundamental change in economic philosophy and in attitudes towards development occurred in the 1930s. 'The Great Depression of the 1930s and the panaceas offered by the New Deal probably did more to alter the course of industrial development than any federal legislation before or since' wrote Collison (1977, p. 12). Prior national policy that affected the development philosophy of the society was an outgrowth of the federal land policies and government policies with respect to the use of the nation's resource base, particularly forests, minerals, and water. In fact, whatever national policy existed with respect to planning and development was rooted in concern for the resource base. Stressing this concern for the physical resources of the country, and probably reflecting a political philosophy that rejected more active government intervention in the development process, the National Resources Committee (1935) insisted that 'Regional planning should, in the main, confine itself to dealing with the physical resources and equipment out of which socio-economic progress arises'.[11]

The federal government introduced numerous programmes into the American society in the depression years to attempt to overcome economic strife and to stimulate the economy, but none altered more dramatically the government's traditional role with respect to regional economic development than the Tennessee Valley Authority created in 1933. For the first time, the national government sought to affect the socio-economic wellbeing of a multistate geographical region by altering its physical resource base and by providing certain basic ingredients to stimulate economic development, in the broad sense, and industrial development, specifically. What Smith (1971, p. 469) has called '... the first major government intervention in regional economic development ...' was not to be the last of its efforts to affect the course of development at the regional level.

In the same period, individual states came to recognize the need for government assistance in the industrial development act. Southern states, suffering from the loss of jobs in agriculture and with no ready industrial base to absorb the displaced workers, were among the first and most active to establish industrial development departments at the state level and to promote activities designed to affect industrial location. Special inducements were introduced to lure northern manufacturers into the region—enticements ranging from free land to tax forgiveness. The programme generally recognized as the first of many was Mississippi's BAWI (Balance Agriculture With Industry) plan, which used industrial revenue bonds and general revenue bonds to attract industry to that state. Whatever its success, the programme was later widely adopted by other states, either in whole or in part,[12] and thus marked an active new stage of involvement in industrial development by the public sector (Hunker, 1974, pp. 40–42). By the later 1930s, many northern industrial states began to establish the equivalent of departments of industrial development in order to compete more effectively in the industrial location process.

There is no question that by 1940 the government, federal and state, had become a more active participant in the business of development. Not only did government attempt to stimulate the economy by various legislative measures, its representatives were becoming involved, slowly at first, in industrial location activity. In addition to the increased amount of government 'thrust upon' it, the profession slowly recognized industry's responsibility and its own to society, although it was not yet prepared to accept the idea that this responsibility compared with the economic contributions that industry could make to a community or state. The issue of social responsibility, so evident in the 1970s, especially with respect to environment concerns, was not a popular topic in the 1930s (Cohick, 1976, p. 12).

The Second World War marked a period of unprecedented federal activity in development including the location of manufacturing facilities. Government investment in manufacturing facilities, either in the form of new plants or in the expansion of existing facilities, stimulated the industrial sector. Federal dollars were directed towards the construction of hundreds of wartime industrial plants—often called 'war babies'—to be operated by the private sector. In several notable instances, government investment was either (a) responsible for the development and location of an entire industry, such as synthetic rubber and the modern petrochemical industry; or (b) had the effect of generating industrial growth in regions that had been up to this time relatively underdeveloped, such as the Gulf South. The net result was a post-economy with a greatly expanded industrial base, with new and increased industrial capacity, and with newly emerging industrial regions. In retrospect, the impact of wartime decisions on the inauguration of new plant and on the location of new facilities was probably a more decisive factor in the industrial redevelopment of the nation than any other government action, certainly up to that time.

In the immediate postwar years, industrial development expanded as a goal in many states and as a professional activity. Because of the growing interest of state government in the industrial development process, representatives of the private sector—chamber officials and others—sought to establish more dynamic industrial development programmes of their own and to thus forestall the time when state involvement would be more active. For example, both Ohio and Pennsylvania created agencies of state government in 1939 to engage in industrial promotion, but also to handle tourist and travel promotion. In 1946, the Ohio Chamber of Commerce, somewhat concerned about the state's role in the promotion process, created its own ID department. By 1948, the Association of Industrial Commissioners of Quebec was formed and included persons engaged in development work for industrial utilities and real estate interests. There were few municipal industrial commissions in Quebec at the time and no provincial activity. That was to come later when, according to Macpherson (1969, p. 1) there was an '. . . almost complete take-over by provincial development personnel . . . '.

The point here is simple: industrial development, long the domain of the private sector, would find increasing government interest in all levels of the development process. If the TVA was the first of the federally supported regional development programmes in the United States, it was not to be the last; the concept of 'area' development was to be expanded upon in the 1960s. Nor was the wartime experience of the government in industrial development to end with the war's conclusion. The postwar years saw increased government efforts to resolve (or attempt to resolve) the socio-economic problems of the nation. Many of the solutions required that the government be a participant in either the redevelopment process or, often indirectly, in the process to promote industry.

Collison (1977, 29) writing of the 1950s as an industrial development professional, puts it bluntly: 'Another problem seemed also to be surfacing—intervention of the Federal Government into industrial development. Noises were being made in Congress for all kinds of panaceas to assist small business people, aid depressed areas etc.' Industrial development was viewed as the principal means by which local and/or regional economic problems could be overcome. The expansion of the manufacturing sector was still believed to be the key to the growth of regional economies; the concept of the multiplier effect was studied and learned, sometimes too well. Given governments' increased role in shaping the socio-economic wellbeing of the people, state and local governments became more involved in the development process than at any previous time.

REGIONAL ECONOMIC PLANNING AND INDUSTRIAL DEVELOPMENT

The postwar years were to see increased government participation at all levels in economic and area development. With respect to industrial development, in particular, Hoover (1948, p. 241) was to observe that 'The power of public control over location is rapidly increasing'. Furthermore, he argued, 'Almost any conceivable action by government, however dissociated it may be from any conscious policy aimed at affecting locations, does, in fact, influence the geographic pattern of locational advantages'. It is true that government has rarely followed a defined policy with respect to industrial location, although the area development programmes of the 1960s would be more clearly defined in this sense than previous programmes. Given these conditions, and recognizing that the location decision rests with the private sector, Hoover (1948, pp. 251–252) suggested that government influence on the decision, especially as it relates to area development, is usually exerted to help achieve one of several goals:

1. 'To increase the total productive activity or total income of the area'.
2. 'To produce a more desirable combination of activities'.
3. 'To improve spatial arrangements within the area'.
4. 'To improve the process of locational selection and adjustment to locational change', relative to job and site information.

Clearly, these goals have not been met ordinarily by direct involvement of the government in the location process; rather, the influence of government is felt in other ways. Indirect influences may include the taxing power of government, legislation aimed at improving the social and/or economic lot of the populace, control of transfer costs, and local and regional infrastructure. It should be noted, as well, that the government can affect the industrial location decision by limiting the freedom of choice of site through the zoning process, by tax penalties, and by other legal restrictions, when the objective of the location policy is to discourage growth in one region in order to stimulate, hopefully, growth in another. Obviously, as Smith (1971, p. 450) concludes, 'Depending on the planning goals, and on the way the economic system functions, some instruments will be more effective than others . . . ' in the decision-making process. Thus, it is correct to state that the increasing role of government in development, whether industrial or areal by definition, reflects an attempt to use location policy to accomplish social and economic goals not otherwise accomplished by the private sector operating in the traditional free enterprise society. This may, in fact, be the key factor distinguishing modern industrial development policy from earlier development efforts.

Government Planning: Distressed Areas

Development activity by the national governments of Canada and the United States is based, at least in part, on the concern that certain regions within these two countries suffer from limited economic growth and, as a result, experience undue social hardships. As Macpherson (1975a, p. 38) has noted with respect to increased Canadian national and provincial economic development efforts, there exists '... an unacceptable degree of economic disparity among regions and provinces'. It is just such recognition of disparity between regions that has led to the broad area development programmes and related development activities in both countries.

We have already noted that the establishment in 1933 of the Tennessee Valley Authority (TVA) was the first evidence of government intervention in economic development in the United States on a large area scale. It was not until 1961 that the federal government initiated a new programme of aid for problem areas with the establishment of the Area Redevelopment Administration (ARA). Its purpose was to provide funds through loans and grants for commercial *and* industrial development in areas of chronic unemployment and low income. Affected counties could seek assistance by preparing an acceptable Overall Economic Development Program (OEDP) that would address these problems by creating programmes to stimulate employment and economic growth.[13] In its conception and goals, this programme resembled international efforts to aid underdeveloped nations.

In 1965, the Appalachian Regional Development Act (ARDA) established an Appalachian Regional Development Commission to administer a wide-ranging set of programmes designed to foster area economic development. As the Act states, its purposes were '... to assist the region in meeting its special problems, to promote its economic development, and to establish a framework for joint Federal and State efforts towards providing the basic facilities essential to its growth'.[14] An important goal, not well-defined in previous legislation, is the one addressing 'joint Federal and State efforts'. This action, as well as future legislation, served to advance the activities of state development departments and agencies, and to make, therefore, state development efforts a significant force in the industrial development business.

The Public Works and Economic Development Act was also legislated in 1965 to provide grants to support public works, development activities, and planning in areas defined as being 'economically distressed'. Five *economic development regions* were created: the Coastal Plain, Four Corners, Ozarks, New England, and the Upper Great Lakes regions. Smaller geographical units were also defined, including *economic development districts* (essentially multicounty areas) and *redevelopment areas* (county or municipal units, or units as large as Indian reservations or labour market areas within a district). With respect to industrial development, specifically, the EDA stood ready to provide funding for industrial expansion by means of loans up to 65 per cent of the total costs of industrial site, building, and equipment.

These programmes added a new dimension to the practice of industrial development. For one thing, they injected the national government more directly into the process than at any previous time in history. While the federal government could not dictate the location choice of private enterprise and could not use inducements to relocate plants, the relocation of which might create unemployment and economic hardship in the original area, it could affect the location and relocation of industry through loans and grants, and attempt to stimulate development in the depressed areas as noted. In accord with this philosophy, the two programmes were committed to the 'growth centre' concept, or a modified version of it. In ARDA, it was clear that public investments were to be made in those areas where a significant potential existed for future growth and where the expected return on the investments would be greatest. EDA stressed that each *economic development district* should have a 'development centre' of such size and potential as to be the basis for future economic growth.

In addition, each programme laid heavy emphasis upon the need for area and economic development *planning*, and placed the responsibility for the development of plans at the action level. The fact is that individual communities or regions engaging in the programmes had to submit the plans for action before funding was forthcoming. Furthermore, each programme brought about increased interaction between the federal and state governments in responding to development issues and problems. In sum, the programmes were evidence of a commitment at the national level to federal involvement in regional development and, to the extent that it is related, in the industrial development process itself. Thus, by the mid-1960s, a growing number of organizations and persons, many of them at federal and state levels, were engaged in development activities. Thus, the industrial development professional, employed in the private sector for the most part, had been joined by a new group of developers whose motivations, goals, and objectives were not necessarily or always consistent with those of the private sector.

The Canadian Experience

Canada's experience was not too dissimilar during this period. Historically, the industrial development business— ' . . . shaping the structure or determining the characteristics of industrial location . . . '—had been left to the private sector in Canada as it had been in the United States. As a result, developers responded to private sector motives (in other words, profit) and thus had '... a strong compulsion ... to consider most favourably the existing growth areas of the nation and to ignore in effect the backward regions ... industrial developers failed to cope with this limitation and this is one of the major reasons for increased government involvement in the industrial and economic development process ...' according to Macpherson (1975b, p. 2). It might be added that industrial developers, in general, were *not* concerned with area development, as such, whether the area was backward or not. Their emphasis, traditionally, was on a relatively small 'action space'. Here, then, is a major cause for increased government input into the development process in Canada.

Not unlike the United States, Canada enacted in 1961 its Area Rural Development Administration (ARDA) legislation to provide strategies for responding to rural povery and unemployment in depressed areas. It was legislation aimed quite clearly at *area* development as opposed to industrial development. But, by 1963, the Area Development Agency (ADA) had been established '... to encourage industrial development in areas of chronic unemployment' (Brewis, no date, p. 1), a policy that tended to lead to a 'worst first' remedial action akin to the early efforts of the EDA in the United States (Todd, 1977, p. 30). Industrial development was to be the device by means of which economic hardship in distressed small communities and/or depressed areas would be relieved. Todd (1977, p. 30) notes that aid took the form of '... a blanket provision of industrial incentives in designated areas ...' but there were failings in the programme: the incentives were rigidly restricted to manufacturing; the manufacturing activity that was generated often did not suit the needs of the designated area; and there was a tendency for capital-intensive firms to take advantage of the grants as opposed to labour-intensive firms so that the efforts to create jobs and relieve unemployment in the distressed areas were frustrated.

By 1969, the federal government established the Department of Regional Economic Expansion (DREE) in an effort to alleviate disparity between regions, an historic and persistent problem in Canada.[15] The Regional Development Incentives Act was passed in the same year to react to criticism of earlier programmes and '... to provide incentives for the development of productive employment opportunities in regions of Canada determined to require special measures to facilitate economic expansion and social adjustment' (Canada, 1976, p. 1). It recognized two kinds of areas requiring attention: *designated areas*, which had to be of sufficient size to be classified as function a areas and, as such, were eligible for manufacturing incentives or grants, and *special areas*, which were eligible for resource and tertiary support, as well as manufacturing incentives, and could receive aid for infrastructure development (Todd, 1977, p. 31). In the latter, there are elements of a growth centre policy, particularly in the provision of infrastructure support for certain urban centres. Thus, the programme was directed to issues of regional economic development, but it is clear that development of an industrial base and of industrial facilities—or industrial development—is a desired feature. Cash grants are, for example, available specifically for industrial development. Investors may be funded if they are willing to establish, expand, or modernize job-creating facilities in a region to which the act applies, the idea being to provide an incentive to locate in slow-growth areas.[16]

Agreements between the federal government and provincial governments are also a feature of the act. 'The Agreements define objectives, a broad strategy to achieve them, the extent of activity, and the types of cooperation and support that will be required. They do not provide for a commitment of resources' (Macpherson, 1975b, p. 5). Individual provinces have, in addition, created their own programmes for area development, usually providing financial incentives, tax concessions, consultation services, and other means of assistance and support to industry. In this sense, provinces engage in competition with each other for industry; often a costly and self-defeating practice in the long-run. Furthermore, and of particular interest in Canada compared to the United States, the national interest may not be as effectively served if the provinces sponsor their own programmes and offer competitive incentives and concessions (Brewis, no date, p. 1).

The Canadian industrial development effort appears to be more closely linked to government policies and programmes, federal, provincial, and local, than is true of the industrial development effort in the United States. Even at the local level, industrial development tends to be seen as the responsibility of the public sector. Clearly, there is an acceptance of the notion in Canada that attempts to encourage industrial development in a municipality should conform to larger city goals leading, ultimately, to integrated community development. This point of view—in other words, recognition of the public sector's responsibility to utilize industrial development efforts to achieve total community development—is only now being accepted slowly in the United States. In both societies, the role of the private sector developer may continue to be diminished if, in fact, the industrial development movement becomes, increasingly, an integral part of larger economic development programmes controlled by the public sector. This may become more obvious, especially if industrial development is viewed and used as a tool of political development by national, provincial, and local governments.

Thus, in both countries, over the last twenty-five years there has been increased participation by government at all levels in development. Furthermore, the expansion of government's role has resulted in the creation of a multitude of development organizations (federal or dominion agencies, state and provincial departments) and an expansion of the numbers of persons practising development in one form or another. This condition has been exacerbated by the increased demands for environmental quality that characterize the past ten years, resulting in further government legislation and participation in the development process.

Current Thrusts of Development

Since the emergence of area development programmes in both the United States and Canada, two major issues have evolved relative to the present and future thrusts of industrial development, as such. The first concerns the historic issue of where in the society the industrial development emphasis is to lie; that is, does the initiative for industrial development derive from the private or public sector? Given the nature of the initiative, whose responsibility is it to carry the process through to its logical conclusion?

The second issue is closely related, and is at the very heart of this essay. Specifically, is the thrust of the development effort to be that of area development, of broad-scale economic development, or, as has been true in the past, development directed more persistently at the industrial sector? In other words, *what is to be the thrust of the development effort specifically engaged in by the industrial development professional?* These are legitimate questions and they are particularly appropriate in terms of charting a course of action or a set of directions that will apply to the industrial developer whether in the United States or Canada.

Despite the historical evidence of innumerable government incursions into the development process, the field of industrial development, as already noted, has been regarded since its inception as the domain of the private sector developer. In part, this emphasis reflects the peculiar attention by the developer to the industrial component of the society during the past 75 years. Those engaged in industrial development were active in the assembling, developing, and marketing of industrial sites; in facilitating the industrial location process; and, in most cases, in profit-generating activity. That is, the act of industrial development was but one more part of the free enterprise system. While industrial developers were individuals engaged in the industrial development business, the business itself was a creation of the free enterprise system and a product of those organizations—railroads, utilities, real estate agencies, banks, chambers of commerce, etc.—which were ardent supporters of that system. There was little pretence that industrial development was more than that.

The area economic development programmes that emerged in the 1930s and have proliferated in recent years, changed the nature of the game in two particular ways. First, they introduced a new and different element into the development process. No longer limited to a concentration on the advancement of the industrial sector, they advocated not programmes of industrial development, *per se*, but programmes directed towards the alleviation of the full range of socio-economic problems of a given region, often depressed, by means of various programmes of economic aid, social assistance, industrial location and/or relocation, infrastructure development, etc. In the second instance, the accomplishment of programme goals was not left to the private sector, but became a task of government. With this fundamental change came a change in the nature of the organizations and individuals engaged in development. Because federal programmes frequently embodied (or required) a concept of area or socio-economic planning, many individuals trained in economics, geography, and planning, became associated with these programmes. The industrial development professional was overwhelmed by the numbers of new 'professionals' engaged in development activity, few of whom, however, viewed industrial development as their particular interest or area of expertise except as it was related to the larger socio-economic development plan for a given area.

Thus, the two major shifts in the direction of development were clear; development was no longer restricted to the type of investment and development judged to be desirable and necessary by the private sector, and the development process, now more broadly defined, was no longer, if it ever was, an exclusive domain of the industrial development professional. In effect, the industrial development process needs to be re-examined in the light of these changes, and the concept of an industrial development profession—that is, reflecting the group of professionals traditionally involved uniquely in industrial development work—has to be reconsidered.

Preston indicates that as early as 1964 the field was, to a degree, 'redefined' so that 'The term "industrial development" was qualified by the words "in its broadest connotation" reflecting the ever-broadening scope of the field'. (AIDC Educational Foundation, 1975, p. 6). He has argued, as well (1974, p. i), 'The field ... is concerned with improving the quality of life through the generation of productive employment opportunities. In seeking balanced, total development for all people, it encompasses all facets of development—economic, social, environmental and political.' It follows from this point that three components must be considered by the private sector as it engages in development: generation of productive economic opportunities, strengthening of the economic base, and production of a competitive or commensurate profit on invested capital. Clearly, the latter is the ultimate goal of the private sector developer. On the other hand, the public sector developer might have a commitment to full employment as a basic goal so that the first component might be ranked as more important and the profit-generating character of the development enterprise as less important in this instance. In effect, Preston addresses the changing character not only of the development process, but of the individual involved in the process, as well. Macpherson (1976, p. 18) supports the tenor of these arguments as he notes that 'Although the nomenclature of this emergent profession seems to indicate concentration on industrial matters, the role of the development officer involves the coordination of all areas of orderly economic development which affects his community'.

In brief, even within the industrial development profession, there is recognition that the concept of the field is undergoing change. To engage in the act of industrial development for profit's sake, while still a goal, is no longer the only task of the developer. If he is to play a meaningful role in society, the industrial developer must broaden his scope to include an understanding of the needs of the larger community. To this end, he must recognize that industry (manufacturing) may not be the only stimulus to a region's economy and that dynamic growth may no longer be forthcoming from further expansion of this sector. The entire spectrum of economic activity is 'fair game' as the developer seeks to provide for balanced community and/or area growth and development. To this end, attention may need to be focused more sharply upon the tertiary sector of the economy, upon its unique location requirements, and upon the total development of the community or region (Hunker, 1974, chapter 2).

Finally, these changes have taken place and are taking place within a changing institutional environment. The necessary enlargement of development goals to reflect both private and public investment in an area is a response to the increased impact of public policy decisions and actions upon the entire development process. If the industrial developer is to continue to function as a critical force in generating interaction between business and government in the development process, an awareness and understanding of these changing conditions and roles is essential.[17]

NOTES

1. To this extent, it is clear that the underlying philosophy of development in the United States and Canada was premised upon Adam Smith's classical model. A major philosophical difference evolved following the development of the Marxian model in the last half of the nineteenth century.
2. Clark (1929, p. 15) quotes from the 'Royal Instructions to Sieur Talon, Intendant in New France'.
3. Not untypical of the responses that Hamilton received are the following remarks contained in a letter from Peter Colt (Hartford Woollen Mill) to Colonel John Chester, Supervisor of Revenue for Connecticut, in July 1791. Chester solicited the information in his state for Hamilton.

> This Company have received some aid from Government—viz a trifling bounty the first Year on Spining—then an exemtion, for two years, of their Workmen from a *Poll Tax*; & their work shops from all taxes for the same term of Time···
>
> Those persons concerned in seting up new Manufactures have every obsticle to surmount which can arrise from clashing Interests, or ancient prejudices; as well as from the smallness of our capitals, the scarcity of Materials & workmen, & the consequent high prices of both (Cole, 1968, pp. 5–6).

4. See Skaggs (1975, p. 484), in which he quotes tariff historian Frank Taussig.

5. See Hedges (1934, p. 3, my italics).
6. The Canadian government had anticipated that the colonization companies would do for Canadian settlement what railways had done in the United States where they saw the railways as '. . . the best immigration agents—in fact, the only immigration agents in the U. S.' (Hedges, 1934, p. 77).
7. 'No further grants of land were made to railways after 1896 and the land was used instead for the free homestead system. . .' according to Glazebrook (1938, p. 316), commenting on the Canadian experience.
8. A land subsidy granted in Alberta for the development of a railway and an irrigation system also resulted in an active colonization and development programme that led to the operation being called '. . . one of the successful agencies of land settlement. . . in Canada (Hedges, 1934, p. 122).
9. The modern corporation had the organizational capability of combining effectively capital and labour in the production process, most particularly in the manufacturing process.
10. Wheat (1973, p. 1) in considering regional growth and industrial location in the United States, notes: 'When one speaks of regional economic growth, thoughts quickly turn to manufacturing. To be sure, increases in employment and income can be achieved, in theory anyhow, in other sectors. . . Yet as a practical matter, the best opportunities for economic development usually lie with manufacturing. . . Manufacturing growth is thus of basic concern for regional growth'.

    Robinson (1965, p. 5) in reflecting on the ambitions of developing countries, observes: It goes without saying that everybody in developing countries wants to industrialize swiftly. Industry glitters with promise. Nothing else seems to hold out much hope of fulfilling the expectations of new nationalism, winning economic independence and raising average prosperity dramatically'.
11. Hunker (1974, p. 26) and quoted in *Regional Factors in National Planning* (Washington: US Government Printing Office, 1935, p. 156).
12. Cohick (1976, p. 15) makes this observation about the Mississippi programme: 'Although this form of financing had been used successfully by Mississippi since 1936, this presentation (to the AIDC annual conference) in 1950 is the first evidence. . . that it had been brought to the attention of industrial developers on a nation-wide basis'. This point is stressed here to indicate the 'state of the art' of industrial development at the time; ID was not well-established nor did it possess a well-developed mechanism for the exchange of information or ideas within the professional group.
13. In the same year, the United States Department of Agriculture established its Office of Rural Areas Development, which was designed to encourage maximum development of human and economic resources in rural areas. Part of this programme was aimed at improved economic conditions through *industrial* development.
14. Programmes were directed towards economic development as such, but, in addition, there were those directed towards related problems associated with regional infrastructure—highway construction, public facilities, etc.—and with social goals—health, vocational education, housing, etc. (Smith, 1971, p. 470).
15. David Walker (1975) addresses this problem as he discusses government initiatives '. . .to raise the Atlantic provinces from their traditionally "disadvantaged" position in the Canadian economy . . . ' in his paper.
16. Other aspects of DREE address needs in agriculture, rural development, etc.
17. The most active force in the development profession in the United States is the American Industrial Development Council (AIDC), first organized informally in 1926. The national organization has a membership of approximately 1200 professionals, but there are several thousand other developers at work in both the private and public

sectors. The AIDC operates an extensive education programme for developers through its basic and advanced development institutes. In addition, there are well-organized regional industrial development councils throughout the country.

In Canada, the Industrial Developers Association of Canada (IDAC), organized in 1969, is the professional group representing the industrial development profession. Many of its members are affiliated to the American Industrial Development Council (AIDC).

REFERENCES

AIDC Educational Foundation (1975). *Fifty Years of American Industrial Development*, South Hamilton, Mass.

Beard, C. A. (1944). *An Economic Interpretation of the Constitution of the United States*, The Macmillan Co.,New York.

Billington, R. A. (1949). *Westward Expansion*, The Macmillan Co., New York.

Brewis, T. N. (no date). *Regional Economic Policy—Introductory Comments by the Chairman* (mimeo).

Canada (1976). *Office Consolidation of the Regional Development Incentives Act, 1976*, Information Canada, Ottawa.

Clark, V. S. (1929). *History of Manufacturers in the United States*, Vol. 1, McGraw-Hill Book Co. Inc., New York.

Cohick, L. D. (1976). *A Review of Industrial Development from Colonial Days to the Present*, (mimeo) remarks presented to the SIDC Annual Conference, Nashville, Tennessee.

Cole, A. H. (ed.) (1968). *Industrial and Commercial Correspondence of Alexander Hamilton Anticipating his Report on Manufacturers*, Augustus M. Kelley, New York.

Collison, K. (1977). *Ohio—Its Development and its Developers*, Ohio Chamber of Commerce. Columbus.

Currie, A. W. (1967). *Canadian Transportation Economics*, University of Toronto Press, Toronto.

Easterbrook, W. T. and Aitken, H. G. J. (1958). *Canadian Economic History*, The Macmillan Co. of Canada, Ltd., Toronto.

Gill, R. T. (1973). *Economic Development: Past and Present*, 3rd edition, Prentice-Hall, Englewood Cliffs, New Jersey.

Glazebrook, G. P. de T. (1938). *A History of Transportation in Canada*, The Ryerson Press, Toronto.

Glazebrook, G. P. de T. (1956). 'Transportation in the Canadian Economy'. In H. A. Innes (ed.) *Essays in Canadian Economic History*, University of Toronto Press, Toronto, pp. 220–232.

Hedges, J. B. (1934). *The Federal Railway Land Subsidy Policy in Canada*, Harvard University Press, Cambridge, Mass.

Hoover, E. M. (1948). *The Location of Economic Activity*, McGraw-Hill Book Co. Inc., New York.

Hunker, H. L. (1974). *Industrial Development: Concepts and Principles*, Lexington Books, D. C. Heath and Co., Lexington, Mass.

Innis, H. A. (1933). *Problems of Staple Production in Canada*, The Ryerson Press, Toronto.

Kirkland, E. C. (1969). *A History of American Economic Life*, 4th edition, Appleton-Century-Crofts, New York.

Macpherson, R. S. (1969). 'Canadian industrial development progress and trends'. *New York Sunday Times*, Special AIDC Supplement, 1.

Macpherson, R. S. (1975a). 'Regional disparity', A paper presented to the Workshop on *Canada—United Through Diversity*, University of Toronto, Toronto.

Macpherson, R. S. (1975b). 'Canada wants your facilities' *Area Development*, **10**, 32–38.
Macpherson, R. S. (1976). 'Rethinking industrial development'. *Executive*, **September**.
Morris, R. B. (ed.) (1953). *Encyclopedia of American History*, Harper and Brothers, New York.
Myrdal, G. (1956). *An International Economy*, Harper and Brothers, New York.
Paquet, G. (1968). 'Some views on the pattern of Canadian economic development'. In T. N. Brewis (ed.) *Growth and the Canadian Economy*, McClelland and Stewart Ltd., Toronto, pp. 34–64.
Paxson, F. L. (1924). *History of the American Frontier, 1763–1893*, Houghton-Mifflin Co., Boston.
Petulla, J. M. (1977). *American Environmental History*, Boyd and Fraser Publishing Co., San Francisco.
Preston, R. (1974). *The Universe of Industrial Development and North American Concepts and Practise*, AIDC Educational Foundation, Wenham, Mass.
Regional Factors in National Planning (1935). US Government Printing Office, Washington, DC.
Robinson, R. (ed.) (1965). *Industrialization in Developing Countries*, Cambridge University Overseas Studies, Cambridge.
Shannon, F. A. (1940). *America's Economic Growth*, The Macmillan Co., New York.
Skaggs, J. M. (1975). *An Interpretive History of the American Economy*, Grid, Inc., Columbus, Ohio.
Smith, D. M. (1971). *Industrial Location: An Economic Geographical Analysis*, John Wiley & Sons, Inc., New York.
Todd, D. (1977). 'Regional intervention in Canada and the evolution of growth centre strategies'. *Growth and Change*, **8**, No. 1, 29–34.
Walker, D. F. (1975). 'Governmental influence on manufacturing location: Canadian experience with special reference to the Atlantic Provinces'. *Regional Studies*, **9**, No. 2, 203–217.
Wheat, L. F. (1973). *Regional Growth and Industrial Location: An Empirical Viewpoint*, Lexington Books, D. C. Heath and Co., Lexington, Mass.

Planning Industrial Development
Edited by David F. Walker

Chapter 3

Problems of Economic Planning for Underdeveloped Socialist Countries

Peter Limqueco and Bruce McFarlane

The problems of socialist economic planning are at the same time ideological and practical. They are matters of both tons of steel and life-and-death struggles over such issues as wage policy, management styles, bureaucratic preferences, economic growth. In the USSR, Eastern Europe and China, (as well as in India) a considerable corpus of knowledge has been accumulated concerning techniques of planning. Some of the background to the appearance (and disappearance) of these techniques remains 'hazy', because it has been connected to particular political struggles (Preobrazhensky versus Bukharan in the USSR and Po I Po versus Mao Tse Tung in China), and because empirical studies as to what actually happened to rural and urban workers in the process of socialist industrialization have been lacking.

Two topics which we consider to be significant in this context are:

1. To what extent do new underdeveloped socialist economies find it useful to draw on USSR/China ('big country') experience?
2. Do familiar problems of bureaucracy, excessive construction patterns, autarchy, and the impact of foreign technology still obtain in such smaller countries?

The remarks which follow in this essay are directed at these issues, in the general context of the actual economic policy problems likely to be faced by countries like Vietnam and Cuba, which have neither the geographical nor the cultural peculiarities which have impinged on Soviet and Chinese planning practice and ideology. Starting from the historical debates about planning in the USSR we examine the financing of socialist industrialization and then problems of planning *methodology*. The conclusion takes up some questions of the planning system, since planning techniques are diffused through a certain planning *system*, but this will not be our main emphasis, which is the investment function, planning methods, and the role of foreign technology.

HISTORICAL LESSONS IN PAST SOCIALIST DEBATES

Our starting-point will be the lessons learnt from the early years of the first experiment in socialist planning and economic policy—that of Soviet Russia in the 1920s. Although Russia was a large country and new socialist states are not, the conflicts between peasant and government objectives, industry and agriculture, autarchy and international trade remain perennial problems of the political economy of socialism.

Lenin, as well as a later Soviet textbook (Kusinen, 1960, p. 710) described the New Economic Policy (NEP) of 1922–26 as a correct course for a transition period between capitalism's abolition and the new era of socialism because it recognized the reality of the need for peasant support. As part of the NEP the legal taxes were set in advance, so the peasants knew that the more they produced, the more would be left for themselves. Lenin allowed the leasing of land and even the hiring of labour as long as family labour predominated in the production process, while the Bolshevik Party allowed both leasing and hired labour as late as 1926. During the NEP, managers of trusts were regarded as quasi-autonomous and were required to work in accordance with 'market criteria'. Payment of subsidies was avoided wherever the living standard was not thereby reduced.

At that time, banking policy was highly orthodox as well. High priority was given to a stable currency, and the authorities tried very hard to accumulate gold and foreign currency. Solovnikov, Commissar of Narcomfin,[1] pursued a four-pronged strategy. First, he practised orthodox financial policy in the credit field; second, he tried for a balanced state budget; third he was prepared to accept Western loans on strict conditions, and finally he pursued the 'golden rule' that credit supply was *not* to be determined by the needs of industry, but vice versa. While all the planners and political leaders did not agree with this line, most did accept the need to stick to a worker-peasant alliance and not to overdo the monopoly position of industry. In 1922 even Trotsky defended the primary role of the market.

The scenario we have outlined so far is *not* remote from the problems facing Vietnam, Laos, China and Cambodia today. In many ways, the NEP experience in Russia is more relevant than the left turn of crash industrialization, rapid collectivization of agriculture, bacchanalian planning and unorthodox finance taken by Stalin in 1929.

The Soviet Industrialization Debate (Erlick, 1960; Preobrazensky, 1965) moreover, which was conducted between 1924 and 1928, *did* raise issues which are still topical and highly relevant for a small country in transition to socialism. Among the most important issues on which clarity was required, the following emerged:

1. What is the key bottleneck? Is it lack of demand (in other words, does the

peasant market need to be protected)? Is it lack of investible funds? Is it a shortage of physical capacity?

2. What are to be the sources of funds to *back up* the development plan? What proportion of these should be external and what internal? If external, what sort, and on what terms? What should be the main *internal* source—agricultural net surplus or the profits of state corporations in light and heavy industry?
3. What is the best way to increase the output of agriculture? Large-scale state farms or smaller family-based farms? The commune or the 'kulak'? Better seeds or more tractors?
4. If the economy *is* able to expand rapidly, is 'balanced' or 'unbalanced' growth more beneficial?
5. What is the right time-scale? What is the right time to *introduce* a policy of stepped-up industrialization or increased integration with the world economy?
6. What role is there for central economic planning? Should it be based on statistics, projections and a careful assessment of objective limits or should it be teleological and achieved by mass mobilization campaigns? What are the best techniques of planning?

In the field of planning techniques and quantitative planning, Russian experience yielded even more extensive positive and negative lessons than did its experiences with collectivization and pre-1940 industrialization. The latter were very specific to Soviet politics—as was the ultimate victory of Stalin in the industrialization debate, and the consequent collectivization and industrialization by his autocratic and coercive methods, backed by a teleological planning philosophy. In the area of qualitative planning, the Russian achievement was much less. China and Vietnam have already shown the importance of modifying policies to suit the different agrarian zones. They have, without withdrawing their interest in the *application* of modern science and technology, suggested that planners seriously need to take into account factors *other than* the rate of return on state funds ('capital effectiveness') and real product per man-hour. Amongst these we now mention (and discuss later in more depth) the need to have participation of ordinary workers in production planning, and the desire to iron out regional inequalities, thereby reducing the gap between urban and rural standards. In the USSR the importance of these things was also realized, but rather too late in the course of Soviet social development. After 1950, average incomes of agricultural workers began to grow closer to average incomes of non-agricultural workers (Millar, 1971; Schroeder and Severin, 1976). The urban–agriculture differential, if measured as a ratio of agricultural incomes (including payment in kind and income from private plots) to non-agricultural incomes rose from 41 per cent in 1950 to 64 per cent in 1960 and to 86 per cent in 1975. The same trend is clear if returns

TABLE 3.1. Relative income of agricultural workers in the USSR

Year	Average income of non-agricultural worker (roubles)	Average money income paid in kolkhoz and State farms[a]	
		Roubles	Percentage
1950	830	90	11
1956	928	209	22
1960	1008	331	33
1965	1190	614	55
1970	1490	961	64
1975	1780	1226	69

[a] Income in kind and income from private plots not included
Sources: Millar (1971) and Schroeder and Severin (1976), 629.

TABLE 3.2. Chemical fertilizer in the USSR

Year	Chemical fertilizer supplied
1932	1 million tons
1953	7 million tons
1967	22 million tons
1970	46 million tons
1975	73 million tons

Source: United States Congress (1976).

from private plots are excluded but the percentages are lower (Table 3.1).

Such a policy can only work, however, if parallel to the 'closing of the gap' policy, solid increases in the use of better inputs are pursued. The USSR eventually had to undertake a virtual 'industrialization of agriculture', featuring more chemical fertilizers, tractors, drainage and irrigation. Chemical inputs rose, as shown in Table 3.2.

The Soviet Union's stand here was theoretically correct in a long-term perspective. They believed that if the 'gap' can be closed, agriculture will ultimately function as efficiently as industry and large-scale transfer of labour to industry will become easier to co-ordinate and finance. What happened in practice in the earlier years, however, was:

1. Hugh investments were swallowed up in agriculture without resulting benefits to productivity (see Table 3.3). This was because political problems remained unsolved—the 'social relations of production' between peasants and workers, and between peasants and the state apparatus were mishandled. This underlines the importance for new socialist states of learning the all-important lesson that 'politics is the concentrated expression of economics'.

TABLE 3.3. USSR gross agricultural output (1940 = 100)

Year	Index
1913	71
1926–29	86
1930–36	78
1937–39	89
1940 (prewar territory)	86
1940 (present territory)	100
1941–45	50
1946–53	93
1954–58	133
1959–65	166
1966–70	205

Sources: Clarke (1972) and *Narodnoe Khoziaistvo V 1974*, 307.

2. The real wage of the non-farm population actually declined and this, in practice, became the *main method* of financing industrialization.

To develop these two points further: in the Soviet industrialization debate political ideas of a struggle against the peasants emerged, due to exaggerated fears of 'capitalist restoration in the wake of the NEP'. In 1925, Preobrazhensky was the chief economic theorist of the left opposition, which held that the retreat to the policies of the NEP heralded a move towards the restoration of capitalism. The left opposition called for a reversal of this process and the rapid development of heavy industry. Unlike the official spokesman for the government, Preobrazhensky did not see the goods famine as being caused by bad management and lack of foresight. Rather, he saw it as being symptomatic of fundamental faults in the structure of the Soviet economy. Preobrazhensky believed that the current shortage of goods was caused by the lack of normal capital formation during the period of war communism. Thus Preobrazhensky advocated a speedy and drastic increase in investment to make up for the depletion of the stock of capital that had occurred during the years of under-replacement. Without this the ceiling for the recovery would be very low indeed.

Preobrazhensky believed that it was not sufficient simply to maintain the stock of capital. Rather, productive capacity had to be greatly increased to cater for the increase in effective demand in the economy, caused by the raising of peasant incomes as a result of the abolition of rents and the reduction of agricultural taxes. If such an increase in productive capacity did not occur, then a further goods famine was likely.

Another argument for rapid industrialization was the need to absorb the surplus rural population. This was even more urgent since technological improvements in industry—for which there was great scope in the derelict Soviet economy—had a labour-displacing effect. On the industry–agriculture ratio, Preobrazhensky argued that it would be self-defeating to retard the development of industry for the sake of agriculture since this would have the effect of slowing down agricultural modernization and reducing the supply of industrial goods, which in turn would reduce the peasant's incentives to increase production.

The method proposed by Preobrazhensky to achieve this massive industrialization programme was that of 'primitive socialist accumulation'. This did not involve ruthless exploitation or the use of violence against the non-socialist sector, but consisted of a transfer of productive resources from the private sector to the socialized sector to a degree not possible under the free operation of the law of value. That is, Preobrazhensky was advocating a system of unequal exchange operating through the price structure. He pointed out that the monopolistic nature of the control of state industry greatly facilitated the implementation of a price policy and described these prices as another form of taxing private production. Preobrazhensky also supported the idea of direct taxation being used to redistribute income to the socialized sector. However, he believed taxation through prices to be a much more effective method—since the taxes were so much easier to collect and a system of direct taxation was dangerous, since it increased the possibility of a break with the peasants.

Bukharin criticized Preobrazhensky on the grounds that his 'superindustrialization' programme would have a long gestation period and would therefore be likely to cause another goods famine. Also Bukharin suggested that Preobrazhensky had misjudged the amount of force that would be needed in the implementation of his programme. Bukharin advocated priority for agriculture and maintenance of the general economic development rate at the same rate of growth produced in agriculture. In articles in *Pravda*, he argued that the left line would lead to the destruction of the worker–peasant alliance *(smyrchna)* built up by Lenin, a key aspect in keeping 'social relations' in harmony with productive forces. He correctly predicted that peasants would react to 'superindustrialization' by cutting back output and backing off from marketing agricultural surplus, and eventually industrialization would be slowed down anyway as the left's policy 'killed the goose that laid the golden egg'. He proposed an alternative policy of priority to agriculture, stability, and support of the successful peasant by way of seeds, mechanization, etc. A higher market level would then encourage industry itself, and harmony in the growth rates between industry and agriculture would be restored. He concluded that socialist forms of organization would have to be *demonstrated* as being superior to win peasant support. In his last work, *Notes of an Economist*, Bukharin made an important point, later taken up by Mao Tse Tung, that industry will decline if it does not develop on the basis of a rapidly expanding agriculture and there will be political dangers 'if the bow is drawn at too high a tension'.[2] Events proved him at least partly right, even if Preobrazensky's *pure logic* was more appealing.[3]

The second issue—which class actually financed the USSR's surplus—is very important. Barsov in the USSR in 1968 reconsidered two old reports on agricultural surplus that were prepared during the first Five-year Plan. These reports raised the issue that most accumulation was in fact achieved in the non-agricultural sectors. Subsequently a debate began between Western economists Nove (1971), Millar (1970) and Ellman (1975) which has had the effect of suggesting that most of Soviet Russia's surplus came from a lowering of the real wages of new and existing industrial workers, especially during 1929–32. Tables 3.4 and 3.5 are suggestive of this. They show strong evidence that the real wages of the non-farm workers *declined*, although per capita consumption went up 10 per cent over the period. Specifically, in summary there was a 40 per cent decline in real wages (Table 3.6).

Real consumption could rise despite a fall in real wages because of the elimination of unemployment after 1928 which, with one and a half million unemployed put to work, allowed more consumption *without* a rise in real wages. There was also a trend towards having more family members at work and a resultant decline in the number of dependants per wage earner, affecting the per capita consumption figure. Most important, too, was the shift from country to towns, where in 1928, average incomes were twice as high as rural incomes. The decline in real wages may also tend to obscure the fact that there was a change in distribution within 'workers'—new ex-agricultural workers

TABLE 3.4. Real wages, consumption and productivity, 1928–58 (1937 = 100)

Year	Real non-farm wages (that is, incomes net of compulsory deductions)	Real consumption per head	Real non-farm output per head
1928	165 (116)	91 (73)	76
1937	100	100	100
1940	94	96	96
1944	79	69	—
1948	76	93	94
1954	145	152	131
1958	167	185	165

Sources: Chapman, (1963a), p. 238; Chapman, (1963b), 144 and 181–2; Bergson, (1961), 303–4.

Notes: Average annual non-farm money wages net of taxes and bonds but including social security benefits, deflated by COL index with 1928 quantity weights. The figure in brackets for 1928 is obtained by using an index for 1928–37 with 1937 quantity weights.

Based on estimates at 1937 adjusted market prices. The alternative figure for 1928 uses 1928 prices for 1928–37.

Based on estimates at 1937 rouble factor cost.

TABLE 3.5. Real consumption per capita, 1950–75 (1958 = 100)*

	1950	1958	1965	1970	1975
Food	72	100	114	136	151
Soft goods	52	100	121	167	191
Durables	32	100	150	238	378
Personal services	72	100	136	178	219
Health and education	75	100	127	148	171
Total	67	100	121	152	177

Source: Schroeder and Severin (1976), p. 646.

Notes: *The underlying series are weighted at 1970 prices.
If we eliminate the war years and take ten years after that—if all benefit of 1930s strategy is available, then political and social history would have been different. Soviet economic strategy would have delivered ten years of stability and ten years of doubling of living standards.

TABLE 3.6. Standards of living 1928 and 1937 (1928 = 100)

Wages in money terms (1937)	400
Cost of living (1937)	700
Real wage (1937)	57
Real wage plus benefits (1937)	61

getting a lower income than older skilled workers. This means that skilled workers may have maintained their real wages. If so, there is less strength in the argument (developed by Ellman in particular) that increases in absolute surplus value as a result of declining real wages was a major source of 'surplus' for Soviet development.

This debate is most important for Vietnam, Laos, Cambodia and other new socialist states. If collectivization makes very heavy demands on labour and material inputs from non-agricultural sectors, the actual net surplus evolving in agriculture itself looks much smaller than is usually assumed, and the contribution of industry and industrial workers to overall surplus looks correspondingly greater. This would seem to challenge quite a few Chinese communist theories and indicates that Vietnam's emphasis on industry in its current Five-year Plan (and Cambodia's neglect of it) becomes crucial, and Vietnam is on the right track. Before the full lessons of the debate can be absorbed, however, it is also necessary to bring out the class changes that were going on in the USSR. The Ellman approach leaves this element out. It was not just a question of more labour inputs into industry and agriculture but a problem of *who* were employed, whether their employment was a result of mass mobilization campaigns; whether the worker's savings were enforced or whether they understood their role and made voluntary savings. We have no space here to go into these questions of 'social relations', but enough has been said to indicate that these are highly relevant factors. We are more likely to learn something from going into them thoroughly than following Charles Bettelheim's (1977) ultra-left attempt to prove the USSR has been 'capitalist' almost from the beginning and to assert that 'state power' was 'captured' because the state apparatus had allowed capitalist social relations to be reborn. Thus workers were separated from the means of production, labour power remained a commodity and the enterprises were separated from and managed independently. Such an approach seems to confuse ideological class struggle in the period after Lenin's death and Stalin's death with the actual fusion of the state apparatus with a new capitalist class by political class struggle, and it is significant that nowhere does Bettelheim specify the mechanism of extraction of surplus value in the USSR in the 1920s.

Planning issues then and now

From 1928–32 Soviet planning began to emerge with its characteristic 'social model' and planning methodology, and some of the questions raised in the previous section were answered. The key bottlenecks proved to be not finance or productive capacity, but the net marketable agricultural surplus and shortages of key inputs, especially new products which tended to be neglected if not already incorporated into the planners' product groups.

It was soon discovered that questions of balanced versus unbalanced growth were closely related to the performance of ministries and whether they tried to set up their own plants and duplicate plants other ministries could have provided.[4]

A very early lesson was learned about time-horizons, but steadfastly ignored: that long periods of gestation for investment projects should be avoided. Not only did they impose substantial 'opportunity costs' on the Soviet economy (in the form of capital that was 'frozen' in unfinished projects), but inflationary pressures were inherently involved as wages were paid before production eventually came 'on stream'.

In the area of planning methods, Strumilin (1963) successfully led a criticism of the concept and strategy of 'balanced growth' and suggested 'taut' plans. As a result maximum targets were set with low estimates of completion time and of required material supplies in order to 'stretch' firms. Consistency and feasibility were rather neglected. 'Balances' were used as guides to planning, but the idea of 'closing' the gap between demand and supply by curbing demand was rejected. Rather, the Soviet approach was that if there was a shortage of inputs of, say, steel for trucks, one did not cut the output of trucks, but instead squeezed more steel out of suppliers *or* ran down strategic stocks or reserves *or* imported steel *or* tightened 'norms' to force enterprises to use scrap and substitutes. Such 'material balances' were selfcontained and were rarely put together. No effective method of determining intersectoral relations emerged until 1959 with the more widespread introduction of the 'input–output' method. The result was that in the 1950s about one-third of industrial plants in the USSR were not fulfilling annual plans because they could not obtain scarce materials.

Finances and taxes played a big role in Soviet planning, but there is no space to discuss them here. In any case, finance, taxation and prices are likely to play a far different role in a small socialist economy which trades with the rest of the world and has a small area, than in the more self-sufficient USSR and China. The huge markets of those countries alter the role of the price mechanism since 'quick' signals to enterprises are less possible there.

Looking back on Chinese and Soviet experience, it is possible to draw conclusions about what to avoid, and what to aim for. Small socialist states such as Vietnam, Cambodia or Laos, as latecomers to the world socialist stage, can take certain steps to improve the *realism* of their plans and the effectiveness of their execution, paying attention to cost effectiveness and incorporating social goals more intelligently into the planning processes themselves. Below we offer some comments on the minimal necessary safeguards for efficient planning, based on our study of Soviet and Chinese experience but eliminating those aspects likely to be irrelevant to smaller socialist states.

Investment Planning is the Key

In order to avoid the 'freezing' of large resources, too many simultaneous projects should not be started. The whole notion of 'investment' must be studied carefully since, as Kalecki (1969) pointed out, investment has two edges —it is a flow of expenditures but is also the creation of physical capacity which remains.

Investment figures, at least for major categories, should always be split into three headings:

1. Value of schemes of fixed investment which are *completed* in the period and so become operational.
2. Value of partly completed projects at the end of the period, *less* corresponding value at beginning of the period.
3. Addition to working capital of the sector, to support the higher flow of output.

Even if this can only be done roughly, it will emphasize the difference between expenditure (which is what the investment figures necessarily are) and *new capacity becoming available*. In detailed planning, information can usefully be given about the value of schemes *started* so that the two components of the second heading above can both be shown. To know 'capacity' (preferably in physical terms) of plants in use at the beginning and end of the period is also valuable.

More specifically, for each industry, (including power and railways) the plan needs an estimate of:

1. The amount of *additional capital in use*, which will be needed between the beginning and end of the Plan, if the output target is to be achieved. Reasonable methods of approximation can be developed. Logically, the process is as follows:
   (a) estimate the amount of plant, or capacity, likely to be available at the start of the Plan;
   (b) estimate output likely to be obtained from this in the final plan year, allowing for assumed changes in shift-working (if any) and for progress in the art of running the plant;
   (c) subtract (b) from output target, and use capital–output ratios for new plants (or extensions, or a mixture) to get additional capital required (including inventories).

2. The increase in the value of partly finished projects between the beginning and end of the Plan. In some cases (for instance, power and perhaps steel) this may be done for individual industries, but at least in the first instance it will be best, as argued above, to make a statistical allowance by some simple rule covering the whole category. The sum of 1. and 2. can then be compared with the (net) investment which had been assumed for the sector.

Investment flows are of three types—flows of heavy equipment, semi-manufactures and construction. To study each case it is possible to apply capital–output ratios (that is, we can assume that for every \$1 million worth of annual output of machine tools, we would need a prior investment of \$5 million of equipment, \$4.5 million of other equipment, \$2 million of construction and \$2.5 million of *stocks* held by producers and trades). This principle allows planning to relate the growth of production to investment over the ten-year span. A simple beginning can be made by assuming a linear relationship. This is a severe restriction on the planner's freedom to manoeuvre, but it makes the issues clear and is not unrealistic. Investment cannot be easily started or stopped from one year to another (nor is it always desirable to do this even where possible).

Consistency and feasibility tests are essential

A vast amount of work is required under this heading. Logically the process is an iterative one, because if serious inconsistencies are revealed, the Plan should be altered and alterations to meet one inconsistency may have serious repercussions on the balance in some other respects. In the first stage this is probably best ignored: in effect we assume *either* that the imbalances are small and can be met without awkward repercussions (for example, that the increase in industrial output requires rather more investment but that transport needs less) *or* that the imbalance which might seem to create bottlenecks can be met by additional imports, and perhaps that big surpluses can be exported, rather than requiring a reduced programme.

On this basis it is probably right to aim at doing all the tests more or less simultaneously (or in whatever order is easiest), using the existing set of figures, rather than try to arrange them in a logical order of 'criticalness' and make revisions in the light of the first before doing the second. Planners should also consider whether the relative order in which industries are developed could be changed, by postponing to a later Plan some investments which have some or all of these characteristics:

1. they require a high proportion of imports;
2. they have to be complemented by big power schemes;
3. they take a long time to complete (and yield no product meanwhile);
4. they yield a relatively small amount of net output and employment when they *are* completed;
5. they produce something which could be imported (or simply foregone), so that their absence does not imply a bottleneck.
6. They fit in better with new political priorities of the country.

They need also to consider whether some investments might be brought forward to the current Plan. These should be *quick* to complete, and preferably:

1. have a fairly low import content;
2. give a high net output and employment;
3. produce something which is useful in one way or another (relieves a bottleneck, saves imports, pleases consumers).

Adjustments to unforeseen events are inevitable

There are three main reasons for trouble developing:

1. An important factor which is outside domestic control may turn out worse than seemed likely. For example, there may be a bad harvest or a fall in demand for export goods, or less capital inflow than was assumed. If export prices fell but import prices remained unchanged, there could be unemployment in export industries.
2. Some important items (such as, import requirements) are extremely *hard* to calculate, and the estimate may prove too low even though internal production targets are in fact achieved.

3. Something which is at least theoretically under domestic control is not achieved—for example, taxes are not imposed as assumed.

An intelligent study should be made of the Plan for possible trouble-spots arising from these factors, and their consequences examined.

Special attention is needed for the construction industry

Construction is an essential element in development. The sort of study needed for a central plan would be on these broad lines (Reddaway, 1965, chapters 3 to 6):

1. From the investment figures plus renewals produce a total value of construction in the plan period. (Logically, repairs and maintenance should also be included, and this would be important for estimating labour and materials). The figure might well give both the gross value and the value added, and it would be useful to preserve the breakdown by type of construction (housing, schools, factories, etc.) which would emerge from the process of making the estimate.
2. Allocate the total and the parts between years in the light of the build-up which is expected and what can be estimated about the position in the end years of the previous period.
3. Split each year's figures into (a) *completions* and (b) *change in work-in-progress*.

Qualitative aspects of planning must be explicitly borne in mind when setting 'quantitative' targets

We must first bear in mind that most works on socialist planning for the Third World have been based on the experience of Russia or China. Both countries are rich in resources and are two of the largest in the world in terms of land and population. Moreover, before their revolutions they had already achieved certain levels of development. These conditions are missing in most Third World countries except Brazil and Argentina and perhaps India, Indonesia and Angola. One problem, which planners do not consider, but that has appeared nakedly since the American defeat in Indochina and in the former Portuguese colonies of Africa, is the lack of cadres properly trained scientifically or in management. One extreme example is Angola. When the Portuguese left, there was just a handful of MPLA cadres who knew how to drive a truck. They could not move coffee from the plantations to the port. Not only are the problems quite different between armed/political revolution and scientific/productive revolution, the solutions are quite often without a base of local historical experience in these countries. Hence manpower planning becomes crucial—the human factor in production needs careful nurturing and, apart from this, the planning system must tackle the problem of the workers' involvement in the planning process and in industrial management. This is the 'social relations of production' aspect which, as discussed in the first section, may put a brake on the expansion of productive forces even when the planning is good.

To take an example, the urban wage-earners in small socialist countries often want land of their own. There is not only a 'proletarianization' of the peasantry going on, but also a 'de-proletarianization' of the workers (Pollitt, 1977). To get people to work to full capacity while they long for a plot of land, chickens, animals, etc., is a task that socialist planning ignores at its peril. (We have already referred to the rather heavy contribution of Soviet urban workers to surplus in this regard.)

Another example is the need to specify which region of a country should have priority in receiving fertilizer, seeds, the best cadres and other essentials. In the southern part of Vietnam, the National Liberation Front (NLF) had already seen this point before the war ended. It was noted that South Vietnam was actually made up of 'zones' where the land was of different fertility and was worked under different kinds of ownership structures. So a different tax and land distribution policy was applied by the NLF. This is a good example of 'qualitative planning'.

What this seems to involve is that, as part of a development plan, a number of criteria *other than* real product per man-hour or the rate of return on state funds should be entered into the planning calculations. Presumably these should include ironing out differences in the contribution expected from rural and urban people (as well as levelling up the standard of living of workers and peasants); redistribution of income in an egalitarian direction; choosing the appropriate technology with some room for human-intensive technology where feasible and ironing out regional differences in incomes and employment opportunities.

Imported technology will be inevitable and must be carefully controlled

We have argued that a nation embarking on industrialization could fairly wisely plan its investment programme. If an adequate and competent number of industrial engineers are not available, surely technical advice can be obtained from the sellers of industrial equipment in more advanced countries. But it is not quite that simple! However technically competent the local engineers may seem to be, they often tend to be overambitious. Nothing less than the most advanced techniques will satisfy them, whether they have been rigorously tested or not. Moreover, the planners may not receive the best advice from foreign equipment salesmen. Indeed they are often induced to buy novel, expensive and sometimes still experimental equipment. Always faced with the need for economizing on foreign exchange outlays, the planners frequently let contracts to unreliable, low-bid contractors only to discover subsequently that contract price is not necessarily the best measure of a good bargain. Moreover, there is a great difference between the total investment programme of a developed industrial country as compared with that of an emergent industrial nation. The former can afford to make technological experiments because it has a sound 'going concern' on which it can depend, whereas the newly industrialized country must rely almost entirely on the one or the few new installations which it builds. Hence a planning blunder, which might affect only a marginal increment of 5 per cent in a mature economy, can become a major tragedy in a newly industrialized country which has staked everything on the success of one new plant. More than that, this one new plant may technically determine the success or failure of a number of other plants with which it is linked in an industrial chain.

However difficult the planning of key industrial projects, the success of the programme will obviously depend on a country's ability to finance the imported components. Very seldom can long-term loans of adequate size be negotiated before the industrialization programme is launched. Consequently, there is the ever-present temptation to buy machinery from foreign manufacturers on short-term credits. A tangled, unco-ordinated mass of external debts can result which, sooner or later, will have to be funded under very disadvantageous circumstances, usually at high interest rates. Even more vexatious is the situation that arises when, by reason of overoptimism, plants are begun before the total financing has been arranged. Half-built structures then stand like spectres, inert and for the time, useless, while heavy overhead costs fall in some untraceable way on the entire economy. Too often the presumption seems to be that it is better to build something large and elaborate for the future at any expense, rather than be content with smaller projects that can be completed swiftly and put into productive operation promptly.

Meantime, a host of difficulties arise from the altogether commendable efforts that are made to construct the largest possible portion of new plants with local materials, funds and labour. Here two kinds of problems emerge, stemming respectively from an overestimation of local engineering skill and from the unforeseen impact of an accelerated investment programme on the going-concern economy. Thus the quality of structural work for buildings, machinery foundations or other construction may prove quite inadequate when the foreign engineers arrive to install the imported equipment. For the most part, precipitate haste and overconfidence are the causes of these troubles and once again attempts to save money can be self-defeating.

In the next section we illustrate some of these points by looking at Vietnamese experience, especially since the year 1975, when socialist economic planning was introduced throughout the country and hard questions had to be faced about sources of finance, foreign technology, and involvement with various agencies such as the Asian Development Bank (which is financing new power schemes for Ho Chi Minh City—formerly Saigon), the World Bank and ASEAN.

VIETNAM: PLANNING AND FOREIGN TECHNOLOGY IMPORTS IN A SMALL SOCIALIST STATE

In the light of what we have just said about the role of foreign finance and technology in the planning process, it is appropriate to look at the Vietnamese Development Plan and the Vietnamese Foreign Investment Law.

Vietnam has been criticized[5] for allowing foreign companies to come into the country with new technology on the licensing system—involving payment partly made according to sales of products from the process. This criticism seems to us to be misplaced. Experience shows that it is important to persuade foreign companies to leave technicians with a real interest in getting a process *working* as distinct from the 'turnkey' system (purchase of whole factories) of merely constructing the plant ready to go on stream. If the experts leave soon after completion, the local people may not know really how to maintain the new blueprint. Moreover, foreigners often prefer to sell a turnkey with a complicated technology to a small Third World country. Why is this so? Because such corporations fear mass copying of their technology and wish to slow down the process. All this imposes unnecessary costs on the recipients. There will be expensive 'shells' in buildings, expensive storage, expensive replacements.

A second point in relation to Vietnamese policy is that, as many of the products will be exported anyway, the 'share' of the foreign company is not crucially related to sales within Vietnam itself. Further it should be noted that Vietnam is looking to France, Australia, Norway, Italy and a number of other countries.[6] It has sought a variety of foreign technology imports from diffuse sources.

Experience in the relatively short period since 1975 already indicates that a determined underdeveloped country can very quickly develop a highly advantageous approach to offshore oil exploration. What the Vietnamese did was to reverse the previous Saigon regime's 'open door' policy to foreign investors which had awarded concessions on highly disadvantageous terms. In its place there is now a two-pronged policy of (a) reserving some of the most promising offshore areas for its own exploration efforts to be undertaken at its risk with technical services and financing from Norway, and (b) negotiating service-contracts with state oil companies of West European States which are particularly anxious to obtain long-term supplies of crude oil—Deminex of West Germany and ENI of Italy. Such service-contracts reportedly provided that the companies will undertake exploration risk and receive the right to buy up to 45 per cent of any oil found at 7 to 10 per cent below world market prices. Accordingly the Vietnamese would end up with 95 per cent of the profits and foreign state oil companies with 5 per cent.

It has become clear that the Vietnamese planners feel that this approach should be extended to each sector of the economy where market conditions allow. This is necessary in order to find what modified versions of the best two or three technologies are most suited to Vietnamese conditions. That is the way Japanese industry developed in the 1950s and 1960s. The ultimate big successes then were Japanese modifications of rather unexpected foreign technologies which worked. With their experience in modifying captured United States' technology and donated Soviet technology during the War of National Independence, the Vietnamese should have few problems on this score. The integument within which foreign technology and planning will interact has two important dimensions: basic ideological choices and strategic planning goals.

Ideological Choice in Economic Policy

Since Vietnam's scientists first shocked some of the neo-Maoist Western left in 1975 with their categorical rejection of two kinds of science—ordinary 'bourgeois' science and 'Shanghai' or 'barefoot' science, a Vietnamese position on social development and the role of technology has clearly emerged.

In the first place, the Vietnamese stress science *qua* science and are keen to use the most modern technology. They have no plans for intellectuals to 'learn from the peasants'; they say their intellectuals mostly *are* peasants. Also rejected were Chinese 'gang of four' or Maoist ideas about 'walking on two legs'[7] in a purist form in industrial policy, as well as autarchy and 'self-reliance' as the main thrust of national economic policy.

The official Vietnamese stance regarding 'walking-on-two-legs' has been put succinctly in a recent interview with Nguyen Khac Vien (Limqueco, 1978):

> The formula walking-on-two-legs makes the real world oversimplified . . .
>
> We must use a formula to change from a simple to a technologically advanced society. This means *many* legs, not only two.
>
> When we talk about economics, we must use precise words instead of *images*. If you go to village committee and tell them to adopt 'walking on two legs', it will be difficult for them to understand what you are talking about.

The place of 'Chinese-line' economic strategy has been taken in Vietnam by the policy of making science and technology the keystone wherever possible.

Associated with this is a policy of pushing ahead fast with industry, especially petrochemicals, and the construction and use of modern machinery. The 1976–80 State Plan has also put forward as its second basic task the building of many new installations in heavy industry, particularly the machine industry.

Now ideological questions do certainly arise from foreign investment and technology in an economy which is socialist yet underdeveloped, and it is appropriate in a survey of this kind to indicate *likely* areas of conflict, without being able to pronounce at this stage on just how serious they are likely to be for Vietnam, Laos and Cambodia or how effectively they are likely to be handled.

1. If such a socialist state embarks on a road of modern technology, it will tend to create a stratum of experts and managers whose ideology can reinforce the *status quo* in respect to present income distribution. Care must be taken that differentials in income do not become ossified and challenge the socialist morality of society.
2. There will be some adjustment problems because the delicate balance between traditional, intermediate and modern technology tends to be disrupted if whole plants are imported.
3. There may be a problem that, in importing foreign technology, the leadership gets 'hooked' on economic growth. There may be a tendency to forget about social transformation. In *this* sense, foreign technology does have an influence on class relations and the issue of 'red' versus 'expert' is almost sure to arise in Vietnam in the future.

Already the Vietnamese leadership has been forced to face up to solving some of these questions. For example it eliminated a clause in the draft (1976) *Regulations on Foreign Investment in the Socialist Republic of Vietnam* which would have required foreign technicians to spend half of their earnings in Vietnam, and has amended another clause which had ruled out negotiation.

The Vietnamese Communist Party's view on handling these issues is that *three* revolutions must accompany developmental efforts in the economic field: (a) the revolution in production relations (classes, income distribution, etc.); (b) the revolution in culture; and (c) the revolution in science and technology. Here the Vietnamese have made their own contribution to the discussion of socialist development, based on their own conditions as a smaller socialist state. In Le Duan's account of the three revolutions, he says that in the revolution of *relations of production* there is a transformation of the systems of ownership, distribution, the organization or production and the managerial system. In the *cultural* revolution there will be a system of values incorporating socialist patriotism, labour collective mastery and Vietnamese poetry and literature. In the *technical* revolution there will be a 'proper combination' of mechanization with handicraft methods, building the large scale and 'using it as the core force' and a training programme for managerial and technical cadres. The cultural revolution, Vietnamese style, is to consist not only of 'mass campaigns' but will aim at an integration of cultural change with the other two 'revolutions' (relations of production, technique) at every level.

The issues of foreign technology and the Vietnamese foreign investment laws should also be seen in a practical context of budgetary and foreign exchange bottlenecks. The desire to get foreign exchange, whether as bilateral aid or from the World Bank and multinationals, is a result of the pivotal role given to the Five-year Plan in overall social development. It is seen as a *stage* in a drive to bring Vietnamese standards up to those of prewar Britain. Given the 'hangover' of bourgeois values in the south, a failure to fulfil the production targets of the Plan would greatly increase social tensions and slow down change.

Similarly foreign capital or foreign exchange is a central point in the budget expenditure within the second Five-year Plan. The Budget has been constructed to spend US $7.5 billion over the five years. Yet in 1976 there was only US $100 million in foreign exchange, with US $75 million frozen in American banks. To meet this the Vietnamese used half of the drawing rights with the International Monetary Fund, and sought economic aid when all attempts to get the US government to honour a US $4.5 billion commitment by former President Nixon failed. By the end of 1976, about US $2.4 billion was received in economic aid from the Communist bloc, and US $0.7 billion from France and Sweden. However, much more will be needed to close the budget and balance-of-payments gap. Hence the 'welcome' to foreign capital inflow on strict terms.

One thing that emerges is the clear desire to get foreign investment into areas where there can be subsequent exports (oil, textiles). The Revised Investment code allows foreign investors to export their share of production duty free and internal investment patterns favour agriculture, timber and fishing. But this just reflects the importance to the Plan of the overall drive to develop agricultural and light industrial exports plus oil.

So this is one area where Vietnam is practising a policy of 'if you want to develop heavy industry, give priority to agriculture and light industry',[8] for Vietnam has, since July 1976, been stepping up agriculture and light industry to increase exports[9] in order to get the capital to finance heavy industry (Chanda, 1976a, 1976b, 1976c); some Vietnamese investment patterns in 1977 resembled those of China in 1956 (a 'moderate' year containing both Maoist and non-Maoist priorities). However, Vietnam can follow neither the Chinese nor the Soviet road for reasons to do with its own internal problems—lack of experience with new industry, a high level of unemployment, a sizeable number of urbanized rootless people, and large numbers of ex-enemy military to put in occupations. Moreover, Vietnam is seeking to widen its former triangular relations with Moscow and Peking into a quadripartite alliance with the USSR, China, the United States and Western Europe, and Japan. Her planning, exchange earnings and decisions on foreign investment will all have to reflect this basic process.

CONCLUSIONS

Although the main emphasis of this review has been on planning techniques for countries like Vietnam, it is appropriate to close with some remarks about the character of the Vietnamese economic and social model in its *operational* aspects, as these affect strategies and planning.

Vietnam's model combines planning with some considerable decentralization of control at the provincial level. Its management structure is not 'mass meeting' control, but there is considerable consultation with workers before plans are submitted to the enterprise board for final decision. Although Party committees are important parts of the control mechanism, they do not appear to have the unheard-of power given to them in China under Teng Hsiaoping since 1977. Rather than describing the Vietnamese system as a 'mixture' of the Chinese and Soviet systems it is probably better to describe its points as constituting a Vietnamese whole, evolving against the specific background of the experience of the National Liberation Front before 1975, and the political configurations since—notably the desire to obtain foreign capital from as widely dispersed sources as possible.

We described the 'distance' between Vietnam and Maoist China on 'walking-on-two-legs' previously in this chapter. Another difference with other socialist countries is the Vietnamese line on the roles of the peasantry and the working class in the process of socialist development. Here again we may return to an authoritative source—the interview with Nguyen Khac Vien (Limqueco, 1978):

> In Vietnam, we say that the peasants cannot 'lead' the revolution. The peasantry is a strong force but without the leadership of the working class, the peasant mass can move dangerously. In the last century, the capitalist led the peasant to overthrow feudalism, but the peasantry cannot lead the road to socialist revolution. Sometimes peasant revolts can lead back to feudalism, as one can witness in some Third World countries.
>
> Can the working class lead the peasantry? Or can the Communist Party be led by the peasants? In agriculture, the peasants have much experience, but they have practically no knowledge of science. Now we must bring science to the countryside, so that not only must one learn from the peasants, one must also provide them with science and technology.
>
> If one has the attitude of not needing to learn from peasants, then one falls into the bourgeois outlook of actually despising the peasantry. If

you only 'learn from the peasants', that is demagogy. Marx says that the proletarian revolution combines the working class with the highest culture of mankind.

As to the question of bureaucracy, the Vietnamese are, of course, aware of it. They know perfectly well that Lenin's government was forced to employ thousands of civil servants from the old Tsarist regime, and of the problems to which this gave rise. They acknowledge their own reliance, in present circumstances, on former 'enemy' administrations. At the same time, they firmly reject the view that is creeping into some Western Marxist discussions that there is a certain 'logic' in adopting heavy industry and science priorities, a logic which ends in the creation of Djilas' 'new class' or some variant of it. According to this interpretation (including some who formerly supported Vietnam in the national independence war), there is an inevitable tendency with such priorities to go the 'Russian way': to neglect service industries and consumer goods,[10] to subsidize excessively blue-collar workers to the detriment of the hard-working professionals, to crack down heavily on intellectual dissent, and to run the economy by bureaucratic decree neglecting the real problems of the population.

It would be a country of miracle-makers which could wholly avoid such a category of pitfalls. Certainly the Vietnamese would not claim to be able to do so. In discussions with them, however, we have found three answers to this general worry about the future coming through, and we will conclude by summarizing them.

1. On the question of the new privileged stratum arising on the wake of rapid industrialization, the Vietnamese see a problem to be solved by carefully balancing the so-called 'imperatives of industrialization' (that is, managerial and executive power) against the gains in real product per man-hour which they seek. They certainly know that uncontrolled forced-draught industrialization transfers power to those with technical knowledge. The role of the conscious socialist forces is to carry out a judicious combination of 'growth' and political democracy:
2. The 'Three' revolutions, it will be noted, include a cultural revolution. Part of this involves reminding a mandarin-inclined administration of the need to remain close to the people. It is a 'cultural' revolution which is to be combined with the technical revolution in a steady, clear way in day-to-day planning and administration. The question of whether institutional-operational mechanisms to ensure that this happens will be successfully established in Vietnam, is of course, still an open question. (Mictal Kalecki once pointed out something about bureaucrats. In a country like Poland they lived little above the average standard; their 'Stalinism' consisted largely in fighting for the principle of subsidies to workers, free health

and education against the demands of 'liberals' and managers to put everything on a productivity basis. They were an important barrier against the abuses of the socialist market system in the headlong rush to economic reform after 1956. This should be borne in mind when assessing the role of 'bureaucrats' in Vietnam.)

3. The problem of bureaucracy in theoretical elaboration, is, moreover, full of pitfalls. Take 'centralization' and 'decentralization'. In any socialist economy, there are always some economic processes in the process of being decentralized. Technology and new blueprints were recentralized in the Soviet reform of 1965 while many areas of light industry were given to local government bodies and the powers of enterprises were strong in relation to the central authority. There is no such thing as a *wholly* centralized economy. Only those mesmerized by American economics books with their absurd exaggerations about 'command economies' would believe that there could be. Apart from flying in the face of the actual situation in Vietnam and China, to say nothing of Eastern Europe, such models as 'state bureaucratic socialism' or 'command economy', so beloved by the second-rate textbooks on 'comparative economic systems' in fact condemn *all* socialist regimes to the 'original sin of irrationality'. For 'rationality' is usually defined by them in terms of non-centralism, of non-planning, being in essence the optimalization theorems of welfare economics—long ago discredited in the 'Cambridge Controversies' by the work of Piero Sraffa, Joan Robinson (1977) and others.

'Bureaucracy' can also be interpreted in different ways. For some it is the number of civil servants;[11] for others it is a vertical system of planning and industrial administration. For yet others bureaucracy should be understood in a *sociological* sense, as a new social caste.[12] We must be careful, moreover, not to let 'bureaucracy' become another one of the 'hang-ups' of the Western left, and especially the United States' radical political economists, that can distort analyses of the realities of the international situation in which a country like Vietnam finds itself, and of the class balance of forces inside the country. Too many of the vital debates and policies of the past in the socialist bloc, instead of being explored, have been dismissed under some such stigmatization as 'Stalinist' or 'bureaucratic' in a way which is the very antithesis of analysis. Such discussions often reflect the way Americans analyse Asia through the prism of their own humanitarian and introspective concerns (Pollitt, 1977), rather than what is the case for peasant, proletarian and planner in places like Cuba or Vietnam.

Any socialist society needs to find a way of carrying through its investment function. To achieve this, certain institutional mechanisms will be set up to carry it out.[13] In some countries like Cuba and Vietnam, some combination of these will be tried out. We have tried to emphasize however, that merely copying one of the communist giants is ruled out, and that the carrying out of the investment function in an efficient way is the major task for small socialist states.

NOTES

1. Narcomfin was the Peoples' Financial Commissariat—roughly the Treasury.
2. Bukharin's views can be seen in Erlick (1960), pp. 24–32 and in Wolfe (1957). In the work by Wolfe, part of Bukharin's 'Notes of an Economist' appear in English in the Appendix.
3. Sartre (1976) makes the point that *voluntarism* was common to Preobrazensky, Trotsky and Stalin, and in fact Stalin was therefore able to take over part of the Preobrazensky line. Like Preobrazensky, Che Guevara developed a voluntarism (which was more mass-based) but as Brian Pollitt (1977) pointed out, he also produced an undemocratic voluntarism for Cuba which turned monstrous.
4. The Soviet term is 'chaotic departmentalism'. For example, the Ministry for Agricultural Machinery in 1932 ended up supplying only 16 per cent of such machinery—the rest was made by farms themselves.
5. There have been many such attacks, but all have been encapsulated in one article of vituperative pessimism on the future of new Asian socialist states, namely André Gunder Frank (1977).
6. Petro-Vietnam and the Italian state oil company AGIP signed an agreement in April 1977 on oil search and exploitation off the Vietnamese coast. France has given Vietnam economic aid, as have Sweden and USSR. It is also reported that Norway will be building an offshore exploration training centre in Vietnam, and has offered a $45 million credit package, backed by Norwegian banks and a consortium of Norwegian oil companies, including $36 million at low interest rate.
7. 'Walking-on-two-legs' refers to the Chinese policy of simultaneously combining large and small-scale: capital-intensive and labour-intensive techniques, and modern and indigenous technology.
8. This is not the paradox it seems; the surpluses earned in agriculture and light industry are useful sources of finance for 'further industrialization'.
9. The export drive is in timber and forestry products; shellfish and shrimps; coffee and tea; and textiles made with Japanese machinery.
10. A recent example is Cutler *et al.* (1977) in its remarks on 'one-sided economic planning' in communist countries. See also discussion with these authors in *Business Week* July 17, 1978, 80) under the title 'A Marxist assault on Marx'.
11. Such a crude analysis of bureaucracy undermines the validity of much of the attack on planned economies in Assar Lindbeck (1977).
12. In which case the 'horizontal' bureaucracy entrenched in enterprises could be more of a problem than the 'Stalinist planners' vertical system of planning.
13. Work on the planning *systems* of Vietnam. North Korea and Cambodia (as against our emphasis on methodology) has been carried out by Suzanne Paine, Economics Faculty, Cambridge University, England.

REFERENCES

Bettelheim, C. (1977). Class Struggle in the U.S.S.R., Harvester Press, London.
Bergson, A. (1961). *The Real National Income of Soviet Russia Since 1928*, Harvard University Press, Cambridge, Mass.

Chanda, N. (1976a). 'Hanoi tries a friendly line'. *Far Eastern Economic Review*, **93**, 13–14.
Chanda, N. (1976b). 'Vietnam banks on industry'. *Far Eastern Economic Review*, **93**, 42–44.
Chanda, N. (1976c). 'The East-West touch'. *Far Eastern Economic Review*, **94**, 20.
Chapman, J. G. (1963a). 'Consumption'. In A. Bergson, and S. Kuznets (eds.) *Economic Trends in the Soviet Union*, Harvard University Press, Cambridge, Mass., pp. 235–282.
Chapman, J. G. (1963b). *Real Wages in Soviet Russia since 1928*, Harvard University Press, Cambridge, Mass.
Clarke, R. A. (1972). *Soviet Economic Facts 1917–1970*, Macmillan, London.
Cutler, A. *et al.*, (1977). *Marx's Capital and Capitalism Today*, 2 vols., Routledge and Kegan Paul, London.
Ellman, M. (1975). 'Did the agricultural surplus provide the resources for the increase in investment in the USSR during the first five year plan?' *Economic Journal*, **85**, 864–883.
Erlick, A. (1960). *The Soviet Industrialization Debate*, Harvard University Press, Cambridge, Mass.
Frank, A. G. (1977). Long live transideological enterprises, *The Review*, **1**, 1.
Kalecki, M. (1969). *Theory of Economic Growth in a Socialist Economy*, Blackwell, Oxford.
Kusinen, O. (ed.) (1960). *Fundamentals of Marxism–Leninism* (English edition), Moscow.
Limqueco, P. (1978). 'Interview with Nguyen Khac Vien'. *Journal of Contemporary Asia*, **8**, 4.
Lindbeck, A. (1977). *The Political Economy of the New Left: An Outsider's View*, New York University Press, New York.
Mao Tse Tung (no date). *Selected Works*, Vol. 5, International Publishers, New York.
Millar, J. R. (1970). 'Soviet rapid development and the agricultural surplus hypothesis'. *Soviet Studies*, **22**, 77–93.
Millar, J. R. (ed.) (1971). *The Soviet Rural Community*, University of Illinois Press, Urbana.
Nove, A. (1971).'The agricultural surplus hypothesis: a comment on James R. Millar's article'. *Soviet Studies*, **22**, 394–401.
Pollitt, B. (1977). 'Moral and material incentives in socialist economic development'. *Journal of Contemporary Asia*, **7**, 1, 116–123.
Preobrazensky, E. (1965). *The New Economics* (translated by Brian Pearce) Clarendon Press, Oxford.
Reddaway, W. B. (1965). *The Development of the Indian Economy*, Allen and Unwin, London.
Robinson, Joan (1977). 'The guidelines of orthodox economics'. *Journal of Contemporary Asia*, **7**, 1, 22–26.
Sartre, J. P. (1976). 'Socialism in one country'. *New Left Review*, **100**, 143–163.
Schroeder, G. E. and Severin, B. S. (1976). 'Soviet consumption and income policies in perspective'. In United States Congress (1976), pp. 620–660.
Strumilin, S. G. (1963). *Na Planovom Fronte (On the Planning Front)*, USSR Academy of Sciences, Moscow.
United States Congress (1976). *Soviet Economy in a New Perspective*, Joint Economic Commitee, Washington, DC.
Wolfe, B. (1957). *Kruschev and Stalin's Ghost*, Praeger, New York.

Planning Industrial Development
Edited by David F. Walker

Chapter 4

Industrialization and Regional Disparities

Jean–Michel Roux

Translated from the French by
Claudette Deschênes and David Walker

Although regions existed first, industry has greatly affected them. While it assures the prosperity of urban poles it also submits most areas to economic exploitation and socio-political domination. Nevertheless, it constitutes the basis of planning to the extent that it promises a diffusion and multiplication of those poles of decision and accumulation, and as far as a social consensus establishes the priority of overall economic growth (with or without internal redistribution of income) as a major indicator of development.

The centres of capitalistic power (whether private or state-controlled) are concentrated in a few areas, while minor tasks are left to the small poles. Decision centres reveal an incapacity to control in detail the micro-disparities which they generate in space. Thus the cultural model of development which is linked to scientific and technical progress is losing its force. This is notably the case in prosperous countries capable of imposing their preferences on the rest of the world.

If new planning procedures that permit the lessening of the disequilibrium which results from industrialization are not found, industrialization itself will remain suspect. To a degree, it will be a sign of underdevelopment. Nevertheless, stimulating the economy remains the only way to raise living standards. How can this contradiction be overcome?

Planners live on a volcano. All their concepts vacillate with the effects of the economic crisis and its corollaries. This implicates both the dominant form of urbanism (Binney, Cantel, and Darley, 1976) and the restructuring of industry. I am taking the opportunity in this essay to criticize terminology, but not just as a basic exercise; it corresponds to a type of planning practice about which a critical examination is urgent. This practice uses a general scheme of the following type:

With acknowledgements to Jérome Lion and Philippe Tourny.

1. Definition of the area to be planned.
2. Analysis of the principal mechanisms by which the area functions. Thus the region is described as a system—certainly an open one but nevertheless restricted.
3. Judgements are then made about disequilibrium and disparity within the region itself and in comparison with its neighbours.
4. The objectives of development are defined.
5. A programme is drawn up which is compatible with the power that the planners have, and with the criteria for locating various types of facility, especially industrial ones.

In this process everything must be discussed as it is impossible to focus solely on industry: the nature of the region, the form of regional analysis, the nature of development, the constraints on the location of new industrial plants.

It is necessary to set in context the criticisms, which are made about industrialization. We discuss industry only as a means of treating regional disparities within a nation or within a group of fairly homogeneous nations, barely touching on the topic of industry as a general means of modernizing the economy. We discuss the underdevelopment of some regions of western Europe, which is not self-evident compared with a country like Bangladesh, for example.

In the realm which concerns us, the newness of some of the problems makes it necessary to refer to a number of recently published works, principally in the French language, since there is often a delay in information from elsewhere.

Lastly, the nature of the debate and the actual direction which regional development policy is going to take, at least in the industrialized countries, forces one to move away from classical theories of industrial location and, more generally, from the principles of marginal economics which inspired them.

THE REGION AS A POLITICAL TRADITION

The notion of region can be employed at a number of scales. Current practice in industrialized countries favours at least two of them: the province (*Land*, state) especially in federal countries, and the small region usually centred on a city and identified by a certain physical and agrarian unity. The Swiss canton would be the best example of the latter. These two types of region are the only ones which cover the whole national territory although they certainly vary in scale from country to country.

In both cases, there is a link with the preindustrial society of Europe or the Middle East. This is true even in new countries which modified this conception of space for their own use. The small region, more than a physical unit, is usually a linguistic and cultural unity corresponding historically to a medieval *seigneurie* in size and with its own regional society *(société environnante)*.

Such a regional society is intermediate between the smaller village type and a much larger, heterogeneous one *(la société englobante)* (Jollivet, 1971; Mendras, 1976)—the small region is the historic location of local characteristics, the large region is much more pragmatic, being a simple political construction, generally the domain of a feudal lord.

Changes in regional boundaries are almost always treated in terms of reform, following a tradition originating from the first revolutionary assemblies in France right up to recent British reforms. But to innovate in this realm can often be a useless exercise. Napoleon's changes, two centuries later, still have no cultural or political existence except to support the weight of bureaucracy. Elsewhere, in countries with tribal and nomadic traditions, the inhabitants have an identity which is scarcely tied to a territorial reality. One can wonder, therefore, if the definition of a region is anything other than a technocratic demarcation, that does not take culture into account, and merely aggravates the disequilibrium which has already been created by an exogenous mode of development.

Of course all observations about industrialization and regional disparities only have meaning when they are linked to the size and cultural significance of the area which is being discussed. We must also distinguish between disparities internal to the region and those between it and its neighbours. The methods employed to analyse these disparities cannot be generalized, as they depend largely on the socio-political conditions of the countries under consideration.

Throughout southern Europe local government barely exists, being no more than a political claim. The only local authorities which count are those of the very large cities and they cover a very restricted area. The English notion of local government does not have an equivalent in French. Neither the relatively recent creation of large regions in France or Italy, nor even the powerful movements towards provincial autonomy which are developing in Spain, can change in an instant this longstanding situation.

The feeble capacity of local authorities to use initiative is not only due to the unitary constitution of a centralized state in contrast to those of federal countries, nor does it stop local leaders taking an important role at the national level. It does, however, lead to a conception of political power which is fundamentally centralized even if, as in Italy, it is not embodied in a single place. This local weakness also holds true for underdeveloped countries, which have been treated as unique regions by the old colonial metropoles and continue to be treated in a similar way by the rich countries on which they now depend.

These simple remarks have major consequences in terms of the perception and management of regional problems and the industrial programmes which follow from them. These programmes are necessarily located on a continuum between the technical optimum and historic and cultural contingency. The unfortunate thing is that the latter dimension has never been developed by planning experts. In a decentralized country, it is possible to envisage planning for a restricted area and there are relatively autonomous administrative and political authorities that correspond to such planning. This allows an emphasis on intraregional socio-economic models using data on flows and physical and financial assets. Regional science is therefore particularly well adapted to the situations in northern Europe and North America.

On the other hand, in a centralized country such as France the tools for describing regional economies are much less developed. Dynamic, operational, economic models are national in scope. The only French one which is somewhat disaggregated, Régina, remains very rudimentary (Courbis *et al.*, 1975). In this, the nation is divided into five regions, in which the urban zones are distinguished. Studies of individual regions as economic systems are also rare, so the accent is placed on indicators of a demographic, economic and social type standardized across the whole national territory—very explicitly defined and capable of being aggregated at whatever scale is desired. They permit interregional comparisons and national checks. Because of the difficulty of performing such studies, multivariate and factorial methods have been developed.

Under these circumstances, the truly regional dimension of industrial problems is rarely identified. Plant location is made more as a result of political influences and municipal industrial park programmes than any calculation of the optimal use of space. In addition, the management of space, divided amongst diverse, specialized administrations with their own administrative regions, has tended to cause a jumble of boundaries, none of which correspond to geographical reality (see Figure 4.1). Using its technical capacity, the central authority gives priority to reducing disparities between large regions, taking little account of other spatial scales. In fact the trend is to consider only the development of a few poles rather than a whole region. Spatial planning is basically planning for urban regions. In contrast, the decentralized authorities of federal countries often accept the differences between themselves and their neighbours, but take steps to deal with their own internal disparities. It is interesting that the first regions in Spain to obtain autonomy are also the richest—Catalonia and the Basque country.

A TERRITORY OR A NETWORK? INDUSTRY VERSUS THE REGION

In ancient Europe all villagers knew the parish boundaries. There, on high festival days, ritual fights between rival localities would break out. Today, such boundaries no longer have the same importance and even landowners and farmers who live right on top of them barely know where they are. They still have the force of law, however, and are used to draw the current map of communes, but there are no longer complementary productive activities and autonomous exchanges taking place in these small areas. Despite this, complementarity is the base upon which the historical and cultural notion of a region is built.

FIGURE 4.1. The boundary problem, *Département* de Bordurie

Industry extends both the volume and area of exchange beyond the regional boundary. It institutes a network of autonomous relationships which do not cover a geographical area. For example, the ore for French aluminium is mainly *extracted* or *imported* in Provence, *refined* in the Alps, *rolled* in Auvergne and Normandy, and *shaped* in Alsace. Producers pay little attention to the neighbourhood around successive operations; the logic of the industrial grouping destroys regional coherence.

In social life, also, the range of relationships and movements of individuals has extended enormously, aided by improved means of transport. Former traditions have been broken. Movements have also become organized towards several centres. The various functions of space, managed in an increasingly centralized fashion by important industrial, commercial and administrative operations, tend to form large specialized zones, but these zones, which can be observed for housing, employment and infrastructure, coincide less and less with each other. (See figure 4.1).

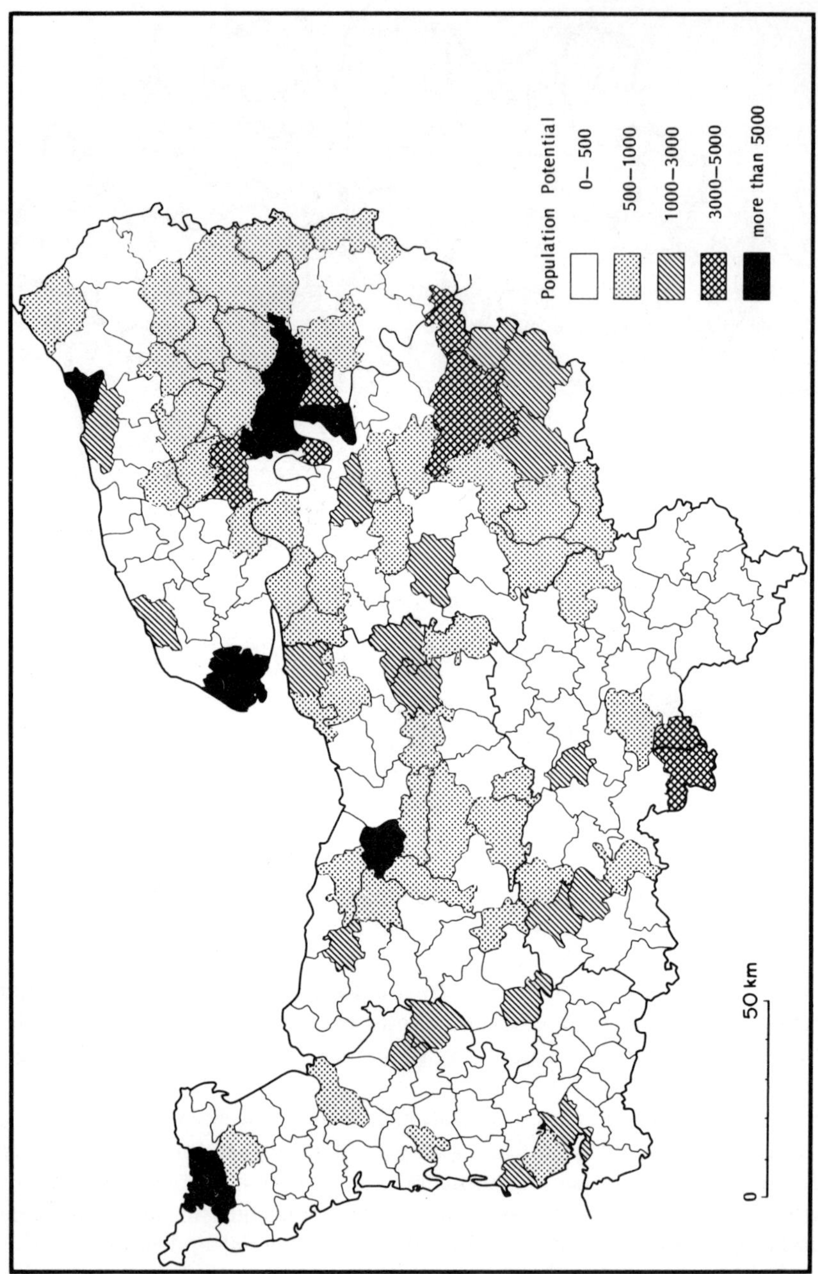

FIGURE 4.2. Population potential in Normandy

Therefore geographical space is overlaid with a series of specialized tiers, each one functionally free of the others. Neighbourhood effects lose their importance, or at least defy systematic analysis. We can see a contradiction between concrete conditions of industrial or agricultural growth on the one hand and the very existence of regions on the other, more so as the concentration of productive capital increases and becomes more internationalized to the profit of some firms and nations. In one way, to fight against regional disparity is to fight the damage caused by modernization, for in a traditional, immobile society the notion of disparity, if it is perceived at all, does not have the progressive dimensions which we give it.

It is already an old idea, firmly held by Marx and shared by other economists of his time, that industry breaks up the unity of an area, that is, the complementarity between town and country. The countryside is turned into a unidimensional area devoted to farming and constituting a territory of reserve labour and land. We share the view that industrialization is closely linked with urbanization, but must add that urbanization destroys the traditional physical limits of cities.

Boundaries between urban and rural areas are generally defined by a complex group of indicators associated with thresholds. Despite some variation by author and country, these cover demographic variables (population density and growth), economic variables (role of agriculture, land prices) and sociological considerations (see Table 4.1, which was inspired by Lefebvre, 1970). Today the application of this battery of indicators to a particular area suggests that rural and urban characteristics are mixed in each area in such a way that a 'pure' city or countryside (physically, economically, sociologically) no longer actually exists. In addition, these local characteristics change rapidly, so that the complementarity between urban and rural areas, uncertain enough at any given moment, is continuously upset (see Figures 4.2 and 4.3).

FIGURE 4.2. Population potential in Normandy. Population potential (V_j) for each canton (j) is made up of two components, external potential (V_{ej}) and internal potential (V_{fj})

$$V_j = V_{ej} + V_{fj}$$

$$V_{ej} = \sum_{i=1}^{k} \frac{P_i}{d_i}$$

when P_i = population of agglomeration i; d_i = distance from i to the largest centre in canton, j if that distance is less than 20 km (the commuting limit for industrial workers).

$$V_{fj} = \frac{P_j}{d_j^{\alpha}}$$

when P = population of the largest centre in canton j; d_j = average distance from the chief centre to the canton's boundary; $\alpha = 2$

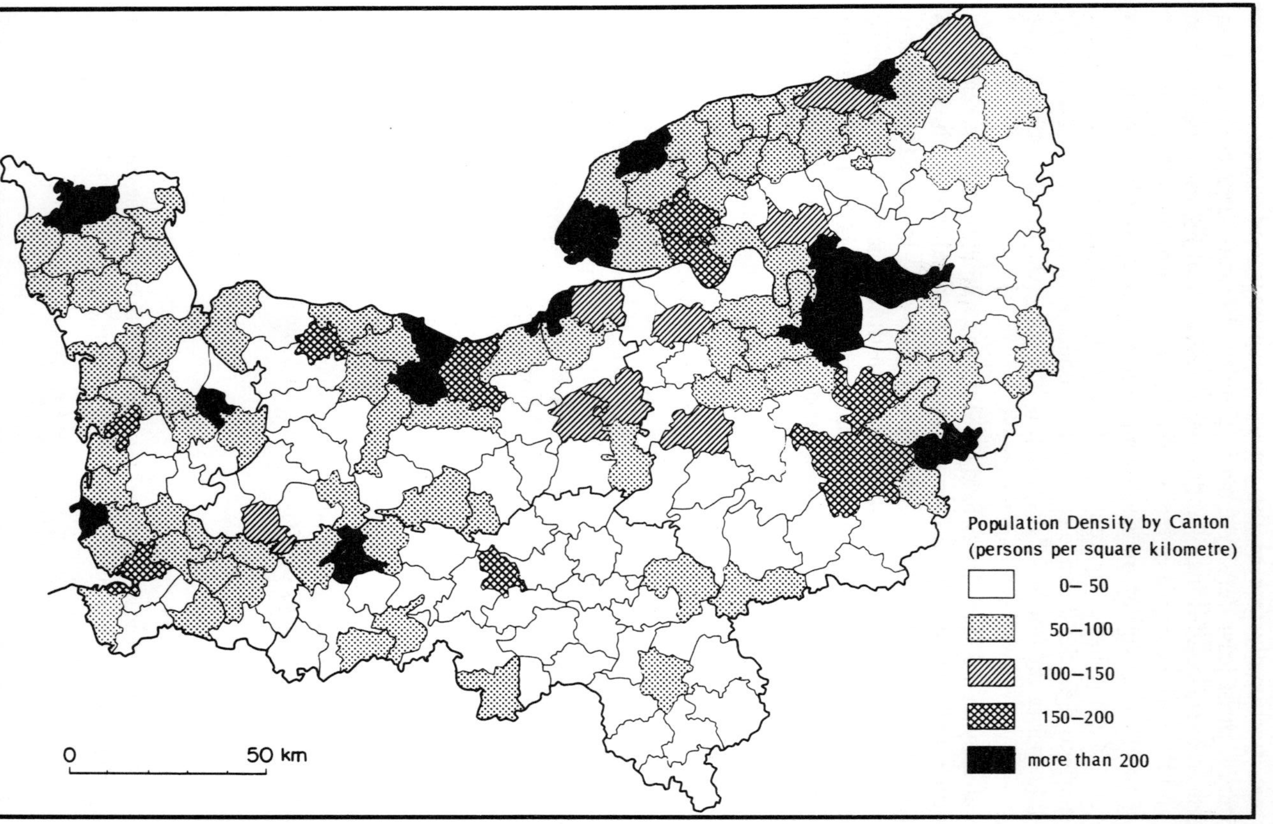

FIGURE 4.3. Population density by canton in Normandy

TABLE 4.1. Urban and rural characteristics

Pure urban model	Pure rural model	Quantitative indicator
Work for a wage	Work often not wage-earning (farmer, craftsman)	Socio-professional composition
Separation of recreation and work	Integration of recreation and work	Nature, form and frequency of recreational Provisions
Choice of consumption as a form of cultural expression	Consumption limited to needs defined by tradition	Importance and form of shopping centres

These observations are particularly valid for western Europe where occupation of the soil is fairly continuous and where industrialization is intense, but they also correspond to general tendencies and concern less prosperous countries. They are thus characteristic of agricultural areas. For example, Morocco is currently a puzzle of very diverse ownership patterns with finely overlapping elements. Each corresponds to an economic and social model which virtually ignores its geographical neighbourhood. Estate lands and communal goods correspond to a precolonial feudal organization; small, single-family farms were laid out in the colonial period on a European model; and large nationalized operations, that arose from the agricultural reform following independence, have an organization similar to that of the collective farms of socialist countries. One can question if these areas, which are so heterogeneous, can still be considered as regions in the sense of a unity for analysis and planning. We know the difficulty which planners in underdeveloped countries have in considering local complex realities and the temptation is always present to erase history in order to recreate new structures in an integrated way.

The model of industrial expansion imposed on a world scale is an urban network, the growth of which is fundamentally aspatial. We therefore observe conquered areas, dependent on a number of centres. In these areas, only historical tradition and popular memory still allow regional boundaries to be drawn.

GROWTH POLE THEORY AS A TOOL OF PLANNING: THE LEGITIMACY OF DISMEMBERMENT

The industrialization of geographical space is dealt with by means of the growth pole concept, which recognizes that growth does not appear everywhere at the same time but appears rather in specific places (Perroux, 1970). These poles are organized and put into a hierarchy; they conform to certain distributions of rank and size in a particular territory; they are linked by communication and exchange networks along which production is brought to fruition. All these observations are made by 'regional science', and even if they are general, they are still empirical. Their application to planning programmes, however, is often made too quickly, causing initially a confusion between observations and aims. The problem arises in translating solutions obtained in abstract space to the real world. To do this requires a mapping from one to the other, but this is never explained. For instance, location theories suggest an optimum-sized centre where particular economic sectors should be located, but this is not detailed enough to determine metropoles (main centres) and secondary centres. For this purpose one must bring cultural considerations to bear on the equilibrium of the socio-economic functions, those very considerations which have nothing to do with global rationality. Each comparison between a real, observed urban network and a theoretical optimal one is accompanied by algorithms or optimum criteria, which reveal the preferences, or interests, of the responsible technostructure and nothing else. Thus the myth of the millionaire and balanced city (respectively in population and function) has been created, especially in France. Worse, these practical applications of theory lead to many bad effects.

To live in a network provides no cultural or political tradition. It is to be uprooted, broken away from all perceived space and subject to an uncontrolled authority. The framework of life loses its historical significance and is replaced by a logic at best non-visible and at worst unbearable. If the problem were just an academic one it would be important, but we could do nothing about it. It is, however, practical in that if we lack regulation of industrial development we will be unable to control its effects.

It is not by chance that the rationally conceived industrialization plan most often cited is that of Puerto Rico. It is an island, and viewed from the air it is almost a point, even if some internal diversity is noticeable to the native or traveller. All the elements of transformation can be delimited, measured and controlled fairly well (Isard, 1967). Even in this favourable case, questions may be asked about the success of the programme. It is quite a different matter, however, to deal with the difficulties of a much larger country in which regional systems are mainly open, even if planning covers all capital and human factors.

Algeria, after independence, opted fully for a policy modelled on growth poles, sometimes on brand new centres (Sari, 1974; Raffinot and Jacquemot, 1977); this also included a focus on propulsive industries (Destanne de Bernis, 1971). Fifteen years later it can be seen that the rural exodus caused by the location of new factories has only aggravated the employment and housing crisis in certain cities. At Guelma (population 60 000), the chief centre in the Wilaya district on the south-east coastal strip of Algeria, planned industrialization from 1966–75 created over 2000 jobs in national companies, as well as some induced employment. However, only 30 per cent of the workers in the new industries originated from the city; another 13 per cent live more than

12 km from the centre and suffer a lack of transport and long journeys to work. So this industrialization makes a constant demand on the surrounding countryside, causing uncontrolled rural migration. Out of 350 000 inhabitants in the rural areas, about 50 000 moved to the cities of the Wilaya in ten years; another 30 000 left the region. Employment and housing in the cities have not improved because, with this migration, the maintenance of full employment demands quick, enormous and centralized industrial investment. Migrants cannot wait long for a job. Meanwhile in the old traditional towns and villages, there are subsistence mechanisms which can cope with the shortages.

The above description only gives a partial image of reality. As in all industrializing countries, movement to nearby medium-sized cities is just a stepping-stone to the larger cities or overseas. Wilaya, for instance, lost 10 per cent of its population in the same period, and most migrants were of an active working age. Such a *noria* cannot be controlled if one's rationale is based on urban areas. It is essential to think regionally and to introduce all kinds of non-economic considerations into the matter.

The concern here is with a fairly benign kind of disequilibrium. The authorities would like to remedy it; there are means of observation available, competence and finance to correct it are at hand, and the directed economy allows at least the advantage of seeing that decisions concerning one place fit into an overall plan. But, for example, it would be interesting to know what it cost France to build the complex at Fos sur Mer, near Marseilles, after market conditions and the economic crisis upset all predictions about it.

From out of all this comes our first sketchy conclusion: there are very few centres which control productive capital, particularly in the economically dominated countries, and those where political traditions make the effect of centralization worse. This system operates over large territories but the decision makers do not know them; they do not continuously respond to the complexity of traditional town and country structures, but rather distort them punctiformly in time and in space. Thus local authorities are left with the task of resolving contradictions between the optimized network of location and the historical organization of regional space. This is equally valid for both so-called socialist countries and capitalist countries.

There remain questions which must take priority in local and regional political life. What size authority is best for marketing purposes—for developing and publicizing industrial and commercial areas—and the accompanying infrastructure? What size authority can best manage the disparities caused by the presence or absence of industry, in terms of lifestyle or social needs? Finally, which regions still function at the cultural level even though industrialization has just about destroyed them?

It is not likely that the replies coincide well with each other even if empirical solutions are proposed. Also, the necessary information upon which to make such judgements is quite insufficient, especially at an international scale.

More than economic models, we need studies about the perception of regional space, institutional analyses, and continuous reports on organizational innovations. This constitutes a research field to be developed and popularized, which is far more political than we have been used to.

MODERNIZATION AND ITS RESULTING SPATIAL DISEQUILIBRIUM

Under an industrial stimulus, organization of space is subject to modernization. This term is purely analytical and does not imply any value-judgement. It simply states that housing, activities and infrastructure are created and moved according to relatively constant rules. From a general point of view, starting from a number of causal relationships which are adopted by models of location, we can observe at almost all scales a functional specialization and a polarized hierarchy of space.

Urbanization, 'Rurbanization'

Population movements are the best overall indicators of these phenomena to the extent that they express all kinds of causal factors—creation of activities and employment, policy concerning land and fixed assets, the overall ideology of a society about space, etc. Virtually over the whole world, such movements take two directions. The first, a well-known direction, is the rural exodus towards urban regions. The second, more recent direction, is the extension and dissemination of urban regions, which we will call 'rurbanization' (Roux and Bauer, 1976). There is a restricted explosion within a major implosion, which no historical frontier has resisted. While the intensity of the two movements varies according to the level and speed of development in a country, it is present everywhere, developments in transportation having increased its size. France is a particularly interesting case in point because industrialization and urban concentration were intense and late in coming. Unlike in northern Europe, the small industrial centres which act as halfway points in migration and preserve a certain rural population density, are not evident. Migratory tendencies favoured abruptly first the largest cities, then towns in the periphery, leaving so radical an emptying of the countryside that even its potential for migration has dried up (see Table 4.2).

For the management of space, this evolution has major consequences. First, it determines rural areas lacking any future; rurbanization will never reach them. Their sole functions are agricultural production, which is becoming less and less labour-intensive, and the regular emission of migrants until they can send no more. Many European rural areas, especially in the South, are already in this position. In the first half of this century in a medium-sized village of 800 to 1000 ha used for mixed farming, the rural population which could make

TABLE 4.2. Migration balance of French population as a percentage of total population: average annual rate 1954–75

	Average annual rate			Total population 1975 in millions
	1954–62	1962–68	1968–75	
Paris agglomeration	+ 1.2	+ 0.5	− 0.4	8.4
Urban areas over 100 000 population	+ 1.2	+ 1.2	+ 0.6	13.3
Urban areas 5000–100000 population	+ 1.1	+ 1.1	+ 0.6	12.7
Urban areas with under 5000 and rural communes with industrial and urban population	− 0.1	+ 0.3	+ 1.1	7.8
Other rural communes	− 1.2	− 0.9	− 0.3	9.9

a living was about 500 (including tradesmen and craftsmen). Today, only 100 people would be comfortably supported under average EEC standards, moreover, the number is constantly declining, even including tradesmen and retired people. Considering the age structure, one can fear a real landslip of population in the 1990s, when those who are still there from before the rural exodus which began in 1945 will die out. Despite variations, similar trends can be expected in many developing countries. Only a detailed and vigorously pursued rural development policy can change this. Apart from China, one can cite the case of West Germany with its central place policy, although the threatened area there is quite small. Except in the United States, a spontaneous shift of population to non-metropolitan areas is not yet evident (Beale, 1977; McCarthy and Morrison, 1977).

Second, these movements create rural–urban fringes, which, although there are no obvious manifestations, await major changes. From experience we now know that the stabilization of these areas is extremely difficult. Even the Dutch, who are usually good regional planners, have been relatively unsuccessful in identifying and protecting the non-builtup area in the centre of the southern urban ring *(Randstad)*.

Lastly, new 'disinherited' areas are opening up right in the centre of cities. The United States, which for a long time contained the only example of this type, is currently undergoing a relative abandonment of whole metropolitan areas, emptying Eastern metropolises and filling those in the South. Although less intense, the same process is growing in Europe and even in the Third World. Recent policy, confirmed in 1976 in Britain, is designed to fight this trend.

In Italy it is even firmer as a collective project (Cervellati, Scannavini, and de Angelis, 1977).

Fragmentation of Space

In detail, such tendencies do not have the force of laws and their rational justification is often quite incomplete. Firstly, different authors have different rationales—which can be based on corporate profit, corporate growth, consumer use, cost of public investment, etc. Next, as we have seen, these tendencies relate to an abstract space far removed from real areas in which are found activities and people and the exchange of goods, services and messages. Real space is marked out by relief, climate, history, and political conditions which theoretical space ignored.

On another level, one finds the reasoning used in theories of urban hierarchy. But modifications of space do not happen mechanically. In the last resort, they are due to decisions made by people to locate a factory, construct a new neighbourhood, or build a transportation route. Such decisions do not always rely on the logic of the socio-economic system. They also result from our ideological models of development and modernization. Now we do not know if the model creates rationality, or vice versa. An understanding of this is vital in order to recognize the level at which regional disparities are found. Such disparities tend to be created within increasingly small areas, resulting initially from the increased number of decision-makers and the differences in the geographical area where they operate. For example, the president of a multinational puts his finger on some place anywhere in a continent and causes a plant, totally at odds with its environment, to appear. Then the operations which follow such decisions have different geographical areas of effect. The optimal location for an urban residential complex, for example, supposing one could find it, is not the same as the one for the activities which employ the residents living there. Lastly investments associated with modernization (residential complexes, factories, offices, industrialized farming) advance into rural areas with little to stop them. The authorities support them and as they can easily pay land costs they are able to locate wherever they wish. Therefore, an extreme dispersal of the elements of transformation is found.

Dispersal of industrial activities, growing with the control of space by firms from outside the region, is one of the causes of disparity within a region (microdisparity) (Keeble, 1972; Van Engelsdorp, Gastelaars, and Cortie, 1973). Perhaps it is not always felt as such but the consequences on income levels, standard of life and housing conditions are directly perceptible. Three examples may be given: the dispersal of privately owned homes around an agglomeration of 400 000 people; average salary levels in a sparsely populated commune; and the chance of rapid changes on agricultural land in the Paris region, measured by a multivariate analysis. The structure of neighbourhood space is permanently broken. The inhabitants recognize it less and less. Relative to current movements, its area is small; it is rarely a city, never a metropolitan area (Lynch, 1969).

Hierarchies

This modernization at a micro-scale is hierarchical. Modern industry consists of a centre of innovation and decision, intermediate locations of management and skilled jobs and peripheral factories with no power. It really does not matter if the latter are decentralized, as the headquarters will protect its own pre-eminence. This is the significance which we must give, after twenty years of experience, to the voluntary policies of decentralization operated by many European countries, even if they were quantitatively successful (Durand, 1972).

Let us now take the consequences of these observations and consider geographical space in general as it is affected by these developments caused by industry.

1. Over large areas and in a continuous fashion, areas are being abandoned or are awaiting new development because their traditional functions (agriculture, forestry, traditional commerce, historical centres, etc.) are dominated by others, are always destructible and do not allow any stabilization of population or services.
2. Within this framework at a more detailed level are some small areas which are adapted to the dominant productive process of today's economy. At first, their heterogeneity and dispersal make it impossible to regard them as areas. If they are close to each other and have a lengthy history, they may become continuous regions; but they are often at the mercy of the obsolescence of their activities as, for example, are the mining areas of Britain, Belgium or France. Further, they are also unequal in function, and hierarchically organized.

Faced with the proliferation of particular situations, the planners are questioning their functions and methods (Cowan, 1973). They are working on regions whose unity and structure are being constantly questioned. They use an approach, zoning, which is completely out of touch with current reality. Their means, industrial and urban investment, follow a logic which feeds the disequilibrium that causes the various, often unpredictable, consequences, with which they must later cope.

Under these circumstances, where does one start an evaluation, at any regional level, of employment induced by industry or of the interrelationships of activities? In fact, in the last few years, programmes and plans have discarded equations of the type which simply copy previous studies made in regions and institutional and economic frameworks that were quite different. Thus some key questions are emerging, though still in a sketchy and simplified way. Why continue to link development with the region, when the one by its very nature destroys the other? In terms of objectives, how can industrialization be used to rectify spatial disparities? The replies fit a particular time and show well that such associations have no absolute character.

On the one hand, the region is always considered as an entity—longlasting, stable, transcending and unifying local disparities. This recalls an epoque in which Burgundy, Württemberg, Galicia or the canton of Lausanne were not only more lively than today but also provided a cultural model for the rest of the world via colonization. This change is not linked to the decline of leadership of growth poles in privileged nations, but rather to the rapid liquidation in these countries of rural society and its unifying image of territory (Mendras, 1976).

On the other hand, since the beginning of the industrial era, there has been a consensus on the content, both implicit and explicit, of the term development and its use for public projects. Yet it has become full of contradictions, and has lost its dynamic and generalized character to become an expression for a particular historical situation, that of the developed countries. This theme will be developed in the next section.

DEVELOPMENT

> Le développement est la combinaison des changements mentaux et sociaux d'une population qui la rendent apte à faire croitre, durablement et cumulativement, son produit réel global (Perroux, 1970).

This definition of development is not the only possible one. It has the merit of stressing both dimensions of the concept: growth (which to be assured must be balanced) and political, social and cultural evolution collectively (if not democratically) accepted with, as the central objective, full employment of human and material resources (productive resources in Marxist terms). Only these allow discussion in a language common to both capitalist and so-called socialist countries. They build up a worldwide vision of a hopeful future based on cities and factories. (Only China is intermittently an exception to such a vision). Today, both dimensions are in a state of crisis.

Unbalanced Growth and Absolute Underdevelopment

Balanced growth consists of the equalization, in each time-period, of overall savings and investment. Capital investment (sometimes with available labour-force substituted for fixed capital) is therefore at the centre of all models, whether national or regional (Sakashita and Kamoike, 1974). But this balance of savings and investment does not take place by itself; the observation is trite at the international level, especially in underdeveloped countries. It also relates to certain regions in developed countries, forcing us to examine the composition of fixed capital formation within a country rather than in global terms.

As an example we will cite the case of a French *département*, Lot, which is primarily rural and agricultural. It covers an area of 5200 sq. km and in 1975 had a population of 150 000. Table 4.3 shows economic relations between the *département* and the exterior, using national accounting methods. It does not deal with production and income, as these are completely external to the region, but they can be considered in an indirect way. The table naturally contains some statistical errors and gaps, especially between the trade deficit and the financial surplus. As there is no boundary control of goods, services and money, construction of the accounts is indirect; details will not be provided here.

TABLE 4.3. Economic relations between the *département* of Lot (Southern Périgord) and the exterior, 1973

Expenses (in millions of francs)		Receipts	
Current account			
Import of goods (of which non-food industrial products = 690.1)	1059.6	Exports of goods (of which non-food industrial products: 305.2)	1061.4
Consumption of energy	187.7	Production of energy	58.0
Import of services (of which tourism = 25.8)	151.3	Export of services (of which tourism: 170.0)	206.3
		Balance (deficit)	72.9
Total	1398.6		1398.6
Capital account			
Movements into banks	215.5	Movements made by bank	150.8
Movements into public financial agencies	40.0	Movements made by public financial agencies	32.6
Contributions to social security (of which, agricultural profession: 20.7)	145.4	Social security allowances (of which agricultural profession: 145.0)	242.1
Government receipts	208.8	Government expenses	250.8
		Salaries paid by exterior public service enterprises to Lot (electricity, railways etc.)	37.4
Balance (positive)			
Total	763.7		763.7

Source: Heymann (1976).

The balance on current account shows a structure that is characteristic of a Third World country lacking raw materials. Farm products and tourism are exported, while manufactured goods and energy are imported. As a result there is a deficit which, though slight, is sufficient to keep a region, already weak and dependent, in a continuous situation of subordination.

The financial balance is much more interesting since it clearly identifies the roles of the various actors in regional development. The state, public services and welfare agencies inject capital into the *département*. This amounts to 188.7 million francs, and pays a large bureaucracy as well as helping an ageing population with pensions, medical assistance, etc. The banking and financial system collects savings in its branches and exports them to wherever investment funds are needed. This amounts to 72.1 million francs. Public service organizations form an intermediate case but do not change the general conclusion. Like the state, they provide wages and investment but they also recoup some of these in the form of payments, included in losses from the banking system.

In this situation, the right hand does not know what the left hand is doing, since the state directly controls the public financial agencies, and the principal savings banks are nationalized. Again this is comparable to the situation in African or South American countries, where the banks collect capital for Switzerland and the Bahamas and where the state or agencies provide food and technical assistance. Lot, however, is not comparable to a Third World country in every respect. Its income levels, even if they are below the West European average, are higher, and personal property (especially housing) is often substantial. The similarity is in the mechanisms of assistance and exploitation, which are quite distinct from the simple poverty usually condescendingly recognized in underdeveloped countries.

If we link this example to the geographical framework sketched above, the following disparities appear.

1. Taking the region as a whole, there is an export of local savings while at the same time external financial support is required for declining sectors, needy social classes and the cost of bureaucracy.
2. In contrast, particular places, sometimes large enough to be regions themselves, raid external savings, industrialize themselves and subsidize underdeveloped areas.
3. Human movements follow the financial flows.

This framework allows enormous variation in both the intensity and size of movements, and the diversity explains the differences between the situation of Lot, which is subsidized by Paris, and the African countries which Paris exploits. The direction of physical and financial movements corresponds largely with the relationship between industrial capitalism (private or state) and its territory of influence. It introduces within the rich countries themselves the same procedures of pillage, long denounced, that take place in the agricultural areas of the Third World (Amin, 1976; Provent and de Ravignan, 1977). Industrial growth, especially if it is rapid, creates inequalities in space (Aydalot, 1976). This process suggests a notion of absolute underdevelopment for most areas, a notion which goes beyond considerations of the level of wealth to consider the network of monetary flows and the pattern of domination that it implies.

The economic crisis: Long-term certainties and the policy response

This section concerns Western Europe, North America and Japan. Elsewhere planning action is subordinated to the raising of average income levels even if it means greater regional and social disparity. We will not forget, however, that models developed in dominant countries can always be applied either well or badly elsewhere.

Present opinion is unanimous on at least one point. We have left the era of rapid and continuous growth. This is so often repeated by all kinds of specialists that it must be taken as a fact if not of objective reality at least of the perception of the future as seen by influential leaders. This conviction of slow growth is based primarily on two observations:

1. Major raw materials are becoming more expensive even if the danger of depletion is less immediate than was once feared (Leontief, 1977; Meadows, 1972).
2. Saturation or near saturation of demand conflicts with the need for industrial expansion and the growth of productive investment, which prevailed until 1973. This has led to a lowering of profit levels (France, INSEE, 1975; CNME, 1976).

These tendencies are leading to the relocation of heavy industry towards mining areas and of labour-intensive manufacturing to Africa or South-east Asia. The international redeployment affects all types of regional concern. Having chosen a continent, industrialists allow themselves to be attracted to the city which will give them the best welcome.

In principle, this relative disinterest of industrialists concerning location and long-term stagnation should leave a wide-open field for concerted planning by the state and local authorities. But, no doubt fearing they might be reduced to a 'green belt' policy, the authorities have gone to the other extreme and put the accent on the productive sector. An official French document (France, DATAR, 1976) states: 'La sagesse commande de mettre en veilleuse toute politique ambitieuse de rédistribution géographique des activités pendant le temps nécessaire à la nouvelle définition des activités'. Even if a general slowdown of developed economies is envisaged, it is dealt with from a productivity point of view as if it were a curable disease. At worst, one hopes to be amongst the countries or sectors which will escape the disease and the unpleasant global prophesies.

It is certain, however, that the notion of productive investment will be modified. Since 1960, it has no longer been at the heart of the American growth model. In the United States, it varies from 5 to 7 per cent of GNP while it is 10 per cent in France and Germany and 25 per cent in Japan. Behind this change is a certain lack of interest in productivity gains and the fact of a reduced profitability for capital. The present economic difficulties encourage other industrial countries to accept the same view. There is a crisis in the accumulation of goods and use of savings (Guillaume, 1977), and a relative, sometimes absolute, decline in industrial investment.

There is little chance of capital being used industrially under conditions of stagnant demand; it must, therefore, be invested in land, buildings, public works and the tertiary sector, which represent a 'sterilization' of capital. There will also be a return to social demands by both the bourgeoisie and the middle classes. Their consumption may no longer be exclusively confined to the accumulation of goods but will go rather towards particular items (for example, related to communication and services—recreation and holidays). Everywhere the consumption of services and a concomitant growth of tertiary employment is becoming a fundamental option, because there is no better alternative.

The End of the Current Era

These symptoms do not only constitute a catalogue of economic reactions and mechanisms. Many imply deep changes in cultural behaviour and should have particularly clear and new effects on geographical space, where their ideological aspects will unfold better than on the abstract and culturally restricted space defined by economics. Thus the social perception of the crisis goes beyond the partial responses given by the present economic and political system. A large body of theoretical knowledge is developing on these themes. Its size is no guarantee of pertinence or objectivity but at least it indicates the existence of the problems which have been posed.

'La crise est un état de conscience. Important en ce qu'il manifeste la fin d'une civilisation, la difficulté croissante a donner un sens à ce qui perd son unité' (Touraine, 1976). In the same paper, he stresses social production and the reduction of our society to a 'pure conflict' in which organizations are becoming the dominant factors, regardless of the actual production process. Naturally, at the centre of everything is the administrative system.

Baudrillard (1976) is even more radical. In his opinion, the value of a product no longer represents any one of its real components (the use to which it is put, the amount of work which went into producing it, for example). Values are becoming topsy-turvy, not linked to measurable reference points such as inputs, cost price, etc.; they are just symbols. Exchange is made according to floating values in a vast simulation process. It is a structural revolution of value: 'Le processus, depuis longtemps opérationnel dans la culture, l'art, la politique (dans les domaines dits superstructurels) affecte aujourd'hui l'économie elle-même, tout le champ dit infrastructurel, la même indetermination regne'. Whether this analysis is valid for all levels of our society or only for understanding new, relatively isolated facts which are significant for the future, it leads to the same conclusions. We are leaving the era in which economics and social decisions based on the productive system were dominant. This is not to say that we are free from the supremacy of capital, because capital itself is largely responsible for the changes. The crisis is perhaps just another name for the movement into a planned society, in which the large bureaucratic systems themselves are a basis for values. At the same time, in human sciences there is a growing pre-eminence of sociology over economics.

Development was the key feature of spatial and economic planning until the crisis began. It has been continuously used in the exact sciences since the seventeenth century (Arendt, 1972), then invaded the political and social fields as soon as they were converted to the idea of progress and the domination of industry and technology over general social behaviour. If we believe that the importance given to development is being re-evaluated, it is because both the quantitative elements of growth and the beneficial effects of development are being questioned. Perhaps development is no longer a goal of society, perhaps it no longer represents the right way ahead.

New themes are arising, therefore, even if they are still imprecisely defined. They concern the environment and quality of life. A perception of new regional disparities based on environmental degradation has appeared. People are no longer satisfied with criticizing the undesirable effects of industry but are hoping to directly question certain projects.

As it is impossible to fully grasp these fertile and innovative ideas and draw indisputable practical consequences from them, national and regional economic policies are still torn between contradictory demands. Traditional indicators of activity and growth must be managed. However, two important tendencies are emerging in the public conscience.

1. The financial network of exploitation and subsidy between dominant poles and dominated regions is associated with a movement of innovation rather than production. There is no reason why this should be reversed. Decentralized industrialization can create intermediate-sized poles, but usually not regional development.
2. Disillusionment with industrial growth is evident in the large centres themselves. In all cases industry is already being carefully watched. New factories will still be built but planning techniques will change.

PLANNING AND LOCATING INDUSTRIAL INVESTMENT

Investment Behaviour

In the last thirty years planning has favoured the micro-economic optimum for residential development as well as for building plants. The latter were concentrated near to the labour force and sometimes also to markets. Industrialists, who were promised an inexhaustible supply of workers, did not hesitate to build large industrial complexes. Industry and sectors with sophisticated technology were concentrated in the largest cities of the most fully developed regions, and those with little investment, and requiring only unskilled labour, located in the small towns of rural areas. But these tendencies are changing. Spatial planning is evolving from a focus on industrial growth poles to a more complete vision of space.

This change of attitude is coming more from industrialists themselves than from planners. A clear preference for small or medium-sized plants (a few hundred workers) outside major industrial regions can be seen whenever the nature of production allows it. In France, a new stimulus has therefore been given to rural development and it is supported in a number of official documents (see, for example, Chavannes, 1975). In Algeria, a Ministry of Light Industry, concerned with reconciling the objectives of geographical decentralization and corporate decentralization, has been created. Many other examples could be given.

The reasons for this change in industrialists' behaviour are well known. For a long time now, labour-force recruitment has been the major factor in the choice of location and workers in the countryside and small towns have a good reputation for serious, even docile, work. Add to this current social, aesthetic and environmental concerns and the rural areas now look even better. Further, firms do not wish to be a major force in any given region. The day of the single-industry town, in which one firm controlled employment, housing and infrastructure, has passed. For ten years now, the European Economic Community has been recommending that a factory does not employ more than a certain percentage (usually 5 to 10 per cent) of workers from its labour-force area. This encourages a reduction of plant size. Finally, a concern for improving the quality of jobs favours the setting up of relatively autonomous workshops with a few dozen workers. A plant of 400 to 500 employees fits these trends well. It is perfectly adapted to the population density (20 to 100 per sq. km) and transport situation of a European region with rural traditions and a population living mostly in villages.

This is now regarded almost as a perfect model but it mainly creates unskilled employment and does not bring about a change of either decision or innovation centres. In reality, there may not even be many such plants. One can doubt it for the following reasons.

1. As investment becomes scarcer, it tends to be used for the modernization of existing plants rather than the creation of new ones.
2. Certain heavy industries resist dispersal.
3. Most importantly, it is proposed that the local authorities deal with the inconvenience caused by new plants and guarantee the provision of the necessary infrastructure that they need. This is what is meant by the 'dialogue' elsewhere between multinationals and Third World countries, financial authorities of the state and regional authorities, in centrally planned countries, and recently between private capitalists and socialist states (Levinson, 1977). All these countries are tending to concentrate investment geographically.

It is difficult to follow, locate and quantitatively compare these diverse trends. Movements of capital are only perceived at the international level and they have intensified since the oil crisis of 1973–74. They suggest that from now on industrial development, if it is based primarily on new plants, will signify a state of underdevelopment. The underdevelopment will express itself at two levels: first, relative poverty compared to richer poles and countries; second, the pursuit of development as a priority policy objective when it is being questioned by the largest decision centres. Under these circumstances, there is no chance that the disparities caused by early industrialization in Europe, North America and Japan, can be avoided in the newly promoted regions. On the contrary, with the desire of such regions to catch up, any delay will make them blind to all the disadvantages.

These problems, posed in a deliberately provocative manner, have no current solution. In conclusion, therefore, a few suggestions are made. One group concerns the institutional framework of planning as it is practised in most capitalist countries. The other group is more innovative.

Local Decision Centres

Modifications decided outside the region cause the breakup of local areas, and therefore increase perceived disparities. It is clear that a detailed understanding can only be guaranteed at the level of a small region. In Western Europe, this would cover some 500 to 5000 sq. km and a population of some 20 000 to 30 000 people, excluding any large city which would tend to have specific and exogenous characteristics.

In most countries, considering the existing institutions, it is difficult to imagine that all planning and decision-making could take place at this scale. The Swiss example proves, if there is any doubt, that the obstacles to a completely decentralized spatial planning are economic and historical. Sometimes these obstacles cannot be overcome, but this is not for the technical reasons which are usually given. In any case, it would be valuable if large regions were conceived as combinations of small ones.

From the point of view of national industrial planning, a number of principles of action must be applied to specific situations.

1. At this level, the only planning must be public. Contemporary industrial firms are not constrained by the boundaries of a small region for supplies, markets, or locational choice.
2. As a high level of prosperity is attained the necessity of creating industrial employment should be questioned more and more. This follows from the previous discussion but many relevant elements have not been considered in this essay.

   Two important questions arise:

   What will the working population do and what will be the role of services and craft industries in the future?
3. We must plan industrial complexes by products and not by industrial activity. At present, public planning tends to express its objectives in terms of the industries and sectors used for national statistical purposes. These categories however, are abstract in comparison to actual industrial processes. Rarely do these statistical industries correspond to a particular firm's specialization, or to such things as manpower policy, infrastructure, marketing or environmental impact.

   If one thinks in terms of products or groups of products, it is easier to handle all the data. Further, by understanding a precise sequence of manufacturing processes, it is possible to trace the location of employment induced by investment at a particular place.

   Is such a change of approach possible? This depends on the level of economic management. In a socialist or state capitalist system, there is in principle no obstacle. One can therefore avoid producing bicycles without saddles or television sets without switches. In addition, though, relatively autonomous small or medium-sized firms (whether private or publicly owned), concerned with service and subcontracting at a regional scale, should be brought back into prominence again. Under economic liberalism, the planner's powers of negotiation and decision are more limited. In our view, however, they would increase in expertise since they would speak the same language as industrialists. This is the only way to obtain some control over the induced effects of investment and to avoid scattering the various stages of manufacturing a product all over the country or even the continent. Under this arrangement, once a propulsive firm had been located in a region, the planning process would effectively link it with small local firms.
4. It is necessary to assure a degree of economic autonomy to the region (Gordon and Moreno, 1976). In the technical field, this is the meaning of planning by product, but it clashes with the intense concentration of capital

and decision-making. How can the regional dimension be returned to the industrial savings and investment cycle?

Currently, in all countries the financial market (that is, private capital placed in shares) forms a declining share of investment. In socialist countries this is practically zero and it is little more in the poorer capitalist ones. In France, it supplies only about 15 per cent of corporate financing. Consequently, an important and growing proportion of savings goes through financial institutions (various types of banks, compulsory savings schemes, etc.). As was demonstrated above, such savings are drained towards the dominant centres. How can financial institutions be set up which are devoted to the needs of the region and not to some national or international arrangement of funds?

There is no one answer to this problem. The most interesting suggestions concern the creation of societies with a regional portfolio which would be guaranteed to some extent by local authorities. In any case, the intervention of such authorities in local and regional industry seems to be increasingly necessary.

Finding a Way to Evaluate Disparities

To question again intensive industrial growth, to base planning policy on a perceived historical tradition and a realistic area of manpower mobility, to assure a degree of technical and financial authority to a planning region—none of these objectives is incompatible with the constraints of capitalist enterprise, but as a group they clash with the way that industry operates. Spatial disparities are measured in the forced mobility induced and the profits assured by industry. To fight against them goes clearly beyond simple financial and technical optimization procedures and moves into the political arena. There, one can find the defenders of self-management and decentralization, including the 'pre-scientific' socialists.

How can a type of planning be conceived which avoids robbing Peter to pay Paul, and without disturbing peripheral regions? Taking into account only disposable capital, and sometimes movements of the labour-force, to analyse a regional situation or to use these factors as criteria for optimization, is both incomplete and poorly adapted as a method. Paradoxically, recent suggestions for measuring disequilibrium have come from some very technical considerations. They concern energy balance and entropy as applied to interregional and intraregional movement (Odum, 1971; Nijkamp, and Paelinck, 1974).

These suggestions must allow preferences so that substitutions can be made between information, socio-cultural organization, preservation of inherited landscape and buildings, and physical production. Approaches to this problem are still rudimentary and their applications few in number. Nevertheless it should be possible to inform the population of the entropy of its regional system as easily as with its gross regional product. Of course, this is only one technique and not even fully developed. Ultimately, everything will depend on the authorities which use the techniques and the democratic system evolving around them.

REFERENCES

Amin, S. (1976). *L'impérialisme et la développement inégal*, Editions de Minuit, Paris.

Arendt, Hannah (1972). *La crise de la culture* (translated into French by P. Levy) Gallimard, Paris.

Aydalot, P. (1976). *Dynamique spatiale et développement inégal*, Economica, Paris.

Baudrillard, J. (1976). *L'échange symbolique et la mort*, Gallimard NRF, Paris.

Beale, C. L. (1977). 'The recent shift of United States population to non-metropolitan areas, 1970–1975. *International Regional Science Review*, **2**, 113–122.

Binney, M., Cantell, T. and Darley, G. (1976). The concrete Jerusalem: the failure of the clean sweep, *New Society*, **38**, I–XVI.

CNME (Caisse Nationale de Marches de I'État) (1976). 'Evolution du taux de profit de l'industrie française'. *Bulletin*, **71**, 2-eme trimestre.

Cervellati, P. L.; Scannavini, R., and de Angelis, C. (1977). *La nuova Cultura della Città*, Mondatori, Milan.

Chavannes, G. (1975). *L'Industrie en milieu rural*, Report to the Ministry of Industry and the Working Group on Industry in Rural Areas, Documentation Française, Paris.

Courbis, R. *et al.* (1975). *Le modèle Régina*, Université Paris Nanterre, Paris.

Cowan, P. (ed.) (1973). *The Future of Planning*, Heinemann Educational, London.

Destanne de Bernis, G. (1971). 'Les industries industrialisants et les options algériennes.' *Revue du Tiers-Monde*, **XII**, 47, 544–555.

Durand, P. (1972). *Industrie et régions*, La Documentation Francaise, Paris.

France (DATAR) (1976) (Delegation à l'aménagement du territoire et à l'action régionale) *La restructuration de l'appareil productif prospective*, La Documentation Française, Paris.

France (INSEE) (1975) (Institut national de la statistique et des études économiques), *La fresque historique du système économique français*, Paris.

Gordon, P. and Moreno, H. (1976). 'The identification of propulsive industrial sectors and their relevance to decision making on spatial development'. *The Annals of Regional Science*, **10**, 67–78

Guillaume, M. (1977). 'Investissement et avenir des sociétés industrielles'. *Les Annales des Mines*, **6–7**, 121–136.

Heymann, Y. (1976). *Les rélations économiques entre un département rural avec l'extérieur. Note méthodologique et application au Lot*, Direction de l'agriculture, Cahors.

Isard, W. (1967). *Methods of Regional Analysis*, MIT (translated into French by A. Sallez and E. Strawczinski), Dunod, Paris.

Jollivet, M. (ed.) (1971). *Collectivités rurales françaises*, 2 volumes, Armand Collin, Paris.

Keeble, D. E. (1972). 'Industrial movement and regional development in the United Kingdom'. *Town Planning Review*, **43**, 3–25.

Lefebvre, H. (1970). *Du rural à l'urbain*, Anthropos, Paris.

Leontief, W. (1977). *The Future of the World Economy* (a United Nations study translated into French as *1999 expertises de W. Leontief*, Dunod, Paris.

Levinson, C. (1977). *Vodka Cola*, Stock, Paris.

Lynch, K. (1969). *The Image of the City* (translated into French by J. L. Venard) Dunod, Paris.

Meadows, D. (1972). *The Limits to Growth (Club of Rome)* (translated into French by J. Delaunay) Fayard, Paris.

McCarthy, K. and Morrison, P. (1977). 'The changing demographic and economic structure of non-metropolitan areas in the United States', *International Regional Science Review*, **2**, 123–143.

Mendras, H. (1976). *Sociétés paysannes*, Armand Collin, Paris.

Nijkamp, P. and Paelinck, J.H.P. (1974). 'A dual interpretation and generalization of entropy-maximizing models in regional science'. *Papers, the Regional Science Association*, **33**, 3–31.

Odum, H. (1971). *Environment, Power and Society*, John Wiley, New York.

Perroux, François (1970). *L'économie du 20 ième Siècle*, PUF, Paris.

Provent, A. and de Ravignan, F. (1977). *Le nouvel ordre de la faim, révolution paysanne*, Editions du Seuil, Paris.

Raffinot, Marc and Jacquemot, Pierre (1977). *Le capitalisme d'état Algérien*, Maspero, Paris.

Roux, J. M. and Bauer, G. (1976). *La rurbanisation ou la ville éparpillée*, Editions du Seuil, Paris.

Sakashita, N. and Kamoike, O. (1974). 'National growth and regional income inequality—further results'. *Journal of Regional Science*, **14**, 81–87.

Sari, D. (1974). *La restructuration des centres urbains en Algérie, dans villes et sociétés au Maghreb, études sur l'urbanisation*, Editions du CNRS, Paris.

Touraine, A. (ed.) (1976). *Au-dela de la crise*, Editions du Seuil, Paris.

Van Engelsdorp R., Gastelaars, R., and Cortie, C. (1973). 'Migration from Amsterdam'. *Tijdschrift voor economische en sociale geographie*, **64**, 206–217.

Planning Industrial Development
Edited by David F. Walker

Chapter 5

Manufacturing in Rural Development

Christopher R. Bryant

Rural development has been the subject of considerable debate during the past three decades. The identity of rural development planning as an activity separate from urban and regional development planning has been questioned (Jung, 1971); and heated debate has arisen over the roles of primary activities, tourism, education and industry, and of concentrated versus dispersed development in rural development. Not surprisingly, then, in answer to the question 'Is it possible to industrialize rural space?', the arguments and the evidence are so contradictory (France, Atelier Central d'Études d'Aménagement Rural, 1977).

The contradictions have arisen partly because of data availability and comparability problems, partly because of underlying 'definitional' issues (for example, what is 'rural'?) but mostly because of the heterogeneity of the issue of the role of manufacturing in rural development. On the one hand, a bewildering variety of industry both by product-mix, size and cost structure, confronts us and, on the other hand, rural space is far from being a homogeneous entity. Rural areas vary in terms of existing activity structure, resource base, degree of integration into the urban-industrial complex and population densities—and when we consider the international scene, the range of variation is even greater. To tackle this situation, two themes are stressed below: (a) the heterogeneity of rural space, and (b) the unity of rural and urban areas, and the essential *regional* character of the problem.

Emphasis is placed on experience in developed countries. The chapter is organized under three principal sections. First, the nature of rural development and the character of the 'rural' context will be discussed. Second, the extent and importance of existing manufacturing in rural areas are identified through an investigation of the structure of, and trends in, employment in selected countries. The characteristics of manufacturing industry in rural areas, the variety of ways in which rural industrialization may occur, and the relationship between manufacturing and rural prosperity are discussed. Finally, and by way of conclusion, the last section is devoted to a consideration of the future of rural industrialization.

RURAL DEVELOPMENT

Development implies a process of *change in structure*, and is not concerned only with *growth* of a system. Placed within an economic context, development implies a modification of the socio-economic structures of production, and not merely an increase in GNP, per capita or globally. Economic development has both *national* and *geographical* dimensions, although in terms of the conscious pursuit of economic development the relative emphasis placed on each differs between the less developed countries and the older industrialized nations (Canada, Department of Regional Economic Expansion, 1973a). The problems of the former include low levels of economic growth and living standards, and the inadequacy of production and institutional structures to cope with the demands of transforming their economies and societies. While internal geographical differences in social and economic welfare certainly exist, the major concern of such countries is with development problems at the national scale. The more industrialized countries have faced a rather different issue; it has become apparent that the process of overall economic growth has not meant that all parts of a country have shared equally in this growth. Except in the case of distressed industrial regions, suffering from obsolescent plant and unfavourable trade conditions, many of the problem areas are characterized by a relatively important rural sector and conversely, a relatively weak urban-industrial sector. Concern over such problem areas is seen in the increasing literature devoted to regional and rural development, and in the myriad of government programmes dealing with such issues.

What, then, is rural development? Why the need for rural development? What distinguishes it from regional development? Are there significant differences between the issues at which the two strategies are levelled?

The need for rural development as conscious direction of change has been related to the creation of relatively stagnant or slow-growing areas in growing economies. Rapid rates of industrialization and urbanization have been associated with increasing polarization of the space economy. Technological change in agriculture has released labour which, given the strong metropolitanization of manufacturing industry, has only served to heighten the differences between fast-growing and slow-growing areas, resulting in massive population movements from many rural areas. The agricultural male labour-force in France, for instance, has declined from 7 772 000 in 1851, to 4 019 000 in 1946 and to 2 060 000 in 1968 (Jung, 1971). The changeover from 'rural' to 'urban' has been equally dramatic: with 'urban' as any commune whose administrative centre exceeds 2000 inhabitants, urban France accounted for 24.4 per cent of the population in 1846, 40.9 per cent in 1901, 53.2 per cent in 1946 and 66.2 per cent in 1968 (Gérard, 1974); broadening the definition to include builtup areas covering more than one commune and totalling at least 2000 inhabitants, the urban population made up 70.2 per cent of the population in 1968 and 71.4

per cent in 1975 (France, Institut National de la Statistique et des Études Économiques (INSEE) 1976). Similarly, in the United States, the 'urban' population (census definition) accounted for 69.9 per cent of the population in 1960 and 73.5 per cent in 1970, while in Canada the shift was from 69.6 per cent in 1961 to 76.1 per cent in 1971.

This dramatic changeover from economies dominated by primary production to domination by secondary and tertiary activities has brought great prosperity to some regions, and very little to others. The now classical models of Hirschmann (1958), Myrdal (1963) and Friedmann (1966) have helped us understand how some regions have moved ahead at the expense of others. In extreme situations, this process has created substantial depressed areas, 'typified by their distance from viable and growing centres of major economic activity and by their dependence on a resource base which is in the process of being depleted or which, because of changing technology, can support only a much reduced work force' (Poetschke, 1968, p. 1). Although there are in fact a wide range of conditions in rural areas, these problem rural areas exhibit low per capita income relative to other areas, predominance of primary activities in the work force, underemployment of labour, population outmigration, shortage of capital and a low propensity for economic and social change—in short, a lack of integration into the mainstream of the economy and society. Rural development is involved in trying to improve this integration. While rural development in developing countries is often oriented to the traditional rural sector (Kulp, 1970), the more industrialized countries have become more and more concerned with the development of alternative employment opportunities. Consequently—and fortunately—it is becoming increasingly difficult to separate rural development from regional development, the latter encompassing the former which has certain sectoral emphases. This implies of course that regional development issues encompass non-rural problem areas as well, such as the distressed industrial region which has often received much more government attention owing to obvious issues of unemployment concentration.

Rural development is, then, concerned with the 'rural' context—what do we mean by 'rural'? We must indicate the main dimensions of this issue to appreciate the data presentation problems on population and manufacturing structures. The most commonly used method of defining 'urban' is based on population levels and/or densities for builtup areas and settlements. The French method mentioned earlier is extremely simple, based only on a simple population threshold for a builtup area. In Canada, the delimitation of 'urban' also includes a density variable (Statistics Canada, 1974) to encompass the fringes of urban places and certain unincorporated settlements; 'rural' is consistently defined as the residual area. Such an approach to definition may be easy to compute, but is not based on a functional notion of 'rural'. All approaches that view urban and rural as 'black' and 'white', while convenient for data presentation, mask the essential unity of rural and urban space. First, many rural centres and market towns are classed as 'urban' by such definitions. It is too easy when looking at employment figures exhibiting concentration of employment in 'urban' areas, to exaggerate the lack of employment in 'rural' areas. The close symbiotic relationship that exists between rural areas and these smaller urban centres cannot be ignored. Second, the definition of 'rural' as a residual ignores the essentially heterogeneous nature of this space. Between the traditional rural area based on agricultural production and the strictly urban environment exists a wide range of zones the population of which is not predominantly dependent upon agriculture or other primary activities; often the population will work principally in an urban unit—such as dormitory or small satellite centres in a metropolitan region—but there are also zones, usually industrial, where the population is dispersed throughout several municipalities, for instance, along a river or some communication axis, or even based on some natural resource such as minerals. This has led a number of countries to modify somewhat their definitional positions. In France, since 1962 (Gérard, 1974) the *Zone de peuplement industriel ou urbain* (ZPIU—or zones of industrial or urban population) which may contain both urban and rural communes has been defined; such zones are delimited on the basis of additional criteria such as the number of employees in commercial, administrative or industrial units, the relative importance of the agricultural population, and the proportion of the labour-force that works outside the commune. The metropolitan and non-metropolitan categories of the United States Census similarly recognizes such broader functioning units.

The point of the previous discussion has been to emphasize that a 'rural' problem is a 'regional' problem, and that rural areas form part of larger functioning economic systems. Rural development may occur without any major development occurring in a 'rural' zone—this, of course, is the reasoning behind the deliberate concentration of investment in the major urban areas of some slow-growing regions such as in France. Nonetheless, despite the logic of dealing with a system in its entirety, the apparent distinction between 'urban' and 'rural' has affected the structuring of the administration of development, and 'rural development' frequently became identified at the outset with agricultural development and forestry, and often involved a resource-orientation initially. Furthermore, regional development planning, despite the holistic nature of the subject, dwelt essentially on urban matters, assuming that investment in key urban centres would lead inevitably to the diffusion of beneficial impact to the remainder of the regional system. Of course, when this diffusion was slow to take place, this only gave further ammunition to the advocates of a distinctive rural development structure (Jung, 1971). While differences clearly exist between urban and rural places in terms of activities, requiring a certain professional specialization in development planning, the emphasis of such differences only serves to detract from *the essential unity of the space-economy*.

RURAL INDUSTRY AND THE ROLE OF MANUFACTURING IN RURAL DEVELOPMENT

Any perspective that views rural development and rural industrialization as synonymous exaggerates the importance of manufacturing and underplays the role of other activities in the development process. Not all prosperous rural areas have achieved their position through industrialization, although it can be argued that most prosperous rural areas owe their status to *favourable relationships with the urban-industrial complex and/or particular physical resource endowments*. But first, to place industry in rural areas into perspective, it is necessary to inspect the overall structure and trends in manufacturing and employment for selected countries.

The Importance of Manufacturing in Rural Areas

Data portraying gross employment structure for a number of countries, representing a wide range of degree of dependence upon primary activities, are shown in Table 5.1. The ubiquitous decline in the relative importance of agriculture and other primary activities is evident. Industrial employment, including construction and public works, continues to account for a significant proportion of total employment in these developed countries, but this proportion has stabilized or decreased in most countries. Italy is an exception to this—evidence of its low level of development in the immediate postwar years; similarly in France, the share of agriculture in total employment declined rapidly from 36 per cent in 1946 to 15 per cent in 1968, while manufacturing employment increased from 22.9 per cent in 1946 to 28 per cent in 1968 (France, Institut National de la Statistique et des Études Économiques (INSEE), 1973). The other ubiquitous trend is the increasing importance of the service sector. It is against this picture of a stable or declining share of employment in manufacturing—even to the extent of an absolute decline such as in the United Kingdom since the mid-1960s (Keeble, 1976)—and an increase in the tertiary sector, that we must view changes taking place in rural areas.

Generally, rural areas exhibit a lower proportion of their employment in manufacturing than urban areas, a lower proportion in services and a much higher proportion in agriculture. In France, in 1962, 28 per cent of employment in rural areas (census definition) was in the secondary sector (39 per cent for all France), while the agricultural sector accounted for 50 per cent and the tertiary for 22 per cent (Jung, 1971). In Canada, manufacturing accounted for 11.7 per cent of the rural labour-force (census definition) in 1961 and 25.3 per cent in urban areas, while service sectors (excluding transportation) accounted for 27.4 per cent in rural and 52.0 per cent in urban areas. Similarly, the 'more rural' provinces have a lower proportion of rural employment in manufacturing than the more urban provinces such as Ontario, Québec and British

TABLE 5.1. Employment structure[1] for selected countries, 1954–72 (per cent national totals)

	1954	1958	1962	1967	1969	1970	1972
			United States				
Agriculture, forestry, etc.	11.5		8.6	5.2		4.4	4.2
Industry[2]	33.8		32.0	33.7		32.2	31.0
Services[3]	54.7		59.5	61.1		63.4	64.8
			United Kingdom				
Agriculture, etc.	5.0		4.0	3.1			4.2
Industry[2]	49.8		46.3	46.9		31.0	
Services[3]	45.2		49.7	50.0			64.8
			Canada				
Agriculture, etc.	18.9		12.2		8.2		6.9
Industry[2]	33.6		31.7		32.3		30.9
Services[3]	47.5		56.1		59.5		62.2
			West Germany				
Agriculture, etc.		16.3[4]	12.8[5]	10.6		8.6	7.8
Industry[2]		47.2	48.2	48.0		50.4	49.6
Services[3]		36.5	39.0	41.4		40.9	42.6
			Italy				
Agriculture, etc.	43.1		29.4	24.1		19.5	18.2
Industry[2]	29.8		38.8	41.1		43.8	44.3
Services[3]	27.1		31.8	34.8		36.7	37.3

Source: compiled from Annuaire Statistique de la France, 1966–75, Partie Internationale, in turn based on UN, FAO, and national yearbooks.

[1] Excluding unemployed and armed forces. Original classification based on the Standard International Industry Classification.

[2] Includes extractive, manufacturing and building/public works industries.

[3] Includes electricity, gas, water and sanitary services; commerce, banks, insurance; transportation and communications; services; other.

[4] Excluding West Berlin.

[5] Including West Berlin.

Columbia (Table 5.2). United States' differences are not so marked, and, based on some sources, may have reversed now (see below); but in 1960, manufacturing accounted for 24.1 per cent of rural employment and 28.2 per cent in urban areas.

TABLE 5.2. Selected indicators of the rural manufacturing labour force for the provinces of Canada, 1961–71

	Per cent of Population 'rural'[1]		Per cent of provincial manufacturing in rural areas		Per cent of rural labour force in manufacturing		Per cent of share of manufacturing employment: total manufacturing		Per cent of share of manufacturing employment: rural	
	1961	1971	1961	1971	1961	1971	1961 base	net change 1961–71	1961 base	net change 1961–71
Newfoundland	49.3	42.8	30.9	37.1	8.1	12.7	0.9	1.8	1.9	5.0
Prince Edward Island	67.6	61.7	56.8	63.6	7.8	10.4	0.2	0.4	0.9	1.7
Nova Scotia	45.7	43.3	41.9	45.6	14.8	16.8	2.4	2.4	7.2	8.1
New Brunswick	53.5	43.1	46.2	45.1	15.9	19.3	2.0	2.6	6.6	5.8
Québec	25.7	19.4	11.1	12.9	13.7	18.6	33.2	11.7	26.0	22.7
Ontario	22.7	17.7	11.9	12.0	16.1	18.5	45.8	58.3	38.5	38.9
Manitoba	36.1	30.5	9.1	11.9	3.9	6.1	3.3	3.4	2.1	4.6
Saskatchewan	57.0	47.0	11.4	16.0	1.0	1.9	1.1	1.6	0.9	2.6
Alberta	36.7	26.5	9.7	11.6	2.4	4.2	3.0	6.7	2.0	5.7
British Columbia	27.5	24.3	24.6	20.8	20.0	15.3	8.0	11.2	13.9	5.0
							100.0	100.0	100.0	100.0

Source: adapted from 1961 and 1971 Canada Census of Population

[1] Census definition of 'rural'

Nonetheless, rural areas are significant in terms of manufacturing employment, and manufacturing in rural areas has quite old roots (France, Atelier Central d'Études d'Aménagement Rural, 1977). First, rural areas account for a significant proportion of total manufacturing employment. In France, 15 per cent of total industrial employment was in rural communes in 1967 (Cazes and Reynaud, 1973); 14 per cent of Canada's manufacturing labour-force was in rural areas in 1961, while the rural proportion of the provincial manufacturing labour-force in the most rural provinces was extremely high (Table 5.2); and in the United States in 1960, rural areas accounted for 23.8 per cent of the total number of employed persons aged 14 years and over in manufacturing. Second, the share of total industrial employment in rural areas, and the importance of manufacturing employment in rural areas, are often found to be increasing. Hence, based on their respective censuses, 15 per cent of Canada's manufacturing labour-force was in rural areas in 1971 (25 per cent if places of less than 10 000 population are included), while the United States figure for

1970 was 26.3 per cent of total manufacturing employment. The shift in the more rural provinces of Canada has been even more striking (Table 5.2). Furthermore, by 1971, manufacturing accounted for 14.1 per cent of Canada's rural labour-force (while the urban figure had declined to 21.3 per cent), and by 1970 in the United States, manufacturing accounted for 27.9 per cent of total rural employment (employed persons aged 16 years and over), while for urban areas the figure had declined to 25.3 per cent. This suggests a movement of industrial employment, and indirectly of industry, into rural areas. While these proportionate shifts may not appear large, the rate of change in manufacturing employment in some rural areas has been large. However, the nature of the data probably overemphasizes the real shift, and we should not ignore the overwhelming dominance by urban areas that these data exhibit.

First, the census data used above on employment relate to place of residence: hence, a shift in employment structure could occur with an increase in commuting without major shifts in industry. As an indication of this, Cazes and Reynaud (1973) note that 30 per cent of the rural non-farm employed labour-force in France work in an adjoining urban area, while the importance of small cities and towns (up to 50 000 inhabitants) as providers of manufacturing employment to surrounding rural areas is stressed elsewhere (France, Commissariat Général du Plan, 1971). In the United States, based on journey-to-work data in the 1960 and 1970 Censuses of Population, 13.6 per cent in 1960 and 24.1 per cent in 1970 of the urban employed worked outside their country of residence, while the respective figures for the rural employed are 14.8 per cent and 28.7 per cent, and the rural non-farm employed 16.7 per cent and 30.0 per cent. This relatively greater shift for the rural workforce is even more significant given that some rural areas close to urban ones in 1960 had been reclassified as urban by 1970.

Second, it is appropriate here to introduce data with more relationship to the idea of functioning regions than the simple rural–urban dichotomy. For Canada, the Census Metropolitan Area (CMA) represents a rather narrow definition of a region, so regions were redefined to incorporate any Census Division, at least half of which was incorporated in a 40 km zone around the edge of each CMA; the exact delimitations are given elsewhere (Bryant, 1976). First, manufacturing in 1961 in the twenty-two regions so defined (Table 5.3) was more important than for Canada as a whole; and while the rural manufacturing labour-force only accounted for 8 per cent of the total manufacturing labour-force in these regions, the rural manufacturing labour-force of these twenty-two regions accounted for a massive 42 per cent of the total Canadian rural manufacturing labour-force. The twenty-two regions still contained 73.1 per cent of Canada's total manufacturing labour-force in 1971, the slight decrease over 1961 being evidence of a slight movement out of the main metropolitan regions. Urban dominance is also shown by provincial data (see Table 5.2). Although intercensal comparisons are always difficult owing to the in-

TABLE 5.3. Selected aspects of the manufacturing labour-force in the twenty-two CMA-based regions of Canada, 1961–71

	1961	1971
The twenty-two regions:		
total labour force	4 248 810	5 848 885
per cent of Canadian total[1]	66.6	67.8
total rural labour force	542 936	NA
per cent of Canadian rural total[1]	31.9	NA
total manufacturing labour-force	1 051 575	1 247 475
per cent of Canadian total[1]	74.7	73.1
total rural manufacturing labour-force	83 722	NA
per cent of Canadian total[1]	42.0	NA
Per cent manufacturing in total of:		
the twenty-two regions	24.8	21.3
Canada[1]	21.7	19.8
Per cent rural employment in total of:		
the twenty-two regions	12.8	NA
Canada[1]	26.3	21.0
Per cent rural manufacturing in total manufacturing employment of:		
the twenty-two regions	8.0	NA
Canada[1]	14.0	15.0

NA Not available
[1] Including Yukon and the North-West Territories

evitable flurry of definitional changes, the three 'most urban' provinces, Ontario, Québec and British Columbia, accounted for more than 80 per cent of the total net increase in the manufacturing labour-force between 1961 and 1971 for the ten Canadian provinces, while Ontario and Québec alone accounted for over 60 per cent of the net increase in the rural manufacturing labour-force. Once again, however, these data do provide evidence of a slight shift towards other regions; for instance, the shares of the four Atlantic provinces and the three Prairie provinces in both total and rural manufacturing employment increase from 1961 to 1971 are greater than their respective initial shares in such employment in 1961.

For the United States, evidence comes from both census data and a recent study on manufacturing employment change (Haren, 1974) using State Employment Security employment estimates. Manufacturing employment (Table 5.4) was initially more important in the metropolitan employment structure than in non-metropolitan areas, but by 1970, the share of manufacturing had considerably declined in metropolitan employment and increased in non-metropolitan employment. These trends, if not the actual levels, are confirmed by Haren (1974). Metropolitan areas account for a substantial share of manufacturing employment, and the data show that the share of United States manufacturing accounted for by metropolitan areas has remained fairly

TABLE 5.4. Selected aspects of manufacturing employment[1] in metropolitan and non-metropolitan areas of the United States, 1960–70

	Metropolitan					Non-metropolitan			
		Urban		Rural			Urban	Rural	
	Total	Central cities	Other	Non-farm	Farm	Total		Non-farm	Farm
Per cent of employment in manufacturing:									
1960	29.0	26.9	31.9	32.0	15.4	23.5	25.2	27.3	11.5
1970	25.8	23.6	27.2	30.7	18.6	26.3	25.1	29.8	15.9
Per cent of United States manufacturing employment:									
1960	70.1	35.0	27.8	7.3		29.9	13.4	16.5	
1970	70.2	29.9	31.5	8.8		29.8	12.3	17.5	
Per cent of workers working outside county of residence:									
1960	14.8	10.1	21.4	17.0	9.2	12.2	9.3	16.6	9.2
1970	25.6	21.0	29.4	31.0	23.4	24.3	19.6	29.5	21.5

Source: adapted from 1960 and 1970 United States Census of Population

[1] Employed persons, aged 14 years and over in 1960, and 16 years and over in 1970

[2] Based on the Standard Metropolitan Statistical Area for each *respective* census

stable. Other sources, however, indicate that non-metropolitan areas have increased their share of United States' manufacturing employment from 22 per cent to 25 per cent, 1960 to 1970 (Haren, 1974). The differences may relate to a number of factors: (a) different data sources, (b) Haren uses the same Standard Metropolitan Statistical Area delimitation to filter both 1970 and 1960 data, and (c) the 1960 census data used above includes 14 and 15-year-olds in the employed workforce; since 14 and 15-year-olds, based on 1970 data, were employed more in non-agricultural activities in metropolitan areas than in non-metropolitan areas and were concentrated mainly in metropolitan areas in 1970 (64.9 per cent of employed 14 and 15-year-olds), it is reasonable to assume that their inclusion in 1960 would serve to inflate the manufacturing numbers in metropolitan as opposed to non-metropolitan areas. But despite data which show a shift to non-metropolitan counties, Haren (1974) notes the tremendous concentration of manufacturing jobs in the non-metropolitan counties in and adjacent to the Great Lakes Industrial Belt, representing a certain amount of infilling and decentralization of activity from centres such as Cleveland, Detroit and Chicago, and also substantial infilling around and in the Southern Industrial Crescent and Carolina Coastal Plain.

The census data also provide evidence of an increasing share of metropolitan manufacturing employment in rural metropolitan areas, underscoring previous comments made with respect to urban and rural differences and commuting trends. Hence, within the 1960 metropolitan areas, 14.8 per cent of all workers and 17 per cent of rural non-farm workers worked outside their county of residence; by 1970, the figures had changed respectively to 25.6 per cent and 31 per cent, a greater increase for the latter group, representing a substantial number of workers since rural metropolitan non-farm workers accounted for 34 per cent of all rural non-farm workers in 1970.

The evidence suggests then, three main observations:

1. That urban areas, and, more generally, metropolitan regions dominate manufacturing employment absolutely. Because of the weight of this structure, dramatic changes are unlikely. Certainly, centripetal or polarization forces still continue to operate; for example, Ontario accounted for 58.3 per cent of net manufacturing employment change from 1961 to 1971 for the ten Canadian provinces while its share of 'initial' 1961 manufacturing employment was only 45.8 per cent.
2. There is an undeniable change taking place in favour of some rural areas and peripheries generally. For the United Kingdom, Keeble (1976) provides evidence that centrifugal forces have become more important in locational change in manufacturing employment since the mid-1960s than centripetal forces, and that these centrifugal forces have operated in favour of the peripheries, including some hitherto non-industrialized, rural areas. He notes that regional employment structures are becoming closer to the

national average, a conclusion supported by the previous evidence given above for the United States and Canada for rural/urban and metropolitan/non-metropolitan breakdowns.

3. This must be qualified by a third observation, that while rural areas are experiencing increases in manufacturing employment, much of this seems related to the extension of broad urban-industrial regions, emphasizing the close relationship between 'urban' and 'rural'.

This dispersal of industry within broad regions is seen by Keeble (1976) as a major component of the overall spread of industry within the United Kingdom, although a broader scale dispersal process is also operative. Increases in 'rural' manufacturing are partly the result of industrial movement, including decentralization, and partly of growth in 'indigenous' manufacturing. Research on industrial movement in the United Kingdom (Sant, 1975) has suggested that many industrial moves are *distributional* rather than *developmental*. The relative importance of short-distance moves represents in some ways an extension of the urban system. Interestingly enough, such broad urban systems are not constrained or delimited by simple commuting constraints. Frequent contact between a unit and the metropolitan core(s) may be insignificant, but the need for regular, but infrequent, contact may permit a move involving road journeys of two hours or more from the core area. *Distributional* moves within such an extended urban-industrial region are unlikely to affect broad regional employment levels, but can be very significant locally. Recent trends within the very broad area of the Paris Basin have been likened to the development of another megalopoitan zone (Atelier de Recherche et d'Études d'Aménagement, 1970 and 1972) in which rural industry accounts for 25 per cent of the industrial potential of the Paris Basin, excluding the Paris agglomeration. The continued development of such 'central' locations for some industries bears witness to the importance of market factors, transportation availability, external scale economies and, as Norcliffe (1975) would add, linkage and contact patterns over relatively short distances.

Interregionally, industrial moves become potentially *developmental*, and have been very important in some regions, such as East Anglia (Sant, 1975) and South-West England (Spooner, 1972) in the United Kingdom. One might argue that such development in 'rural peripheries' is only feasible because of increasingly better links between them and the main urban-industrial core regions. When such peripheral regions are indeed close to the main core areas, as with East Anglia in the United Kingdom, it is difficult to argue against considering them as part of the core (Spooner, 1972), and from this perspective, some of the observed disperal of industry in the United Kingdom (Keeble, 1976) could be regarded equally as representing integration of former peripheries into the 'core'. However, manufacturing has developed in some of the more remote rural regions; hence, in France, a recent study (France, Atelier Central d'Études d'Aménagement Rural, 1977) notes that 40 per cent of industrial jobs being created were in rural communes *outside* ZPIU.

The Structure of Manufacturing in Rural Areas

We must now turn to the structure of manufacturing and the types of industry developing in rural areas, and, data permitting, in the remoter rural areas. First, rural areas are often characterized by concentration of manufacturing activities in industries that, *in terms of employment* at least, are growing slowly or are experiencing a contraction nationally. Census data show that in the Canadian Atlantic provinces, 33.8 per cent of the 1961 labour-force was in food and beverage industries (15.6 per cent for Canada), and 13.1 per cent in wood industries (7.0 per cent for Canada), groups that experienced respectively 10.6 per cent and 1.7 per cent increases in their labour-force overall 1961 to 1971 (all manufacturing employment increased by 21.5 per cent). In the United States, rural areas exhibit a greater concentration of employment in wood industries (including furniture), food and textiles than in urban areas (Table 5.5); this relative concentration is even stronger if non-metropolitan and metropolitan categories are considered. All these sectors contain nationally slow-growing or declining industries in terms of employment. Industries particularly susceptible to decline or even closure include old sawmills, certain woodworking establishments, and textile and clothing mills (Haren, 1974). This phenomenon is not peculiar to the United States; in France, rural industries are often concentrated in sectors in recession nationally such as textiles, clothing, agricultural supplies and food processing (Cazes and Reynaud, 1973; France, Commissariat Général du Plan, 1971; France, Atelier Central d'Études d'Aménagement Rural, 1977). Indigenous industry in South-west England similarly appears concentrated in nationally slow-growing industries (Spooner, 1972). This general picture, of course, is not unexpected—it is one of the characteristics of rural problem regions.

What is perhaps more disconcerting is the frequent concentration of growth in these areas in those very same slow-growth sectors. Despite the variety of industry currently locating in rural areas, much of this diversity is found within the orbit of the principal urban-industrial concentrations. Till, cited in Hansen (1973, 1974), found from an analysis of manufacturing trends in 'distant non-metro' counties of the Southern United States, that growth was predominantly in nationally slow-growth industries; and the share of the national labour-force in food and beverage industries, a nationally slow-growing industry in Canada, accounted for by the Atlantic provinces, increased from 12 per cent to 16 per cent from 1961 to 1971. Even under government programmes to assist industrial job creation, supported jobs are often dominated by the sectors initially predominant; such is the case with the Regional Development Incentives Programme in the Canadian Atlantic provinces (Canada, Department of

TABLE 5.5. Structure of manufacturing employment[1] by industry for urban/rural[2] and metropolitan/non-metropolitan areas, United States, 1970

	Urban	Rural	Metropolitan	Non-metropolitan
Per cent of manufacturing employment in:				
furniture, lumber, wood	3.3	9.6	2.7	10.1
primary metals	6.3	5.5	6.7	4.6
fabricated metals	7.8	6.1	8.1	5.6
machinery	10.4	8.9	10.7	8.4
electrical machinery and supplies	10.2	7.8	10.5	7.6
motor vehicles	11.5	8.7	12.6	6.5
other durables	10.7	9.4	10.8	9.2
food and kindred industries	6.9	7.4	6.5	8.2
textiles and allied industries	8.9	16.8	7.7	18.7
printing, publishing, etc.	7.0	3.2	7.0	3.8
chemicals and allied industries	5.2	4.5	5.1	4.6
other non-durables	11.7	12.0	11.4	12.8
Labour-force participation rate:				
male	77.6 per cent	73.9 per cent	78.3 per cent	72.9 per cent
female	43.1 per cent	36.0 per cent	42.8 per cent	38.0 per cent
Unemployment in Labour force:		Non-farm / Farm		
male	3.9	4.2 / 2.2	3.8	4.0
female	5.0	5.7 / 4.6	5.0	5.6

Source: adapted from the 1970 United States Census of Population
[1] Employed persons, 16 years and over
[2] Based on 1970 Census definitions

Regional Economic Expansion, 1973b), despite a detectable move towards diversification in some provinces. This process of concentration of slow-growing industries in rural peripheries has been explained by a 'filtering down' process (Thompson, 1969) whereby such industries might actively seek out areas of cheap, unskilled labour and where little competition exists from other industries. It is, of course, possible that regionally concentrated growth in some national slow-growth industries may reflect changing comparative advantages or the realization of real potential. Hence, for instance, food processing industries have played a significant role in development in East Anglia (Ward, 1977), taking advantage of the obvious resource endowments of the region and the improving position with respect to markets. The key would be to possess data on industrial performance, which unfortunately are lacking for the geographical breakdown required.

Not all industries developing in rural peripheries are slow-growth ones however. Keeble (1976) suggests that industries differ with respect to their 'locational net benefit surfaces' which influence an industry's propensity to move to peripheral areas. The case of interest to us is where net benefits increase away from core or traditional centres; in this case, movement and/or differential growth occurs favouring the peripheries—such would be the case of textiles and clothing, both sectors suffering overall employment decline in many developed countries, and of the consumer electronics industries, a major growth sector in the 1960s. Thus, certain types of both nationally declining and growing industries may be attracted to peripheries, in both instances here on account of some aspect of their labour situation.

Other evidence, however, is indicative of a certain fragility of rural industry. Rural plants tend to be small which, in the face of general trends towards concentration and consolidation nationally, is a real handicap in terms of achieving scale economies (Jung, 1971; Chabert, 1972; Veyret-Verner, 1971). That rural industries are frequently small is incontestable—given the labour pool constraints in many areas, they could hardly be otherwise. The close positive correlation between size of centre and size of industrial unit established is further testimony to this (Spooner, 1972; Haren, 1974; France, Commissariat Général du Plan, 1971). Industries established in South-west England between 1939 and 1967 were considerably smaller than the United Kingdom average (Spooner, 1972), and in Norfolk, East Anglia, there were only five employers with more than 2000 employees in 1977 (Holmes, 1977) despite the existence of quite large urban centres. Rural industries in France are also small (Jung, 1971); between 1962 and 1967, 84 per cent of the industrial units created in rural areas had no more than fifty employees, and only 2 per cent had more than 200 employees. However, the evidence relating to problems created by small size alone is not clear; frequently, in rural industrial zones where industry is small-scale and in difficulties, other structural difficulties exist as well, as with many Alpine industries (Veyret-Verner, 1971; Bouclier and David, 1967; Chabert, 1972). In any case, certain recent observations of a reduction in size of industrial unit (Atelier de Recherche et d'Études d'Aménagement, 1970), partly related to possibilities of considerable subdivision of the production process in certain industries, might act to counter the criticism based on small size.

Finally, another indication of fragility relates to the frequent observation of high rates of turnover in industrial job creation in rural areas. In France, between 1962 and 1967, while 256 000 new industrial jobs were created in rural areas, 202 000 were suppressed because of industrial closures (Cazes and Reynaud, 1973). The same is often true of development areas generally; induced industrial moves often apparently lead to disappointing changes in total employment through being offset by closures in other sectors (Sant, 1975). The strong attention given by some government industrial job creation programmes to existing industry is not, therefore, necessarily misguided. Attraction of growth industries should not detract attention from the existing major employers.

The previous discussion has provided evidence of the urban-orientation of much manufacturing in rural areas; but we should recognize a wide range of types of rural industrialization, ranging from the large-scale development of natural resources in a rural context to the development of small craft-type industries in villages. The former extreme may not represent *rural* industrialization to some (see, for example, Singh, 1968)—they may simply see the implantation of an urban complex in a hitherto rural area. But it still deserves consideration under 'rural development' particularly on account of the impact such development might have on surrounding rural areas. The latter—the craft industries—seems to represent some idyllic goal for others! The truth is, both exist; but equally there is a wide range between them. This variety should be recognized (Atelier de Recherche et d'Études d'Aménagement, 1972; France, Atelier Central d'Études d'Aménagement Rural, 1972) if only to counter the notions that urbanization and industrialization equal 'bigness' and that development effort must be concentrated at major 'growth centres'. Two major dimensions differentiate between different types of situation—scale of industrial development, and nature of the recipient area, in terms of links to metropolitan core regions (accessibility notion, including not only transportation considerations but also contact and linkage considerations generally) and of size of centre (labour threshold notion to which could also be added (Norcliffe, 1975) that of infrastructure availability). These are suggested as important in considering the chances of success of rural industrialization, the type of industry involved and also the impact of development.

To illustrate a number of points, some examples are given from one country, France, standardizing therefore for distances within a country. First, the broad sense given to 'metropolitan' is akin to the megalopolis concept. 'Rural development' can occur, and be a problem, within such a highly urbanized region, such as the Paris Basin (Atelier de Recherche et d'Études d'Aménagement, 1970). Polarization of economic activities has occurred *within* the region leading to the development of large rural areas where labour supply and job creation is limited, and jobs concentrated in non-dynamic sectors, such as the northern plateaux of the Lower Seine planning region (Atelier de Recherche et d'Études d'Aménagement, 1972). Development has been pulled to major centres within the region, or to particular axes of development. But, conversely, a more recent dispersal of industry has also been taking place. Large-scale development has occurred in some 'rural' areas without labour supply problems, being able to draw workers from other centres while still maintaining close contact with core areas; such is the case with the plants built by Simca and Antar in rural areas within France's Northern Industrial Zone (Henniquau, 1973). Such development often reflects the infilling and increasing integration of the physical parts of a megalopolitan area. The areas affected can be associated with Friedmann's 'upward transitional' areas (Friedmann, 1966), and extension of the megalopolitan structure may even integrate parts of the 'periphery'.

Beyond the metropolitan cores are the peripheries, often rural in character. Industrial development takes place in a variety of forms, although the orientation is essentially urban. Major urban centres are often selected, and as we go down the population scale, industrial development tends to become smaller in scale. Naturally if sufficient reason exists (for example, special natural resource endowment), massive inmigration can occur, as happened with the Lacq natural gas exploitation in South-west France. Numerous examples exist of *diffuse industrial zones*, based either on medium-scale industrial activity —such as the Choletais region (Paris Région, Institut d'Aménagement et d'Urbanisme de la Région Parisienne, 1975), the South-west area of Eure (Atelier de Recherche et d'Études d'Aménagement, 1971) and some Alpine valleys—or on more of a craft or artisan scale.

This suggested structuring of rural industrialization must not be construed as implying that all centres can experience development. Based on the previous evidence and discussion, we can postulate, particularly in the case of rural peripheries, a decreasing probability of receiving industrial development with decreasing population size and density.

The emphasis in our previous discussion given to differences between metropolitan and non-metropolitan areas and the importance of size of centre has much in common with Norcliffe's (1975) tentative ideas concerning a general theory of manufacturing places. In addition to processing activities which are found in both heartland and hinterland, he suggests a three-fold categorization of activities within manufacturing: fabricating activities, often involving the production of intermediate products; integrative activities, such as production processes involving assembly; and 'administrative' activities involving on the one hand the key decision-making activities of a manufacturing firm and on the other hand, certain sectors such as computer electronics where contact with research facilities is critical. His suggested 'theory' is summarized thus (1975, p. 52):

> Specifically, the following relations are anticipated: a positive relationship between plant size and city size; a concentration of administrative activities in metropoles, integrative activities in large towns and fabricating activities in medium-sized and smaller towns; and particular types of industries to be well represented in towns of a given size group.

MANUFACTURING AND RURAL PROSPERITY

The basic question to be tackled in this section is this: Assuming manufacturing development in a rural context, what effect does it have on rural prosperity? It is essentially an impact question. More specifically, can manufacturing absorb the underemployed labour? Does it increase incomes? Does it stimulate development of the primary sector? Does it lead to the development of other activities, either close by or in other parts of the region through some linkage effect?

Research has tackled these issues at two levels:

1. General studies of association between manufacturing (often submerged in a 'general urban-industrial' factor) and rural prosperity, and
2. Case studies, often involving interviews of employees and employers.

First, the positive relationship between urban-industrial development and rural prosperity is now widely accepted, and has been extensively corroborated (Sisler, 1959; Ruttan, 1955). This does not mean urban-industrial development accounts for all, or even a major portion, of rural prosperity. This is evident from the large amounts of 'residual' variation in rural prosperity in such studies; hence, Sisler (1959) using county data for the United States found that roughly 15 per cent of the variation in farm income and 31 per cent of non-farm income was associated with variation in the level of urbanization. The regional pattern produced by analysis of each region as a separate data set, however, produced more interesting results, the strongest associations being found in regions characterized by significant urban-industrial concentrations. This integration takes place through the markets in capital, goods and labour, the stress being placed on the labour market in most studies. For farm families, for instance, the impact is transmitted through developments in part-time farming, and more generally the participation of farm family members in non-farm employment. Generally, however, such studies do not tackle the notion of spatial impact directly, although one can infer the existence of strong distance-decay phenomena from the marked regional variations in Sisler's (1959) results. The question of spatial impact has been addressed directly in a recent study (Moseley, 1973) dealing with levels of rural prosperity around the major growth centre, Rennes, in Brittany, France; the conclusions confirm the existence of other factors influencing the level of rural prosperity. The positive relationship between the growth centre and rural prosperity around the centre was confined essentially to the commuting area. This confirms the previous comment that the major channel of integration is via the labour market, and additionally suggests that 'spread' is quite limited.

The case study approach allows for more detailed investigation, and the impact on demography, labour, other activities and the local municipality are treated briefly in turn. Size of development is important in considering impact on *demography*. A large enough development can lead to stabilization, even expansion, of population. The Lacq natural gas development in Southwest France and its associated industrial development necessitated substantial inmigration of workers, interestingly enough from areas beyond the immediate zone (Larbriou, 1973). Local labour for this development was rarely drawn from a wider radius than 20 km. In an analysis of two small growth centres in East Anglia (Moseley, 1973), the initial thrust for industrial development was associated with inmigration of London 'overspill' population and over the expansion period, 1958–71, households migrating to the centres or their commuting areas and originating in East Anglia accounted for roughly 20 per cent of all immigrant households. A criticism that has been levelled particularly at the larger-scale growth-centre developments has been the possibility of creation of yet another polarized space (see, for example, Heady, 1974).

The effect on *labour* is also linked to scale of development. The obvious and most general impact is an increase in alternative job opportunities. Increase in employment may stem from several sources, such as *direct* employment from the industrial unit itself, *indirect* employment resulting from demands generated for materials, goods and services by the initial development, and *induced* employment related to increases in demand because of general increases in income in the area. Whether *indirect* and *induced* employment generated are located in the same region is, of course, related to the nature of the industry's linkages and the existing level and structure of activities. The labour market, as noted earlier, seems to be the main channel through which beneficial impact is spread to surrounding communities, but this seems limited to broad commuting zones (Moseley, 1973; Larbriou, 1973). This is not to be discredited for, even with smaller centres, the level of commuting can be quite high; in Thetford, a centre of approximately 18 000 population in East Anglia, over 2000 workers commute daily to its industrial estates (Ward, 1977); and in a Louisiana study (Bertrand and Osborne, 1959) two-thirds of the 500 employees in the plant studied lived in rural areas near the plant. But beyond the commuting zone in rural peripheries, the long-established trends of population decline continue (Larbriou, 1973), and the vicious circle of stagnation persists.

The effect on incomes is partly related to type of industry, particularly important in rural peripheries where a major attraction has often been a large pool of female labour. The effect of such employment may even be to depress average wages owing to the predominance of low-paid unskilled jobs, although family income and living standards of those involved certainly improve (Bertrand and Osborne, 1959). Industries that focus on female recruitment do not absorb labour released from reorganization of the primary sectors. Furthermore, when dealing with relatively isolated centres as opposed to dispersed industrial zones, a commonly observed problem is that of the monoindustry centre; this creates rigidity in local labour market opportunities, and ties the fate of a centre to one industry. Even smaller centres with relatively diversified bases suffer badly with closure of a single major unit. The problem often seems to be accentuated when a rural region has received branch plants of large corporations. The South Norfolk area of East Anglia has until recently possessed a mix of such branch units and smaller, independent operations. But during an economic squeeze, the larger corporations begin sacrificing some of their branch plants. As a recent survey of industry there noted: 'Big may be beautiful, but the diverse and determined crop of modest-sized firms . . . are busily proving that small is safer' (Eastern Daily Press, 1977, p. XVIII). The point is that even though employment may increase with branch plant development, the 'exploitative' nature of core–periphery relationships may still remain with control over such activities being located outside the region. Furthermore, some industries are more prone to ups and downs than others; for instance, severe weather conditions can hurt food-processing industries dependent upon local resources for raw materials, and layoffs are not uncommon.

Frequently, new manufacturing has less of an impact on unemployment than expected (Petersen, 1974). This may be partly due to a concentration on female recruitment in some cases (Sant, 1975), and partly because other industries are declining regionally. Finally, overall regional disparities may persist simply because of rapid growth in service employment in core regions (Sant, 1975). It is no coincidence that the success of regional development in France up to the 1980s is considered to rest with the ability and success in manipulating the distribution of tertiary employment.

With respect to *agriculture*, the most obvious beneficial impacts are the absorption of surplus labour and the addition of non-farm income to family income. This may involve development of part-time farming, on which opinion is divided. On the 'for' side, part-time farming permits a form of adaptation of local labour without breaking former social and cultural ties completely; some of the additional income may be used to improve farming technology. On the other side, it has been argued that part-time farming represents a transitional phase; the evidence against this view is very strong, however, especially in North America, where part-time farming has developed more extensively than in Western Europe (de Farcy, 1977). Part-time farming may discourage farm amalgamation, and may crystallize the agricultural structure, leading to the demise of competitive agriculture.

At the limit, the effect on farm labour leads to the abandonment of agriculture completely. Naturally, in some highly developed agricultural regions, this very process permitted a considerable amount of farm amalgamation and consolidation. Conversely, in some regions, the lack of farm consolidation and improvement has been attributed to slow growth in non-farm employment and the attendant slow decline in the farming population (Rodd, 1965). However, in the poorer rural peripheries, simple abandonment of the land often occurs, a phenomenon exacerbated by land speculation which sometimes accompanies large-scale industrial development (Larbriou, 1973). A final comment on labour concerns the increasing competition between industry and agriculture for labour, and the resulting scarcity of agricultural labour. Again, historically, this process only served to encourage more capital-intensive farming in many currently prosperous agricultural regions. This form of relationship does not necessarily hold, however, in poorer rural regions because a more capital-intensive technology is often lacking to cope with their particular physical conditions. Of course, both processes of crystallization and consolidation may occur simultaneously, with a resulting stronger differentiation within the agricultural sector (Kotter, 1962). Furthermore, significant industrial development can result potentially in an increased local concentration of demand for agricultural produce. However, in the poorest rural peripheries, the prospect for stimulation of local agricultural activity is very limited because of the natural resource base for agriculture; other, better endowed, regions are more likely to benefit from any increased demand.

As for the impact on *other industrial activity*, the hopes of many have rested with the mechanisms underlying the notion of the *growth pole*, or its more limited geographical expression, the *growth centre*. The idea is that development concentrated at such centres will provide the force for transferring economic pulses to other parts of a region, via the satisfaction of indirect and induced demand. However, the evidence suggests the extreme difficulties of inducing further industrial activity in this way, at least when this 'spread' is assumed to take place naturally. Backward linkages (for materials, etc.) of new development are frequently directed outside the region or to other urban centres in the region. Linkages to the local region may be very important *locally* (Moseley, 1973), but the magnitude of linkages to other areas may only serve to heighten disparities. Even large developments can experience difficulties in attracting other industry; for instance, many of the economic impulses generated by the Lacq natural gas development in France are transmitted to other metropolitan centres beyond the region (de Vanssay, 1959; Larbriou, 1973). So while the *growth pole* may stimulate growth in other sectors, the *growth centre* may have a limited effect spatially on its surrounding region. Similarly, induced activity serving the local population is inevitably faced with market-size problems, although this type of activity is more reasonably viewed at a regional scale than at the individual centre level.

Again, activity stimulated in *services* can be both direct and induced. As with industry, indirectly stimulated activity is a function of type of unit, and it appears, for instance, that smaller firms have closer ties with their regions (Moseley, 1973). The tertiary sector, although expanding rapidly nationally in most countries, is not generally regarded as susceptible to easy dispersal. Important exceptions exist (such as universities, government offices) which can stimulate additional activity; but such developments are generally restricted to the larger urban centres, even in the rural peripheries. Induced tertiary activity, related to general income and population changes, tends to favour the immediate centre of development as well as convenience stores within the commuting area. This cannot be expected to generate large increases in employment, but rather might stabilize what otherwise could be declining establishments.

In terms of the *local community*, at one extreme of development, industrial expansion may create considerable increases in local municipal income—often an attraction for the local rural community—and an improvement in services offered. Frequently, however, such growth brings with it dependency problems, local planning problems that are beyond the competence of local officials, soaring municipal costs and social segregation which may sour the benefits of industrialization. At the other extreme, the 'rural' character of a centre may simply be maintained with the stabilization or addition of a few small-scale industrial units.

The fact that many of the impacts may be limited in geographical extent around the recipient centre, and that much of the total impact is transmitted to other centres and regions, should not surprise us. It simply reflects the first stages of integration into the urban-industrial complex. With time, some links may be strengthened with the local area. Our conclusions so far only stress the point that rural industrialization is often a long and difficult process. Overnight solutions are rare and far between. Naturally, the role of other sectors in rural development cannot be ignored; undoubtedly agriculture will remain the principal support of most rural areas. Even with agriculture though, the more prosperous areas are often associated with the urban-industrial complex. It is no coincidence that many urban centres developed initially in areas of good agricultural land resources. Furthermore, agricultural structures have evolved more rapidly in urban-industrial regions than elsewhere. Pautard (1965) has argued that French agricultural regions have evolved differentially over the last 150 years, in terms of farm size and technology, in direct response to degree of contact with the main urban-industrial concentrations. Such proximity effected substantial transfers of farmers and farm labour out of agriculture permitting farm amalgamation and encouraging substitution of capital for labour. The poorer rural peripheries are unlikely to benefit from this historical relationship between farm improvement and urbanization/industrial development to the same degree simply because modern farm technology is less adaptable to the harsher physical environments. Similarly, urban markets initially encouraged the development of intensive farming nearby, for example in market gardening zones. This particular relationship is weaker now due to declining transportation costs, hence benefiting areas with better resource endowments rather than the poorer rural regions.

Recreation is another sector that holds out hope for some rural areas, but cannot be viewed as a panacea for development. The key to success in commercial recreation ventures seems to lie in market accessibility and/or the possession of significant resources, such as in scenery (Burton, 1967; Jung, 1971). This means that (a) the spatial incidence of demand must fall within relatively limited areas, and (b) not all rural areas possess potential because of lack of significant physical attractions. Even where physical resources do permit the development of recreation and tourism, such development has its own problems, such as seasonality and predominance of low-paid service employment (Spooner, 1972). Hence, tourism and recreation are now generally regarded as only being able to provide a temporary and partial complement to the activities in rural areas.

The dilemma is this: to maintain population levels regionally, alternative employment opportunities are required. Employment in primary sectors, whilst still important, has been decimated in the last century and cannot be expected to provide expanded employment opportunities. Recreation and tourism are limited from an employment perspective, although they may be a perfectly legitimate object of development for other reasons. We have then come full circle back to industry, and it is to the question of getting industry moving in some rural areas that we now turn in the final section.

THE FUTURE OF RURAL INDUSTRIALIZATION

Some have seen rural industrialization as the panacea for rural development. Jung (1971, p. 111) sums up this overoptimistic situation well: 'L'enfer, dit-on, est pavé de bonnes intentions. La France, depuis quinze ans, s'est pavé de zones industrielles ... dont beaucoup n'ont pas dépassé le stade des bonnes intentions'. While regionally, industrialization in rural peripheries is still seen as playing a major role in providing the job diversification (France, Délégation à l'Aménagement du Territoire et à l'Action Régionale, 1973) and the impetus for social and economic adjustment (Canada, Department of Regional Economic Expansion, 1973c) necessary to maintain regional population levels and balanced communities (Nolan, 1977), individual rural communities have often misunderstood the facts of life about industry.

The structure and geographical distribution of manufacturing industry are testimony to the overwhelming dominance of urban areas in manufacturing. The slight swing towards rural areas, even beyond the major metropolitan zones in some countries, obviously holds out some hope for future industrialization—but under what conditions, and where? While such movements may not seem large viewed against the total weight of manufacturing employment, they may be critical turning-points for the communities affected.

First, what makes industry move to a rural area or setting? There are both 'push' and 'pull' factors. 'Push' factors involve the disadvantages of urban location which are most explicit in the context of industrial decentralization. External diseconomies develop in major urban-industrial concentrations, including traffic congestion, lack of space and a highly competitive labour market (Spooner, 1972; Sant, 1975; France, Atelier Central d'Études d'Aménagement Rural, 1977; Fulton, 1974). In the United Kingdom, it has been suggested (Keeble, 1976) that such factors are particularly strong now and have contributed in a major way to the recent dispersal of manufacturing activities. The 'pull' factors relate to the advantages of being in a rural area. Frequently, a bewildering list of advantages is presented (see, for example, Fulton, 1974), but an interesting survey of industrial plants in Nebraska, USA (Shively, 1974) provides evidence that economic factors are listed by firms as the most positive aspects of their particular location, with labour cost and availability, and transportation being rated as most important, while 'community' factors were given a low weighting.

Accessibility to other regions is clearly a key factor regionally, especially given the extraregional ties of many firms. Highway development and construction programmes have brought many a community 'closer' to the metropolitan cores (Haren, 1974), and the need for regular, albeit infrequent, contact between plant and market clearly conveys a locational advantage to rural areas adjacent to the metropolitan core regions. But generally, accessibility may be regarded as a permissive factor for most industries. The scale of the space-economy under discussion is however of great importance—compare for instance the United States and Canada on the one hand and the United Kingdom on the other.

Labour considerations appear to be emphasized most. Expansion is cited most frequently as motivation for industrial moves (Sant, 1975; Spooner, 1972), with problems of labour supply—and land supply—prominent in creating difficulties in areas of origin; and rural areas have traditionally been regarded as cheap, often non-unionized, labour areas. Rural areas, partly because of lack of industry, also seem attractive to industries seeking situations of little labour competition—obviously this can be shortlived; in addition, competition from Third World countries where labour costs are relatively low casts further doubt on the long-term stability of certain industrial movements into rural peripheries in developed countries, such as that of the consumer electronics industries. Nevertheless, rural areas are frequently seen as areas of *plentiful* labour. An indication of the potential attraction is seen in the lower rates of participation in the workforce in rural areas (and non-metropolitan areas) in the United States, especially for female labour, as well as higher rates of unemployment. Obviously, there exist minimum thresholds for labour supplies, both in quantity and quality. Accepting a common rule of thumb that a unit should not employ more than 10 per cent of the labour-force in the catchment area (Atelier de Recherche et d'Études d'Aménagement, 1970) imposes further constraints, although some industries apparently search out situations where they are major employers in an area—the 'big fish in a little pond syndrome' is not entirely without advantages. It is easy to understand the positive relationship between size of new units and size of centre. Overall, then, industries developing in rural areas tend to be labour-intensive (Hansen, 1973; Petersen,

1974), using low-skill, often female labour. This accords with observations on the clothing industry in the United Kingdom (Keeble, 1976), an industry that has experienced shortage of labour and high labour costs in its traditional centres, resulting in the dispersal of smaller units in rural areas to tap local supplies of underemployed female workers. Low wages, however, are not necessarily to be equated with low labour costs, as some of the earlier industrial decentralizations in the Paris Basin experienced (Parry, 1963); the rates of labour turnover, and hence training costs, were very high. *Land availability*, and cheapness, is another often-cited advantage of rural areas; room for expansion has played an important role in many short-distance moves within broad metropolitan regions. Some rural areas, however, with fairly long histories of rural industry are also at a disadvantage because of lack of appropriate space for expansion, as in some Alpine valleys (Chabert, 1972).

Furthermore, the attractiveness of living in rural areas seems more important now (Hansen, 1974; Fulton, 1974; Keeble, 1976). Local area/municipality characteristics seem generally to play an important role only in site selection as opposed to regional selection. Availability of premises is often significant in the final stages; for instance, out of 3000 new industrial units created in rural communes in France between 1962 and 1967, only 1300 required construction of new buildings (France, Commissariat Général du Plan, 1971). Other factors often cited as affecting specific locational choices include the prior existence of industry and minimum levels of infrastructure (Norcliffe, 1975), both of which exert pulls to larger, existing centres. Access to energy supplies, and specific material sources, while once very important (for example, in many Alpine valleys), has become much less so (Chabert, 1972; Bouclier and David, 1967). Where access is important, it is rather access to a potentially wide range of sources than to a specific one. The movement of industry in many Alpine valleys to the valley mouths provides evidence of this (Veyret-Verner, 1971).

We can place the above discussion into a geographical context by considering various types of rural industrialization. Clearly, with resource-based industries the key is availability of the resource at a comparative advantage over other sources, although raw material sources are less important now than hitherto, particularly for the secondary processing stages. While such development is attracted to existing centres, a sufficiently important resource can call for the development of a new town such as Moureux in South-west France. Here, many of the above-mentioned location factors are of little consequence—but the attraction of subsequent development is another matter, and many resource-oriented centres find it difficult to diversify. Indeed, the distinction sometimes made between resource centre, growth centre and service centre (see, for example, Canada, Atlantic Development Council, 1971) emphasizes the low probability of resource-centres expanding into a more diversified base. Equally interesting has been the strong resource-orientation of many industrial development programmes in rural peripheries (Canada, Department of Regional Economic Expansion, 1973b).

Within the broad context of metropolitan regions, accessibility is still an important consideration, both to market and to branches of the same and other industries. In industries where subdivision of processes has progressed substantially (electronics, for instance), examples of concentrated dispersal exist (see Parry, 1963), permitting the maintenance of contact while being able to use a dispersed labour-force and at the same time providing opportunities for living in rural areas. But generally, labour supply presents serious constraints in many rural areas, and even busing is not going to ease matters except in limited cases. Beyond the main core regions, labour supply is also significant, both in terms of attraction, and also in terms of constraints on expansion. Many rural peripheries are thinly populated as a result of narrow and unstable economic bases, and a long history of outmigration. Thus, their future for industrial development is strictly limited, even with active resettlement and concentration of population. Small-scale industry, particularly of the craft-type, could be developed in places, but is unlikely to turn into a flood. Denser populated rural peripheries present more of an attraction in terms of cheap, unskilled/semi-skilled labour (Brittany in France, for example). This has attracted both labour-intensive industries whose technology has been developed to the point where tasks are routine—hence, the developments very often in nationally slow-growing industries—and some high technology industries, such as assembly of consumer electronic goods, where a supply of female labour has also been a powerful attraction.

Inevitably, we are faced with the conclusion that most rural communities are not destined for industrialization. Rural space is heterogeneous, and this must be appreciated fully in order to develop successful government programmes. Heady (1974) has suggested three types of community in terms of industrial prospects: (a) 'endowed' communities with some hope of industrialization. We have argued that the main chances of success fall within the orbit of existing urban-industrial complexes; (b) 'bootstrap' communities which are more numerous, where development is possible but where, if it occurs, is due to a 'lucky break'; and (c) the purely agricultural communities in which long-run prospects lie with restructuring the community to cope with a declining resource base. The aim of planning in the latter case is to prevent these areas becoming 'dead' zones (France, Délégation à l'Aménagement du Territoire et à l'Action Régionale, 1973).

Rural development requires a regional approach which in turn demands recognizing the essential symbiotic relationship between urban and rural areas. Manufacturing has an increasingly important role to play in those rural regions that are able to develop links to the main core regions. However, this does not mean that we can be content in such regions only with concentration of investment/effort at 'growth centres' and waiting for 'spread' to occur. The evidence stands against this position—the impulses generated serve simply to tie that particular centre into the economy, without pulling many other areas with it. The term 'growth centre' might fruitfully be given a wider meaning to include a dispersed clustering of activities, reaching out to a broader population. The suggestion is reminiscent in some ways of the 'agrarian' (small-scale) versus the 'modern' approach to industrialization in developing countries (Robinson, 1964). Manufacturing within metropolitan regions can be expected to experience continued dispersal, and the form of dispersed industrial zones developing in some areas may become a model, on a different scale, for some rural peripheries. Where manufacturing is feasible in rural peripheries, its full potential can only be realized through integrated efforts aimed at industry, settlement, population, primary activities and training. But above all else, rural industrialization is not the solution to the development of large areas of the space economy, and in many of the remote rural areas, rural exodus has progressed so far that it would be illusory to try to turn the clock back.

As a final comment, it is worth noting that our state of knowledge about manufacturing in rural regions is deficient in one major respect. While it is possible to document the magnitude and development of manufacturing employment in rural regions to a certain extent, we lack data pertaining to the viability of enterprises being created. Government intervention may lead to job creation and support of manufacturing in rural peripheries, but we possess no easy method with which to evaluate the economic viability of such activity. Hence, where government intervention may have played an important role in the observed dispersal of industry, for example in the United Kingdom (Keeble, 1976), this hiatus means that we must at least raise a question about the extent to which such dispersal really does imply a reversal of polarization forces. Clearly, future research into the geographical structure and pattern of change in manufacturing needs to be complemented by more critical evaluatory analyses. Otherwise, our knowledge about the processes involved will continue to be based on educated guesswork.

REFERENCES

Atelier de Recherche et d'Études d'Aménagement (AREA) (1970). *La vie rurale dans le bassin parisienne*, Paris, Study commissioned by the Ministère de l'Agriculture. France.

Atelier de Recherche et d' Études d'Aménagement (AREA) (1971). *Le sud ouest de l'Eure, programme d'aménagement rural*, Paris, Study commissioned by the Direction Départmentale de l'Agriculture de l'Eure, France.

Atelier de Recherche et d'Études d'Aménagement (AREA) (1972). *Programme d'aménagement rural de la Seine Maritime*, Paris, Study commissioned by the Direction Départmentale de l'Agriculture de la Seine Maritime, France.

Bertrand, A. L. and Osborne, H. W. (1959). *Rural Industrialisation in a Louisiana Community*, United States Department of Agriculture, Agricultural Economics Division, Bulletin No. 524.

Bouclier, C. and David, S. (1967). 'La papéterie en Grésivaudan: un problème d'imlantation industrielle an montagne'. *Revue de Géographie Alpine*, **55**, 4, 665–691.

Bryant, C. R. (1976). *Farm-generated determinants of land use changes in the rural–urban fringe in Canada, 1961–1975*, Environment Canada, Lands Directorate, Technical Report, Ottawa.

Burton, T. L. (1967). Outdoor recreation enterprises in problem rural areas, Studies in Rural Land Use, Report No. 9, Wye College, Kent, England.

Canada, Atlantic Development Council (A.D.C.) (1971). *A Strategy for the Economic Development of the Atlantic Region, 1971–1981*, Atlantic Development Council.

Canada, Department of Regional Economic Expansion (DREE) (1973a). *Regional Development and Regional Policy: Some* issues *and Recent Canadian Experience*, Queen's Printer, Ottawa.

Canada, Department of Regional Economic Expansion (DREE) (1973b). *Assessment of the Regional Development Incentives Program*, Queen's Printer, Ottawa.

Canada, Department of Regional Economic Expansion (DREE) (1973c). *Regional Development Programs by Province*, Queen's Printer, Ottawa.

Cazes, G. and Reynaud, A. (1973). *Les mutations récentes de l'économie française: de la croissance à l'aménagement*, Doin, Paris.

Chabert, L. (1972). 'L'industrie en Maurienne et en Tarentaise: les fabrications disparues ou en difficulté'. *Revue de Géographie Alpine*, **60**, 75–100.

de Farcy, H. (1977). *Les emplois non agricoles aux Etats-Unis*, Bulletin d'information de l'ACEAR, fascicule 2.5.

de Vanssay, R. (1959). 'Le gaz de Lacq au service de l'économie du centre-est'. *Revue de Géographie de Lyons*, **35**, 285–290.

Eastern Daily Press (1977). *Supplement: Industrial East Anglia*, Norwich **March 15th,** 18.

France, Atelier Central d'Études d'Aménagement Rural (ACEAR) (1972). *Projet de programme de travail pluriennal*, Ministère de I'Agriculture, France.

France, Atelier Central d'Études d'Aménagement Rural (ACEAR) (1977). *Industrie en milieu rural*, Bulletin d'information de I'ACEAR, fascicule 13.103.

France, Commissariat Générale du Plan (1971) *Espace rural—rapport pour la préparation du VI Plan 1971–1975*, La Documentation Française, Paris.

France, Délégation à I'Aménagement du Territoire et à I'Action Régionale (DATAR) (1973). *La politique d'aménagement du territoire*. Ministère de I'Aménagement du Territoire, de l'Equipment, du Logement et du Tourisme, Paris.

France, Institut National de la Statistique et des Études Économiques (INSEE) (1973). Données sociales: première édition 1973 Collections de l'INSEE, vol. M24, No. 101.

France, Institut National de la Statistique et des Études Économiques (INSEE) (1976). *Résultats provisoires du recensement de la population de 1975*, INSEE, Paris.

Friedmann, J. R. (1966). *Regional Development Policy: A Case Study of Venezuela*, MIT Press, Cambridge, Mass.

Fulton, M. (1974). 'Industry's viewpoint of rural areas'. In, L. R. Whiting, (ed.) *Rural Industrialization: Problems and Potentials*, The Iowa State University Press, Ames, Iowa, pp. 68–78.

Gérard, M. C. (1974). *Aspects démographiques de l'urbanisation: analyse 1968*. Collections de l'INSEE, Series D30.

Hansen, N. M. (1973). *The Future of Nonmetropolitan America: Studies in Rural and Small Town Population Decline*, Lexington Books, Lexington, Mass.

Hansen, N. M. (1974). 'Factors determining the location of industrial activity'. In L. R. Whiting, (ed.) *Rural Industrialization: Problems and Potentials*, The Iowa State University Press, Ames, Iowa, pp. 27–45.

Haren, C. C. (1974). 'Location of industrial production and distribution'. In L. R. Whiting, (ed.) *Rural Industrialization: Problems and Potentials*, The Iowa State University Press, Ames, Iowa, pp. 3–26.

Heady, E. O. (1974). 'Rural development and rural communities of the future'. In L. R. Whiting, (ed.) *Rural Industrialization: Problems and Potentials*, The Iowa State University Press, Ames, Iowa, pp. 136–150.

Henniquau, T. (1973). 'L'influence des implantations industrielles sur les exploitations agricoles'. *Études Rurales*, **49–50**, 160–180.

Hirschmann, A. O. (1958). *The Strategy of Economic Development*, Yale University Press, New Haven.

Holmes, K. (1977). 'Employment: worst may be over'. *Eastern Daily Press*, Norwich, Supplement: Industrial East Anglia, **March 15th**, 2.

Jung, J. (1971). *L'aménagement de l'espace rural: une illusion économique*, Calmann-Levy, Perspectives de l'économique: économie contemporaine, Paris.

Keeble, D. (1976). *Industrial Location and Planning in the United Kingdom*, Methuen, London.

Kotter, H. (1962). 'Economic and social implications of rural industrialisation'. *International Labour Review*, **86**, 1–14.

Kulp, E. M. (1970). *Rural Development Planning: Systems Analysis and Working Method*, Special Series in International Economics and Development, Praeger.

Larbriou, S. (1973). 'Industrialisation-urbanisation? L'example de Lacq'. *Études Rurales*, **49–50**, 245–264.

Moseley, M. J. (1973). 'The impact of growth centres in rural regions'. *Regional Studies*, **7**, 57–75.

Myrdal, G. M. (1963). *Economic Theory and Underdeveloped Regions*, Methuen, London.

Nolan, T. V. (1977). 'Imbalance of rural populations a major problem'. *Eastern Daily Press*, Norwich, Supplement: Industrial East Anglia, **March 15th**, 9.

Norcliffe, G. B. (1975). 'A theory of manufacturing places'. In L. Collins, and D. F. Walker, (eds.) *Locational Dynamics of Manufacturing Activity*, John Wiley and Sons, Ltd, London, pp. 19–57.

Paris Region, Institut d'Aménagement et d'Urbanisme de la Région Parisienne (IAURP) (1975). Le Choletais, *Cahiers de l'IAURP*, **40–41**, 78–90.

Parry, C. (1963). 'Un example de décentralisation industrielle: la dispersion des usines de "La Radiotechnique" à l'ouest de Paris'. *Annales de Géographie*, **72**, 148–161.

Pautard, J. (1965). *Les disparités régionales dans la croissance de l'agriculture française*, Gauthier-Villars, Série Espace Economique, Paris.

Petersen, J. M. (1974). 'Effects of rural industrialisation on labour demand and employment'. In L. R. Whiting, (ed.) *Rural Industrialization: Problems and Potentials*, The Iowa State University Press, Ames, Iowa, pp. 108–118.

Poetschke, L. E. (1968). *Regional Planning for Depressed Rural Areas: The Canadian experience*, Department of Forestry and Rural Development, ARDA reports and digests, Canada.

Robinson, R. (1964). 'The role of industry in development'. In R. Robinson, (ed.), *4th Cambridge Conference on the Role of Industrialisation Development*, Jesus College, Cambridge, pp. 5–11.

Rodd, R. S. (1965). *An Economic Analysis of the Manitoulin District*. Department of Agricultural Economics, University of Guelph, No. AE/65–66/6.

Ruttan, V. W. (1955). 'The impact of urban-industrial development on agriculture in the Tennessee Valley and the Southeast'. *Journal of Farm Economics*, **37**, 38–56.

Sant, M. (1975). *Industrial Movement and Regional Development: The British Case*, Pergamon Press: Urban and Regional Planning Series, London.

Shively, R. W. (1974). 'Corporate and community decision-making to attract industry'. In L. R. Whiting, (ed.) *Rural Industrialization: Problems and Potentials.* The Iowa State University Press, Ames, Iowa, pp. 89–93.

Singh, T. (1968). 'Planning the rural sector in the national economy'. In R. Robinson, and P. Johnston, (eds.) *The Rural Base for National Development, 6th Cambridge Conference on Development Problems*, Jesus College, Cambridge, 109–118.

Sisler, D. G. (1959). 'Regional differences in the impact of urban-industrial development on farm and non-farm income'. *Journal of Farm Economics*, **41**, 1100–1112.

Spooner, D. J. (1972). 'Industrial movement and the rural periphery: the case of Devon and Cornwall'. *Regional Studies*, **6**, 197–215.

Statistics Canada (1974). *1971* Census of Population, Vol. III, Part 4–Industries, Bulletin 3.4–4, Statistics Canada, Ottawa.

Thompson, W. R. (1969). 'The econômic base of urban problems'. In W. W. Chamberlain, (ed.) *Contemporary Economic Issues*, R. D. Irwin, Homewood, Ill. pp. 1–47.

Till, T. E. (1972). Rural industrialisation and southern rural poverty in the 1960's: patterns of labour demand in southern non-metropolitan labour markets and their impact on local poverty, University of Texas, unpublished doctoral dissertation.

Veyret-Verner, G. (1971). 'Aménager les Alpes—mythes et réalités'. *Revue de Géographie Alpine*, **59**, 1, 5–62.

Ward, B. A. W. (1977). 'Plan now to meet needs of future growth'. *Eastern Daily Press*, Norwich, Supplement: Industrial East Anglia, **March 15th,** 1–2.

Planning Industrial Development
Edited by David F. Walker

Chapter 6

Political Aspects of Regional Industrial Development

David F. Walker

As economic development is a vital topic for any administration it is not surprising that it is usually of great interest to political representatives as well as those with a professional interest in it. The professionals may not like to see their carefully developed models interfered with, but the fact of the matter is that political influence is almost inevitable. Indeed, many politicians may have been elected to carry through some specific development programme, whether it be for expansion or slow growth. Thus the industrial developer works within a policy framework laid down by elected representatives, even if it is not to his liking, and this makes it difficult to build a good development programme. Add to this the fact that there are tiers of political power and boundaries between different units at the same level of authority, and it is clear that textbook examples of industrial development planning are hard to carry through.

Nowhere are these problems more complex than in democratic federal states, and therefore this essay will focus on them. In federal countries, provinces (or states) have considerable political powers with complete jurisdiction over many facets of life. Thus an extra tier of government is placed between local and national authorities. On the positive side, this allows regional variations to prevail against the centralizing tendencies emanating from the capital. At the same time, however, federalism provides an additional source of jurisdictional wrangling which could be highly counterproductive. A federal state represents a compact and a compromise between authorities which desire union without complete unity (Dikshit, 1976, pp. 1–4). 'The phenomenon that is so created', however, 'is not static but dynamic' (p. 2), which means that development practitioners may face fairly important changes in the parameters under which they work. A good current example is the discussion about changing the Canadian constitution and particularly the uncertainty surrounding the status of Québéc with its separatist Parti Québecois government.

An important but neglected work by Bökemann (1974) stresses that an adequate approach to regional development must include consideration of the role of the state and that this role 'is determined by the hierarchical organization of territories and the organization of departmental agencies' (p. 55). Any given site can be considered to be a product, the value of which is determined by its potential uses. Various levels of political authority may have noticeable effects on such potential. Consideration of Figure 6.1 illustrates the hierarchy of influences affecting the quality of a site. The main effects are in the form of communication opportunities, utility opportunities (water, gas, power, sewage, etc.) and boundary conditions (such as legal safeguards, land-use restrictions). Any particular governmental authority produces sites by combining the opportunities arising from the activities of a higher government with its own investments. Thus, for example, if the Austrian federal government builds an expressway from Salzburg to Vienna, the province of Upper Austria could establish an industrial park beside it while a municipal authority may concern itself with providing necessary housing and services for the workers. Effects from above may, however, be negative. A clampdown of federal spending on defence could reduce income in many provinces and cities while a land-use restriction to protect agricultural land would probably reduce the return a farmer could make by selling it. The characteristics of specific hierarchical relationships in a country, therefore, are clearly of fundamental importance in providing the framework for industrial development opportunities.

This essay examines the way political factors affect industrial development strategy and practice. Further, it considers approaches that have been used to minimize difficulties and encourage as fruitful a development programme as possible. Two countries are mainly used for examples, Austria and Canada. Both are federal in constitution but their sizes are vastly different and there are considerable contrasts in history and traditions.

Canada is the world's second largest country with a land area of nearly 10 million sq. km and a vast northern territory that is almost uninhabited. It became a confederation in 1867, formed from several British colonies. One of the colonies, Québec, was and still is primarily French-speaking, having been taken from France in the eighteenth century. There are ten provinces in Canada today, with populations (1976) ranging from 118 000 in Prince Edward Island to 8 260 000 in Ontario (Figure 6.2). In addition, two territories (Yukon and North West Territories) are administered from Ottawa. Population and wealth has gradually spread westwards as Canada developed, leaving lower income levels and higher unemployment in Atlantic Canada for most of the twentieth century and increasing problems in Québec since the 1930s. Meanwhile in the post-second World War period, Alberta and British Columbia have grown rapidly.

Present-day Austria represents the German-speaking remnant of the pre-

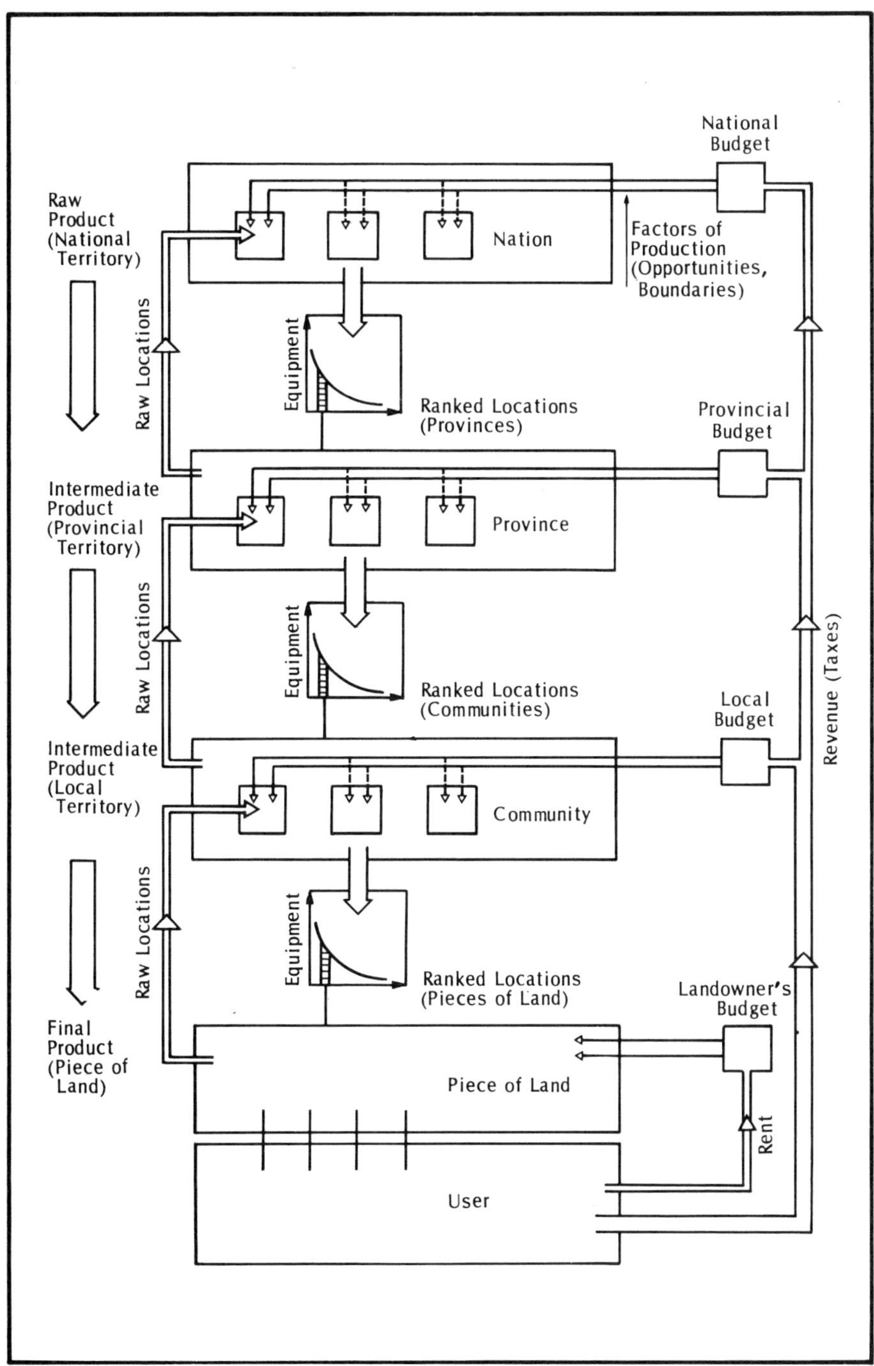

FIGURE 6.1. Institutional structure of the 'production of locations' process (Bökemann (1974), **38**)

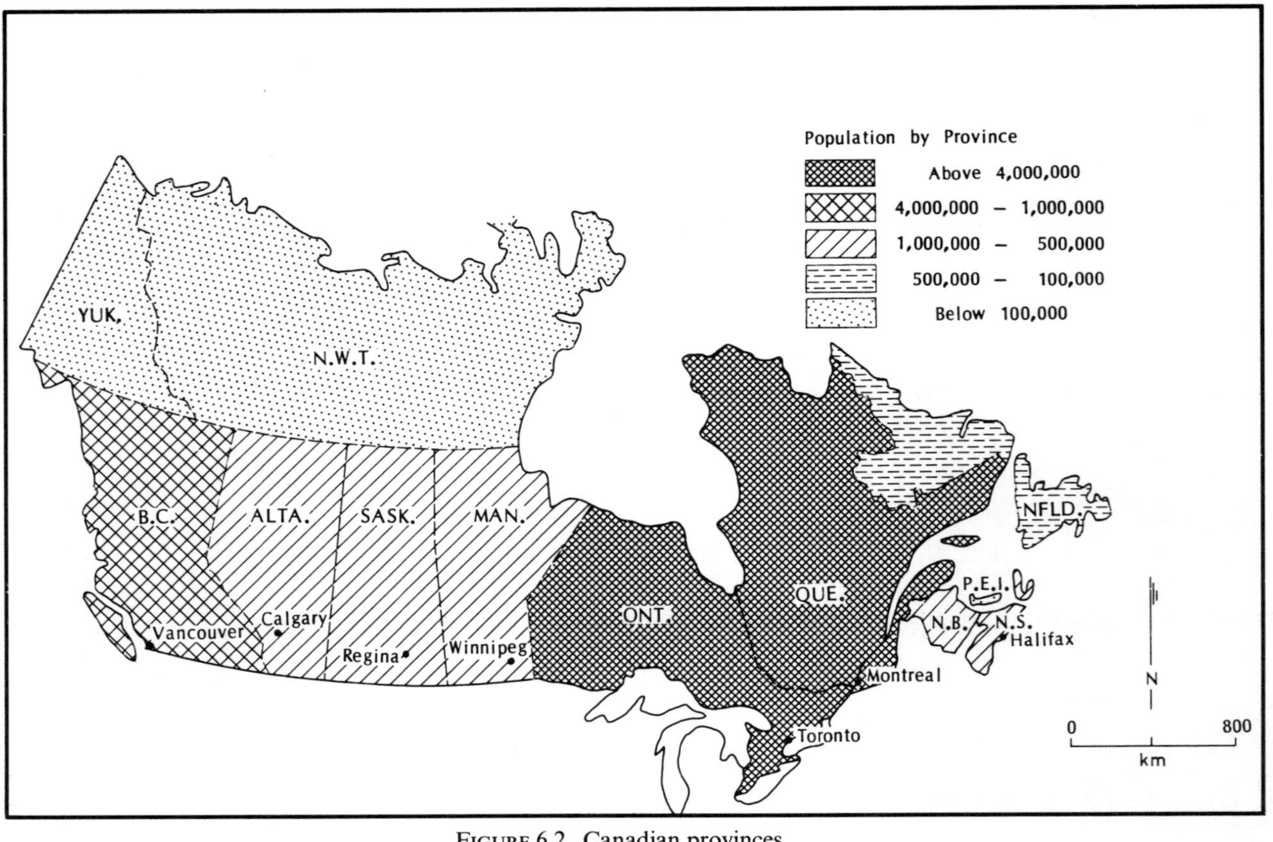

FIGURE 6.2. Canadian provinces

First World War Austro-Hungarian Empire. It is a small country of some seven-and-a-half million people and 83 800 sq. km. Austria has been a federal republic since 1918 and comprises nine provinces (*Länder*) varying in population (1971) from 271 500 (Vorarlberg) to 1 628 000 (Vienna) (Figure 6.3). The central government (*Bund*) has very considerable power over most important aspects of government (Dikshit, 1976, p. 159). In the realm of regional planning and development, however, it has no formal control over what happens within a province. Like Canada, Austria has been characterized by a westward spread of population and wealth since the Second World War. This has been encouraged by the limitations imposed by a long boundary with communist countries, limitations not fully compensated by the relative prosperity of Vienna. The large Alpine area also poses special development problems for the country.

REGIONAL IMPLICATIONS OF NATIONAL POLICY

It is often forgotten that enormous sums of money are spent across a country by federal governments in programmes with no specific regional intent. Regional programmes are usually a relatively late addition to the policy arsenal and even when well established, may compete for funds and priority against well-entrenched ministries operating with a broad national interest in mind. Thus it is not uncommon to find that the spending of other federal units undermines that of the ministry concerned with regional affairs.

In Canada, there are a number of federal economic policies, which clearly have important regional effects; chief of these are tariff and transport policies. Tariff policy in Canada has been protective for about a century. As manufacturing has grown up mainly in Québec and Ontario, tariff protection benefits the two central provinces. At the same time it often prevents the peripheral areas from obtaining products cheaper at nearby United States locations or from offshore. Thus the cost of living is increased and manufacturers needing semifinished products or machinery must cope with higher costs. Transport policy is more controversial in its effects. Rail policy, for example, opened up the west while port expenditures clearly benefit coastal areas. On the other hand, easterners claim that the St Lawrence Seaway benefits central Canada at their expense while westerners complain about unfair rail freight rates, which encourage shipment of raw materials eastward for manufacturing. All in all, it would seem that both of these policies reinforce core-periphery relationships within Canada by aiding Ontario and, to a lesser extent, Québec. In a smaller country such as Austria effects of this type are certainly less, but trade relationships do affect the provinces differentially. In the east, only limited trade takes place with the Comecom block (not mainly as a result of Austrian decisions) while locations to the west of the country benefit from its associate status with the prosperous EEC countries.

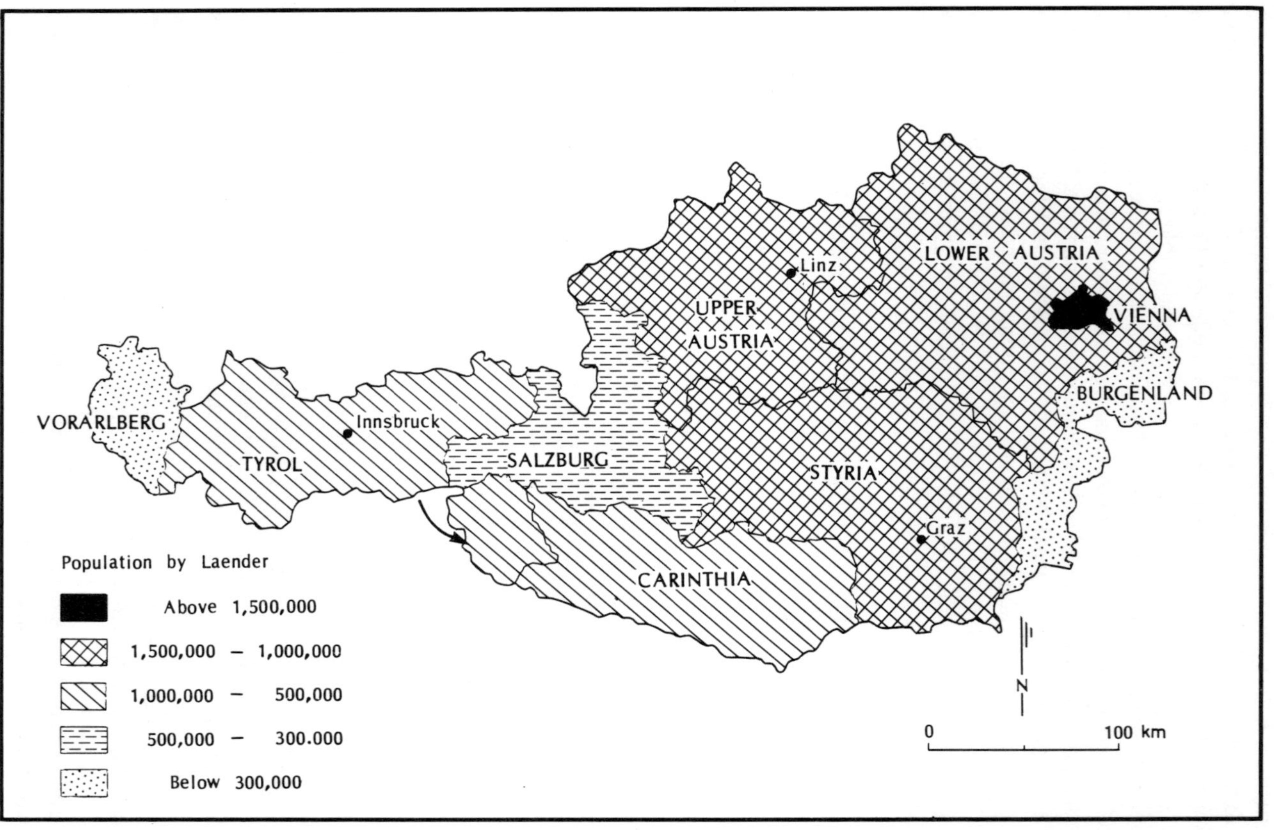

FIGURE 6.3. Austrian *Länder*

TABLE 6.1. Grants, contributions, and subsidies to business, Canada, by Region, 1974–75

	Atlantic region	Québec	Ontario	Prairie region	British Columbia	Canada	Total assistance
			(Dollars per capita)				($ Million)
IT & C industrial assistance programmes	8	6	.9	1	11	7	158.7
DREE	8	6	1	3	—	3	69.7
Agriculture	3	19	12	35	3	16	357.1
M & I industry training programme	3	2	1	1	2	2	36.9
Total	23	33	23	40	17	28	622.4

Source: Economic Council of Canada (1977), 1970.

National concerns prompt many kinds of supports directly to business as well. Frequently aid for management, marketing, and research and development are available to all companies regardless of location. Such support tends to benefit the developed areas most and counterbalance spending for regional priorities. In Canada, for example, support from the Department of Industry, Trade and Commerce is higher in Ontario and British Columbia than in Atlantic Canada and Québec reflecting existing industrial strengths (Table 6.1.). The Atlantic Provinces particularly lose out because high per capita agricultural support programmes do not help them much. If these per capita figures are translated into dollar terms, it can easily be seen how large federal supports are to the richer parts of the country. Austria, however, has tended to avoid some

TABLE 6.2. Aid as percentage of total provincial industrial investment, Austria 1966–1970

Province*	ERP	Provincial	KKAG	Total
Vienna	6.7	0.9	0.7	8.3
Salzburg	5.8	1.2	0.1	7.1
Vorarlberg	5.7	0.4	0.0	6.1
Tirol	6.3	1.5	0.7	8.5
Upper Austria	3.7	0.7	0.2	4.6
Styria	4.9	1.0	1.3	7.2
Lower Austria	5.1	2.5	0.8	8.4
Carinthia	3.7	0.4	3.5	7.6
Burgenland	16.7	9.2	16.2	42.1

KKAG = loans from Kommunalkredit A. G. and transport tax reductions.
Provincial = aid to industry and commerce from provinces.
ERP = loans from the E.R.P.
°Provinces are listed in a generally accepted rank order from wealthiest to poorest.
Source: Betensen (1978), 118

TABLE 6.3. Federal transfers to provinces and local governments, Canada, by province and territories, 1971–75

	Newfoundland	Prince Edward Island	Nova Scotia	New Brunswick	Québec	Ontario	Manitoba	Saskatchewan	Alberta	British Columbia	Total, all provinces	Yukon and Northwest Territories	Canada
(Millions of dollars)													
Transfers to provinces													
Unconditional grants	208.9	44.2	233.9	191.6	1093.1	227.9	156.4	117.8	156.6	32.4	2462.2	94.9	2557.7
Equalization	186.6	40.5	215.8	172.9	974.7	—	122.0	82.4	—	—	1795.0	—	1795.0
Other	22.3	3.7	18.1	18.6	118.3	227.9	34.4	35.4	156.6	32.4	667.2	94.9	762.7
Conditional grants	168.0	38.5	178.1	178.7	1705.3	1755.2	247.5	202.6	409.2	528.9	5411.9	15.2	5427.1
Health	68.3	11.9	89.9	74.6	781.4[1]	934.4	120.4	104.1	203.7	269.4	2658.3	8.2	2666.4
Postsecondary education[2]	13.5	2.8	35.7	18.9	402.3	447.2	42.6	35.9	110.5	102.3	1211.7	—	1211.7
Welfare	34.9	7.1	32.0	37.0	396.6[1]	320.0	52.5	35.6	70.1	139.8	1125.6	6.9	1132.5
Other	51.3	16.6	20.5	48.2	124.9	53.5	32.0	27.0	24.9	17.4	416.3	0.1	416.5
Total	376.9	82.6	412.0	370.3	2798.4	1983.1	403.8	320.5	565.9	561.3	7874.7	110.7	7985.4
Transfers to local governments													
Unconditional—grants in lie of taxes	0.7	—	4.3	—	14.6	33.1	5.1	1.9	3.5	5.5	69.0	0.5	69.5
Conditional grants	2.5	0.5	2.4	1.8	14.1	20.5	1.6	0.7	4.2	7.1	55.4	0.2	55.6
Welfare	1.9	0.2	0.9	0.9	6.1	3.6	0.4	0.3	0.6	2.1	17.0	0.1	17.2
Other	0.6	0.2	1.5	0.9	8.0	17.0	1.2	0.4	3.5	5.0	38.4	—	38.4
Total	3.3	0.5	6.8	1.8	28.7	53.6	6.8	2.6	7.7	12.6	124.5	0.6	125.1
Transfers to provinces and local governments	380.2	83.2	418.7	372.1	2827.1	2036.7	410.6	323.1	573.6	573.9	7999.2	111.3	8110.5
(Dollars per capita)													
Transfers to provinces													
Unconditional grants	385	376	288	289	178	28	155	130	91	14	110		
Equalization	344	347	265	261	159		121	91			80		
Other	41	31	22	28	19	28	34	39	91	14	30		
Conditional grants	310	329	219	270	278	217	245	224	238	221	242		

Health	126	102	111	113	127	115	119	115	119	112	119
Postsecondary education	25	24	44	29	66	55	42	40	64	43	54
Welfare	64	61	39	56	65	40	52	39	41	58	50
Other	96	142	25	73	20	7	32	30	15	7	19
Total	695	708	507	559	456	245	399	353	330	234	352
Transfers to local governments	6	5	8	3	5	7	7	3	4	5	6
Transfers to provinces and local governments	701	713	515	562	461	252	406	356	335	240	358

[1] Special arrangements including a federal tax abatement have been made for the province of Québec for these programmes. Amounts shown are the federal contribution including the tax abatement.

[2] The total contribution includes (a) a federal personal tax abatement of 4.357 points and a federal corporate tax abatement of 1 point; (b) the equalization (where applicable) and the revenue guarantee arising from those tax points; and (c) a cash transfer to bring the total contribution to the eligible contribution. The equalization of $72 thousand is included with equalization payments above and the revenue guarantee of $1.8 million is included with other unconditional grants.

Source: Estimates by the Economic Council of Canada, based on data from Statistics Canada (Economic Council of Canada, 1977, Table C-1).

of these problems by establishing regional goals that are followed by all ministries, rather than setting up a separate ministry for regional problems. Thus Table 6.2, showing support for industry (mainly loans), indicates a reasonable correspondence between support and need.

FISCAL ADJUSTMENT

In federal state, both provinces and the federal authority have powers of taxation to cover the respective services they provide. This frequently poses a problem of social justice because poorer provinces are unable to provide the same level of service as richer ones. As a result, the federal government usually provides much higher payments per capita to the poorer provinces, rather like a modern-day Robin Hood. The size and type of such adjustments play an important role in affecting relative attractions for industry through their influence on services and infrastructure. Large adjustments allow poor provinces to maintain good general services affecting the standard of living (such as health and education) and thus attractiveness to labour and management, as well as infrastructure of direct importance to industry (for instance, roads, rail, power, industrial parks).

The favoured approach in North America is, by means of equalization payments from the federal government, to allow all provinces to treat their citizens equally in terms of services provided for the tax dollar (Maxwell, 1970). The general approach derives from Buchanan (1950), but has been developed by Graham (1964) specifically for the Canadian context. He argues that 'Fiscal transfers, once regarded mainly as a price for holding the country together, have come to be supported on social grounds as well' (p. 7). For Graham, fiscal equity 'simply means that similarly situated individuals in different provinces and localities should receive equal fiscal treatment, taking both benefits from public services and burdens of taxation into account' (p. 10). This places the focus on individuals rather than on political entities. Adjustments are required at both federal-provincial and provincial-municipal scales.

Payments by higher-level governments in accordance with fiscal equity may be made in the form of conditional or unconditional grants, the former being for specific purposes and the latter allowing freedom to set spending priorities. Graham (1964, pp. 20–21) argues that conditional grants conform to a tradition of national financial responsibility and have been common in the United States. Unconditional grants, however, correspond better to the principal of fiscal equity by allowing the transfer of funds as a right to be used as the recipient chooses. In the context of development policy, unconditional grants allow choices to be made by the smaller political entities. Table 6.3 shows transfers between 1971 and 1975, by the Canadian federal government, illustrating the preponderance of conditional grants.

In Austria, also, there is an intergovernmental fiscal adjustment system (*Finanzausgleich*) (The Austrian Conference on Regional Planning (1973, pp. 104–7). Taxation is allocated to provinces (*Länder*) and local communities on the basis of size of population and number of communities in different size categories. There are conditional and unconditional federal grants, conditional provincial grants, and equalization payments designed to reduce the revenue gaps between provinces and communities to a defined minimum percentage level. Table 6.4 shows the effect of these measures.

REGIONAL DEVELOPMENT POLICY

Most countries in the West now have policies specifically designed to change the regional pattern of income, policies which almost always stress the manufacturing sector. Many discussions on the relative merits of particular policy instruments may be found—whether to encourage people to move or to bring industry to them, whether loans or grants are more effective, whether improvement of infrastructure is as necessary as direct support for manufacturing, etc. Less often discussed is the question of who should make the

TABLE 6.4. Gains from redistributed taxes as a percentage of municipal and provincial budgets, Austria 1970*

Vienna	0.0 per cent
Salzburg	0.0 per cent
Vorarlberg	0.0 per cent
Tirol	0.3 per cent
Upper Austria	2.4 per cent
Styria	5.1 per cent
Lower Austria	6.9 per cent
Carinthia	4.2 per cent
Burgenland	12.9 per cent

*Actual gains are greater, but a two-third reduction was made to account for the centralized tax collection procedure. In this procedure tax sums are redirected to poorer provinces to compensate for taxes lost from branch plants of large corporations which have their headquarters in wealthier provinces and pay all their taxes in those provinces. Thus, some redistributed taxes just recompense provinces for the effects of centralized tax collection. The remainder is a true 'gain' in tax revenues.

Source: Berentsen (1978), 119

decisions about policy. In a federal country this issue focuses primarily on the topic of degree of decentralization.

Canada

In Canada, despite the fact that there are definite limitations to its jurisdiction (Van Loon and Whittington, 1971, pp. 522–9, 531), the early leadership in regional policy came from the federal government and a number of different programmes were established, each concentrating on separate aspects of the problem (Brewis, 1969; Richards, 1965). In 1968, a new federal department, that of Regional Economic Expansion (DREE), was created to co-ordinate all regional work. Existing separate programmes were placed under its wing, frequently being modified considerably in the process. A determined effort was made to develop a united approach to regional problems and to remove former conflicts between the separate federal programmes. Officers were appointed within the department who were responsible for specific regions.

Within this broad framework of a department concerned with all aspects of regional development, a new incentive scheme for manufacturers was soon announced. In July 1969 it was put into legislation as the Regional Development Incentives Act (RDIA). As in the case of its predecessor, the Area Development programme, a system of regions designated as being eligible for support was used, but their minimum size was larger (8000 sq. km). Also the criteria for designation indicate that designated areas should have potential for development or improvement. The Regional Development Incentive Act (RDIA) continues the earlier practice of giving grants to firms to cover part of the cost of new plant and machinery. Maximum possible grants vary according to region, with the highest available in Canada's main problem region, the Atlantic Provinces.

One of the more interesting changes under the new department was implemented in March 1970 with the arrangements for Special Areas. These respond to arguments for growth centres which were so frequently made in criticism of the earlier incentive scheme (Walker, 1975, p. 208). Special Areas are designed 'to promote economic expansion in selected areas by enhancing their attractiveness as locations for new job-creating activities' (Canada, Department of Regional Economic Expansion, 1972, p. 16). Relatively small-sized areas (usually urban ones) are provided with finances to improve their infrastructure—for example water supply, transport, sewage treatment facilities, industrial parks, schools or assembly of residential land. The places are chosen on the basis of some existing attractiveness for growth and potential for development. The intent of the special area approach is to make them even more attractive by concentrating available funds on them.

Although this new department was welcomed initially as a genuine response to criticisms of earlier federal development efforts, it too began to attract its critics after a few years of operation. The focal point of dissatisfaction concerned decentralization. A private group in Atlantic Canada, the Atlantic Provinces Economic Council, argued that DREE should station more of its officials in the region if true regional planning were to take place. In fact it recommended that 'all DREE planning, implementation, industrial intelligence and promotion for the Atlantic Provinces be transferred to a regional office headed by an assistant deputy minister' (Atlantic Provinces Economic Council, 1971, p. 100). This view found supporters in other parts of the country and became an election issue in 1972. After nearly losing power, the Liberal government implemented a major reorganization of DREE. Two principal elements were involved in the changes: firstly, a greater degree of decentralization, and secondly, a move towards overall regional economic planning.

In response to charges that Ottawa-based officials are too far removed from regional situations to be able to respond to their real needs, the department committed itself to a policy of basing about 70 per cent of its staff outside of the capital. Four regions were set up, each under an Assistant Deputy Minister, with regional headquarters at Moncton (Atlantic), Montreal (Québec), Toronto (Ontario) and Saskatoon (Western). The regional offices have considerable power and can authorize incentive grants for projects with capital costs between $500 000 and $1.5 million and up to 100 jobs. At the same time, provincial offices were also enlarged and can now deal with smaller grants. By 1975, over 60 per cent of DREE personnel were located outside Ottawa and the proportion of senior executives was over 70 per cent (Canada, Department of Regional Economic Expansion, 1975, pp. 2–3).

Decentralization was closely linked with an increase of cooperation between the federal government and the provinces. Before 1974 federal regional policy tended to be imposed upon the country but the new system involves consultation leading to the signing of ten-year General Development Agreements between Ottawa and each province. These agreements map out the main elements of a socio-economic strategy, which Ottawa will support within the province. By 1975 an agreement had been signed with every province except Prince Edward Island, for which a comprehensive plan already existed. More detailed subsidiary agreements have since been signed, covering specific sectors or areas. Existing agreements are summarized in annual reports.

This thrust towards overall regional economic development follows a series of working papers produced by DREE during the reorganization and published in 1973 under the title 'Economic Circumstances and Opportunities'. A separate report on each province and region evaluated past performance and suggested future policies. Another series in 1976 was entitled 'Climate for Development'. The whole approach has moved to one of regional economic planning, with defined regional objectives and a conscious effort to work to the policy objectives. The success of this approach will not be clear for some years but at least it is conceptually sound. Closer interrelationship with the provinces is also welcome because each province has its own policies and, in the past, these have not always been in harmony with the federal approach.

Austria

In the years after the Second World War, Austria was mainly concerned with national rehabilitation after Nazi and Russian occupation. The Russians did not move out from the east, in fact, until 1955. National economic policy was undertaken without clear enunciation of regional objectives. Around 1957, special policies were set up to deal with certain problem areas such as those facing declining farm population or mine closures. Over the years different regional policies were pursued in various sectors but only since the 1960s has there been a recognition of the need for co-ordinated objectives to underlie regional policy. Out of this awareness the current approach has evolved (The Austrian Conference on Regional Planning, 1973, pp. 47–9).

Like Canada, Austria faces the problems posed by a 'high degree of dispersion of regional planning responsibilities' (The Austrian Conference on Regional Planning, 1973, p. 66). Certain areas are under entirely federal control:

1. Matters pertaining to universities and higher secondary schools;
2. Transport as regards railways, shipping, aviation, and the national highway system;
3. Postal services and telecommunications;
4. Mining;
5. Agriculture (partially) and forestry;
6. Water regulations, flood control, inland waterways;
7. High-voltage transmission lines;
8. Protection of historic monuments;
9. National censuses.

The rest are in the provincial domain, while local planning comes under municipalities. All three governments can take measures concerning the private sector (such as, provide subsidies to companies).

At the instigation of the federal government, a forum for research, consultation and policy initiation has therefore been established. This is the Austrian Conference on Regional Planning (Österreichische Raumordnungskonferenz) or ÖROK. Set up in 1971, it includes the following bodies:

1. The conference proper consisting of:
   (a) The federal chancellor and relevant ministers;
   (b) Provincial governors;

(c) Representatives of the two associations of local authorities (Austrian Federation of Cities and the Austrian Federation of Communities);

(d) Presidents of employers' and employees' associations. This last point needs some explanation as such associations (*Kammer*) play an important role in Austrian business life. Every employer and employee must belong to the relevant association and many decisions, particularly concerning wages, are taken as a result of bargaining between the appropriate employers' and employees' association.

2. The Deputy Commission consists of officials representing the members of the Conference. This is a real working group as opposed to a decision-making one.
3. The Austrian Advisory Board on Regional Planning includes experts, who frequently study particular problems in working groups.

A great deal of research has been carried out by ÖROK. Subcommittees are usually responsible for organizing particular topics and presenting reports based on their work. The conference's own staff co-operate with experts in the actual research.

An important focus of ÖROK's work has been to document the planning actually being carried out in Austria and to give some consideration to appropriate goals and programmes for the country (Österreichischer Raumordnungskonferenz, 1974). This, as well, has provided an incentive for the federal and provincial governments to enunciate their regional policies more clearly. Each government has been obliged to articulate its position within the ÖROK framework.

The way in which Austria has chosen to cope with its federal structure in dealing with regional development is fundamentally different from the approach now in operation in Canada. Like Canada, questions of industrial growth are considered along with the topic of overall economic development but there the similarity ends. Economic, social and environmental elements are being dealt with together in a comprehensive approach instead of being separated. Where in Canada there is a Department of Regional Economic Expansion specifically concerned with regional economic problems, Austria has only an inter-governmental conference looking after regional planning as a whole. The effects of this difference are quite important. No one department at the federal level has a vested interest in regional development and fights for it organizationally against others, who may well feel their position is being challenged (for example, regional policy encouraging a certain location of industry and industrial policy trying to improve efficiency). Rather representatives of each department, whose policies affect regional planning, are forced to sit down together and come up with a co-ordinated approach to solve regional problems identified by the planning conference. Each group has a voice in deciding on problems and policies, each must also share responsibility for implementing appropriate programmes. The same kind of co-ordination operates within each province. Planning groups then have no real power in and of themselves but every relevant ministry develops units specially concerned with regional issues.

In 1970, an advisory group in Vienna put forward its proposals for an industrial policy (Beirat für Wirtschafts-und Sozialfragen, 1970). They included suggestions for investment in new, research-based products, high-valued quality products, items with good long-term growth prospects and those which have interlinkage. The group also commented on improvements in financing and research. No word was written about the location of industry. This kind of sectoral thinking also dominated the relevant trade and industry ministry (Bundesministerium für Handel, Gewerbe und Industrie) well into the 1970s but under the regional conference system, it has been forced to elaborate a regional policy and contribute to the dialogue on regional problems. Industrial support programmes, which take the form of low-interest loans to manufacturers, have been channelled mainly to problem regions (rural areas, especially near the eastern borders, and areas with structural problems). Such industrial supports complement aid for improved infrastructure in similar regions (Berentsen, 1978, pp. 119–120).

At a provincial level, this kind of interrelationship has been especially well developed in Lower Austria. The province has decided to maintain population in its rural areas, an objective very much in line with Austrian regional policy ideals. Therefore it has established a number of subregions, in each of which there is an urban centre currently of about 10 000 people or capable of being developed to that size. These towns are attainable in not more than an hour by the population of the surrounding subregion and, additionally, public transportation and roads leading to them are being improved. Those urban centres are now the focus for the more expensive type of services such as sizeable hospitals and vocational schools (Amt der Niederösterreichischen Landesregierung, no date b). Industrial policy corresponds to this approach by encouraging important industries to settle at the chosen urban centres where they have a better chance of success than if they were scattered throughout the rural areas. Rejected, however, is the view that industry must locate in the absolute best spot if this means too great a concentration (Amt der Niederösterreichischen Landesregierung, no date a). In general, therefore, the rural population will have jobs and services within easy commuting range. It will no longer be necessary to move away permanently to enjoy a good standard of living.

MUNICIPAL DEVELOPMENT

As Bökemann's diagram (Figure 6.1) suggests, the same questions of interrelationship arise between municipal and provincial governments as at the provincial–federal level. Municipal authorities usually have powers over land-use, subject to provincial supervision, but their influence is normally curbed by limited finances and a dependence on higher levels of government for funds. Thus questions of fiscal equalization and conditional or unconditional monies arise here too. Differential effects of regional policy and problems of co-ordination between levels of government are certainly relevant.

In industrial development, it has become usual for local authorities in Canada to take an active role in promoting the development of the business sector. In the nineteenth and early twentieth centuries, this took the form of bonuses to companies, tax exemptions or low taxes to attract companies (Naylor, 1975, pp. 104–61). More recently, the usual pattern has been for an industrial development department to concern itself with advertising the community, making contacts with firms and trying to encourage them to locate in the municipality. The role of the industrial commissioner is more complicated than this but he is essentially concerned with job creation and preservation (Walker, forthcoming, Chapter 8). At the community level this has almost always caused some tensions with the planning department, which has to balance economic with social and environmental concerns. There has been a slight trend towards combined planning and development departments, which could encourage co-ordination, but the basic mistrust between two groups with very different backgrounds is hard to overcome. On the one hand are usually career civil servants with a public welfare orientation, academic education and, frequently, an anti-business stance. In contrast, development commissioners usually have either no university background or one in engineering or business followed by a long business career. Either the educational background of the two groups will need to be more balanced or joint in-career education is essential.

The activities of promotionally minded development commissioners working for particular communities could, of course, easily undermine any efforts to establish spatial strategies at provincial or federal levels. In Ontario, where local authority commissioners are well entrenched, the provincial government is not very effective in carrying through development strategies even if it has published many plans (see for example, Ontario, 1976). In many other provinces, however, effective control is with the province as community influence was originally lacking. Some provinces (such as Alberta) have set up regional offices to stimulate development in particular areas, others (such as New Brunswick and Manitoba) have encouraged the creation of regional boards with local directors but partly funded by the province. Québec has provided funds for both community and regional commissions but retains a major say on the appointment of commissioners. All in all, provincial powers in industrial development have been growing.

These problems scarcely arise in Austria because community industrial development has not emerged as a separate occupation and because most local authorities have a role restricted to controlling land-use. Economic development, then, is handled within the provincial planning group and every planner is expected to be aware of industrial issues. The local authorities are represented on the Regional Planning Conference, but their voice there is relatively small. On the other hand, the Conference does provide an opportunity to comment directly on federal policies, something generally denied to Canadian third-tier authorities. Vienna, it should be noted, is an exception to these comments because it is a province and has all provincial rights.

THE DYNAMISM OF POLITICAL RELATIONSHIPS

Evident from the above discussions is the fact that objectives, policies and programmes are in an almost continuous state of flux. He who wishes to work in the area of industrial development cannot sit back and make calculations based upon the assumption of a continuation of today's trends. This is perhaps more evident at present in Canada than in Austria because the whole structure of the Canada's federation is under threat. Québec has a separatist government committed to a referendum which will allow its population the chance to vote for or against independence. The province has always pressed for more powers than other provinces because it feels inhibited in its ability to preserve and enhance the Québecois language and culture. Thus, regardless of the results of the referendum or the party in power, it can be expected that pressures to decentralization will strengthen. In fact the new leader of the liberal opposition, Claude Ryan, has bemoaned Québec's lack of control in key areas of public policy as well as in indigenous private enterprise (Ryan, 1976, p. 588).

The Québec case may be the most serious, but other voices are also being raised against the existing character of the Canadian confederation. The tensions are strongest in the West, where discrimination in favour of central Canada has often been claimed and occasional suggestions for independence are made (Blackman, 1977). While Graham (1977, p. 473) argues that 'provincialism outside of Québec is largely economically oriented, particularly with respect to development policy', there certainly are pressures for greater decentralization (Emerson, 1978).

The degree of decentralization of power will have an important effect on manufacturing location because it is likely that provinces would initiate policies to increase their manufacturing sector if they were able to do so. If some degree of regional protection were developed, the manufacture of consumer-oriented products could well become more decentralized, especially to the West. Moreover, resource-serving sectors could also increase more rapidly in the West. Meanwhile Ontario, and probably Québec, would lose, although Québec might make some gains at Ontario's expense. Greater regional self-sufficiency has been proposed as a strong policy option by the Canadian

Federation of Independent Businessmen. In the view of a growing number of Canadians, then, even a decentralized policy under DREE is not enough. A broader discussion of economic policy is desired (Fréchette, 1977, pp. 439–40).

Two things about possible decentralization in Canada must be recognized. Firstly, in the East and West, regions (in the sense of areas with similar backgrounds and problems) are more extensive that provinces. Thus some combined effort will be required by the provinces if they are to deal most successfully with problems such as freight rates or industrial diversification. This, of course, brings into play yet another problem of co-operative action. The second is that it may be easier to persuade the federal government to decentralize its offices than the large private corporations to move their headquarters. Thus, without indigenous companies, economic dependence on central Canada will remain.

In addition to these possibilities of structural change, there is the whole question of parties and personalities. Politicians vary in character: some co-operate well, while others are abrasive. Thus the same structure could work or fail depending on the people concerned. No essay can do justice to the topic of the political personality and no attempt will be made to examine it here. It could, however, be very important. More amenable to analysis are party platforms and here critical distinctions may be observed. In Austria, the Social Democrats set up ÖROK and are for co-operative planning, while the Conservatives prefer reduced federal power and indeed governmental power in general. Similarly in Canada, the Conservatives are for more decentralization and greater provincial authority. There, the Liberal party is for a strong federal government and a well-articulated regional programme. A switch of governments in either country could affect industrial development quite drastically.

One can only conclude by reiterating the fact that industrial development is only useful if it serves the people as a whole. Opinions change about development as they do on any issue, and both political structures and politicians change with them. This could lead to some disastrous decisions from the professional point of view, but it may also challenge the professional to ask whether his cherished opinions are based on solid ground. Professionals have the opportunity to express their views and to sway both public opinion in general and politicians in particular. If their efforts at education and persuasion are not met with success, perhaps they should rethink their position. In any case, industrial developers must ultimately come to terms with political reality.

REFERENCES

Amt der Niederösterreichischen Landesregierung (no date a), *Gute Arbeitsplätze im ganzen Land*, Vienna.

Amt der Niederösterreichischen Landesregierung (no date b), *Raumordnung in Niederösterreich*, Vienna.

Atlantic Provinces Economic Council (1971). *Fifth Annual Review. The Atlantic Economy. Summary*, Halifax.

The Austrian Conference on Regional Planning (1973). *Regional Development Policy in Austria*, Vienna.

Beirat für Wirtschafts-und Sozialfragen (1970). *Vorschläge zur Industriepolitik*, Vienna.

Berentsen, W. H. (1978). 'Austrian regional development policy: the impact of policy on the achievement of planning goals'. *Economic Geography*, **54**, 115–134.

Blackman, W. J. (1977). 'A Western Canadian perspective on the economics of Confederation'. *Canadian Public Policy*, **3**, 43–44.

Bökemann, D. (1974). 'A framework for the technological theory of regional development'. *Papers, Regional Science Association*, **33**, 33–58.

Brewis, T. N. (1969). *Regional Economic Policies in Canada*, Macmillan Company of Canada, Toronto.

Buchanan, J. M. (1950). 'Federalism and fiscal equity', *American Economic Review*, **40**, 583–99.

Canada, Department of Regional Economic Expansion (1972). *Annual Report 70–71*, Information Canada, Ottawa.

Canada, Department of Regional Economic Expansion (1975). *Annual Report 1974–75*, Information Canada, Ottawa.

Dikshit, R. D. (1976). *The Political Geography of Federalism: An Inquiry into Origins and Stability*, Macmillan of India, Delhi.

Economic Council of Canada (1977). *Living Together: A Study of Regional Disparities*, Ottawa.

Emerson, D. L. (1978). 'Comments'. *Canadian Public Policy*, **4**, 71–76.

Fréchette, Pierre (1977). 'L'économie de la Confédération: un point de vue québecois'. *Canadian Public Policy*, **3**, 431–440.

Graham, J. F. (1964). *Fiscal Adjustment in a Federal Country*, Canadian Tax Foundation, Toronto.

Graham, J. F. (1977). 'Comments'. *Canadian Public Policy*, **3**, 470.

Maxwell, J. A. (1970). 'Fiscal equity and federalism'. *Growth and Change*, **1**, 39–45.

Naylor, R. T. (1975). *The History of Canadian Business 1867–1914, Volume 2: Industrial Development*, James Lorimer & Co., Toronto.

Ontario, (1976). *Ontario's Future: Trends and Options*, Ministry of Treasury, Economics and Intergovernmental Affairs, Regional Planning Branch, Toronto.

Osterreichischer Raumordnungskonferenz (1974). *Einheitliche Grundsätze für die Anzustrebende Raumordnung*, Vienna.

Richards, J. H. (1965). 'Provincialism, regionalism and federalism as seen in joint resource development programmes'. *Canadian Geographer*, **9**, 205–215.

Ryan, Claude (1976). 'Un cas pertinent: le Québec'. *Canadian Public Policy*, **2**, 487–595.

Van Loon, R. J. and Whittington, M. S. (1971). *The Canadian Political System*, McGraw-Hill Co. of Canada, Toronto.

Walker, D. F. (1975). 'Governmental influence on manufacturing location: Canadian experience with special reference to the Atlantic Provinces'. *Regional Studies*, **9**, 203–217.

Walker, D. F. (forthcoming). *Canada's Industrial Space-Economy*, Bell, London.

Planning Industrial Development
Edited by David F. Walker

Chapter 7

Development of 'Holdings' in Turkey and their Organization in Space

Ilhan Tekeli and Gökhan Menteş

INTRODUCTION: THE PURPOSE OF THE STUDY

Since 1908, industrialization and the creation of a bourgeois class in the private sector have been two dominant desires in Turkish political life. Even during the global crisis of the 1930s, when the industrialization of the country was attempted by means of a 'statist' policy, the desire to develop a Turkish bourgeoisie continued to be a matter of primary importance. As a result of efforts that have lasted for more than half a century, capitalist groups of considerable size have been established in today's private sector of Turkey.

Especially since the early 1960s, these monopolist groups have organized multiplant and multifirm corporate systems. To give an idea of the dimensions they have reached, it will be useful to mention a few indicators of the three largest corporations in 1976. When the Koç Group celebrated its fiftieth year of establishment, it consisted of 59 different firms. Of these, nine were amongst the largest 100 industrial establishments of the country. In the same year, 26 000 people were directly employed in the holding company. An additional 50 000 were employed in 566 industrial establishments engaged in producing various parts necessary for the final output of the corporation. In 1977, it ranked as the 212th largest industrial establishment in the world, excluding American corporations.

In 1976, the Sabancı Group celebrated its twenty-eighth anniversary, owning major share portions of fifty-six different firms. One of these firms, Akbank, stood out as the third largest bank of the private sector of the country with 503 branch-offices. Eight firms of the Group were listed amongst the largest 100 firms. A total of 26 000 people were directly employed in its firms.

İş Bankası, on the other hand, was in its 52nd year of establishment and occupied 174th place on the list of the largest 300 banks in the world. It was the largest bank in the private sector of Turkey and, in 1976, had 718 branch-offices spread out all over the country. It held shares in 78 firms, of which nine were amongst the largest 100 industrial establishments.

Despite the fact that these multifirm and multiplant systems are very important in Turkey's economic scene, they have quite limited status at the international scale. None has yet become multinational in its operations. On the other hand, they act as partners and mediators to the multinational corporations operating in Turkey.

Even if they are not multinational in character, it is hard to comprehend the locational behaviour of such multifirm and multiplant systems within the framework of 'classical' location theory. The phenomenon of the corporation represents a new stage in the organizational evolution of firms. Thus new theories are needed to understand their locational behaviour. Although pioneering observations regarding corporation geography were made as early as two decades ago (McNee, 1958), studies aimed at explaining the locational behaviour of these giants are quite new. The only book devoted specifically to this purpose has been edited recently by Hamilton (1974). One possible path towards the development of a 'modern' location theory is to synthesize the experiences of different nations. To aid such an effort, this chapter documents the Turkish experience.

In addition to its significance for location theory, the article presents a series of hypotheses concerning the organizational form and the behaviour of 'domestic' finance capital emerging in the capitalist countries on the periphery of the Western capitalist system. The organizational and locational behaviour of finance capital has strong implications for the national and spatial development strategy of the Third World. According to Hymer (1972), the large corporation illustrates how real and important are the advantages of large-scale planning but it does not tell us how best to achieve wider domains of conscious coordination. It reveals the power of size and the danger of leaving it uncontrolled. What can regional or national planners do against the antisocial development of the corporate phenomenon? In order to answer this question one should first understand how and why the corporation behaves as it does.

The Method of the Study

The method followed in this study consists of two main steps:

1. The emergence of the Turkish corporations is explained with reference to the conditions of the country. Here, the evolution of the basic elements of the organizational structure of corporations is investigated.
2. The spatial reflection of the new organizational scheme is put forward. In other words, the organizational structure of the corporation is used as an independent variable to explain its spatial reflection. It is assumed that an understanding of the organizational evolution of the system is necessary to comprehend the evolution of its spatial structure.

A rough examination of the multiplant/multifirm system in Turkey reveals two types of organizations. The first type is controlled and integrated by a holding company—a company controlling one or more other companies through stock ownership. The second distinctive type consists of a system controlled by a bank. The developments that have taken place in the last few years indicate that such a distinction as suggested by Hilferding (1910) is no longer meaningful. Recent experience shows that these two systems have entered into a process of mutual transformation resulting in a new type of organization which carries the seeds, and advantages, of the two previous systems. This transformation manifests itself in an integration of and a flow between the capital invested in different activities such as manufacturing, commerce, insurance and banking. In other words 'finance capital' as described by Lenin (1939) has emerged.[1]

The Turkish corporations are now in the process of approaching a *maximalist*[2] organizational form which accelerates their growth and which reduces the risk element in their actions—to the extent allowed by the existing legal and institutional possibilities. By examining the legal and institutional opportunities available for corporations in present day Turkey, it is possible to establish a rough maximalist organizational scheme. This scheme, even if not yet fully practised by the existing corporations, is assumed to show the structure they will have in the near future. Once such an organization plan is obtained, the type of spatial structure that it produces can be easily demonstrated.

This kind of synchronic analysis has two drawbacks. First, there is the danger of interpreting the maximalist scheme as the ultimate step in the evolutionary process of firms. This plan, however, is described with reference to the existing institutional structure (see Figure 7.1). Parallel to the development of the power of finance capital, the presumed institutional structure, and subsequently, the organizational form, will be surpassed. On the other hand, this kind of analysis is not very helpful in understanding the *process* by which the multiplant/multifirm system has come into existence through time. It has to be supported by complementary interpretations. Still, the existence of such a scheme facilitates the comparison of evolutions of different groups of finance capital. It is convenient in the sense that distinctive stages of evolution can be easily identified relative to the unique organizational form reached by the largest corporations today.

For these reasons, the present chapter first elaborates upon the maximalist organizational scheme that emerged within the contemporary institutional possibilities of Turkey. Next, the concern will be to indicate the different evolutionary paths pursued by various capitalist groups in trying to reach such a stage in their organizational structure. In the Turkish case, there are sufficient examples to compare the divergent paths. Third, parallel to the changes in the organizational structure of firms over time, changes in their locational behaviour will be shown. This analysis provides a basis for a series of both dynamic and static hypothesis developed to expound the spatial organization of the multifirm/multiplant system of finance capital. Finally, these hypotheses give a framework for the evaluation of classical location theory, which has concerned itself for so long with the location of a single firm.

THE ORGANIZATIONAL SCHEME OF THE TURKISH HOLDING COMPANIES

The emergence of *holdings*[3] in Turkey started in the year 1963 but the increase in their numbers is a phenomenon of the 1970s; in 1976, there were 115. These developments match deliberate changes introduced into Turkish commercial law. One of the preconditions to sustain capital accumulation and secure the growth of capitalism is to modify the legal measures in favour of the capitalist groups. The Turkish example gives clear proof of this fact. During the genesis and growth of the Republican bourgeoisie, laws regulating economic life were altered in order to realize these conditions. For instance, it is well known that the Koç Group has spent much energy in encouraging the passing of the two important laws which provided the bases for the establishment of the holdings system in Turkey. Only after the modification of the Corporation Tax Law in 1963, and legislation that enabled the establishment of foundations as effective entities in the control mechanism of holding systems in 1967, did the Koç Group truly form its new organization and set up an example that was immediately followed up by the other groups in succeeding years.

Although the legal developments that finalized the contemporary maximalist scheme took place between 1963 and 1967, the preconditions which formed the cornerstones of the corporate system (that is, joint-stock companies, banks, insurance companies and foundations) were realized much earlier.

The Development of Joint-Stock Companies

The emergence of joint-stock companies is the most important creation paving the path towards the development of multifirm/multiplant systems. In stock companies the capital is divided into shares which are transferable and represented by the stock. The liability of the owners is limited by their assets. There is no upper limit to the number of shareholders. The company is governed by a board of directors, elected by the owners, whose voting rights are limited to the number of shares they hold. These characteristics of stock companies provide the basis for a shares and securities market where the exchange of shares may result in changes in the governing bodies of firms. They also allow for the transformation of the savings of small depositors into large-scale investments conducted by such companies. Finally, a firm may control the management and the activities of another firm by holding its shares. The latter, in turn, may control a third firm and so on, creating a control system in echelons. This is how the interfirm hierarchy is set up.

The establishment of incorporated joint-stock companies in Turkey dates back to the year 1850, when the Code of Overland Commerce was passed. Until 1926, however, when the Turkish Code of Commerce no. 865 was legislated, the number of such companies remained quite small, and they were basically foreign establishments. Even with the second legislation, an interfirm system failed to develop. This was because the legislation contained a provision that put an upper limit of ten to the number of votes that a shareholder could use, regardless of the percentage of shares he held in the company. This provision was dropped by Commercial Code no. 6762 passed in 1957. By easing the requirements for the establishment of stock companies, this legislative change resulted in an increase in the number of such firms. More importantly, term no. 466 of this code introduced a definition of *holding* for the first time in Turkish commercial legislation. The code defines the term *holding* as 'a firm whose basic purpose is to participate in the activities of other firms'.

Although the Code mentioned 'holdings', the terms of the Corporation Tax Code of that time prevented their establishment. The prevailing code envisaged a double taxation system—the profits of the subsidiary company and the portion transferred to the parent holding company were subject to independent taxing. Thus, it was not feasible to establish a system of interfirm control relations. In 1963, however, this possibility arose when, as a result of the pressures imposed by the Koç Group, the double taxation system was cancelled by Code no. 192. Since than, not only were holding companies established but the joint-stock companies also multiplied in number.

The Development of Banks

Banks are the second most important phenomenon in the emergence of corporations. As in the case of joint-stock companies, the establishment of banks in Turkey dates back to the nineteenth century. Initiated in 1856, the first banking establishments had their origins in the West. Attempts to found national banks commenced during the first World War but remained diffused and ineffective until 1936, when the first law (no. 2999) concerning banks was passed. However, it was really Code no. 7129, passed in 1958, that provided the necessary basis upon which the present system of finance capital was built. According to this code, private banks could only be established as joint-stock entities.

The code also introduced several measures regulating the relationship of banks and their affiliated firms. According to term 38, a bank can at the most give 10 per cent of its capital as credit to a firm. Nevertheless, if the bank owns 25 per cent of the firm, there is no upper limit placed on the amount of money that can be loaned. These conveniences encouraged the large capitalist groups to form their industrial enterprises in partnership with banks. This explains the existence of multifirm/multiplant systems formed around banks such as Akbank, Yapı ve Kredi Bankası and Iş Bankası even before 1963.

Actually, the provision of the possibilities for the establishment of banks and joint-stock companies and the changes made in the Corporation Tax Code have provided sufficient preconditions for the development of the holding bank systems encountered in Turkey today. In order to grasp the full possibilities of this system, however, it is necessary to describe the development of two complementary elements, insurance companies and foundations.

The Development of Insurance Companies

The first legal terms concerning the issue of insurance arose in the year 1860. Just as in the case of joint-stock companies and banks, the insurance companies were under the control of foreign capital until 1926. The terms brought in with the Code of Commerce in 1926, the Code no. 1149 regulating the control of insurance companies, and the Code no. 1160 related to the establishment of monopolies in the reinsurance business in 1927 sped up the growth of Turkish insurance companies. Again similar to the case of stock companies and banks, the present legal framework of the insurance companies came into existence in the 1950s. The relevance of the Code no. 7397, passed in 1959, to the present topic is that it carried terms envisaging the establishment of insurance firms as incorporated entities, as well as terms preventing liberal competition in the field. In addition, the terms regarding the prohibition of discounts were to increase the profits in a positive direction.

The Development of Foundations

Foundations, which are referred to as the fourth institutional cornerstone of the maximalist organizational plan, followed quite a different path of evolution. They had long existed in the legal system of the Ottoman Empire and were built upon the divine laws of Islam. In 1926, when the Republican Regime reformed the Civic Code, it replaced the pious foundation (*vakıf*) by another form of charitable trust called *tesis*. The preindustrial entity of *vakıf* was abolished. Later, in 1967, the institution was re-established by Code no. 903. This time, however, it was to function as an institution of the capitalist system. According to this Code, which owes much to the pressures of the Koç Group, a *vakıf* may be established as a legal or private entity with the allotment of the goods and/or money to realize a given goal. If a *vakıf* devotes 80 per cent of its income to services normally provided by the state, it is exempted from almost all taxes as decided by the Council of Ministers.

The changed status of foundations gave them the right to own shares of joint-stock companies and, therefore, the possibility of having organic relations with the corporations. Since the governing body of a *vakıf* is appointed by its founder it can be a suitable tool for exercising control over various firms of the maximalist organization. Moreover, it acts as a mechanism which lightens the tax-load of the holdings system.

The Maximalist Scheme

Having examined the four institutional developments of the period 1957–67, it is now possible to enter into the discussion of the maximalist organizational scheme presented in Figure 7.1. This figure, as has been mentioned above (page 151), has been drawn to represent the internal structure of an organization that uses all the institutional possibilities available to it.

At the top of the system is the 'holding company', which is the central decision-making unit. Here, all the policies and vital planning strategies concerning the system are determined. The holding company keeps a file of shares sufficient to sustain the control of the firms within the system. It can also issue securities and shares to generate a monetary source serving the whole system. At the present stage of development of finance capital in Turkey, major portions of the stocks of holding companies are controlled by the families that founded the holdings. In other words, the stocks have not yet been divided or scattered among many shareholders. That the holdings still preserve their family-firm characteristic is an indication of the fact that the corporate system in Turkey is in its preliminary stage of development.

The second important element in the system, 'the bank', carries out a series of quite different functions simultaneously. First of all, it collects the small savings of the public and channels the collected total to the companies within the holding system through its credit mechanisms. Considering the fact that most investments of such companies are realized not by auto-financing but through credits, the banks stand out as very important elements in the chart. In addition, banking also offers an attractive opportunity for corporations because of the high rates of profit in the field of banking. This implies that, even without their resource-supplying functions, the banks would still remain in the maximalist diagram.

A third interesting function of banks is to increase the number of hierarchical levels in the system. This proves beneficial in two respects. First, by delaying the payment of the corporation's taxes, it relieves the system of some of its tax load. Under the Turkish tax system, a firm that profits from the shares of another firm is taxed for these profits in the following financial year. To give an example, a given portion of tax payments can be postponed for five years in a system consisting of five levels. In countries such as Turkey, where the economy is experiencing a rapid rate of inflation, such delays are highly significant. Secondly, by multiplying the number of levels the amount of controlled stock belonging to ineffective shareholders (that is, the public) is increased.

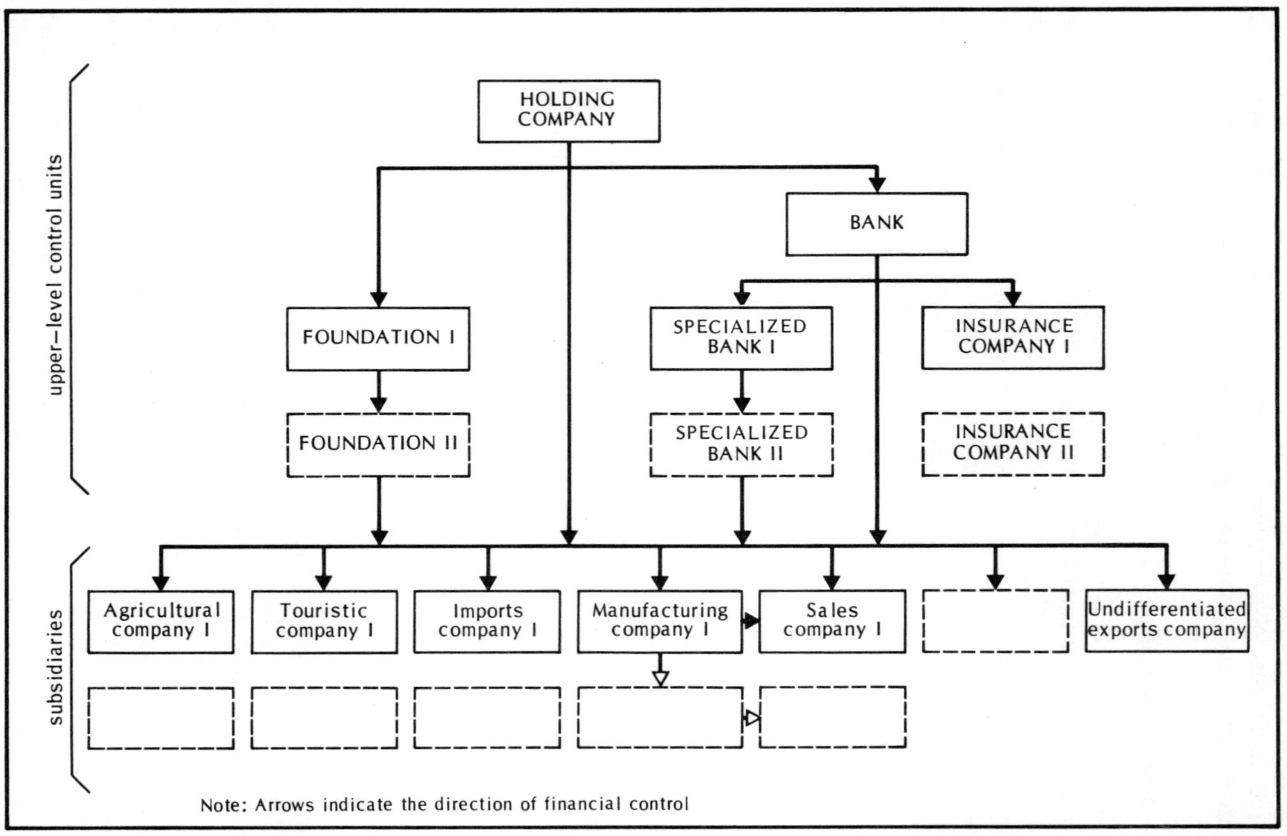

Note: Arrows indicate the direction of financial control

FIGURE 7.1. The maximalist organization scheme of corporations in Turkey

Due to their highly critical role within the system, the banks sometimes change places in the chart. Instead of holding companies, they might function at the highest controlling point of the system. This structure, as is the case for İş Bankası and Yapı ve Kredi Bankası, is observed when (a) the shares are spread out among several holders instead of being owned by a single family, and (b) the stocks are controlled by institutions rather than by private individuals. In Figure 7.1, the bank is not given as a single entity in itself but as a complex consisting of two other elements. Together with 'insurance companies' and 'specialized banks' it forms a subsystem within the larger system of the corporation.

Insurance companies perform the function of collecting cheap funds for the banks, more cheaply than any other fund on which the banks may rely. To increase their effectiveness in the field, the banks establish subsidiary companies in insurance and/or increase the number of such affiliates. A final reason for the existence of insurance companies is that through them the insurance expenditures of member companies are internalized.

Another element that has a place within the subsystem is the specialized banks. By specializing in a certain field (such as the supply of credits for just the manufacturing sector) they increase control of the system. Furthermore, they are functional in terms of increasing the number of hierarchical levels.

The third multifunctional element of the corporation, the foundation (*vakıf*), is also an upper-level unit performing financing and controlling functions. Generally there are two types of foundations. One of these, commonly called a 'retirement and mutual aid foundation', provides additional social security for people working in the establishments of the system. This way such funds are internalized. The other type, usually named after the founder of the holding, aims at keeping up a respectable image for the corporation in the eyes of the public by engaging in various socio-cultural activities. Foundations also perform other functions, however. Through them it is possible to control certain companies with fewer shares. Moreover, they reduce the tax-load of the system, as explained in detail above.

The remaining elements in Figure 7.1 are the companies and factories which are directly engaged in the production and distribution of the goods and services generated by the system. These include such entities as large agricultural establishments, tourist establishments, manufacturing firms, large commercial establishments, and delivery companies. The dominant trend in multifirm/multiplant holding systems is widespread dispersion in several sectors rather than a perfect monopoly in a given sector of the economy, a strategy which decreases the economic and socio-political risks associated with concentration and prevents the trust-like image.

The diversification of the activities of the system does not take place in the form of random leaps, but rather in a given order influenced by the type of activities in which the holding company is already engaged. The initial activity of the holding company partially determines the next area of concern. As new areas of opportunity are perceived further diversification becomes possible. In the Turkish case the diversification of the activities of holding companies take place through two basic channels. The first is the establishment of production firms through import substitution. If the initial activity of the holding company is an import business and the delivery of imported goods within the country, the growth of the domestic demand may reach a level where it may be feasible to establish a domestic production plant. Several advantages accrue to the entrepreneurs. First and foremost, they are able to use the existing distribution mechanism for an already existing market. Meanwhile, they have the opportunity to transfer technology from abroad or to start a joint-venture with the foreign corporation with which they already have import relations. Once such a production unit is established the sales and distribution activity within the 'import firm' separate and a new firm shouldering the sales function is created. As a result, each production activity in the maximalist chart generates a subsystem of trading and distribution businesses. Depending upon the nature of the production activity, there may be more than one factory and several distribution firms. For instance, it is possible to organize the distributive function by establishing many regional firms.

The second channel of diversification is to the supply of inputs and the organization of marketing of outputs from existing activities. In other words, the opportunities arising from the forward and backward linkages of the firm are utilized. In this way the firm reduces its sensitivity to outside changes and achieves a less risky structure.

The existing practice of holding companies in Turkey indicates that they feel the need to enter foreign markets after their production activities reach a certain level of maturity. This is achieved by means of the 'undifferentiated exports firm' indicated in Figure 7.1. It is not specialized by the goods and services produced by the production firms of the holding company. Instead, it performs the marketing functions for the whole system.

Up to this point the analysis has concentrated upon the nature of the integration between the firms that function within the holdings system. Not indicated in the maximalist scheme are numerous small entrepreneurs who, in reality, are organized and controlled by the holdings system. Yet, to be able to understand the real controlling power of these giants, one must have a grasp of this army of small entrepreneurs surrounding the holdings. Because they comprise an important extension of the system in the economy, they have to be thought of as part of the maximalist scheme.

The production firms in the holding system have a secure, continuous supply of raw or semi-processed materials which become their inputs into the production process. Successful management of the supply of inputs is vital when the firm enters a new field of production. Here the holding company is faced with two alternatives. The first alternative is to internalize these functions within the holdings system. The second is to leave these fields to others and create a network of small entrepreneurs surrounding the system. In Turkey such branches as side-industries of the automotive sector, and the retail dealers of the sales and distributing firms are left to the small entrepreneurs, whereas the contact with small depositors is organized by the bank systems.

The establishment of a network of small entrepreneurs around a holdings system can be justified in some instances by economic considerations, but in many cases it is motivated by socio-political factors. Such an organization silences the reaction that will certainly arise in the community of small entrepreneurs if such functions are internalized. At Turkey's present stage of development, it is easy enough to organize retailing outlets in the form of chain stores and department stores. In fact, there have already been such attempts but they became the target of strong opposition from small entrepreneurs organized by the Confederation of the Guild of Shopkeepers. For the time being, this has discouraged further efforts at chain expansion.

The management of the multiplant/multifirm structure of the corporation necessitates an active central control mechanism which, in turn, demands an effective system of data processing. For this reason holding companies rely heavily on computers. In some cases, independent data processing firms are established within the system, for example, Koç Burroughs located in Istanbul with a branch-office in İzmir.

Some Characteristics of Holding Companies in a Peripheral Country

The maximalist scheme developed for the emerging corporations in Turkey underlines interesting characteristics which arise from the *peripheral*[4] position of the country. One such characteristic is the lack of a unit responsible for research and development functions. Because existing systems rely upon technology transfer instead of technological discovery, research and development functions either do not exist at all or are not sufficiently differentiated to warrant an independent unit serving the system. If holding companies eventually acquire technology-producing functions, there are two available places for such functions. One possibility is to establish a new foundation for this purpose. Another alternative is to organize a specialized department in one of the large production firms of the system.

A second reflection of Turkey's peripheral position can be identified in the undifferentiated and poorly organized quality of the export firm. The present holding systems in Turkey are completely oriented to the opportunities of the domestic market. For instance, the most developed of the export organizations amongst the Turkish holding companies, EXSA of the Sabancı Group, has entries into twenty-seven foreign markets but the marketing functions are performed basically through intermediaries. It is possible to interpret this situation as a first step towards becoming multinational, but that would be an overly optimistic appraisal. None of the Turkish holding companies has production units in foreign countries which is, mainly, a reflection of the fact that Turkey occupies a place on the periphery of the western capitalist system.

Different Models of Evolution Towards the Maximalist Scheme

The capitalist groups in Turkey that now have similar maximalist structures have followed strikingly different lines of evolution. In order to comprehend their evolutionary history it is useful to examine some concrete examples.

The development path of the Koç Group, which began over fifty years ago, started from commerce (Koç, 1973). Beginning with a local trading house in Ankara in 1917, Mr Koç's firm became the first agency for foreign corporations in 1928. After diversifying his activities, he founded his first joint-stock company in 1938. In 1948 he entered production by establishing plants for import substitution. In time he continued to enlarge his business by setting up new production companies. When he founded Koç Holding in 1963, it was the first system of its kind. Finally, he established the Koç Foundation as an upper-level control unit in 1967. For many years, the Koç Holding stood as an example of a corporate scheme without a bank. Eventually, in 1976, the corporation bought the majority of shares of Garanti Bankası thus coming very close to the maximalist scheme at its upper level control units. In sum, the Koç Group's capital has assumed its multidirectional and flexible quality *via* first commerce, next manufacturing and, finally, banking.

Another establishment of 50 years' standing, İş Bankası, diversified its activities in quite a different manner. The bank was founded right after the War of Independence with the use of a considerable sum of money donated to Mustafa Kemal, the victorious commander of the war. It originated out of the desire to establish a national bank and was founded by the national leader and his close friends as an incorporated joint-stock company in 1924. Consequently, the organization has received state support whenever necessary. The initial diversification of the bank took place with entrance into the insurance business. Also, it played an active role in setting up several leading manufacturing establishments. It still maintains a monopolistic position in some sectors, among them glassworks. In 1934, it organized the 'Retirement Fund of the Members of İş Bankası,' which performs the function of the foundations indicated in Figure 7.1. After the death of Mustafa Kemal (Atatürk) in 1938, the shares of the bank were transferred to institutions such as the Republican People's Party, the Institute of Language and the Institute of History, all founded by Atatürk. Also the retirement fund of the bank bought a majority of the shares owned by private people, creating an interesting pattern of institutional ownership. Over the following years, the bank continuously increased its diversification by co-operating with some trade companies, establishing specialized banks, new insurance companies and manufacturing plants. After 1963, it set up holding companies in sectors under its control, thus approaching the maximalist scheme. It should be noted, however, in the example of İş Bankası, that the positions of the bank and the holding company are interchanged since the bank occupies the highest level of the hierarchy. Starting its business with an accumulated sum of capital, İş Bankası diversified its activities in the following order: (1) insurance and banking, (2) manufacturing, and (3) commerce.

The father of H.Ö. Sabancı Holding, on the other hand, commenced his business life as a porter in the cottonfields of Çukurova and entered the cotton trade in the 1920s (Arzık, date unknown). Later, he set up a business in order to export the product to Europe. Mr Sabancı used his accumulated capital to establish large agricultural farms for raising cotton. In 1948, he was one of the 83 founders of Akbank in Adana; some years later a majority of its shares were to be controlled by the Sabancı Group. During this time, Mr Sabancı undertook further diversification by opening the Erciyas Hotel, which later proved to be an invaluable contact place for business opportunities. The hotel became a meeting place for many businessmen and statesmen. Mr Sabancı also benefited from the support of the President of the Republic (C. Bayar) which enabled him to establish the large textile factory, BOSSA, in 1954. Despite the fact that a bank was already in the system, its growth did not accelerate until after 1960. Akbank then began to diversify its activity and created its subsystem by entering the insurance business. It grew rapidly after 1962 enlarging its participation in the manufacturing industry. In 1967, Mr Sabancı's sons established the H. Ö. Sabancı Holding. A few years later, the Sabancı Foundation was formed by the Sabancı brothers. By the 1970s, the maximalist scheme had been attained. In retrospect, the evolution of the Sabancı holding company proceeded from agrocommerce into banking and finally into manufacturing.

The analysis of roughly 50 years of development experienced by the three largest corporations, Koç Holding, İş Bankası and Sabancı Holding, indicates that despite their different origins they ultimately emerged with similar structures after a long period of divergent evolution. The maximalist scheme defined by available institutional opportunities has been nearly fulfilled by each of the capitalist groups. Having tested the validity of the maximalist scheme for the three largest corporations, by examining the nature of institutional units, it is now time to say a few words regarding the performance characteristics of this type of organization.

Performance Characteristics of the Maximalist Scheme

In the scheme, there is a subsystem centred on a bank which brings the small savings of the society into the larger system and a hierarchical structure which reduces the tax-load of the system. There is also the possibility of selling a large number of shares to the public without having to give up the control of the firms under domination. Furthermore, there is a monopolistic price policy that emerges within the oligopolistic structure of the economy. All these arrangements create an environment, which is very conducive to high profits and thus to high rates of growth for such systems.

The real bottlenecks in the development of holding companies in contemporary Turkey are not the scarcity of capital but the scarcity of qualified personnel and difficulties imposed by the country's balance of payments. In the past, corporations have been able to overcome their personnel problem by attracting experienced people from the public sector, but this source is no longer sufficient for the needs of their large-scale projects. Now, they are trying to train their own staff. They make arrangements to recruit their personnel from the graduates of Turkey's leading universities and then support their further specialization abroad in a predetermined field.

The organizational scheme explained above concerns itself with the characteristics of a single holdings system, with the assumption that big capitalist groups would achieve a similar structure after a period of activity in various sectors. When this is the case, it is not difficult to infer that oligopolistic control mechanisms will emerge in these sectors. If the holding systems are to sustain their profitability, the rules and norms regulating the partition of the market and the determination of prices have to be respected in the business environment. But because the corporate phenomenon is in its first stage of development in Turkey, such rules have not been laid down yet. Instead, a holding company desires to continue its growth as a monopoly in a given sector.

When, however, another corporation wishes to enter the same sector, intercorporate conflict occurs. For instance, a conflict took place in 1975 between H. Ö. Sabancı Holding and Koç Holding when the former attempted to enter the tyre and automotive industry, in which the latter had a monopoly. Later, the two groups came to an agreement. İş Bankası, on the other hand, has been successful at preserving its monopolistic position in the glass industry. It can be asserted that such conflicts are likely to occur in the first stages of corporatization. In time, the tensions ease and, finally, corporations co-operate.

The increase in the number of corporations in the country reduces their bargaining power against the multinational corporations. To give an example, the Koç Group had three joint ventures with three different multinational firms in the tyre industry. In that situation, it was the Koç Group that had the final say in the apportionment of the domestic market. When the new and powerful Sabancı Holding Company emerged, a fourth multinational company could take the advantage of the competition and take a share of the market. Since Koç Holding was no longer the only alternative, the fourth multinational corporation did not have to agree to abide by Mr Koç's decision to share the Turkish market.

Perhaps more important are the conflicts that occur between the holding companies and the small entrepreneurs eliminated from business life because of the large-scale developments. As already mentioned, holding companies will try to weaken the conflict by establishing a large network of small entrepreneurs centred on their system. The conflict, however, is structural and cannot be avoided. It occurs even between the dealers in the system and the holding company. It is known that such a conflict clearly surfaced in a meeting between the Koç Holding and the Koç dealers held in the early 1970s at the Çinar Hotel.

THE SPATIAL ORGANIZATION OF HOLDING COMPANIES

In analysing the spatial organization of the corporations, the method used in the previous section is used. First, the type of spatial organization corresponding to the maximalist scheme is investigated. Later, the study focuses upon the type of transformation experienced in achieving this type of organization of space by tracing the pattern of individual companies.

Figure 7.2. summarizes the spatial organization corresponding to the maximalist scheme in Figure 7.1. As can be seen, the headquarters of the upper level control and finance units of the system, (the holding company, the bank and the foundation) are located in the largest settlement of the country. The highest order centre within national space provides the most suitable location for obtaining the information flows necessary for corporate decision-making. It is the most convenient place to perceive and evaluate investment opportunities in the country and the point of highest interaction with metropolises abroad.

As in some other countries, the political centre of Turkey is not its largest city. The nation's largest population centre is Metropolitan Istanbul, whereas the political capital is Ankara. This dichotomy may be observed in the location of the upper level units of corporations. Out of 111 holding companies established between 1963–76, 69 chose Istanbul and eighteen preferred Ankara for the location of their headquarters. This clearly indicates that Istanbul weighs more heavily in locational decisions for the control units of the corporations. Nevertheless, the decision to locate in Istanbul cannot occur to the complete exclusion of Ankara because the corporation has to have close contacts with politicians and statesmen in order to secure tax returns in exports and to obtain import permissions, price controls and promotion certificates, for which the state remains the ultimate body of approval. The internationalization of such 'economies' is achieved by means of a 'liaison office' established in Ankara.

The second important locational issue of the holdings system concerns the location of its production plants. The corporation is in a position to perceive the investment opportunities throughout the nation and able to comprehend the relative locational advantages of alternative places. It chooses the activity

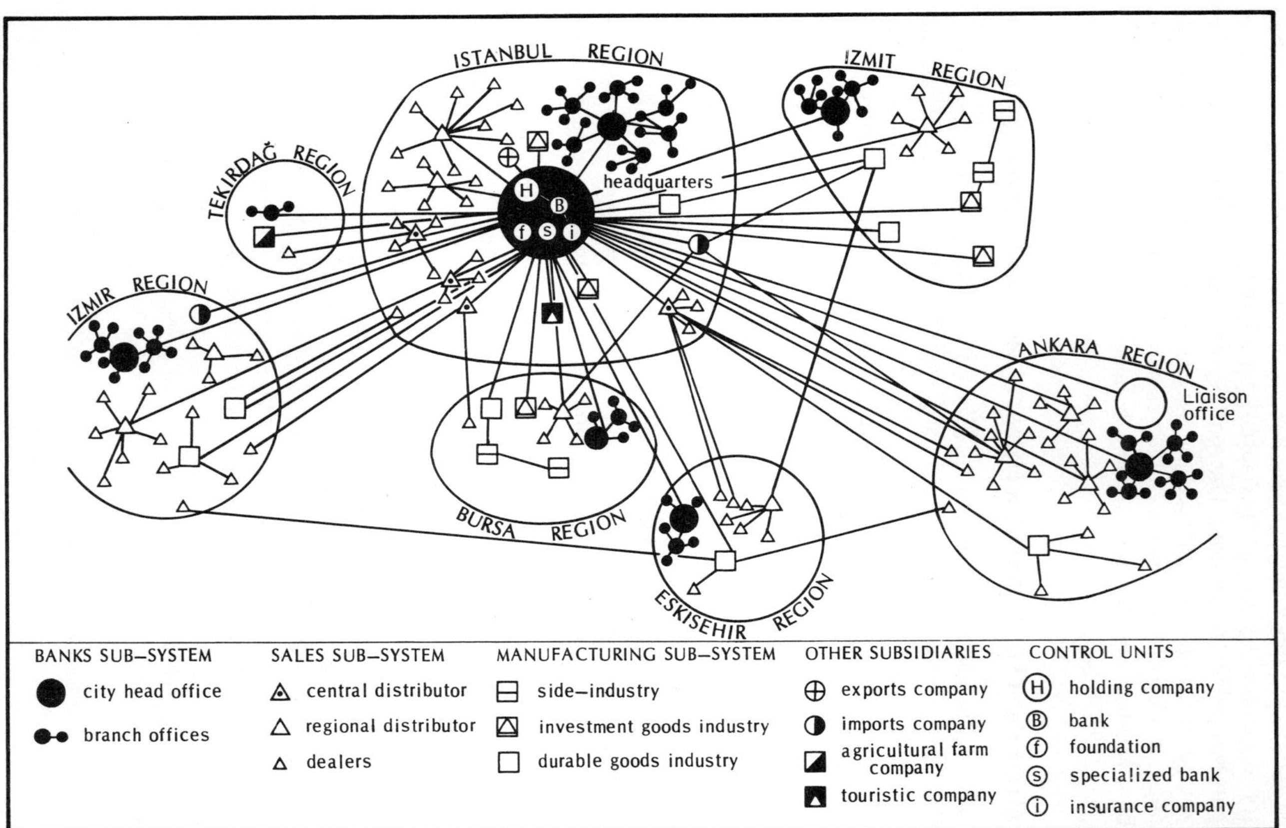

FIGURE 7.2. An illustrative diagram of corporate spatial organization in Turkey

and the place which are the most suitable for its operations. Naturally, the location chosen for the plant need not coincide with the location of the entrepreneur. However, in determining its 'optimum' location, the corporation does not investigate all possible locations as would a planner in a state planning organization. It will only consider that part of national space in which its distribution and collection channels may operate. The 'optimum', in other words, will be a function of the organizational level of the holding company.

In spite of the fact that holding companies conduct scientific research prior to their locational decisions, the empirical evidence indicates that the differences concerning the ownership of capital still affect the spatial distribution of production plants. The production establishments which belong to groups under the control of a single family tend to spread within the boundaries of only one or two regions. In a sense, they remain within a distance that can be easily controlled from the residence of the family's members, On the other hand, when such establishments are controlled and owned by institutions, they seem to diffuse throughout national space, as in the case of İş Bankası.

The second type of holding in the maximalist scheme of the corporation is the sales or distribution firm. There is a basic rule for these distributory activities; the locational behaviour of the sales firms is closely associated with the central-place hierarchy. This rule alone, however, is not sufficient to explain their pattern. It must be supported by additional hypotheses which should be capable of answering the following two questions: First, down to what level of the central-place hierarchy will these distributors diffuse? Second, into which regions (inside or outside the country) will these commercial activities penetrate?

The downward diffusion of the distributory activities of a holding company may be said to be a function of two factors. The first is the type of the goods distributed, characterized by the nature and frequency of the demand existing for them. The second is the decision to make on the amount of the distribution to be carried by the system, and the portion to be left to small entrepreneurs outside the system.

In the organization of its 'sales field', the behaviour of the corporation varies, depending upon the nature of the product. If it is an investment good, there is no reason to separate the place of production and the place of distribution. This is because the demand for such goods is infrequent and not standardized. On the other hand, a firm producing durable consumer goods has to send them to the third-order places (towns) or even second-order places (central villages). Finally, the non-durable and daily goods industry has to have an organization that can secure the penetration into first-order settlements (villages and hamlets).

If durable and non-durable consumer goods are produced in a holding system, the managers of the company have to decide on the type and amount of the distributory activities to be internalized in sales firms controlled by the system. In Turkey, there are alternative arrangements for this situation. In some cases, a commercial subsidiary is established in the centre where company headquartes are located. Through this company, goods are transported to the dealers located in the second and third-order places. Another alternative is the establishment of a central firm coupled with several regional sales firms. Depending upon its nature, the product is either transferred to the dealers or delivered directly to the consumers from these regional sales firms. These two alternatives are largely valid for the distribution of durable goods. If daily consumer goods are produced, a possible arrangement is to set up regional distribution centres or warehouses and transport the goods from such centres to the retail shops of the first-order settlements. Regardless of the alternative chosen, holding companies generally prefer to include the regional sales centres in their system, leaving the lower order activities to small entrepreneurs.

The decision on the determination of the lowest hierarchical level to locate sales companies of the corporation brings with it the question of the degree of internalization of the transport activities. After agreeing on the portion of sales activities to be performed by the system, the holding company has to decide on whether this service will be realized by a transportation company within the system or is to be conducted by entrepreneurs external to the system. In Turkey the practice is for such services to be externalized because there is a competitive market of small entrepreneurs in the transport sector.

In organizing the sales fields for durable goods the corporation must consider the service and repair of such commodities. The behaviour of holding companies in this regard is similar to that of sales organizations. Generally, large service establishments in regional centres are owned by the corporation, leaving the small service stations at lower order centres to other entrepreneurs.

The corporation organizes national space not only to carry out its sales activity but also to accumulate small savings for the purposes of the system, to provide banking services to the public and to sustain an orderly flow of raw materials to its factories. The organization of the 'accumulation fields' follows a central-place pattern just like the one observed in commercial activities, except that the branch-offices in the lowest order settlements are internalized by the system, and never left to small entrepreneurs. At present, branch-offices are organized at third and sometimes second-order centres in Turkey. The 'field of raw material flows' is also organized along hierarchical lines, but not in a uniform fashion. The location of raw materials forces such fields to exhibit discontinuities in certain regions.

By relying upon the assumptions behind the maximalist scheme, it can be said that the corporation will organize all national space in the manner explained above. Naturally, in their early stage of development the organization of corporations will be limited to one or two regions. The holding system is in a position to organize itself in foreign countries as well but due to the underdeveloped nature of the exports departments of corporations, a 'field-like' organization does not reach out to other countries. There are, however, some 'point-like' units in a few foreign metropolises. Turkey sent over a million workers to Europe, especially to Germany, after 1960 and this has increased the importance of organizing accumulation fields in Europe. At present, Turkish capitalist groups are in the process of developing more effective schemes to tap the savings of the workers in Europe.

Different Models of Evolution Toward the Maximalist Spatial Organization

The synchronic structure of corporate spatial organization as analyzed above has provided certain clues about the way corporations may grow in spatial terms, but it does not say anything about the stages of development that corporations go through in organizing their space. Yet, corporations show quite important behavioural differences, depending upon their stages of development. The examples presented in Figure 7.3 make it possible to develop some general hypotheses about the spatial evolution of Turkish corporations.

The first stage in the evolution starts with the location of the family firm, owned by a single entrepreneur or by a group of family members. At this stage, the entrepreneur does not face any locational problem. His location is predetermined. The concern is with the choice of a profitable area of business activity rather than with the choice of place. This ethnocentric (home-oriented) behaviour of the entrepreneur is caused by his 'action space' being limited to the settlement where he lives. There, he can perceive and control business opportunities better than anywhere else. He knows the conditions of that business environment and is faced with less risk in establishing a new line of business. Thus, the location of the family and the location of the family firm coincide at the outset without creating a decision problem.

If the family firms continues to grow by perceiving new opportunities and entering into new businesses, a differentiation of business establishments will take place within the same city. When more than one establishment emerges, one of them will become the decision centre of the firm. Parallel to the expansion of the activities of the family firm, both the environment within which business opportunities are perceived and the 'action space' are enlarged. The firm begins to perceive operations and projects of a larger scale in a wider environment, necessitating a transition to the structure of an incorporated joint-stock company, on the one hand, and an intraregional decentralization, on the other. At this stage, the firm is no longer influenced by the residence of its controllers; it has reached a regional level of operation.

After a period of further diversification in the region, a multiplant/multifirm structure emerges which is conducive to more effective organizational control through a holding system. The action space of the organization will continue to enlarge within the new structure, creating pressure for 'relocation', depending upon the characteristics of the region. The aim of the corporation,

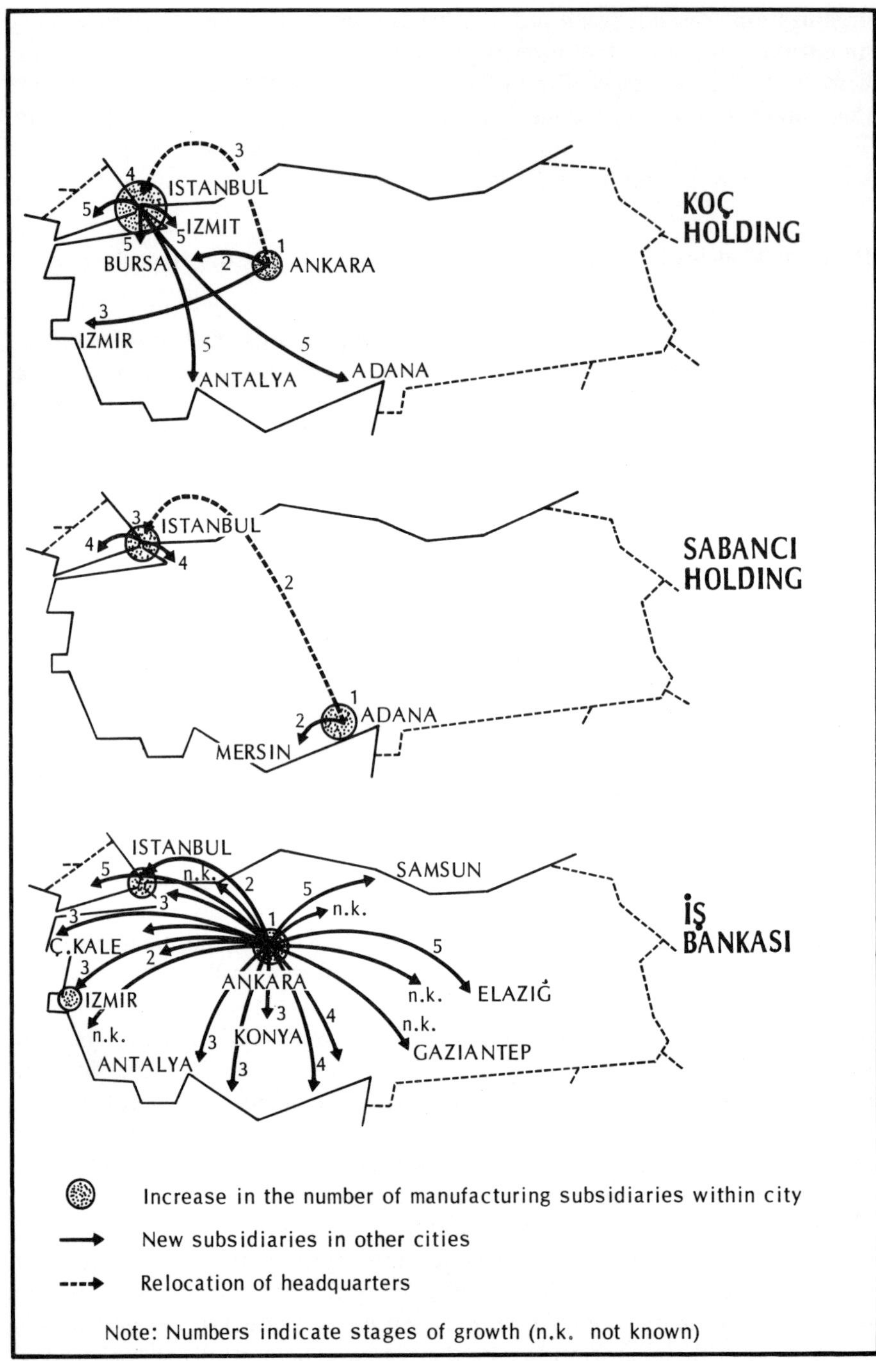

FIGURE 7.3. Spatial growth of the three largest Turkish corporations

to exploit all business opportunities available in the nation, will necessitate that it locate its controlling functions in the largest city of the country. If the corporate headquarters are not there already, but located in a regional centre, it will jump to the economic centre of the nation and decentralize its new plants around this new location. It can be hypothesized that when the holding company remains under the control of a single family, this duocentric structure will persist even though the holding system may have an action space that can stretch all over the nation. If the ownership of the company is not the monopoly of a single family, however, the activities of the company will tend to spread out over national space, as may be the case for institutionally owned establishments.

The spatial development patterns shown in Figure 7.3 indicate that the two largest corporations of the country, Koç Holding and Sabancı Holding, relocated their headquarters after going through the stages described above. These corporations were located in the second and fourth largest cities of the country—Ankara and Adana, respectively—when first established but later felt the need to leap to the highest order centre to take advantage of the larger action space. After this, decisions to expand and decentralize their activities were taken in their new headquarters in Istanbul.

On the other hand, Yaşar Holding of İzmir located in the third largest settlement of Turkey, has not yet relocated its controlling activities. This fact can be explained by two factors both delaying opportunity-seeking attempts at the national level. Either it has not received the scale sufficient for such a jump or has not yet exhausted the business opportunies in the rich region of İzmir. Naturally, corporations such as Transtürk Holding and Profilo Holding, initially established in Istanbul, have not faced the problem of relocating their headquarters in the process of corporate development.

Because of the institutionalized nature of its capital, İş Bankası manifests a plan of spatial organization that deviates from the other examples. One observable difference lies in its action space which is not regionally biased, its plants being distributed all over the nation. Another deviation occurs because its headquarters have remained fixed in the capital city of Ankara since the foundation of the system. The national scope assumed from its establishment onwards has not created any tension within its system to force it to relocate its headquarters.

The examples emphasize two factors which influence the locational behaviour of a subsidiary company. The first is the nature of its ownership, while the second is the stage of development of the parent company to which it belongs.

NEW QUESTIONS FOR LOCATION THEORY AND IMPLICATIONS FOR SPATIAL DEVELOPMENT STRATEGY

Having examined the development and patterns of spatial organization observed for holding companies in Turkey, it is now possible to discuss whether classical location theory is sufficient to explain the behaviour of these dynamic corporate systems. It might seem logical to infer that classical location theory is irrelevant for the explanation of the multiplant/multifirm systems, since it concerns itself with the locational question of a single firm at a given point in time. Such an inference, however, has to be carefully qualified. In explaining the pattern of spatial development of the holdings system, this study relied heavily upon the concepts of central place theory. As is known, Christaller (1933), and Lösch (1954), used classical location theory to develop and formulate various aspects of central-place theory.

In recent years the use of various programming techniques within the scope of the location theory (Serck-Hanssen, 1970; Scott, 1971) may be interpreted as an indication of the fact that location theory is convertible into a context capable of dealing with the new locational questions posed by holdings systems. Here one is faced with the conceptual problem of defining the boundaries of a theory in evolution. For the above reasons, the remaining section of this essay concentrates upon new questions raised by corporate systems, instead of elaborating further on the inadequacy of 'classical' location theory.

The development of corporations as systems raises five important questions:

1. The first question is related to the type of pressure exerted on the elements of the system during the growth of the corporation and the adaptation of these units to their changing environment. A comparison of the elements of a holding company in two temporal cross-sections reveals one of the following conditions:
   (a) both the size and the functions of some elements remain unchanged;
   (b) Some elements grow in size while their functions remain the same;
   (c) the functions of some elements are diversified; while a part of these functions are passed to new establishments (such as a new plant), others are still conducted by the old units;
   (d) the functions of some units are completely abandoned and replaced by new functions;
   (e) some elements are relocated elsewhere at larger scales, abandoning their previous locations;
   (f) both the location and the function of a part of the elements are completely dropped.

   It may be said that each element will be under strain because of the growth of the holdings system. In specific periods, the management will apply one of these decision alternatives to each element of the system. Generally, the probability of preserving established units is high because of their inertia.

   The type of changes experienced by the establishments within the holdings scheme is greatly affected by the economic conditions of the country. It is possible, however, to mention a few general principles. The points at the outlets of the distribution and accumulation channels of the holding company, (that is, the branch-offices and dealers found in the lowest order settlements) will not undergo major changes in their size and functions. However, there will be a tendency in the long run for their complete abandonment if radical technological changes take place. Medium or small-size production plants, on the other hand, will counteract the tension either by differentiating or by renewing their functions. If these two alternatives are not applicable they will be abandoned. Finally, the large-scale production units of the system are likely to maintain themselves either by expanding in the same location or by differentiating one of their functions in another location. The probability of closing down such units is very low.

The story of the Arçelik Company, one of the largest holdings of the Koç Group, gives a synthetic example of the above hypotheses. The location of the first plant of this establishment, engaged in the production of durable houseware, was in Sütlüce, a district of Istanbul close to the Golden Horn. The inadequacy of its operations relative to increasing demand forced the plant location to be abandoned and re-established at a much larger scale in Çayirova, a suburban district of the metropolis. Later, the company underwent further pressure to enlarge its operations. This time, however, the need was satisfied by separating one line of activity, refrigerator production, and locating it in the inland city of Eskişehir. The large-scale plant in Çayirova was preserved and continued production in the previous branches of business.

Naturally, those elements with the most easily transferable functions, those that have the least inertia, are commercial establishments.

2. The second question concerns the way that establishments owned by two different holding companies will choose their relative locations in space. Or to put it differently, how will they share the domestic market?

In classical location theory each production plant is surrounded by a continuous market not served by any other production unit. Yet, in holding companies, the production and sales units are spatially differentiated. The sales functions are organized, in many cases, independent of the place of production. In addition, the market is never under the complete control of a single company. Thus the division of a regional market between two competing corporations will not be realized in a geometrical manner but in terms of the percentage of sales. In this case, the competitive corporations will establish their sales units around the same place in a given city, just like in Hotelling's (1929) example of ice-cream vendors on the beach. Also, the sales units of such corporations will show a tendency to agglomerate in central places whose order depends upon the type of the product sold. The picture resulting from such a tendency of concentration of private initiative differs from that of the public interest, as clearly explained by Alonso (1964). An alternative to this practice would be to plan the size and location of service units parallel to the needs of the users—for example see the solution provided by Mycielski and Trzěciakowski (1963) concerning regional and roadside service stations.

3. The third question is concerned with the spatial differentiation of price. In an economic system consisting of individual firms there is an areal division of the market between firms. The price of the service or the product sold is subject to spatial differentiation. The price paid by the consumer consists of the factory price plus the transportation cost. What happens in a market controlled by corporations? The holding systems that are in the position to share the national market have to pursue a uniform price policy. In such a situation, the corporations seem to pay for a portion of the transportation cost. Actually, this is made possible through the monopolistic price system of the oligopolistic structure of the economy. In other words, a uniform price policy emerges as a result of the agreement between 'competing' corporations. This implies that the consumers who are close to the production place bear the extra transportation cost to distant consumers. Turkey has experienced this phenomenon since the 1960s.
4. The fourth question brought about by corporations concerns the extent to which their locational decisions are bounded by their earlier locational decisions and environmental conditions. As active systems, corporations are capable of following strategies aiming at changing their environment rather than simply taking it as given during their adaptation process. The degree of flexibility that corporate systems can have in their spatial organization remains as an important theoretical problem.
5. The fifth question concerns the multiplier effects of these systems in their vicinity. In the earlier sections it was shown that a single entrepreneur was faced with the choice of activity rather than the choice of place. This behaviour leads the entrepreneur to reinvest his earned income in the same region. On the other hand, the profits of a holding company in a region are easily transferred to the centre of the system. Very possibly, the money transferred this way will not be reinvested in that region but channelled to other places evaluated by the board of directors to be more appropriate. This is why the spread (regional multiplier) effects of corporate establishments might be nil. Furthermore, the plants belonging to such systems do not have to depend on the inputs supplied in their locality but may get them from firms controlled by or in agreement with the holding company, which may be located at distant places. Thus the forward and backward linkage effects of the corporation are not necessarily limited to the immediate regions of their holdings but extend in a much broader region. As with material inputs, so labour inputs too need not be obtained from the local area. The corporation may appoint its professionals to wherever it wishes. This, besides giving a locational flexibility to the corporation and reducing risks, decreases the contributions to the local economy. This is another significant point for regional and national planners. It implies

that, unless other measures are taken, the net impact of a corporation on its immediate environment will be negative. The point is especially important for underdeveloped countries where the 'spread effects' are weaker as a rule (Myrdal, 1957, Chapter 4).

The locational questions touched upon in the final section of this study indicate some interesting areas of research for the analysts of the spatial organization of corporations. It appears that, in addition to the classical location theory, the insights and conceptual frameworks provided by general systems theory and the theory of organization have the potential to make important contributions for the development of the field.

NOTES

1. It should be pointed out that Lenin's definition of finance capital was in regard to the dominating core of the Western imperialist system. He referred to the coalescence of the industrial monopolies and banking monopolies that were the results of the enormous accumulation of capital and the intensification of production during the advanced stage of capitalism (Lenin, 1939). The definition used here, on the other hand, refers to a small number of monopolies controlling the economy of Turkey which were formed after a similar coalescence during the Republican era. The definition does not imply that Turkish finance capital has developed independent of the western imperialist system. Quite the opposite is true. The growth and the present structure of finance capital in this country can not be interpreted meaningfully in isolation from the international finance capital with which it continues to have strong interest relationships.
2. The term 'maximalist' has been deliberately used in its normative meaning to describe the strategy adopted by Turkish corporations in forming their multifirm system of holdings. It is used relative to the institutional structure of the economy to emphasize the fact that the large corporations take the *full* advantage of the legal opportunities for the expansion of their multiplant/multifirm system. The 'maximalist organizational scheme' that results from adopting such a strategy characterizes the structure of the largest corporations today. It is also aspired to by the developing monopolies in the economy.
3. The word 'holding' in English refers to a company owned by a holding company. The same word in Turkish usage, however, refers to the holding company itself rather than one of its subsidiary establishment. It is not by coincidence that this word was introduced into the Turkish Commercial legislation in the late 1950s, during the time of maturing brotherhood with the United States. Thus, the terms 'holding company', 'holding system' and 'corporation' in this paper are used interchangeably to denote a control system consisting of affiliated companies of a monopolistic group organized as a *holding* in Turkey. As clarified later in the article, the term 'holding company' also refers to the uppermost control unit of such a system, that is the 'mother' company of the system of holdings.
4. Here a brief explanation of the core–periphery model might be useful. The model echoes the argument that the core appropriate to itself the surplus of the periphery for its own development (de Souza and Porter, 1974, p. 60). The centre is capable of spatial definition at the world, national or subnational scales depending upon which is considered to be the most approriate for a particular set of authority-dependency

relationships. As Friedmann (1974, p. 2) puts it, at whatever scale of analysis, core and periphery stand in an asymmetrical relationship of dominance-dependency that is articulated through four major spatial processes: (1) decision-making and control; the spatial and distribution of power, (2) capital flows; investments and the location of economic activities, (3) the spatial diffusion of innovations, and (4) migration and settlement. The spatial relations of power (that is, decision-making and control) are identified as the most critical process to which all others are ultimately related.

REFERENCES

Alonso, W. (1964). 'Location theory', In John Friedmann and William Alonso (eds.), *Regional Development and Planning*, MIT Press, Cambridge, 78–106.

Arzik, N. (date unknown). *Ak Altinin Agasi* (The Lord of White Gold), Ajans-Turk Matbaasi, Ankara.

Christaller, W. (1933). Translated by Carlisle W. Baskin (1966). *Central Places in Southern Germany*, Prentice Hall, Englewood Cliffs.

de Souza, A. R. and Porter, P. W. (1974). *The Underdevelopment and Modernization of the Third World*, Association of American Geographers, Resource Paper No. 28, Washington.

Friedmann, J. (1974). *Urbanization, Planning and National Development*, Sage Publications, Beverly Hills.

Hamilton, F. E. I. (1974). *Spatial Perspectives on Industrial Organization and Decision-Making*, John Wiley Sons, London.

Hilferding, R. (1910). *Das Finanzkapital*, Volksbuchhandlung, Vienna.

Hotelling, H. (1929). 'Stability in competition'. *Economic Journal*, **39**, 41–57.

Hymer, S. (1972). 'The efficiency (contradictions) of multinational corporations'. In Gilles Paquet (ed.) *The Multinational Firm and the Nation State*, Collier-Macmillan Canada, Don Mills.

Koç, Vehbi (1973). *Hayat Hikayem* (My Life Story). Apa Ofset Basimevi, Istanbul.

Lenin, P. V. (1939). *Imperialism: The Highest Stage of Capitalism*, International Publishers, New York.

Lösch, A. (1954). *The Economics of Location*, Yale University Press, New Haven.

McNee, R. B. (1958). 'Functional geography of the firm with an illustrative case study from the petroleum industry'. *Economic Geography*, **34**, 321–337.

Mycielski, J. and Trzeciakowski, W. (1963); 'Optimization of the size and location of service stations, *Journal of Regional Science*, **5**, 59–68.

Myrdal, G. (1957). *Economic Theory and Underdeveloped Regions*, Harper Torchbooks, 1971 Edition, New York.

Scott, A. J. (1971). *Combinatorial Programming, Spatial Analysis and Planning*, Methuen and Co., London.

Serck-Hanssen, J. (1970). *Optimal Patterns of Location*, North-Holland Publishing Co., Amsterdam.

Planning Industrial Development
Edited by David F. Walker

Chapter 8

Perspectives on Transnational Corporations in South-east Asia

Christine Flores

From the 1960s to the present day, the major influences on the understanding of social phenomena and, as a result, on the bulk of planning activities in the South-east Asian open economies (the Philippines, Malaysia, Indonesia, Singapore and Thailand) have been the viewpoints of conventional modernization theorists. They postulate that economic development is a smooth and continuous process activated by economists, planners, key decision-makers and entrepreneurs. Second, they believe that changes in the economy and society are made gradually by making adjustments from one internal sector to another—for example shifts from farming and primary industries to processing and manufacturing industries. This process guarantees that benefits will somehow, sometime, percolate from highly capitalized groups to the low-income groups and that both work together to satisfy their mutual interests. Planning for development is then viewed as consisting of efforts to transform a society, backward and poor, into an ideal type characterized by features which originate from the developed countries. In achieving this transformation it was thought that the principal role would be played by high economic growth rates gained through sectoral development planning and fostered by external assistance. One need not repeat in depth the details of this all-too-familiar perspective, one that has been critically summarized time and again (Hoogvelt, 1976; Frank, 1971; and Portes, 1976).

While much of planning policy in these open economies is swayed by these influences, recent events in Vietnam, Laos and Cambodia, as well as internal pressures from within the countries themselves, have been forcing attention on a different set of explanations of social change. Most if not all of the South east Asian countries have in recent years suffered sudden convulsions within their social fabric that gradualist development theories find difficulty in explaining. Against these explanations a considerable body of literature has emerged under the rubric of dependency theory. This perspective proposes that there is little that is useful in modernization thinking or the 'developmentalist' attitude. Underdevelopment is the consequence of development. This perspective directs attention to forces, structures, and causal relationships between metropolitan, developed countries and peripheral, Third World ones. Hoogvelt (1976, p. 67) stresses that fundamental to the theory is the conception of a *dialectic* relationship between the development of the First World and the underdevelopment of the Third World. Over the years, a two-way causal connection has developed between the West, which gained ascendancy precisely because it was underdeveloping the Third World, and the countries it dominated. This dialectical relationship has unfolded in three distinct stages: a mercantilist–capitalist stage, a colonial stage and neocolonial stage.

THE TRANSNATIONAL FIRM

One central force is the transnational corporation. It remains ambiguously defined, however, and this ambiguity is a disadvantage for researchers and students concerned with the subject. There is a lack of international consensus on its definition, resulting in our inability to monitor the activities of such corporations with precision. Differences in current working definitions of foreign investments (the Organization for Economic Co-operation and Development even uses direct foreign investment as a designation for its long-term loans) add to confusion. The tendency of some investigators to define foreign firms in terms of the citizenship of the board of directors rather than by the proportion of equity leads to inconsistencies especially when comparisons are attempted.

Added to this definitional obstacle is the difficulty with which researchers are able to cast off the convenient fiction of 'value-freedom'. Analysis of the transnational corporation with the supposedly neutral concepts utilized by the modernization stream only muddles thinking on the subject. There is a marked disinclination to clarify the different interests that are at stake in their operations. This has led to the belief that a transnational is simply one more good 'corporate citizen' that can help achieve the development programme of a Third World country. The ancient observation that foreign investment is a crucial economic act with vital social and political consequences is overlooked. In spite of the ITT episode, for instance, leading to destabilization activities and the 1973 Allende tragedy in Chile, an episode which gave evidence that the transnational corporation is a central element, a central force, one is often led to believe that it is an isolated and negligible intrusion into political and economic systems.

This trend is reinforced by the difficulty with which researchers with a critical focus can gain access to research funding on the topic, one that alienates many philanthropically inclined sources. Further, a measure of co-operation in the investigation of the activities of these corporations from those close to their operations is hard to come by. Another bedevilling factor is the inherent difficulties in detailing the exact techniques by which transnationals exercise power. Lastly, research methods on the transnational which will lead to information having comparative value need to be developed. As a result of the present ambiguity surrounding the question of transnationals and their operations, allegations of their meddling in national and local affairs are often overlooked by academic researchers, who could provide some empirical data. The mass media is quick to point out that they are benevolent institutions.

In popular mythology transnational corporations are thus seen as positive agents providing capital, technology, skills, employment opportunities and taxable enterprises. They make basic contributions of transportation, housing, education and medical care. They help alleviate the balance-of-payments deficit of their host countries through the finance capital they bring in, the production of formerly imported items and their large exports relative to local firms. They often stimulate host country business by training indigenous personnel, by creating new activities linked with the investor's primary business and by demonstrating techniques that can be imitated (Wilkins, 1974).

THE TRANSNATIONAL CORPORATION IN SOUTH-EAST ASIA TODAY

The present constellation of governmental attitudes towards foreign investment in South-east Asia remains under the hypnosis of this thinking. Except perhaps on the question of land development, where the countries are more or less selective and stringent in controlling outsiders, attitudes regarding natural and human resources tend to favour foreign investment. Economic nationalists who insist on self-reliance do exist but, if they are not silenced, they are unable to make significant dents in public policy and are placated by half-hearted measures.

Key decision-makers have been encouraging transnationals, often uncritically, through specific incentives, which provide handsome privileges for their business. Government policies try to create the general and political conditions that will achieve a hospitable atmosphere to attract foreign firms.

Links between Malaysian and Filipino political élites and multinationals operating within their countries have been forged in many ways. The Philippines and Malaysia currently offer the best climates for foreign investments in South-east Asia. The colonial pattern persists and major concessions to firms include payment of only nominal prices for leasing rich mining and agricultural estates, while large sums of money get repatriated.

In Indonesia, a Foreign Investments Law Instituted in 1967 has since guaranteed very advantageous privileges on behalf of the transnationals. In 1974, new policies were announced in the aftermath of the anti-Tanaka (then the Japanese Prime Minister) riots. Those sought to exercise some controls such as requiring a payment of $ 100 US per month per foreign employee from foreign companies, which had not yet 'Indonesianized' the labour force. Implementation, however, appears, to be sketchy and quite contrary to these moves. Indonesia, along with the other four countries, was in fact quite eager in the 1977 Association of South-east Asian Nations (ASEAN) conference to encourage the expansion of economic cooperation with Japan.

Singapore has had a long tradition of engaging in entrepôt trade and its economic development cannot be divorced from this activity. Transnational corporations play an integral role in its economy and lately the state has displayed a very aggressive attitude in the 'competitive concessions' war which has found the ASEAN members competing with one another to host transnational firms.

Thailand ranks third as the world's tin exporter, next to Malaysia and Bolivia. United States' influence in the mining and smelting of the mineral is substantial and mediated by high-ranking government officials.

PERSPECTIVES

More efforts should be directed to study the implications of transnational involvement in these economies. The balance of this article discusses some perspectives by which this may be done. Hopefully it will be of some use for people in host countries who feel that they must remain in the driver's seat in spite of the difficulties involved. National governments, which are determined to make independent decisions, still possess certain 'degrees of freedom' by which they can carry out policies to control transnational activities.

By its very nature, deciding on a framework for investigating impacts of transnational corporations, especially on the local level, means engaging in partisan scholarship. The framework would begin where people feel most intensely the pressure of the corporations on their own lives. This means that the presupposition that there is a mutuality of interests between the people of the host countries and the transnationals is laid to rest. One need not go far for some, even institutional, supports for rejecting this assumption.

What else could be the intent behind all the major documents from the conferences of the non-aligned nations and the recently incorporated Centre for Transnational Corporations at the United Nations, which collects information on impacts on countries and advises governments on how to curb transnational excesses, if such a mutuality of interests actually existed? Since its inception, the Centre has given top priority to the creation and implementation of a code of conduct defining some fundamental rules for transnational corporations. In fact, remaining on this issue, it may be worth referring to the criticisms that a body such as the United Nations is receiving in its attachment to the assumption (as reflected in its reports), that many contemporary governments have the true 'national interests' at heart. One sees that the composition of many governments in Third World countries is often elitist, corrupted by external influences, including the transnationals. In fact, host country ambivalence and hostility have not only been directed at the investors but also at the national leaders.

As early as the landmark 1970 Lusaka Declaration on Non-alignment and Economic Progress, which involved Indonesia, Malaysia and Singapore among our subjects, positions relating to these crucial issues were articulated. The heads of state of the participating countries: 'realising that the occupation of parts of territories of non-aligned developing counties and dependent nations by aggressors or minority governments deprives these groups of their resources and constitutes a hindrance to their development. . . pledged themselves among others "to ensure that external components of the developmental process further national objectives and conform to national needs" (Barratt-Brown, 1974).

Critics of multinational activities, especially those whose normative perspective consists of the interests of the people of the host countries, in my view deserve first hearing as to which elements need to be included in a critical research framework.

Four sets of criticisms, kindred in some way but sorted out for the sake of analysis, appear to be repeated again and again in the literature, and an exploration of their contents is useful. Criticisms on the operations of transnationals have been launched:

1. From a conceptual viewpoint heavily influenced by both mercantilist and Marxist critiques.
2. Related to the first, a viewpoint which looks at the potential and actual dilemmas faced by the host countries in their dealings with the corporations. The very co-existence of the political logic of the national community is seen as conflicting with the economic logic that motivates the multinational corporation;
3. From a more specific perspective that sees multinational involvement within a historical and structural framework. Attention is focused on how colonial history has deeply moulded the present economic and social structures. This includes looking at the historical roots of dependency of the countries under study;
4. From a micro-level perspective that looks at the ways by which independence in decision-making on national and more local issues is compromised by the pervasive presence of foreign investments. The exercise of multinational influence and its outcome on certain points of the political system is studied.

The Mercantilist and Marxist Critique

Mercantilists, represented by Kari Levitt (1970) in *Silent Surrender*, and Marxists, represented by Stephen Hymer (1974), alike begin with the premise that economic relations must essentially be in conflict. These relationships and the distribution of gains are essentially zero-sum games and there could be no harmony underlying these processes—unlike Wilkins (1974), who stressed the optimally efficient use of scarce resources without making value-judgements about income distribution, mercantilist and Marxist critics stress the latter.

To them the goal of economic and political activities is the redistribution of wealth and power. To the mercantilist critic, redistribution among nation-states is important. Particular powerful nation-states have utilized the multinational as an instrument of expansion so that weaker nation-states are at present forced into a defensive position. The latter, reacting against economic exploitation, political dependence, and cultural inundation, organize to set up countervailing institutions.

To the Marxists, the principal actors within the economy are classes. Class justice becomes significant. Hymer (1974, p. 114) posits that two laws working together—the *law of increasing firm size* and the *law of uneven development*—produce the following consequence:

> a regime of North Atlantic Multinational Corporations would tend to produce hierarchical division of labor between geographical regions corresponding to the vertical division of labor within the firm. It would tend to centralize high-level decision-making occupations in a few key cities in the advanced countries, surrounded by a number of regional sub-capitals, and confine the rest of the world to lower levels of activity and income, i.e. to the status of towns and villages in a new Imperial system. Income, status, authority, and consumption patterns would radiate out from these centres along a declining curve, and the existing pattern of inequality and dependency would be perpetuated. The pattern would be complex, but the basic relationship between different countries would be one of superior and subordinate, head office and branch plant.

The law of increasing firm size states that, from the Industrial Revolution on there has been qualitative as well as quantitative growth in the size of firms, from the workshop to the factory to the national corporation to the multi-divisional corporation and finally to the multinational corporation. Each step is marked by the acquisition of a more complex administrative structure and a larger brain to co-ordinate activities and to ensure survival and growth. *The law of uneven development* states that the tendency of this industrial organization is to simultaneously produce underdevelopment in some geographical regions and development in others.

The structure of this Imperial system, or in the words of Sklar (1976) 'corporate internationalism', sees a metropolitan bourgeoisie in the industrial capitalist countries and a managerial national bourgeoisie in the Third World. Both groups work in conclave (Sklar, 1976; Martin, 1976). Both of these groups recognize their mutual interest in maintaining the *status quo* but in time their competing interests will surface.

Conflicts of Interest between Multinational Corporations and Nation-States

Where multinationals predominate dilemmas arise in two areas. First, a large number of the nation's economic actors become responsible to superiors and stockholders of the firms—that is, to people who most likely are the nationals of other countries. At the same time, the state apparatus, assuming its benevolence, is unable in many cases to investigate whether commercial and business laws designed to protect these actors are being enforced. This often occurs due to the lack of adequately trained civil servants cognisant of the transnationals, as well as their use of antiquated laws (Muller, 1975). Likewise the weakness or the absence of organized labour could mean the lack of another counterbalancing force against the power of the corporation.

Secondly, through the diffusion of ideas and values from the rich countries, the values and ideas of citizens of poor countries are affected and shaped. This adds to the previous conditioning of the reactions of colonized peoples. Directly affected are the consumption habits and, in an indirect way, attitude formation especially of the nationals working within the transnationals. Inappropriate patterns of consumption are encouraged as cultural standards by generous advertising budgets that give the multinational corporation: 'enormous power to determine what does or does not give "psychological satisfaction". It is disingenuous to talk about the "dictates of the consumer" when the consumer is so thoroughly subject to the dictation of the modern technology of manipulation' (Barnet and Muller, 1974, p. 177). These authors, for instance, recount how findings from a study of a village in Mexico reveal that peasants who come into contact with advertising messages want and buy white bread and soft drinks—nutritionally marginal foods attractively packaged for economically marginal people.

It was also found that Brazilian entrepreneurs in firms dependent on foreign investments felt that the proper functioning of a society required only an alliance of upper-class groups. This was in contrast to entrepreneurs in independent firms who believed that political power ought to be shared by salaried employees and wage workers. An explanation of how these linkages between economic roles and attitudes towards domestic politics occur is provided by Evans (1971, p. 689):

> Nationals working at the local level strive to absorb the cultural perspective of the organizations that provide their livelihood and their work environ-

ment. The ability to identify with the corporation as an organization and to acquire the cognitive and stylistic norms that prevail within it is an important prerequisite of executive success. The socialization of local elite personnel is reinforced by the employment of foreign personnel in key high-level positions. If corporations are successful in inculcating a sense of organizational identity, the probability that the local economic élite will act on the basis of national identification diminishes.

Multinational Involvement in South-East Asia: An Historical Perspective

The present development of South-east Asia and the role of the transnational corporation in this development can be understood within a historical framework (Catley, 1976). In an analysis of countries where foreign investments still play an active role, an historical analysis would cover precolonial life in South-east Asia, the period of early mercantilism (1511 to 1870), late mercantilism (1870 to the Second World War), and neocolonialism (the Second World War to the present day). These periods have general application to the region as a whole but would need greater precision if applied to individual countries.

A basic pattern of South-east Asian precolonial life was discernible. Wet rice cultivation was supplemented by other activities such as handicrafts and livestock raising. Communal irrigation, planting and harvesting were the norm and enforced cooperative labour was undertaken at crucial times (to build dykes or for terracing, for instance). There was a concentrated social life in the villages and state power over these communities was restricted.

European-based trading companies appeared with the growth of European commercial capital in the early sixteenth century. Products provided by the existing mode of production were extracted either by exchange or force with the co-operation of the ruling classes. European expansion by and large remained patchy until the mid-nineteenth century when new methods of production (such as rubber estates, and sugar plantations) were introduced and greater demands were made on the region's resources. After the Second World War, metropolitan interests and access to the commodities and markets required that different political structures were necessary.

During this period, élites from the landed classes, indigenous bourgeoisie and merchants created a language of quasi-national identity as a reaction to Western colonialism. They formed natural alliances with metropolitan capital and looked to their colonial masters as models for nation-building, thus preserving in modified form the colonial situation. This structure remains in the open economies—a functional but not necessarily ideological convergence of interests among the purveyors of metropolitan capital, the transnational corporations, the landed classes and the indigenous bourgeoisie. Their interests, competing but as of now not yet antagonistic, are presently mediated within the nation-states by technocratic élites—mainly bureaucratic and military. These élites, who are mostly similar in policy orientations, create social and political arrangements which favour the prerogatives of foreign capital, through a judicious application of planning mechanisms. Since national planning is carried out by an apparatus that is extensively manipulated by the propertied classes, the perspective and goals of the transnational remain virtually unchecked. The kinds of institutional and political constraints which ought to be imposed on multinational firms give way to bland measures that do not effectively channel their activities to developmental goals benefiting the majority of people in host countries. In fact, the competition for foreign investments among the countries in the region supplants any efforts to institute such constraints which even the industrialized countries feel compelled to apply. Such measures at present include a screening process, on foreign operations, the refusal of permits to certain industries and restrictions on domestic borrowing.

Because of the symbiotic relationships between élites and transnational corporations the range of options open to governments to control the latter's activities is severely restricted. Governments have become so tightly linked to decision-making structures located outside the countries that transnationals occupy a pre-eminent position in the country's political, economic, and social structures. Logically the formulation of internal policies cannot withstand pressures from the popular classes but the present regimes in fact do not require any popular mandate because the people are inherently outside of the technocratic process. They are to be controlled and mobilized for the task of economic development, in other words, only to be rendered productive (Bock and Harvey, 1976). Popular participation is ruled out and is seen as inconvenient and irrational. Antipopulist sectors convinced of the necessity of piecemeal welfare measures if not suppression of political rights as a way of dealing with social unrest, are those enshrined.

Implications at the Local Level

Specific studies which examine the micro-level effects of multinational activities in South-east Asia are available but are very few in number. They include profiles of specific firms or groups of industries. Their development over time is investigated and the concessions gained from the governments which have made expansion possible are documented. Studies, some with more detail than others, are available on such agribusiness concerns as Del Monte Castle and Cooke in the Philippines. Descriptions of their origins from the turn of the century to their present expansion reflect their capabilities to manipulate governments to grant concessions favourable to them, including the leasing of land acreage over and above the limits imposed by the constitution. The tin smelting company, Thaisaco in Thailand has been granted the right to monopolize the smelting and the exporting of tin in Thailand, which ranks third in the world as an exporter of the commodity. The electronics industry in West Malaysia (Bock and Harvey, 1976) is one of the most important in the country in terms of generation of employment but, because of its footloose character, creates problems for the local economy. In the more recent past, research on the Export Processing Zone in the Philippines and the condition of workers in this area has become available (Snow, 1976).

Research along these lines, although crucial, is proceeding at a glacial speed. There are likewise the essential problem areas where the effects of multinational activities are felt directly—on consumers, on sectors of population affected by the pollution from their factories and on communities in the vicinity of company towns. In fact community studies of these company towns could provide comparisons between firms and throw some empirical light on their 'corporate conscience'. Lastly, the acceleration of assimilation of groups in the hinterland resulting from the operation of remote or strategically located enterprises needs documentation.

Studies could be undertaken on government policy outcomes which seem to reflect corporate drives quite faithfully in their accommodating stance towards foreign investments. Illustrations from the historic past could inform those interested in how reciprocal obligations between political élites and multinational firms are created and eventually evolve into symbiotic relationships. Relating to this is the investigation into how far diplomatic protection of multinational firms by the home countries has been or needs to be exercised within the host countries.

Illustration from the recent past sustain the speculation that the transnational corporations remain pre-eminent in the region and that their development needs to be watched. Of course, the most recent instance is shown by the facility with which Japan seemed to call the tune in the ASEAN 1977 ministerial conference in Kuala Lumpur. Prospects to establish pan-ASEAN investment criteria were watered down. Opposition came from a variety of sources. Some thought that the centralization of rules and regulations within one body may in fact enlighten investors, a criticism also faced by the UN Centre for Transnational Corporations. The possibility that one single information point may prejudice some countries exists. Finally, others were wary of the bureaucratic overtones that such an entiry could have. While all these criticisms have some validity, activities that relate to curbing the power of the transnationals in the region are essential, especially from the viewpoint of the long-term political and economic interests of the region. Assessments of the costs and benefits of individual investment projects finding their way into these countries are important. Likewise, the political conduct of corporations already in the region needs to the evaluated and rapidly so. Delays in recognizing consequences of foreign investments mean more opportunities for these firms for manipulation, less control by the countries in minimizing these attempts, and the failure to mould these firms by selective counterpressures to suit national development objectives. Perspectives on the study of the multinational firms in the South-east Asian region will multiply. The challenge though is how to adopt formats that will have the most impact and not lead to confusing people who are seeking change from the alienating, brutalizing structures brought about by their monopolization of power and wealth.

IMPLICATIONS FOR PLANNING

Transnational involvement has significant impacts on planning in the areas where investments are located. Ideally, to plan is to choose, but where choices are limited by the power of the transnational corporation, planning becomes a mere ritual devoted only to cosmetic changes within the environment and often to the benefit of the transnational. Not only are company towns, for instance, managed as independently as possible but on a broader scale, weaker states are treated much like fiefdoms since *de facto* sovereignty in these nations actually belongs to the transnational corporation.

Employment becomes very vulnerable to world demands and to decisions made by headquarters. Allegiance to local and national governments by the transnational workforce and their dependents is undermined by daily reminders that the multinational employee is primarily responsible to the firm's stockholders and decision-makers. The planning of overall economic policies and allocation of resources is influenced by transnational activities. Powerful lobbies backed by wealthy foreign business are able to subvert protectionist policies formulated by the most staunch economic nationalists.

Many governments influenced by a strong colonial history and composed of members with ties to the transnational firms are incapable of controlling and ordering the processes of production so that the internal needs of the society are first met. In fact, in many of the weaker countries, a reverse phenomenon has occurred whereby the enterprises have gained tremendous influence over the workings of government. Certain conditions to guarantee that the abilities of these enterprises function, often in unrestricted ways, are created and sustained by those in authority. These conditions take the form of the banning of strikes and lockouts among workers, the suspension of civil liberties and the repression of human rights to ensure that opposition against transnational practices is controlled. Many of the repressive governments depend on the transnational's presence and continuity for their power and legitimacy, and vice versa. The resources, which the firms are able to create to keep political configurations favourably to their operations intact, are enormous.

The values of the transnational firms become the dominant values which dictate planning orientations. Politics which reflect the people's demands are ignored by the planning process. Popular participation is ruled out and instead, élite guidance and technocratic decision-making are enshrined. Since popular views on the broader social goals are ignored, planning élites never attain as much clarity as to the nature of appropriate national objectives as they need and are unable to effectively release the creative resources for development which could be generated by the population. Only a thin strata linked somehow to the transnational workforce and consumption values benefits.

Where social reforms exist, they are merely given lip service. Moreover, the criteria by which social services such as health, education and housing are judged often relate to the extent that they contribute to productivity, political stability, or satisfactory economic performance.

Careful selection of planning techniques and frameworks appropriate to the internal needs of the society is often disregarded. Instead a cadre of experts is formed, with globally oriented loyalties taking priority, instead of preference for improving local standards. Their function becomes one of legitimizing the interests of those who hold political and economic power, and of acting as the legitimate filter of 'reputable' opinion on public policy (Goulet, 1977).

Planning techniques, organizational systems and work modes begin to follow the capital-intensive models utilized by cities of the industrialized economies. That which pleases the educated eye, usually shaped by images from the industrialized world, becomes the norm. Thus, even though cheaper alternatives may be available by using indigenous resources, they are often incompatible with the planners' preferred images of order and easy management of public affairs. It appears that, as long as the transnational corporations remain so powerful in the region that they can strongly influence the parameters within which national and local planning is carried out, the socio-political and economic changes called for to satisfy the *internal* needs of the general population are unlikely to come about.

REFERENCES

Barratt-Brown, M. (ed.) (1974). *The Anatomy of Underdevelopment*, Spokesman Books, London.

Barnet, R. and Muller, R. (1974). *Global Reach*, Simon and Schuster, New York.

Bock, K. Y. and Harvey, P. (ed.) (1976). *People Toiling Under Pharoah*, Urban Rural Mission, Christian Conference of Asia, Tokyo.

Catley, B. (1976). 'The development of underdevelopment in South-east Asia'. *Journal of Contemporary Asia*, **6**, 54–74.

Drysdale, P. (1972). *Direct Foreign Investment in Asia and the Pacific*, University of Toronto Press, Toronto.

Evans, P. B. (1971). 'National autonomy and economic development, critical perspectives on multinational corporations in poor countries'. *International Organization*, **25**, 656–692.

Frank, A. G. (1971). *Sociology of Development and the Underdevelopment of Sociology*, Pluto Press, London.

Goulet, D. (1977). *The Uncertain Promise: Value Conflicts in Technology Transfer*, IDOC/ North America, New York.

Hoogvelt, A. (1976). *The Sociology of Developing Societies*, The Macmillan Press, London.

Hymer, S. (1974). 'The Multinational Corporation and the Law of Uneven Development'. In J. Bhagwati (ed.), *Economics and the World Order from the 1970s to the 1990s*, The Free Press, New York, pp. 113–141.

Levitt, Kari (1970). *Silent Surrender*, Macmillan of Canada, Toronto.

Martin, R. (1976). 'Who suffers whom? Notes on a Canadian policy towards the Third World'. *Canadian Forum*, **56**, 12–20.

Muller, R. (1975). 'The MNC and the exercise of power: Latin America'. In Abdill Said and Luiz R. Simon (eds.), *The New Sovereigns, MNC's as World Powers*, Prentice-Hall, Englewood Cliffs, New Jersey, pp. 55–67.

Portes, A. (1976). 'On the sociology of national development: theories and issues'. *American Journal of Sociology*, **82**, 55–85.

Sklar, R. L. (1976). 'Postimperialism: A class analysis of multinational corporate expansion'. *Comparative Politics*, **9**, 75–91.

Snow, J. (1976). 'The export processing zone of Asia: The Social impact'. Unpublished Ph.D. thesis, Harvard University.

Wilkins, Mira (1974). *The Maturing of Multinational Enterprise*, Harvard University Press, Cambridge, Massachusetts.

Planning Industrial Development
Edited by David F. Walker

Chapter 9

Industrial Development and Regional Standards of Living in Finland

Mauri Palomäki

Discussions on how to promote regional development through industrialization began in Finland in the early 1960s after a group of studies had shown remarkable differences in the living standards of people in different parts of the country. Planning for development—especially for industrial growth—led to legislation to promote and support enterprises in the development areas. The support has been distributed throughout the development areas but, if calculated either by enterprise or per capita, Northern and Eastern Finland have gained the most. This has resulted in the relatively greater growth of manufacturing employment in development areas than in industrial Finland, so that the importance of industry has grown in underdeveloped parts of the country. During the ongoing period of economic depression the unemployment rate has been one of the lowest in the administrative province of Vaasa, an underdeveloped area of the country where industrialization was strongest a few years earlier. Whether or not all the favourable results can be attributed to regional policy is still an open question.

ADVANCEMENT OF RESEARCH AND SOME CENTRAL CONCEPTS

Research on regional development has a long tradition in Finland. Hustich and Wahlbeck (1952), and Wahlbeck (1955), described the regional distribution of income and the factors affecting it—studies originating from the personal interest of individual researchers unconnected to regional planning as such. Although differences in income interpreted regionally were most remarkable, there was no immediate reason to change them.

Later, and especially amongst the political decision-makers, the regional differences in income level were considered to be unjustifiable, and efforts were made to improve the situation. In the State Planning Office, which at that time was responsible for regional planning on a national level, a study on the regional divergencies of development in Finland was begun (Palmgren, 1964). For the first time in the progress of research in Finland, this study attempted to construct a 'synthetic indicator of development' using as elements many individual factors connected with stages of economic, social and cultural development. The ultimate aim was to find an objective measure which could be used for dividing Finland into zones of development. Palmgren, however, stressed that the concept of development was poorly defined and, in any case, relative in character.

Riihinen (1965) also succeeded in improving the definition of concepts. He divided the concept of development into two parts: goal-development and facilities-development. Goal development is concerned with what all citizens of a country should have—that is prerequisites for a good standard of living, including nourishment, housing, services and employment. This kind of development ought to have the same measured rate in all parts of the country. Facilities-development refers to the means whereby the population reaches its standard of living. The same goal can be obtained in one part of the country with advanced agriculture, in another with industry, or in a third region where services form the basis for equally good living standards.

The concepts formulated by Riihinen can be used as a starting point for this article. They focus on the way the ultimate objective of regional policy in Finland, an even standard of living (goal-development), has been approached by using one measure or policy for increasing the degree of industrialization (facilities-development). Unfortunately, such a clearcut dichotomy of concepts does not lead very far. In the progress of research there have been two areas of difficulty. The precise definition of 'standard of living' itself has turned out to be complicated, and the measurement of the regional variation operationally problematic.

As a concept, standard of living comes close to that of social welfare. The latter, obviously, is wider and more general. Social welfare could be analysed by using as a criterion: the extent to which the human needs of a society have been satisfied. This leads to the task of defining operationally human needs, and everything becomes even more complicated. It is easy to enumerate normal human needs and even to put them into an order of importance but researchers have found so many needs that the handling of their lists creates new difficulties (Allardt, 1976). The solution has been an introduction of need-hierarchies, but even this direction has proved to be problematic.

It is very difficult to measure the degree of the need-satisfaction of different kinds of social groups. Even within a group individual opinions on the degree of need-satisfaction vary widely. It is even possible to manipulate the opinions in a positive or negative direction. So it is quite understandable that no ready statistics exist covering large areas and illuminating the degree of people's welfare. Consequently, at this stage of research one must abandon the welfare concept as an indicator of regional development, however good it may be in principle.

The concept 'standard of living' is more restricted. It has, however, so much in common with welfare that measuring the standard of living gives a fair understanding of the extent to which the needs of a social group have been satisfied. The level of income was earlier considered as an excellent indicator of standard of living—in fact, it was thought that all other possible factors should be of a secondary importance. Lately the views have been so oriented, in fact, that the level of income in the Western way of life can be considered as a basis for creating the standard of living (Hustich, 1968, p. 157). When measuring the standard of living one has to fix attention on the things which can be bought by money directly or indirectly. If selection of this kind of indicator is successful and produces rationally explainable regional variation, it is also suitable to measure regional development.

THE REGIONAL VARIATION OF DEVELOPMENT IN FINLAND

Among the many studies made for practical regional policy in Finland, those by Lauri Hautamäki (1969; 1973) seem to me to be the most remarkable. They describe the phenomenon and its regional variation in a very clear way, with opportunities for immediate application. They have been of great significance in planning regional policy and programmes in Finland. The following description of the problem is based mainly on a study for controlling the division of Finland into development zones (Kehitysalueiden neuvottelukunta, 1973).

In order to analyse development in Finland's various regions, considerable statistical material was collected. Of four groups, the first consisted of ten variables selected with a view to their capability of measuring the standard of living, such as level of housing, employment, schooling and contentment. A second group consisted of eighteen variables describing the structure of the population and the economy of municipalities. They are not direct measures of standard of living, but have influence on the potential for providing a good standard of living. The third group was formed by eight variables describing the special preconditions of different economic activities. The needs of industry and services were especially considered, such as access to traffic arteries and service equipment. The final group of eleven variables describe the economic strength of municipalities, such as the number of income tax units, the value of a tax unit, self-sufficiency with regard to jobs and location in the network of central places. Altogether, forty-seven different variables were involved in the analysis.

The Factor of Industrialization

Principal component analysis was used as the statistical method to determine general features in the material, and this gave easily interpretable results. The first factor (1) was characterized as the factor of industrialization. Heavy loadings accumulated on the following variables: number of tax units per inhabitant, high income per inhabitant, high proportion of matriculated and intermediate grade students, positive balance of migration and the share of economically active population in industry.

After rotating, other factors could be interpreted as follows: (2) factor of an unfavourable population structure, (3) factor of Swedish-speaking archipelago, (4) factor of small and non-self-sufficient municipalities and (5) factor of periphery.

Obviously the factor of industrialization is best suited for describing the regional development of Finland, because it is the most general of all factors found by principal component analysis and the components characterizing it are also easily understood as components of the standard of living. For regionalization of the results, factor points for each municipality were calculated in such a way that the national mean would be 500 with the variation occurring around it so that the lower the number, the higher the standard of living and the better the municipality's state of development.

The results of the latest study(Hautamäki, 1973) do not differ in any great degree from the earlier ones of Palmgren (1964), Riihinen (1965), and Hautamäki (1969). Figure 9.1 shows that the high state of development is insular in character. Cities and nearby rural municipalities are well-developed areas, while even in prosperous parts of the country there are peripheral municipalities with a remarkably low state of development. It is possible, however, to find that the degree of underdevelopment increases from the south-west to the north-east of the country. This happens to the lowest values in the region as well as to the highest ones.

The latter result justifies dividing Finland into broad development zones according to the industrialization factor. Again the result comes close to that obtained by earlier pieces of research (Hustich, 1971). In the analysis of the degree of homogeneity of the zones (Hautamäki, 1975, p. 112), it was found that the variation of development inside the zones was smaller than between them. Differences between the rural municipalities belonging to separate zones are particularly clear. The degree of development also varies according to zone in the group of urban municipalities, but the differences are not as clear as in rural areas. In fact, in a statistical analysis, the administrative status of a municipality explains the variation of development better than the other factors. Basically this depends on the fact that the economic and social conditions prevailing in urbanized areas have been defined as 'developed'.

Consequently, Finland maintains the same situation found in all well-developed countries. There is a highly developed prosperous core area and underdeveloped peripheral areas. In Finland the underdeveloped part covers a much larger area than the core, but far more people live in the core area. The underdeveloped areas are characterized by an old-fashioned economic structure with a high proportion of primary activities and consequent high structural unemployment. The income level of the population is growing more slowly

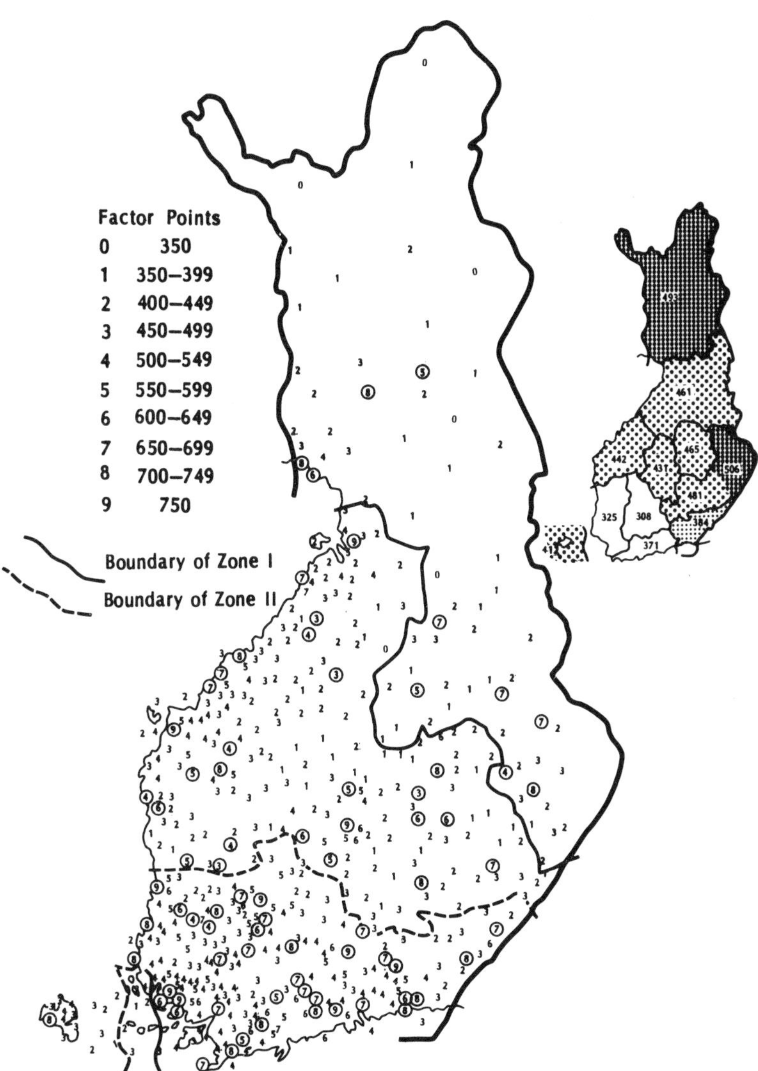

FIGURE 9.1. Degree of development in Finland and the development zones. The higher the sum of factor points, the more developed the municipality. The numbers on the map have been located at the centre of the municipality. Numbers referring to the urban municipalties are encircled. The inset map shows development by lääni

than in other parts of the country. The population is diminishing as a result of rapid out-migration, which also leads to an ageing population with a shortage of working age people. The service equipment of centres is also less developed and therefore education, medical care, variety of retail trade and even the quality of administration lag behind the average level of the country.

Zones of Development Areas

Northern and Eastern Finland are most backward, and therefore together they form the 'first zone' of development areas. In Central and Western Finland the situation is clearly healthier, so that the most developed parts correspond well with the areas in industrial Finland. It is appropriate, however, to form a wide area in Central Finland as the 'second zone' of development areas, to carry on a feasible regional policy. Because of their insular nature and position, the municipalities of the south-western archipelago also belong to the development areas. The rest of the country makes up industrial Finland. In demarcating the zones of development the functional regions have been used, especially the present-day provinces (Palomäki, 1968, p. 284).

The factor analysis showed qualitative differences in the state of development which must have significance for the selection of the measures to be taken in development policy. They may cause differences even inside a single zone. For instance, the archipelago is characterized by a relatively high standard of living, but also by an ageing and declining population. In the northern and eastern periphery the situation is reversed. The standard of living is low, but both population growth and especially its structure are favourable. The former regions, according to Hustich (1968, p. 166), are secondary underdeveloped areas where the economic activity has earlier been more lively compared to the national average. The latter are primary underdeveloped areas, where the economic activity has never been higher than at present. Hustich (1968, p. 165) considers them as economic reserve areas.

WORKING AND PLANNING FOR CHANGE

Policies to improve the standard of living in underdeveloped areas had already begun before the study mentioned above was published. At the beginning of the 1960s the State Planning Office was founded, and one of its important duties was to influence, by means of research and proposals for action, the equalization of development in the different regions. Unfortunately, this arrangement did not prove to be satisfactory. To make planning more efficient, the Council of Underdeveloped Areas was founded on a very high level in the Finnish administrative hierarchy. This council, with its many special sections, was to play the leading role in the formation of legislation concerning the underdeveloped areas.

There were lively discussions about the goals of development and the methods to be used. Help should be given to all main occupations. New methods of support are necessary to develop agriculture and related occupations, such as forestry, fur farming, fisheries, and market gardening using greenhouses, in addition to traditional means of support. However, prompting the industrialization process was considered the most important means of development because it was believed that results would ensue most rapidly from this measure. Tourism was found as an occupation with possibilities for expansion, especially in North and East Finland. Services were considered only as far as there was a need to support retail trade in areas of diminishing population with scattered settlement (Kehitysalueiden neuvottelukunta, 1974a).

Two kinds of opinions arose in Finland on how to direct the support regionally. The agrarian parties and those connected with them, in particular, demanded a basically even support across the development zones (with some weighting according to need). Such a policy was considered as the most equitable. Finland, however, is a big country with a small population. In planning for development policies, very sizeable areas were proposed for support. Quite soon a question of efficiency arose. It was doubted whether it was possible to reach satisfactory results everywhere, because such widely spread and scanty resources diminished the economic efficiency of operations. This brought forth a school of growth centre policy, which placed efficiency objectives as the most important criteria for development aid. This policy would concentrate the support in a few centres to make sure that exceptional results would be obtained somewhere. As objectives of support, only those centres were to be selected where possibilities of growth were judged to be good once they received an impulse to begin. Several alternative systems of central places for growth centre policy were presented; they were even structured hierarchically into three levels: growth areas, growth centres proper, and growth points (Kehitysalueiden neuvottelukunta, 1974b).

Nevertheless, plans to start the growth centre policy in Finland did not get under way as no means could be found for the development of centres on different levels. The selection among alternative central place systems also proved to be overwhelmingly difficult. For these reasons, there was stronger support for an evenly distributed development policy, regulated through a division into zones. Thus the two first acts for development regions, each of five years' duration, were implemented according to the ideology of aiming for strict regional equality.

Planning Policies for Underdeveloped Areas

Outside the legislation for development regions proper there has also been another kind of planning to improve the living standard in underdeveloped areas. Several policies are currently in operation—the government has supported significantly *the production of housing facilities*. In recent years the share given to the underdeveloped areas has grown in relation to other parts of Finland. The classification of municipalities *according to the cost of living* is a tool to regulate the size of salaries and some social income transfers, and it is designed to compensate for the differences in living costs between the municipalities (established by comparing the prices of the most important commodities).

The system of social security services and the social policy planning in Finland is, in general, confused, and neither regional policy nor circumstances prevailing in underdeveloped areas have been taken into consideration. There are no national-level goals, or even norms, to follow so the variation between individual municipalities is considerable.

According to a *system of additional payment in peripheral areas* civil servants receive higher wages (up to 20 per cent) than elsewhere in Finland. So-called peripheral points are calculated for every municipality. The additional payment is measured according to these points. Population density, the distance from central places, coldness of the climate, the nearness of Finland's land boundary, circumstances of the archipelago and lack of roads are taken into account in the calculation. This kind of support applies particularly to the underdeveloped areas.

There is also a special *classification of municipalities according to their capacity to carry the costs of certain services*. Through this system (which has ten grades) the government supports municipalities in different degrees to level the disparities in municipal services caused by the varying wealth of municipalities; medical care and education are especially involved. The work began in 1969, and its field has been constantly enlarged.

The *regional support of agriculture* is directed through the aid of milk and meat production and milk transportation. There are, furthermore, subsidies for cattle farming, the keeping of a cow and production of rye, as well as aid for transportation of agricultural products and supplies in Northern Finland. There are ten support measures and unfortunately each one has a regional division of its own, none of which corresponds to the development zones. The support for agriculture is particularly important to the underdeveloped areas, because an economy with a predominating agriculture is a distinctive feature of underdevelopment.

The investment tax also has regional consequences, because it hits industrial Finland. It is based on the construction of non-residential buildings, both public and private. The amount of the tax can be 40 per cent of costs of construction.

Planning which was not geared to the economy has also brought progress to the economy of underdeveloped areas. The distribution of university level education and research was still centralized in southern Finland to a great extent just after the Second World War. In addition to Helsinki (the capital), only Turku, the former national centre, had a university. Nearly all other tertiary-level special institutions, with the exception of a college of education in Jyväskylä, were located in Helsinki and Turku. Now, however, new universities operate in several locations: there are fully fledged universities in Tampere, Oulu, and Jyväskylä, a School of Economics in Vaasa, a Medical School in Kuopio, a Humanistic-Pedagogic School in Joensuu, and a College of Technology in Lappeenranta and Tampere. The situation has altered greatly (Palomäki and Taina, 1973, pp. 43–46).

The regional expansion of Finland's tertiary education has brought many remarkable benefits. Now that it is possible to study academically in the underdeveloped areas, costs of studying have decreased, encouraging long-term university studies. Graduates have taken jobs near the university, raising the level of knowledge in general as well as the level of management in enterprises. Considerable sums of money have been channelled into university centres, not only from public funds, but also from students coming from surrounding areas and all over the country. The university centres of underdeveloped areas have established their academic credibility and are now on a more equal basis with the centres of industrial Finland.

It is worth mentioning that there is still one ambitious plan for locating considerable capital city functions outside Helsinki. The system of administration in Finland has always been quite centralized, and the power of decision-making even in small affairs has been, to a high degree, concentrated on Helsinki. To redress the situation, a three-phase plan was drawn up to transfer offices, including those in the highest bureaucratic hierarchy, into nineteen other cities (Decentralization Committee, 1974, p. 47). The plan raised a storm of discussion and opposition in the capital and surroundings, and no firm decisions to move have yet been made. The economic depression, with difficulties even in government finance, has proved to be an additional obstacle to decentralization.

I have presented here many such plans and development measures which have a more or less conscious goal for decreasing the regional differences of development. There are still more similar measures in operation. The purpose of my list is to show the different kinds and more or less parallel measures which have been undertaken. I hope this illustrates that it is difficult to measure and judge the effects of only one kind of support—the support of industry—and to separate it from the effects of other measures.

SUPPORT FOR INDUSTRY IN UNDERDEVELOPED AREAS

The first law concerning underdeveloped regions proper was an act to promote the economy of underdeveloped areas, in force between 1966–69. Simultaneously the laws on tax reliefs and investment credits were implemented (EFTA Committee, 1971, p. 134). The second phase was during 1974–75, when another law for promoting the economy in development regions was in force. This formed a basis for a body of special laws serving the same purpose. It included the law on credits to those firms operating in development regions, the law on tax relief for promoting the production activities in developing areas, the law on labour financing of productive activities in development areas, the law on transport subsidies in development areas, the law on the Regional Development Fund, the law on credits, with subsidized interest to the municipalities of development areas in order to promote enterprise activities, and the law on professional schooling in development areas (EFTA Committee, 1971, pp. 134–137).

There have also been attempts to evaluate the general effects of the laws mentioned above. It has been found that they have really benefited growth of production, increase of employment and earnings, and the standard of living in underdeveloped areas. The developmental measures have not resulted in a great movement of firms into the underdeveloped areas; they have, however, encouraged the growth of production in underdeveloped areas and, especially, the foundation of new enterprises in middle-sized centres and their commuting areas. Despite this, the population of underdeveloped areas still decreased as a consequence of migration.

The developments which have taken place and the estimates of future conditions showed that the second round of development legislation did not have enough strength to balance regional development. The experience of applying the measures brought to light limitations in their internal structure. The measures were directed at too a narrow a field of activities with influence on development. They also proved ineffective because they limited development policy to the less developed parts of the country.

In 1975, the third body of development laws was established. The general law is now called the law on the promotion of regional development, and it defines the main principles and premises of developmental activities. In this legislation one can notice a clear shift from an underdeveloped area policy towards a more comprehensive regional policy. The division of the country into zones will be preserved, but adjustments will allow the most underdeveloped parts to be defined as areas of additional support, where the measures are stronger than in other areas. The importance of the regional aspect in all planning will be stressed, especially at national and provincial levels of government.

THE FLOW OF CAPITAL INTO UNDERDEVELOPED AREAS

It is highly laborious, if not impossible, to clarify precisely the amounts of money that were directed to industry in underdeveloped areas during the two first periods of legislation on development area policies. This is very important information for judging the results of activities and comparing them to changes in the standard of living in different parts of the country. It would have been useful to have information on the amount of support to every municipality, but this proved impossible. However, countywise there was sufficient statistical data available.

During the period of the *first laws* on development areas (1966–69), the laws on investment credits and tax concessions proved to be the most remarkable. The law on investment credits was based on the principle of assistance on interest charges. The loan was obtained from an ordinary bank, but the debtor paid 5 per cent interest at most while the state covered the rest, which in general meant more than a half of it. Underdeveloped Finland received a total of about 230 million Fmk as loans in this way, which were used for a total of 105 objectives. It has been calculated that with this aid about 3400 new jobs were established mainly (75 per cent) in the first zone. But, as about two-thirds of all these jobs could have been established even without any assistance on interest charges, one has to estimate the total effect of this law as 1100 new jobs (Lehikoinen, 1972, p. 10).

The law on tax concessions provided two kinds of tax relief. Under certain conditions the firms enjoy the right of free depreciation on fixed assets in the years of acquisition and for nine subsequent years. In the first zone the taxpayer may, for a period of ten years, deduct a further 3 per cent per year of the purchase value of the working assets used in the project. The investments under tax concessions produced more than 8000 new jobs, of which about 6500 were in the first zone.

During the period of validity of the *second generation* of development laws (1970–76), banks and other financial institutions granted 1.2 milliard Fmk loans on development area terms. It has been estimated that this money has created altogether 42 000 new jobs in underdeveloped areas. The second zone received 72 per cent of the loans.

The foundation of the Regional Development Fund (RDF) in 1971 was a very significant additional measure in development policy. It is a credit company and the majority of its shares are state-owned; the RDF finances enterprises operating in underdeveloped areas or are moving there. As well as providing finance, the Fund has as a further objective to advance economic activity in underdeveloped areas through research and product development. In addition to industrial enterprises, the Fund finances tourist, fur farming, market gardening, nurseries and service enterprises. Its prime objectives are small and medium-sized or other labour-dominated enterprises, who are exporting their products or substituting for imported goods. Another goal is the growth of the size of firms and the raising of the level of management in all fields of economic activity. The RDF during the first five years of activity has used about 740 million Fmk, which has created an estimated 28 000 new jobs in underdeveloped areas; about 63 per cent of the money was invested in the second zone.

To judge the results of development policy for industry regionally, the main task of this article, one must first have a picture of the intensity of measures

TABLE 9.1. Comparison of the change in development and the volume of development aid by *läänis*

Lääni	Development			Development aid 1970–76		
	1964	1974	Differ-ence	m. Fmk	1000 Fmk/ enterprise	Fmk/inhabitant
Uusimaa	29	33	4	1	1	1
Turku and Pori	20	28	8	125	103	181
Ahvenanmaa	12	20	8	12	322	554
Häme	23	28	5	36	30	55
Kymi	19	26	7	11	26	33
Mikkeli	12	18	6	303	1130	1422
Pohjois-Karjala	10	20	10	373	2192	2090
Kuopio	12	22	10	447	1781	1776
Keski-Suomi	15	23	8	338	1305	1429
Vaasa	14	24	10	732	948	1730
Oulu	12	23	11	461	1078	1154
Lappi	12	20	8	459	2650	2332

as a whole and the regional division. Unfortunately, no overall calculation of the sums of money used or of the new jobs created exists. I have, therefore, tried to collect material from the sources mentioned above.

In preparing Figure 9.2 and Table 9.1 only data which are directed to promoting industrial growth have been used. As a source one synopsis made by the planning board of the Prime Minister's office (Valtioneuvoston Kanslia, Katsaus 1, 1977) was valuable. In the calculation the development region credits (1.8 milliard Fmk) provided by the Ministry of Commerce and Industry between 1970 and 1976 were included. These loans carry assistance on interest charges. Also involved are the investment, start-up, and labour training programmes, which have brought direct financial aid to the firms since 1975 (125 million Fmk) as well as the support for transportation in underdeveloped areas since 1973 (71.8 million Fmk). The loans provided by the RDF between 1970 and 1976 are, of course, a very significant item (1.3 milliard Fmk) in the calculation. Because of the strong inflation prevalent in Finland during the period studied, the sums of money have been adjusted to the value of money in 1976.

The southernmost administrative *läänis** of Finland have gained very little from these aids because only their most peripheral sections belong to the underdeveloped areas. Even the relative significance of support there is negligible.

*It is inaccurate to translate the name of the Finnish regional administrative body, *lääni*, as having general administrative duties. It is more or less a representative of central government on a regional level and, therefore, differs functionally from the Anglo-Saxon county or province. It is regionally different, too. Counties are, especially compared with America, smaller than *läänis*, and in Finland there might be several provinces in one *lääni*. Because of this and its shortness, the Finnish form, *lääni*, is used here.

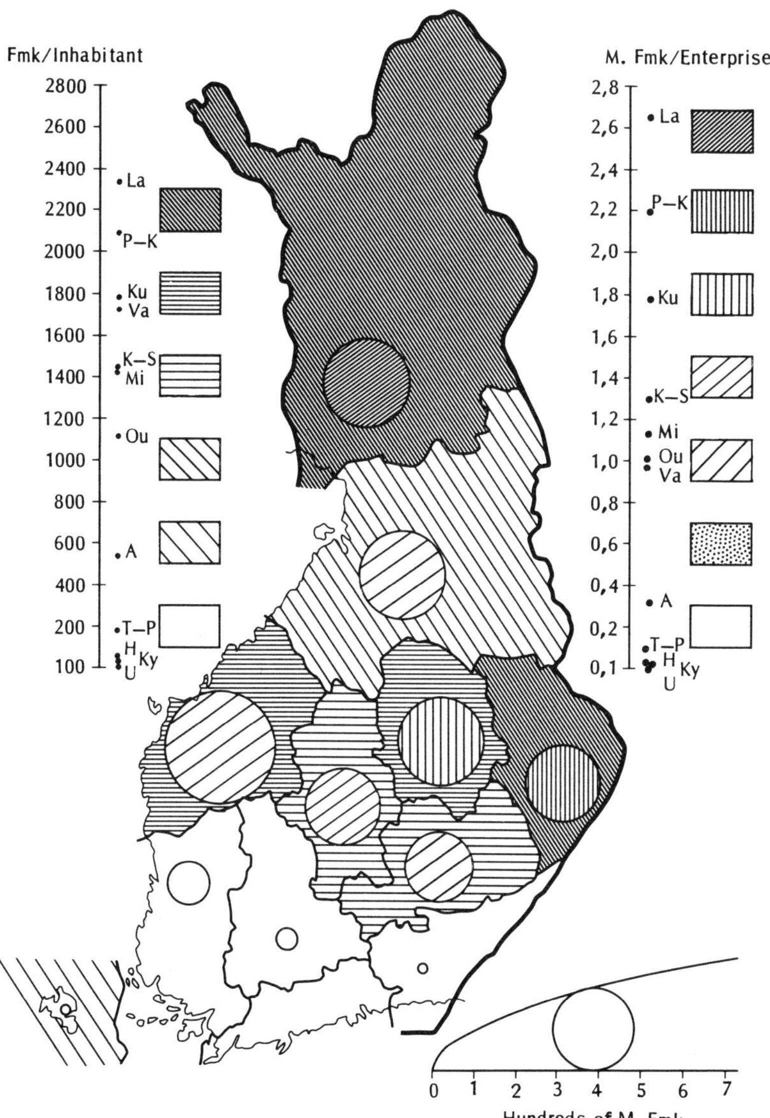

FIGURE 9.2. Development aid to the Finnish counties. The letters in the appended diagrams are shortenings of the names of Läänis (see Figure 9.4)

The largest sum of money was directed to the *lääni* of Vaasa (about 730 million Fmk). The *läänis* of Oulu, Lappi and Kuopio have received approximately 460 million Fmk each. The *lääni* of Pohjois-Karjala received nearly 400 million Fmk, and the *läänis* of Keski-Suomi and Mikkeli more than 300 million Fmk. Of the support as a whole, (3.3 milliard Fmk) the second zone of underdeveloped regions received more than two-thirds. This contrasts with an emphasis on zone 1 under the first development laws.

The *läänis* of development regions are, however, very different from each other with regard to their economic structure and population. Therefore, the relative distribution of support varies regionally in ways other than the absolute sums of money. The support per establishment in industry is by far the biggest, for instance, in the *lääni* of Lappi and considerable too in Pohjois-Karjala and Kuopio. Support calculated in this manner is smallest in Vaasa, a region characterized by a great number of small enterprises. On a per capita basis, the support is divided more evenly, but in its main features it is the same as the distribution counted per establishment. The *lääni* of Vaasa is, however, among those with plenty of support.

If the development measures directed mainly to support industry have the desired effect, the results ought to be seen most clearly in Northern and Eastern Finland and in the *lääni* of Vaasa. This is true, assuming the other measures with an influence on the degree of development are regionally directed in the same way. However, this assumption, obviously, is true only in some cases.

RESULTS OF DEVELOPMENT POLICIES

In order to estimate the success of the development policies practised in Finland, there must be new studies of the distribution of development using the same indicators and methods as Hautamäki (1973) (Figure 9.1). That, however, is not possible for this article. Hautamäki used much data which is available only from population censuses or special studies. Omissions in the published statistics mean that data must be collected from archives to reach an adequate degree of accuracy for municipalities. On the other hand, there is plenty of such data available which suits the estimation of development in a coarser regional division. This has been used here.

The factors have been chosen from the matrix of all variables in the principal component analysis presented by Hautamäki (1973, p. 57). The heaviest loadings on its factor of industrialization were received by the variables connected with income level (taxed income per inhabitant), variables connected with the level of education (persons with matriculation examination as per cent of population) and degree of industrialization. Variables describing population changes (net migration and increasing or decreasing population) are also important as are some variables depicting contentment (density of television licences in population). The rate of unemployment, furthermore, can be considered as a strong factor influencing the regional behaviour of people. The division of Finland into *läänis* was the only possible regional framework in this comparison.

To describe the changes in the degree of development, data concerning the above-mentioned variables were taken before the laws on regional development were in power and as late as statistics permitted. The data show mainly the changes in the period from 1964–74. Mean values for three-year phases were also calculated and the mean was centred to 1964 and 1974.

Figure 9.3 gives an overall picture of the results of development activities. The size of the sectors shows the distribution of actual values of selected variables. Such values have been changed into index values with that for the whole country in 1964 equal to 100, and every *lääni* gets its share. The values for 1974 have been calculated using as a base the value in 1964 for the country as a whole. This brings out the absolute growth of different variables and keeps the different components of development comparable. The relative values depicting the state of development have been marked in sectors using shadings. The principle on which it is based is: the greater the development, the darker the shading.

The numbers describing the state of development have been marked on Figure 9.4. The situation before development laws can be seen on the left-hand side, and that after the law's influence on the right-hand side. Each *lääni* has its own symbol. The angle of the line connecting the symbols can be interpreted for visualizing the speed of development in the *lääni* in question.

Degree of Industrialization

Most of the money used for the growth of the economy in underdeveloped areas has been directed towards industry. During the study period, Finland lived through a strong phase of industrialization. One-sided orientation to wood and wood-related industries, so characteristic of Finland earlier, clearly changed towards a more varied industrial structure. To describe the regional changes in industrial activity, changes in labour force (salaried employees and wage earners) between 1964–74 were chosen (Official Statistics of Finland, 1967 and 1977), because the first objective of development policy has been to increase employment in underdeveloped regions.

During the period studied the industrial labour force in Finland grew from 425 000 to 556 000, and the rate of industrialization from 93 to 188 employees per 1000 inhabitants. Growth was distributed in all *läänis*, but was fastest in the western part of industrial Finland. In Vaasa the growth was great too, but it was only small in the *lääni* of Kymi.

The degree of industrialization rose everywhere except Uusimaa, where the increase of industry was smaller than the expansion of other occupations. It increased fastest in the *lääni* of Turku and Pori (36 per cent), but in Vaasa the

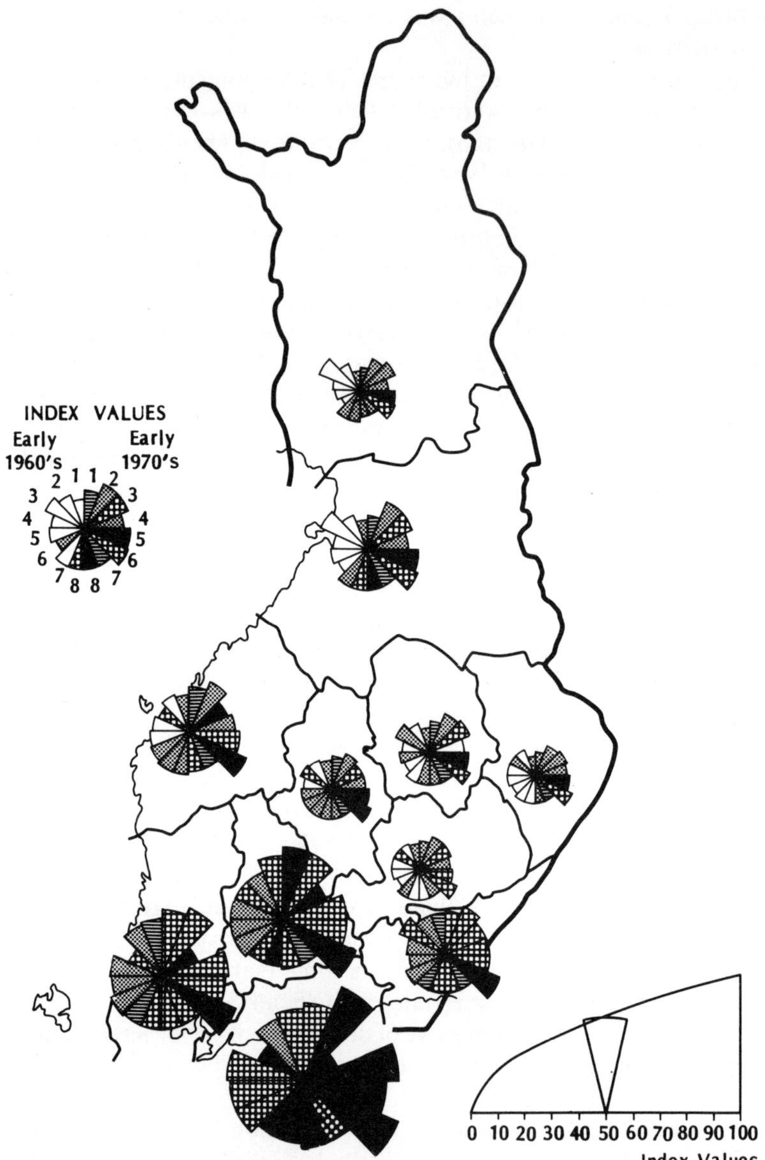

FIGURE 9.3. Growth of selected indicators. (1) Industry. (2) Gross national product. (3) Unemployment. (4) Incomes. (5) Students in senior secondary schools. (6) Television licences. (7) Migrants. (8) Change of population. The meaning of shadings can be read from the diagrams in Figure 9.4

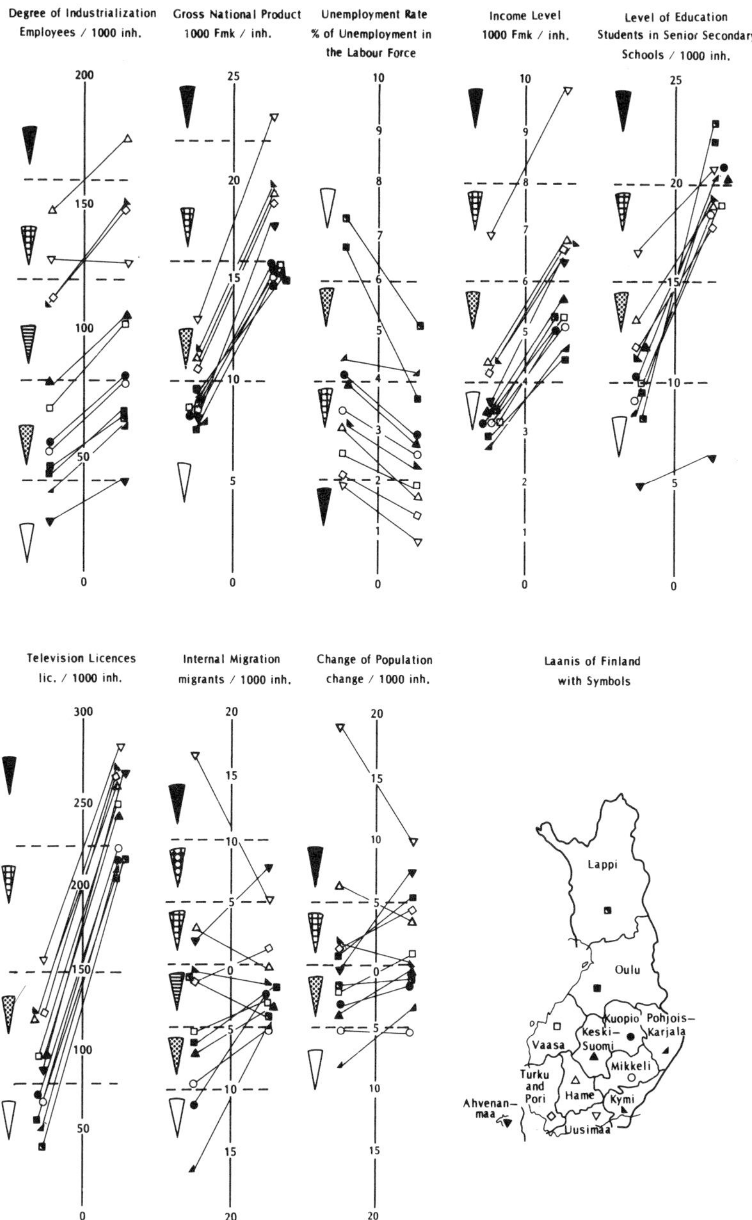

FIGURE 9.4. Change of the degree of development. The situation in the early 1960s is on the left- and that of the early 1970s on the right-hand side of the diagrams. The shaded sectors are explanations for Figure 9.3

growth was only slightly slower (34 per cent). The speed of increase varied between 21 and 28 per cent in other parts of underdeveloped areas. The average growth in underdeveloped areas was 25 per cent, while in industrial Finland it was 21 per cent.

It appears the industrialization policy has succeeded in speeding up the growth of industry in underdeveloped areas, especially the degree of industrialization. Taking the crude number of new jobs in industry as a measure one can, however, find that the increase in Industrial Finland has been nearly double that of underdeveloped areas. This fact shows concretely that factors other than development area policy influence the industrialization process, and that the total force of the other factors is greater than the strength of the regional policy practised until now.

Gross National Product

The way of keeping accounts in the Finnish economy makes it possible to calculate regional cross-sections and to follow development over time. The main difficulty is that about 9 per cent of total production cannot be regionalized. In the source used here (the Prime Minister's Office, 1977) the data was from the years 1960 and 1973, which made the period under comparison longer than that employed in the other analyses.

The gross national product nearly doubled in Finland in thirteen years, from 48.7 milliard Fmk in 1960 to 95.0 milliard Fmk in 1973 as calculated in 1976 money value. Regionally the growth has been balanced in the sense that there was a strong increase in all *läänis*. The growth was fastest in the *läänis* of Uusimaa, Häme and Oulu (Figure 9.3). Progress was slow in the *läänis* of Mikkeli and Pohjois-Karjala and it also seems to have become slower in the *läänis* of Lappi and Keski-Suomi.

The growth of gross national product (Figure 9.4) calculated on a per capita basis has also been remarkable. Even the poorest *läänis* in 1973 have surpassed the richest ones in 1960. Differences between *läänis* have, however, become clearer. There are now three clearcut groups while in the earlier situation they were far less definite. The *lääni* of Uusimaa stands in proud solitude as a consequence of very rapid growth. The other *läänis* of industrial Finland form a firm group in which Ahvenanmaa can now be incorporated. In the group of *läänis* in underdeveloped areas the growth seems to be slower than elsewhere.

The analysis carried out with the help of gross national product exposes a type of development in which there is growth in the whole region, but those parts best developed in the beginning have made the greatest progress.

Unemployment

There are problems in using unemployment as a measure of development. In Finland unemployment can be characterized as structural because even in economically favourable years there is unemployment in the underdeveloped parts of the country. Yet in industrialized regions there prevails at the same time a severe shortage of labour. In underdeveloped areas, people have been released from agriculture faster than new jobs in other occupations have been established. Unemployment depends much on economic fluctuations, too. A depression affecting forest industries causes difficulties in employment everywhere in the country. The rate of unemployment also varies according to the seasons, with summer as the best and late winter the worst time.

To take into account the great variability of unemployment, three-year averages of unemployment were calculated. Because of the quality of statistics (Ministry of Labour, 1976) a short period from 1967–69 and 1973–75 was used, which does not correspond well with other material used in this section of the article. The regional divisions have also caused difficulties, because the authorities responsible for employment administration have a division of their own. With some difficulty this was converted into the *lääni*-division.

The presentation of unemployment in Figures 9.3 and 9.4 also caused technical inconsistency, because development lines going down to the right on Figure 9.4 must be interpreted as favourable. The shadings of sectors in Figure 9.3 have, however, been kept comparable to the other sectors. In other words, the darker the shading, the more favourable the development.

Few dramatic differences exist in the amount of unemployed but the total labour force in the area naturally affects the rate of unemployment. The regional variation of this rate follows the variation in development quite consistently. The *lääni* of Vaasa is quite close to the *läänis* in industrial Finland. The *läänis* of Oulu, Lappi and Pohjois-Karjala belong to the most difficult areas. Changes were favourable overall especially in the *läänis* of Lappi and Oulu. As was the case with gross national product, no groups are formed on the basis of the unemployment rate. The *läänis* in the figure are only in an order of superiority and are nearly equally spaced. The difference between the best and the worst is, nevertheless, great, and it did not decrease to a noteworthy extent during the period studied.

Since 1975 the economy of Finland has fallen into difficulties, because the worldwide depression has hit the most important industrial sector, wood-related industries. Since investment decreased, the machine industry and shipbuilding have also been unable to operate to full capacity, causing large-scale unemployment not only in the periphery but also in the industrialized core areas. Regions such as the *läänis* of Uusimaa and Vaasa, with varied industries seem to have succeeded best in their campaign against unemployment.

Income Level

Statistics covering every aspect of Finnish income do not exist. The data on the regional variation of income level must be gathered from municipal taxation statistics (Central Statistical Office, 1963 and 1973). As an indicator of the development of the regional income level, the per capita taxable income in *läänis* in the years 1963 and 1973 was used. Data were converted into 1973 money value using the consumer price index. Thus income increased during the period studied in Finland from 19.2 milliard Fmk to 31.9 milliard Fmk.

Regionally, the amount of income seems to have grown quite evenly. In the *lääni* of Uusimaa, however, the increase has been the greatest. The growth of income level per person resembles that of gross national product to a great degree. Uusimaa, again, is distinguished clearly, with the fastest growth of income level. The group of the developed *läänis* was cohesive at the beginning and by the end Ahvenanmaa had joined the group. The rate of growth of income level has been slower than that of other variables. The *lääni* of Keski-Suomi has succeeded best, while Oulu was the weakest.

Number of Students in Senior Secondary Schools

The number of students in senior secondary schools has been selected here to describe the level of education of the population. The period studied is between 1964–65 and 1974–75 (Central Statistical Office, 1965 and 1975). Senior secondary schools in Finland have concentrated on giving a good standard education in order to prepare young people for university. From the point of view of economic growth the share of university graduates in the population would be an even more interesting figure, but it is available only from population censuses and does not fit in the time-division used here. The mass of students in senior secondary schools grew briskly in every *lääni* (Figure 9.3). The regional division of growth has been characterized by a special feature. The growth in the *läänis* of Uusimaa and Ahvenanmaa was only 1.5-fold, and the further north and east the *lääni* is located, the higher the coefficient of growth: in Pohjois-Karjala 2.1, in Oulu 2.2, in Lappi not less than 2.6. A growth of this kind can be interpreted to mean that the crest of the innovation wave of study in senior secondary schools has just now reached the most underdeveloped parts of Finland.

The change in the relative number of students in senior secondary schools has been very impressive regionally (Figure 9.4). Ahvenanmaa, with its weak position, is a special case. The *läänis* with the *lowest* positions in the school year 1964–65 can be found at the *top* of the list ten years later. The change can be best interpreted to mean that more alternative places have been available for young people to study in developed *läänis* (for example, in technical, commercial, and agricultural institutes). As a matter of fact, a balanced schooling system better represents a high rate of development than an overproportional growth of any part of education. It is interesting to find such an excessive growth as a type of development.

Television Licences

The study period happens to cover the time when television really became common in Finland. Every television set needs a licence before it can be used, so the growth of the number of licences mirrors well how this innovation has been diffused through the country. In 1963 there were about 476 000 licences and in 1972 about 1 182 000 (Central Statistical Office, 1963 and 1972). The growth was not less than 2.5-fold.

In the southern and western *läänis* the growth has been 'only' 2 to 2.5-fold, but in eastern and northern *läänis* 3 to 4-fold, and in Lappi, the most extreme *lääni*, 5.5-fold. The growth resembles that of students in senior secondary school, but is more evenly distributed regionally. The density of television licences varied in 1963 from 40 to 155 per 1000 inhabitants, and the *läänis* had the usual order as shown in Figure 9.4. In 1972 the order was nearly the same, but the differences in density had become much narrower: from 210 to 280. This type of development represents a model of equalized regional growth. This is what the development area policy is striving for.

Internal Migration

Internal migration has been described here through net migration. In order to lessen the influence of random fluctuations, three-year averages at the beginning and at the end (1962–63 and 1974–76) of the period (1963–76) are taken. Migration has decreased considerably, but because of the method of presentation, it cannot be so easily seen in Figure 9.3. In relative terms the change comes strongly to the foreground. The enormous increase in population through migration in the *lääni* of Uusimaa at the beginning of the 1960s was later reduced to a moderate size; even Ahvenanmaa surpassed it. The *läänis* with a severe decrease through migration at the beginning now have a much better position, especially the *lääni* of Pohjois-Karjala.

There is, of course, a great temptation to explain such positive development as an outcome of a successful industrialization policy. It could, unfortunately, be only partly true. The decreasing volume of internal migration is to a great extent a consequence of the diminishing pull of economic core areas caused by the depression. It is highly probable that when the business boom comes once again, it will reach Southern Finland first, and cause a new wave of internal migration away from the underdeveloped areas. The increase of emigration (mainly to Sweden) shows that the pressure for migration is growing. Emigration was favourable to Finland in 1973 (+ 6200), and in 1974 (+ 1300), but already unfavourable in 1975 (– 4400) and in 1976 (– 9400).

In internal migration trends there are, however, features to which the development laws have been aimed. Migration is now regionally more balanced than before.

Change of Population

Total changes in population are not likely to be very dramatic during such a short time as the period studied. The development during one decade shows a decrease, which can be seen from Figure 9.3, in the *läänis* of Lappi and Vaasa and increase in those of Uusimaa and Häme. Other changes are not revealed by the method applied. In a more detailed analysis, of course, more minor changes would also be revealed.

The relative change in the 1960s divides the *läänis* along the full length of the scale in Figure 9.4. At the end of period again the *läänis* lay closer together. Vaasa and Ahvenanmaa have moved from the group of *läänis* with diminishing population to that with growing population. The position of Oulu has especially been improved. Uusimaa and Häme have lost their former special position. The positive change very much resembles that of internal migration; the phenomena are in fact closely interwoven.

CONCLUSIONS

There have been remarkable changes in Finland during the period of validity of development area legislation. The standard of living in the country as a whole and in all its *läänis* has risen. To be a little more precise, using the same indicators as earlier, the coefficient of regional association (Chorley and Haggett, 1967, pp. 240–242) from the map in Figure 9.3, and the variation coefficient (the standard deviations in per cent from the mean) from Figure 9.4 were calculated. The method was kept simple because of the coarseness of regional division and the quality of material. The value of the coefficient of regional association (I_d) implies how much the map describing the end of the study period differs in percentage terms from that at the beginning. The predominantly negative value of the variation coefficient (V_d) shows how much the dispersion shown in Figure 9.4 has diminished.

Table 9.2 shows that, during the period studied, population change and internal migration have altered regionally more than the other indicators of development. Changes in industrialization and income level have been smallest. The change as a whole has been 10 to 11 per cent during the period studied. (Because of the method of calculation the values of variation coefficients are useless in those cases where there are positive and negative values and a mean near zero as in the case of migration and population change. Values in parentheses have therefore been omitted in determining means and medians). The change to a magnitude of about 10 per cent can be considered as a result of efforts in which the development area policy has been one component.

In general the underdeveloped *läänis* have developed fastest, but there are exceptions. To elucidate this the change by *läänis* has been calculated roughly using the sums of the shading classes in Figure 9.3 as measures of development.

TABLE 9.2. Relative regional change of the distribution of selected indicators

Indicators	Coefficient of regional association I_d	Variation Coefficient V_d
Industrialization	3.5	−9.7
Gross national product	8.2	−3.0
Unemployment	11.2	−13.4
Income level	2.0	−6.1
Students in secondary schools	6.3	−5.9
Television licences	8.2	−26.0
Internal migration	21.3	(+68.4)
Population change	19.4	(−1129.6)
Mean	10.0	−10.7
Median	8.2	−11.6

It can also be understood as a summary of Figures 9.3 and 9.4. At the beginning of the period of this study the differences were great. The *lääni* of Uusimaa was clearly more developed than the other *läänis* in industrial Finland. The differences between other developed *läänis* were smaller. Keski-Suomi and Vaasa formed an intermediate group towards the underdeveloped *läänis*. Differences there were small, but Pohjois-Karjala was the weakest. At the end of the period studied differences had clearly diminished. Uusimaa is still leading, but Turku and Pori and Häme have come closer and are on the same level; Kymi lags behind only slightly. The level of its development is now closer to that of industrial Finland. The order of underdeveloped *läänis* has also changed. Vaasa is now the first in line, and Oulu has risen to the same position as Keski-Suomi. Kuopio now belongs to the intermediate group. All the other *läänis* are now in the same level except Mikkeli, which has remained last.

The rise of underdeveloped *läänis* has been faster than that of better developed ones. Even the weakest underdeveloped *lääni* is now on the same level as the last of those in industrial Finland at the beginning of the period studied; so the differences have been smoothed, although they have not disappeared totally.

Aid to industry in underdeveloped *läänis* in Table 9.1 is presented in three different ways (compare Figure 9.2) to make the comparison of the results easier. There is a correlation between the rapidity of development aid that, calculated per inhabitant, seems to reflect best the speed of development. The volume of support per enterprise is nearly as good an indicator. Amount of money as such does not seem to be important in causing a faster rise in the standard of living.

Industrial Finland has had so little support of any kind that it cannot have had any influence on development, except perhaps in the *lääni* of Ahvenanmaa.

The development there has been prompted by other factors.

In Central Finland, or the Second Zone, changes correlate very well with the support given through development laws. In Northern Finland the situation is more complicated. Oulu has developed fastest in the whole country, but the support given to its industry is smaller than what one could expect. A great deal of its development must be explained by other factors such as the growing university of Oulu with its multiplier effects; the low degree of industrialization as such has also influenced its development. This might be the main explanation in the case of Lappi, where the support per enterprise, especially, has been remarkably great, but the results in the overall growth of the standard of living are modest.

In spite of the changes in Finland's economic geographical situation there is dissatisfaction within the country about the results of the development policy. It is, however, easily forgotten how short a time and how little money has been at the disposal of regional policy. Of all investments in Finland, only 31 to 34 per cent have taken place in the underdeveloped areas. The effects on the standard of living seem to be greater in underdeveloped areas than in the industrialized part of the country.

The economic core of Finland still lies in Southern Finland and, as a consequence, the standard of living has remained higher than elsewhere in the country. This situation will continue for a long time in the future. It is based on many geographical factors, whose joint effect is such that conditions for economic activities are better in Southern Finland than elsewhere in the country. It is easy to imagine chains of cause and effect brought about primarily by the physical geography of Finland, which lead to better conditions for farming, denser settlement, larger population, more intensive industrialization, a denser network of central areas with large centres, and to a political hegemony, which ultimately dictates the substance of future legislation on underdeveloped regions.

REFERENCES

Allardt, E. (1976). 'Dimensions of welfare in a comparative Scandinavian study'. *Acta sociologica*, **19**, 227–239.

Central Statistical Office (1962–76). *Statistical Yearbook of Finland*, (LIX–LXXII, Helsinki.

Chorley, R. J. and Haggett, P. (1967). *Frontiers in Geographical Teaching*, Methuen, London.

Decentralization Committee (1974). *Virastojen ja laitosten hajasijoittaminen*, Hajasijoituskomitean loppumietintö, Helsinki.

EFTA, Economic Development Committee (1971). *Industrial Mobility*, Geneva.

Hautamäki, L. (1969). Kehittyneisyyden alueittaisista erosta Suomessa, *Helsingin Yliopiston Maantieteen laitoksen julkaisuja*, Sarja B, **3**, 1–55.

Hautamäki, L. (1973). Selvitys kehittyneisyyden alueellisista eroista ja aluejakovaihtoehdoista aluepolitiikassa, *Valtioneuvoston Kanslian julkaisuja*, **2**, 1–139.

Hautamäki, L. (1975). Kehitysalueiden tarkoituksenmukaisuudesta ja rajauksesta maamme aluepolitiikassa kehittyneisyyden alueittaisten erojen valossa, *Terra*, **87**, 104–114.

Hustich, I. (1968). 'Finland, a developed and an underdeveloped country'. *Acta Geographica*, **20**, 155–173.

Hustich, I. (1971). 'Om avgränsningen av utvecklingsområden i Finland'. *Terra*, **83**, 25–38.

Hustich, I. and Wahlbeck, L. (1952). 'Inkomstinivåns geografi i Finland år 1948'. *Meddelanden av Ekonomisk—Georafiska Institutionen vid Svenska Handelshöqskolan*, **1**, 1–46.

Kehitysalueiden neuvottelukunta (1973). Vyöhykejaon tarkistustyöryhmån raportti, *Valtioneuvoston kanslian julkaisuja*, **2**, Helsinki, 1–139.

Kehitysalueiden neuvottelukunta (1974a). 'Elinkeinopoliittisen jaoston raportti'. *Valtioneuvoston kanslian julkaisuja*, **1**, Helsinki, 1–138.

Kehitysalueiden neuvottelukunta (1974b). 'Kasvukeskuspoliittisen jaoston mientintö'. *Valtioneuvoston kanslian julkaisuja*, **2**, Helsinki, 1–199.

Kehitysaluerahasto Oy (1976). *Vuosikertomus*, *1975*, Kuopio.

Lehikoinen, Irma (1972). 'Kehitysaluelainsäädännöstä ja sen vaikutuksesta yritystoimintaan'. *Yhteistyön korkeakoulu*, Vaasa, 7–11.

Ministry of Labour, Planning Division (1976). *Työvoimakatsaus*, Helsinki.

Official Statistics of Finland XVIII A:80 (1967). *Teollisuustilasto*, Osa 1, **1**, Helsinki.

Official Statistics of Finland XVIII A:95 (1977). *Teollisuustilasto*, *1974*, Osa 1, **1**, Helsinki.

Palmgren, Kai (1964). Kehittyneisyyden alueittaisista eroavuuksista Suomessa, *Publications of the National Planning Office*, A: 15, Helsinki, 1–160.

Palomäki, M. (1968). 'On the concept and delimitation of the present-day provinces of Finland'. *Acta Geographica*, **20**, 279–295.

Palomäki, M. and Taina, J. (1973). 'The distribution and regional balance of university level education in Finland'. *Acta Wasaensia*, **3**, 1–57.

Prime Minister's Office (1977). *Valtioneuvoston Kanslia*, *Katsaus 1*, Helsinki, mimeo.

Riihinen, O. (1965). Teollistuvan yhteiskunnan alueellinen erikoistuminen, Helsinki.

Wahlbeck, L. (1955). *Om inkomstnivåns geografi i Finland år 1950*, Helsingfors.

Planning Industrial Development
Edited by David F. Walker

Chapter 10

Industry in Metropolitan Area Plans: Proposals and Experience in the West Midlands County, England

Barbara M. D. Smith

1. SETTING THE SCENE FOR INDUSTRIAL PLANS IN THE WEST MIDLANDS COUNTY IN THE 1970S

(i) Setting the Scene of the Paper

Planning involves purposive intervention in the existing situation to change it in a preferred direction. Means and ends have to be identified. Planning in the industrial sphere will aim to serve industry as provider and promoter (Camina, 1974), but also on occasion, to control its activities in the public interest in terms of distribution, nuisance and working conditions. The balance between promotion and regulation will vary and both may conflict with the rule of the market over industrial firms in a free enterprise economy.

Industry in metropolitan area plans, whether these are formal or not, can be considered either broadly, without restriction as to whose planning is involved, or narrowly, confining the planning to that of the metropolitan authority. The latter's role can be described as gap filler, acting where the private sector, other levels of government or statutory undertakers (water, power, etc.) are not considered to be meeting the needs of the metropolitan economy. Willingness to recognize and step into such a gap is a political decision.

This paper considers first the meaning and context of metropolitan planning in terms of planning responsibilities, the industrial problems and trends facing the planners and the institutional framework of past and present plans at local, regional and national levels. The second section examines constraints on industrial planners. These derive from their lack of power, legal or practical, over the ingredients of economic activity and over industrial investment decisions. Nevertheless, an extensive list of policies already introduced in Britain can be provided. It is against this background that industrial planning in the West Midlands County area is considered in the third section. The subject is divided into structure planning and economic planning as they affect industry and as practised by the West Midlands County and its districts in the 1970s. A conclusion attempts some evaluation of the pragmatic, incomplete and badly co-ordinated industrial planning operative in the West Midlands at the present time, against a background of serious industrial problems and often rather unhelpful national policies.

The concern is with industrial or industrial development planning rather than with either economic or employment planning. Industrial planning deals more specifically with employers, plants and firms as institutions and with the demand for labour rather than with employees and labour supply, but industrial planning is often little more than an adjunct of planning for the employment of residents and commuters. The assumption has been implicit that what is good for people is good for firms (Smith, 1974b)—and the firms' satisfaction with plans and their relative performance have been neglected. Some efforts to force them to match the needs of people have caused fatal damage. Vociferous pressure groups now snap at many industrial proposals on environmental grounds putting constraints on industrial planning.

Local or metropolitan planning is concerned with industrial development through anxiety about both the volume and kind of local investment and employment and their location. Both involve planning powers and plans at levels below, above and within the metropolitan one. Below can mean district, community and plant, and above regional and national. The latter level has the crucial powers over industrial development outside the firm through its policies for the economy as a whole, for the industrial strategy (Treasury, 1975) and sectoral plans (*Trade and Industry*, 12 November and 10 December 1976), and for the assisted area regions and nationalized industries. Regional policy sustained over forty years has affected the distribution of industry through controls and incentives and through the location of infrastructure investment (McCrone, 1969; *Trade and Industry*, 11, 18 and 25 February 1977; OECD, 1977).

What is metropolitan in this context? In England, since the local government reform of 1974, it has specifically referred to the governing body in the metropolitan county. Two tiers of local government were created, the top tier of the metropolitan county, and the lower one of the metropolitan district. The metropolitan county was set up to provide a conurbation authority to plan cohesively for the whole urban area but, in so doing, challenged the autonomy of the districts (Royal Commission on Local Government, 1969; Local Government Act, 1972).

The 1974 reform gave strategic planning powers to the metropolitan county and local planning powers to the district. Strategic planning involves the making of structure plans, indicating the broad, significant existing structure of land-use and the major changes intended; it leaves the translation of these into plans for particular localities and parcels of land to local planning. The metropolitan county also plans transportation, working with and through the nationalized railway and private and public bus undertakings. Great importance has been attached to the conjunction of these two planning roles but executive powers over the constituents that operationalize such plans mainly lie elsewhere. The districts are the housing authorities, for instance, and regional bodies control water, health and sport (though there is no elected, executive regional government in England). However, the generous boundaries consistent with this planning role were not obtained by the West Midlands Metropolitan County because of the opposition of the shire counties (Hall *et al.*, 1973; Department of the Environment, 1971).

It remains to touch on what constitutes industry in this context. The principal concern will be with manufacturing industry, extended in practice to include associated sectors such as the expanding metal stockholding industry which also occupy industrial land (Central Statistical Office, 1968; Ministry of Housing, 1963). This manufacturing industry in the West Midlands County is predominantly in private hands. Thus, industrial planning is by government in relation to the private sector using its powers of persuasion through advice, pressure and example, backed up by some financial incentives and occasional straight direction or use of sanctions. However, in this mixed economy, the division between private and public is less clear. With few manufacturing plants in formally nationalized industries, there are now a number of plants in the County in groups under the aegis of the National Enterprise Board and many others dependent upon these plants or public contracts for much of their business.

(ii) Background Problems and Planning Practice

A. Planning and the Local Industrial Environment in the 1960s

The relationship between planning and industry in the 1960s is relevant to the 1970s as a background to contemporary industrial planning and as a source of problems. Planning impinged directly upon manufacturing concerns in five situations in what is now the West Midlands County area in the 1960s. These situations arose when a concern was located in the way of a redevelopment or road scheme; when it was a non-conforming user on land not zoned for industrial use under a development plan; when it grew out of its premises and needed to extend or, more particularly, to move to larger (or occasionally smaller) premises; or when a new concern or a new branch factory to employ more than about thirty employees was to be established in new premises. (Thirty employees was approximately the number capable of being employed in a building below the industrial development certificate [i.d.c.] limit in operation at that time.) All these involved a move, a forced move for planning reasons or a voluntary move for reasons internal to the firm. Such concerns came up against the local planning authority when seeking permission (planning permission and an i.d.c. from the Board of Trade without which that permission could not be given) to build or alter industrial floor space. The need for permission could be avoided by taking over existing premises. Economic forces could also affect firms seeking to expand their supply of labour or premises. The fifth situation occurred when a firm was a bad neighbour to a degree that forced the local authority to act. Compensation was paid to the owner of premises affected by planning policy but this was invariably inadequate to install the concern in equivalent premises. Help in finding alternative premises was usually given by the local authority and the Board of Trade, but many firms closed down and some moved out of the area.

It was the proposals involving growth and diversification that were diverted out of the County area. These were often the larger developments involving branch factories in growth industries such as engineering or motor vehicles and components or new products unable to claim ties to the area (Howard, 1968; House of Commons Expenditure Committee, 1973). Modernization schemes were also held back to the detriment of efficiency until the concession of 1973 (*Trade and Industry*, 14 January and 27 February 1977). Thirty years of i.d.c. control (combined with industrial location and structural factors) have been instrumental in confining the County industrial structure to a straightjacket designed in 1947 (Smith, 1971). The relative importance of this in explaining the present situation is disputed (City of Birmingham, 1973a; Barlow and Downing, 1976; Carter, 1977).

The economic environment seemed to change for the worse after 1967. Why? Why then? A number of trends, some reaching back well before 1967 (Maton, 1966), gain significance in conjunction with other factors in the local and national situation. These trends can be listed as: first, increased productivity per head, reducing the labour force needed for the same output; second, changes in labour legislation and practices, encouraging employers to save costly and difficult-to-dismiss labour; third, continued decentralization of industry and population, representing the results of differential growth as well as actual movement, the latter being only a small part of the whole (Smith, 1973, 1977b; Hall *et al.*, 1973; Department of the Environment, 1976b); fourth, decline in the number of plants in the conurbation as a result of death, merger, and outward movement and decline in the significance of linkage and agglomeration economies to firms, affecting particularly the number of small firms; and, fifth, increased importance attached to lower costs and competitiveness in order to maintain or increase profits or sales, forcing firms to consider the costs of overmanning and of inefficient, old premises. Between 1959 and 1973, in the Birmingham employment exchange area the number of plants with 11 to 99 employees declined by 41 per cent compared to a fall of 23 per cent in those with over 500 employees.

These trends confronted industrial planners with serious implications for the county economy.

B. Problems for Industrial Planning to Face: Economic and Industrial Problems Ongoing into the 1970s

What industrial problems have been recognized in the County area and who has been responsible for their diagnosis? Symptoms and causes are difficult to separate. There are short-term problems of inadequate demand in the national economy on which are superimposed much longer-term problems deriving from the local industrial structure, lack of investment and inner city decline.

Analysis and diagnosis has taken place principally in three bodies. First in the field was the West Midlands Regional Economic Planning Council with *The West Midlands: An Economic Appraisal* (1971). Its message was stark but its power to generate change small. Second in the field was the West Midlands County with its two editions of *A Time For Action* in 1974 and 1975. Third, alongside, came the tripartite work of the West Midlands Planning Authorities Conference (West Midlands Planning Authorities Conference, 1975) and Joint Monitoring Steering Group set out in their *Annual Reports* of 1975 and 1976. Analysis has shown increasing sophistication, moving on from simply employment and unemployment to measures of industrial performance. Nationally, there have been signs of the same malaise and analysis.

The following long-term problems provide direction to industrial planning in the County area (West Midlands County Council, 1975a).

1. Problems of structure

(a) The local economy is vulnerable to rapid changes of fortune as demand for its products can shut off suddenly.

(b) The major industries of the local economy (metal manufacture, engineering, vehicles and metal goods), the growth industries of the 1930s and 1950s, are now neither growing nor competitive and immediate prospects are poor.

(c) The industries that have been growing nationally are not growing as fast locally. Having benefited in the past from the absence of nationally declining industries, the area has now a concentration of the declining industries of the present generation.

(d) The local economy is short of firms in the current national growth industries such as chemicals, plastics, timber and furniture. Locational unsuitability, relative costs and regional policy explain this.

(e) The local economy is concentrated on a few industries, and diversification out of traditional metal industries has been slight since the war. Firstly, manufacturing in 1975 still provided 50 per cent of employment in the County (Great Britain, 33 per cent); secondly, metal manufacturing (metal manufacture, engineering, vehicles and metal goods) provided 41 per cent of employment in the County in 1975 (Great Britain, 17 per cent), with around a sixth of all manufacturing employment connected closely with the motor vehicle industry (House of Commons Expenditure Committee, 1975); and, thirdly, non-metal manufacturing provided 9 per cent of employment in the County in 1975 compared to 13 per cent in 1961 (Great Britain 19 per cent in both years). Increases in productivity have cut employment in brewing, chemicals, tyres, glass and cocoa while new industries like plastics have not developed.

(f) There has been some diversification into services but the service sector remains relatively small.

(g) Service growth has, in any case, been concentrated in the public sector in education, health and local government where public expenditure cuts make continued growth unlikely. The other national growth sector, financial services, remains small in the County.

2. Problems of investment and performance

(h) These problems of structure and lack of growth are closely related to lack of investment, lack of profits either to invest or as a motive for investment and high operating costs. Labour costs are high in the County in terms of net output per employee (Department of Employment, 1973). Investment is said to be sparse, ill-chosen and underutilized (Dudley, 1975; Treasury, 1975).

(i) Investment abroad, or in other directions, earns higher profits than local manufacturing and is therefore preferred by investors.

(j) The local economy's poor performance is not explained simply by an adverse industrial structure; there are some additional locational or other factors present (West Midlands County Council, 1976d; Joint Monitoring Steering Group, 1976a). In 1958, the West Midlands Region had a net output per employee in manufacturing industry equivalent to 98 per cent of that of the United Kingdom; by 1972, it had fallen to 89 per cent, with only Northern Ireland recording a lower figure amongst the regions (West Midlands County Council, 1977; see also Wood, 1976).

3. Problems of employment

(k) The number of jobs available has fallen by 9 per cent since the peak of 1966 while the potential working population including commuters has been maintained for demographic reasons (*Department of Employment Gazette*, 1977).

(l) The population of working age has fallen as a proportion of total population producing more dependants per wage-earner.

4. Problems of unemployment

(m) Unemployment has been increasing in both scale and duration since 1966. At times, the County rate has exceeded that for Great Britain and matched those of some assisted areas. As nationally, unemployment is disproportionately high amongst the young, the old, the least skilled and the black, and in particular inner localities, the latter only in part reflecting the place of the residence of these groups.

(n) Yet there is said to be a shortage of apprentice-trained skilled workers in manufacturing in the County (as elsewhere), such that production is being held up in some plants (but see Needham, 1977 and Smith, 1975).

5. Problems of location

(o) Decline in employment and investment has tended to be concentrated in the older, inner areas, especially in Birmingham, and growth in newer areas, often outside the County boundary but also in Dudley, Alridge-Brownhills and Solihull. The inner decline has tended to be concentrated in male, manual, manufacturing jobs and the outer growth in female service jobs.

(p) Redistribution of population has produced social polarization so that those travelling into the County to work tend to include disproportionately employers, managers and white-collar workers, limiting the practicality of cutting in-commuting.

6. Problems of land shortage

(q) There is a lack of large, prime industrial sites in the County to attract in new investment and to permit restructuring and development of existing industry.

7. Problems of relative regional comparisons

(r) A number of indicators for the West Midlands Region and County now compare unfavourably with those for other regions and especially the South-east. The latter indicates that the explanation is not simply the success of regional policy.

To sum up, a combination of concentrations of manufacturing, manual socio-economic groups and immigrants with recession and structural economic problems has built up serious short and long-term industrial problems in the County and its inner areas, notably in Birmingham. Loss of freedom to take decisions locally and of dynamic local entrepreneurs and the influence of mergers and trade unions can also be mentioned (Liggins, 1977). This list indicates many issues of relevance to industrial policy-makers in the County area.

(iii) The Institutional Framework of Planning and Past Plans Prior to 1970: Their Character and Aims

A. Development Plans

The Town and Country Planning Act, 1947, introduced the development plan system in England and Wales (Cullingworth, 1964). The Act reduced the number of planning authorities to nine in the conurbation. Each had to prepare what was basically a land-use map of its area, indicating present uses and future planned uses of all land. This involved surveys of the present and estimates of the future population and its employment, housing, shopping and other needs over the next fifteen years. Land was zoned in broad lots for particular uses, this zoning to be maintained through subsequent development control. The development plan and town map, once accepted by the local council, had to be approved by the Minister of Town and Country Planning.

Co-ordination between planning authorities was limited but there was an official regional framework and an unofficial one in existence from 1948 (Ministry of Town and Country Planning, 1948; West Midland Group for Planning and Post-War Reconstruction, 1948). Dispersal of population and employment, and of the firms that produced that employment, was accepted as a general principle to control the size of the conurbation. Arrangements were made to provide land for housing and industry in reception towns across the green belt. Little further effort was directed to persuading firms or people to move; the attractions of overspill reception areas and the dis-attractions of the conurbation (shortages, costs and congestion) were assumed to be adequate incentives. Industrial movement (firms without employees) to development areas was also introduced by central government backed up by financial incentives and industrial development certificates (Smith, 1972; Sutcliffe and Smith, 1974).

Decisions about population and housing often virtually dictated industrial planning. Shortages of housing land put pressure on its availability for industry; slum clearance of housing inevitably involved the adjacent industrial premises; population estimates implied the employment requirement. Other concerns were unemployment, pollution and the separation of industry from residential areas; footloose industries, that it was considered could move out, were identified. Plans failed to take account of the realities of industrial operations.

The industrial aspects of these development plans involved mainly redevelopment schemes; industrial land estimates and zoning to provide the needed land for existing firms, and to segregate industry from other uses; recognition and treatment of industrial non-conforming users; and, where required, industrial overspill to accompany population to development areas. The flow of industry was to be outwards; no arrangements were made in terms of land, or housing for additional workers, to accommodate incoming firms—few have arrived though there was no means of stopping outsiders from buying property on the market. Some parts of the Black Country were conscious of the need for diversification and expected some industry to arrive from Birmingham. Most authorities restricted disposal of their own land to local firms.

B. Structure Plans

Development plans envisaged changing the local situation to a desired end state in a finite period of time. This was impractical. Population growth and movement far exceeded expectations and proved difficult to accommodate in accordance with the plans. A Planning Advisory Group Report (Ministry of Housing and Local Government, 1965) proposed a new system of development plans that was implemented in the Town and Country Planning Acts of 1968 (Bor, 1974) and 1971 (Cullingworth, 1974).

Flexibility, public participation and co-ordination round a regional strategy were new influences. Economic and employment issues featured strongly (Palmer, 1975). The new development plans were to comprise structure plans at the strategic level and local plans, for district, action area or subject, at the detailed level (Department of the Environment, 1977b). Amongst the dozen aspects of society to be covered were employment and industry (Ministry of Housing and Local Government, 1970). The written statement was to identify aims, objectives (operational aims), problems, optional strategies for meeting objectives or for dealing with problems taking into account constraints, internal and external to the authority. It was also to set out the preferred strategy and an implementation programme, bearing in mind resource limitations. The process started informally in the West Midlands in 1969; it is not yet complete.

C. The Regional Context

Structure plans, including that of the West Midlands County, are required to be consistent with the regional strategy agreed locally in 1972 (West Midlands Planning Authorities Conference, 1974). This appeared in 1974 with the Minister's approving statement of 1973 and some updating amendments to population and economic forecasts. The three in combination constitute the strategy. While this short strategy is specifically the outcome of the work of the West Midland Regional Study reported on in 1971 (West Midland Regional Study, 1971b), it represents ongoing activity in three or four distinct, even if overlapping, camps—the local planning authorities through the West Midlands Planning Authorities Conference and their small, full-time Regional Study team, the regional offices of central government departments (directly or collectively through the Regional Economic Planning Board), and the Economic Planning Council (Saunders, 1977).

These regional strategies largely concentrate on the choice of locations in the Region to receive population and industry from the conurbation and on the scale of this overspill (Department of Economic Affairs, 1965; West Midlands Economic Planning Council, 1967). The main choice has lain between close-in dormitory housing development without industry or farther-off self-contained development in new towns and town development schemes against a backcloth of economic, political and financial constraints affecting implementation of the chosen strategy. The amount of potential industrial movement, its willingness and economic ability to move to these self-contained towns a dozen miles away (relative to remaining in the industrial complex or moving with incentives to development areas) and ways of generating such movement were key issues, uncertainly assessed (West Midland Regional Study, 1971b). Close-in development has generally been considered easier to arrange and more likely to succeed but environmentally less desirable. The regional strategy is currently being re-examined jointly by the tripartite team (Joint Monitoring Steering Group, 1975 and 1976a). Real concern about the health of the whole regional economy has developed, calling into question the continued reality of the overspill issue.

D. The National Element

Currently in Britain there is no national plan, though individual ministries have policies that may fit together into a national strategy. There is at the moment a specific industrial strategy (Treasury, 1975). Economic policy (Treasury), employment policies (Department of Employment, partly hived off to the Manpower Services Commission), the industrial strategy and inter-regional policy (Department of Industry), and intraregional and inner city policies and structure planning (Department of the Environment) are threads in this. Both regional and metropolitan plans have to fit into this framework.

On the industrial planning side, government now consults and works with the Confederation of British Industry (Confederation of British Industry, 1976 and 1977; Grant and Marsh, 1977) and the Trades Union Congress (Trades Union Congress, 1974). There are echoes of this at County level. It is difficult to estimate how fruitful these consultations are; it is not clear how valuable a collective voice can be when the circumstances of firms differ so considerably. Moreover, neither the CBI nor the TUC appeared at the structure plan public examination and the Department of Industry, manufacturing's sponsoring ministry, only appeared briefly. Thus, the voice of manufacturing was not heard directly and structure plans have relied once again on planners' interpretation of industrial needs. Doubtless the planners will be accused next of misunderstanding these.

II. CONSTITUENTS OF INDUSTRIAL PLANNING IN THE WEST MIDLANDS COUNTY AREA IN THE 1970s: THE POSSIBILITIES

This section reviews the range of possibilities that forms a backcloth to the industrial planning that could be adopted in the West Midlands County area. It reviews these in terms of the broad powers, aims and policies available to the planners there. Constraints on the use of these possibilities and on their effectiveness in changing the industrial situation are also considered.

(i) Broad Powers Available to Industrial Planners

Local planners are legally restricted in their industrial and other activities to those permitted them under either general legislation or special private acts. The latter are receding in importance as the Local Government Act 1972 decreed the termination of existing private legislation in 1979 and fresh proposals have been deterred.

Apart from land-use planning legislation, the key legislation giving local authorities powers to assist industrial planning includes the Local Authorities (Land) Act 1963, the Local Government (Financial Provisions) Act 1963, the Local Government Act 1972 and the Community Land Act 1975 (Camina, 1974; Handley, 1977; Rogers and Smith, 1977). These cover land acquisition, land development, loans, derelict land reclamation, etc. and allow the spending of the equivalent of a twopenny rate on anything considered in the interests of the area and its inhabitants. Arguments about the range of the powers and need to obtain the approval of the Secretary of State and of the district auditor constrain what can be done. Much greater powers to influence industrial development remain with central government using the Industrial Development Act 1966 or the Industry Acts 1972 and 1975.

Legal powers are exercised subject to political and financial commitments. Many authorities do not exploit their powers or available funds to the full. Authorities have generally been unwilling to assist firms if the market could provide capital, premises, etc. Some find an advocacy role important and inexpensive or concentrate on improving the service offered to local industry in as many directions as possible and/or on making the area known as a suitable location for industry. The powers of the metropolitan authorities remain at best ancillary and often both marginal in effect and subject to conflict with other economic assessments of the local situation. For instance, central government may assess other areas as far more needy while the individual concern may find local sites less than optimal in terms of private costs and available alternatives.

(ii) A Conceptual Framework for Industrial Planning by Central or Local Government in a Particular Area

Industrial planning aims and policies have to fit into an existing industrial situation reflecting economic and power relationships. This is spelt out in the conceptual framework for industrial planning posited below. The aim of industrial planning is assumed to be to ensure an adequate local economy and industry to provide for the needs of residents and in-commuters. If market forces fail to produce this situation, the industrial planner can intervene to do so, supplementing or countering market forces. Ability to ensure either the industrial conditions or the performance required is limited by the planners' powers over the factors of production, investment decisions, internal firm efficiency and the economic climate. So planners need to consider the ingredients of economic activity and the accessibility to their influence of industrial employers in terms of location and seat of control so that aims and policies can be designed consistent with this situation.

1. Basic ingredients of economic activity whose supply needs to be assured and, if necessary, planned

Industrial planners at local and central government level need to ensure a satisfactory supply of the factors of production and motivation in quantity, quality, location and price (Smith, 1977a). Obviously, these factors include: (a) land and premises; (b) labour; (c) capital to finance investment and to operate it; and, much less obviously, (d) entrepreneurship and management; (e) motive for operation and development (demand for output at a price that leaves a relatively satisfactory margin after financing and meeting the costs of operation in the local area in the eyes of management, be it in the private or public sector); (f) a helpful planning and government environment; and (g) other ingredients such as access to suppliers, a pleasant environment, etc. The test of whether such supply is satisfactory will be seen in the relative performance, survival and growth of local industrial employers.

By their policies industrial planners can exercise direct and indirect influence on the supply of these ingredients of economic activity as well as manufacturers' performance in using them. They can extend their influence by adding to their range of activities, for example by building factories, running children's crêches or even becoming entrepreneurs (Minns and Thornley, 1976). But there are constraints on their ability to influence individual employers.

2. Types of industrial employer by locational position vis-à-vis *the local area*

This locational position affects where industrial planning contact has to be made and the ease of that contact. Industrial employers can be divided into (a) the non-mobile, or the indigenous and ongoing employers in the local area; (b) the mobile, divided into those potentially coming into and going out of the local area; and (c) the new, divided into those setting up from local and non-local initiatives.

Planners need to have different plans to contact and influence each type of employer, increasing difficulty being experienced outside the non-mobile indigenous ones. In particular, the new and mobile have to be diverted from alternative locations by relatively better communication, planning and ingredients of economic activity in the local area. But there are other problems.

3. Types of industrial employer by control position

This affects by whom and where the investment decision is actually taken and thus where industrial planning contact and influence has to be directed. Each of the previous locational types, therefore, subdivide according to organization and location of control. Again, difficulty of contact and influence increases where headquarters lie outside the local area. Division is necessary into private and public sector and some further subdivision by industry, size of plant, existing location and space conditions, etc.

The above framework conditions the viability of the more general aims of industrial planning and of the economic and employment planning of which it is part. The latter produces a rather different structure of aims and policies to implement them, leaving out completely measures of openness to contact and influence.

(iii) Broad Aims and Policy Possibilities

The broad aims of industrial planning at the local level usually involve seeking to influence jobs, investment or rateable income in order to diversify, replace, increase, redistribute or improve the contribution of existing industry to the local economy. Such aims in the West Midlands recently had absorbed the neutral aims of providing an efficient service to industry and put in abeyance the negative aim of regulation to prevent industrial abuses except in most flagrant cases.

The primary constraint on industrial planning is the need for the aims/problems to be recognized for themselves, for subsequent diagnosis and, then, as being a fit objective of planning and, in particular, of local planning.

Two problems confront the industrial planners in meeting these aims (in addition to those in the previous framework). There is the lack of industrial or infrastructure investment to plan because of, first, the current industrial situation and, second, the inertia generated by the existing stock of industrial buildings and machinery. Change is difficult to generate when few decisions to invest are being taken, little mobile or new industry can be contacted, and substantial spare capacity already exists. Even active policies may then produce only marginal outcomes (Department of the Environment, 1973; and 1976a). There are also few funds to back industrial planning given commitments in other fields.

An attempt has been made in the next section to summarize industrial policies practised in Britain to indicate the context in which the local industrial planner would be working and the range of possibilities of which advantage could be taken. Five groups of aims are set out with policy possibilities under each but no attempt is made to price or scale the practice as an indication of resource allocation.

Broad aims and policy possibilities in industrial planning in the West Midland County area

1. Aim: to affect the location of industrial investment and employment in order to reduce unemployment in particular areas, to reduce congestion in others, to promote industrial efficiency and growth, to improve the environment and to reduce travel to work.

(i) Sub-aims

(a) *to affect location between regions in Great Britain:* work to workers policy involving pressure (i.d. c.s and incentives) on manufacturing firms in the West Midlands County to locate growth and new developments in assisted areas outside the County.

(b) *to affect location between areas within the West Midlands Region:* policy on distribution of population and industry to divert 'surplus' from the conurbation to new and expanded towns across the green belt and, more recently, to rejuvenate inner areas.

(c) *to affect location within the West Midlands County area:* via land-use planning, especially to promote environmental improvement, efficiency and renewal, to reduce travel to work, to permit adjustment and growth of existing firms and to admit new ones, especially in inner areas.

(ii) Policies and measures involving area discrimination in favour of priority areas

To attract employers to one place rather than another	Central	Regional WMEPC	Regional WMPAC	Local City	Local District
(a) Overall character of policies	Yes	(i)	(i)	(i)	(i)
(b) Designation of priority areas	*Yes; DI	(i)	(i)	(i)	(i)
e.g. assisted areas	*Yes; DI				
new towns, etc.	Yes; DOE	(i)	(i)		(ii)
inner areas	1977; DOE			Yes	Yes
growth centres	*				
outlying residential areas to help women work				Yes	Yes
(c) Extra incentives in priority areas					
e.g. labour subsidy (REP) 1967–78	*Yes; DE				
investment subsidy/grants	*Yes; DI			F	F
other (training, removal)	*Yes; DE/DI			F	F
small firms employment subsidy	*Yes; DE				
(d) Extra public expenditure in priority areas on, e.g.					
infrastructure	*Yes; all			F	F
industrial sites	*Yes; DI			Yes	Yes
advance factories	*Yes; DI			Yes	Yes
industrial estates	*Yes; DI			F	Yes
extra facilities	*			F	F
subsidies on these	*			F	F
e.g. rent/rate rebates	*			F	F
(e) Locating advice in favour of priority areas	*Yes; DI			Yes	Yes
(f) Public sector investment location					
(i) nationalized industries	*Yes; all			(i)	(i)
(ii) central government offices	*Yes; CSC			(i)	(i)
(iii) other public sector				F	F
(iv) National Enterprise Board	*Yes; NEB			(i)	(i)
(g) Differential i.d.c. control	*Yes; DI	(ii)		(ii)	(ii)
(h) Differential o.d.p., control 1966–70	*Past; DOE				

To attract employers to one place rather than another	Central	Regional WMEPC	Regional WMPAC	Local City	Local District
(i) Differential zoning and land allocation	Yes; DOE	(i)	(i)	Yes	Yes
(j) Plan-making and approval					
(i) national (covert)	Yes; all	(i)	(i)	(ii)	
(ii) regional	Yes; DOE	Yes	Yes	(ii)	(ii)
(iii) structure	Approve; DOE	(i)	(i)	Yes	(ii)
(iv) local		(i)	(i)	(ii)	Yes
(k) Relocation of nuisance makers and concerns from redevelopment areas and non-industrial land	(i); DOE/DI			(ii)	Yes

Abbreviations

*	these priority areas only exist outside West Midlands County area;
(i)	right to discuss and comment on; advocacy role;
(ii)	right to discuss exercised;
Yes	policy is used;
F	feasible policy to be used in theory;
DI	Department of Industry;
DOE	Department of the Environment;
CSC	Civil Service Commission
DE	Department of Employment
ESA	Employment Services Agency, part of Manpower Services Commission (MSC);
TSA	Training Services Agency, part of MSC;
DT	Department of Trade;
DoT	Department of Transport;

ITB Industrial Training Board; all seven districts not equally involved.
WMEPC West Midlands Economic Planning Council;
WMPAC West Midlands Planning Authorities Conference.

2. (i) Aim: to foster industrial development and investment in general in order to aid 'lame ducks', reduce bottlenecks, improve efficiency, investment and private and public planning, and to reduce unemployment generally. These policies are not discriminatory by area and their effect in a particular area will depend on its structure in relation to industries encouraged (locally important due to presence of car industry), the extent to which manufacturers actually use the help offered to them, and productivity effects on employment.

(ii) Policies and measures to foster and sustain development

To foster development and competitiveness anywhere	Central	Regional WMEPC	Regional WMPAC	Local City	Local District
(a) Industrial strategy (Cmnd. 5710/6315)	Yes; DI	(i)	(i)	(ii)	(i)
(b) Industry Act 1972 and 1975					
(i) selective assistance to firms in need	Yes; DI	(ii)	(ii)	(ii)F	(ii)F

To foster development and competitiveness anywhere	Central	Regional		Local	
		WMEPC	WMPAC	City	District
(ii) selective assistance to industries/firms to reduce bottlenecks, etc.	Yes; DI				
e.g. ferrous foundaries machine tool non-ferrous foundries					
(c) Accelerated investment scheme, 1975–76	Yes; DI				
(d) Industry Act 1975					
(i) planning agreements (only one made)	Yes; DI			F	F
(ii) National Enterprise Board	Yes; DI				
selective assistance to needy	Yes; NEB			(i)	
investment to promote growth/ efficiency	Yes; NEB			(i)	
provision of land and premises	Yes; NEB			(i)	
(e) Advice and information	Yes; DI			Yes	Yes
e.g. Small Firms Information Service	Yes; DI				
(f) Export promotion	Yes; DT			Yes	
(g) Financial incentives for investment					
e.g. tax allowances	Yes; Inland Revenue				
other	Yes; DI				
(h) Public expenditure in general on					
(i) infrastructure (roads, etc.)	Yes; DoT			Yes	Yes
(ii) industrial sites	F			Yes	Yes
(iii) advance factories (need i.d.c.)	F			Yes	Yes
(iv) industrial estates	F			Yes	Yes
(v) extra facilities	F			F	F
(vi) industrial improvement areas (coming)	F			F	F
(vii) subsidies on these, e.g. rent/rate rebate	F			F	F
(viii) training facilities (see mainly in 4)	Yes; DE/MSC			(ii)	Yes

To foster development and competitiveness anywhere	Central	Regional WMEPC	Regional WMPAC	Local City	Local District
(i) Positive, helpful land-use planning				Yes	Yes
(i) structure planning, including local				Yes	Yes
(ii) zoning and allocation of land including rezoning to help firms					Yes
(iii) reclamation and rezoning of derelict land	Yes; DOE			Yes	Yes
(iv) reconsideration of redevelopment and renewal policies to avoid harming firms					Yes
(v) reconsideration of non-conforming use policy to avoid harming good neighbour firms				Yes	Yes
(vi) development control tightened to				Yes	Yes
improve environment					Yes
regulations relaxed to help employment				Yes	Yes
used to support i.d.c. applications				Yes	Yes
used to speed up industrial planning applications				Yes	Yes
(j) promotion and information services	Yes; DI			Yes	Yes
advertising of sites and services				Yes	Yes
brochures				Yes	Yes
industrial development/ promotion officer				Yes	Yes
statistical publication				Yes	One
industrial development budget				Yes	Yes
industrial liaison officer (as in Belfast LED Unit)				F	F
(k) selective encouragement of:					
growth				Yes	Yes
diversification of industry				Yes	Yes

To foster development and competitiveness anywhere	Central	Regional WMEPC	Regional WMPAC	Local City	Local District
new industrial firms	Yes; DI			Yes	Yes
small firms	Yes; DI			Yes	Yes
offices				No	Yes
warehouses (take too much land)				Yes	Yes
labour intensive firms				Yes	Yes
science based industrial firms				Yes	Yes
light industry on residential estates				Yes	Yes
(l) advocacy and pressure group role				Yes	Yes
(m) employment protection and aid to needy firms					
(i) temporary employment subsidy	Yes; ESA			(i)	(i)
(ii) advance notice of redundancy	Yes; ESA				

3. *(i) Aim: to promote the spatial mobility of workers* in order to improve the matching of supply and demand (workers to work policy).

(ii) Policies and measures to promote worker mobility over space

To transfer workers to work	Central	Regional WMEPC	Regional WMPAC	Local City	Local District
(a) Employment transfer service	Yes; DE				F
(b) New town housing allied to job (industrial selection scheme)	Yes; DOE			F	F
(c) Assistance to keyworkers and others					
(i) removal expenses	*Yes; DE			F	F
(ii) allocation of council houses					F
(iii) building of council houses					F
(iv) encouragement of private housebuilding				F	F
(d) Improvement of transport to link houses/jobs better				F	
(e) Provision of day nurseries to allow women to work				F	Yes

4. *(i) Aim: to promote occupational mobility of workers* in order to improve the matching of supply and demand to reduce mismatches between types of workers and jobs (training and placement policies).

(ii) Policies and measures to promote worker mobility between occupation, skills, and industries

To match workers to work locally	Central	Regional		Local	
		WMEPC	WMPAC	City	District
(a) Training, retraining		(i)		(i)	
(i) training opportunities scheme	Yes; TSA				Yes
(ii) skill centres	Yes; TSA				
(iii) wider opportunities courses	Yes; TSA				Yes
(iv) industrial training boards	Yes; ITBs				
(v) apprenticeship support schemes	Yes; TSA			Yes	Yes
(vi) apprenticeships with local authorities				Yes	Yes
(vii) vocational courses	Yes; TSA				Yes
(viii) adult education					Yes
(ix) adult literacy and English language training					Yes
(b) Placement and guidance					
(i) employment office services, information; advice	Yes; ESA				
(ii) job centres (job displays, on main streets)	Yes; ESA				
(iii) careers office (16–17 year olds)	Yes; ESA				Yes
(iv) careers advisory service, including advisers from ethnic groups	Yes; (ESA)				Yes
(v) services to disabled and those with employment problems	Yes; ESA				

5. (i) Aim: to facilitate job creation and saving temporarily during recession or school-leaver bulge.

(ii) Policies and measures to create and maintain jobs

To create and maintain jobs	Central	Regional		Local	
		WMEPC	WMPAC	City	District
(a) Job creation programme 1975–77	Yes; MSC			Yes	Yes
(b) Community industry (school-leavers)	Yes; DE				
(c) Work experience (school-leavers; 1976–)	Yes; DE				
(d) Recruitment subsidy for unemployed school leavers (–1976)	Yes; ESA				
(e) Job release scheme (early retirement; (1976–)	Yes; ESA				
(f) Youth employment subsidy (under 20s; 1976–77)	Yes; ESA				
(g) Job introduction scheme for disabled	Yes; ESA				
(h) Small firms employment subsidy in special development areas	*Yes; DE				

Sources: *Department of Employment Gazette; Trade and Industry; Annual Reports of Manpower Services Commission* (relevant issues)

III. INDUSTRIAL PLANNING IN THE WEST MIDLANDS COUNTY AREA IN THE 1970s: INTENTIONS AND PRACTICE

(i) Structure Planning and Industrial Policies at Local Level

The final section of the paper turns to the practice of industrial planning in the County area. As it is difficult to summarize the contents of the eleven structure plans relevant to the West Midlands County area in a few words, this section concentrates on the industrial aspects of the plans of two of the pre-1974 county boroughs. This illustrates the fact that structure plans were the outcome of differing economic, political and land supply conditions. Some reference is made to the industrial policies of these areas after 1974 before turning to the County itself and its structure and economic planning activity. Until the County appeared, there was no overall view at County or conurbation level but many shared problems and policy proposals.

A. Coventry County Borough and Metropolitan District

Coventry has been chosen for special study because it was and is exceptional. It had adopted corporate planning and fitted structure planning into this framework (City of Coventry, 1972). It had an updated development plan and, currently, it is one of only four areas in the County with an approved structure plan. The City Council was committed to dealing with the serious unemployment connected with the slump in the car and machine tool industries and the lack of job variety. Related to this, Coventry acquired new private statutory powers to foster industrial development.

In summary form, the economic objectives of the Coventry structure plan were the promotion of industrial development, the provision of employment, the stimulation and attraction of investment, and the efficient use of physical and manpower resources (City of Coventry, 1973). The implementation programme included spending nearly £1 million on land acquisition, unit factory and industrial loop road building. This commitment followed a decision to allocate 10 per cent of the capital budget each year for five years to industrial and commercial development.

Subsequently, Coventry Corporation Act 1972 enabled the City to provide financial assistance as an incentive to invest in Coventry rather than elsewhere. The incentives, introduced in March 1977 and backed up with £250 000, include loans, grants, rent guarantees and rent free periods (West Midlands County Council, 1977; *Birmingham Post*, 1977a). Help can be generous but it is carefully allocated to encourage a spread of projects and those producing jobs and diversification or developing local skills. A register of vacant sites and premises is maintained with the help of local estate agents and the City has been advertised as a 'positive centre' that 'offers opportunities' (*Birmingham Post*, 1976).

Coventry City Council is itself a substantial industrial developer with 230 acres of industrial land inside and outside the City. Three main sites contain 77 factories and more are being built each year, especially at Aldermans Green Estate. The private sector is also active; for example, an old colliery is being redeveloped to provide another 500,000 sq.ft. The City has also pressed the government to extend the machine tool industry scheme to a wider spectrum of concerns so that smaller and local firms can benefit. Direct action has been taken to relieve unemployment through training schemes and relief work and job creation.

Corporate planning, general efficiency, special powers, determination and a serious problem have in Coventry combined to produce a drive for development that is already having effect—though, in August 1977, the unemployment rate of 8.0 per cent (Birmingham 7.6 per cent; Great Britain 6.8 per cent) indicated that further results were urgently needed.

B. Birmingham County Borough and Metropolitan District

Birmingham County Borough's policy towards industrial development changed formally in October 1971. Prior to that, industrial overspill had been supported and industrial land in the City had been reserved for local firms to the exclusion of outsiders (Sutcliffe and Smith, 1974). Nothing was done to attract firms in; jobs seemed plentiful and the future secure. But, by the late 1960s rising unemployment had ended the labour shortage and job losses were a source of concern. The City resolved 'to deliberately encourage the retention and expansion of existing industry within the City boundary', and to back this up with its land allocation policies in its structure plan and its publicity campaign for the City as an industrial location (City of Birmingham, 1973b). The selective introduction of new, especially science-based, industries was sought plus a business school and investment in infrastructure to attract service jobs.

Birmingham's objectives and policies can be summarized to provide a useful example of the approach and content of industrial planning in a structure plan. They were:

1. *To restructure the economy and retain employment* by allocating land for development and servicing it to provide sites for firms affected by Council action and for small unit factories.
2. *To diversify the manufacturing employment structure* by promoting the locational advantages of the City to outsiders, allocating sites to newcomers, especially those with growth potential, and pressing the Department of Industry for i.d.c.'s to attract 'some major firms' to the City in new (but unspecified) growth industries.
3. *To improve industrial efficiency by developing a stock of modern factory buildings* by encouraging redevelopment, conversion and modernization.
4. *To limit the take up of land by warehouses and distribution centres* by discriminating against such proposals.
5. *To help areas of the City where employment was short for residents or for certain groups* by defining land for light industry in residential areas.
6. *To reduce journeys to work and to encourage the local relationship* of homes and jobs by moderating policies towards segregation of uses and non-conforming use.

Policies were also to be introduced to provide jobs in greater variety and number, notably in service industries, to monitor the employment situation and to watch environmental standards.

The implementation of such general policies is difficult to assess but Birmingham has acted to assist industrial development in specific ways. From the past, it owns flatted factories, industrial estates and factories, though the provision of these related to the relocation of concerns affected by planning action rather than to the positive assistance of industrial development. More recently, Birmingham has organized a promotion campaign round a brochure entitled *Birmingham Means Business;* it has a team in the estates office to assist industrial development particularly with information about sites and premises through a commercial officer; it has organized a drive to fill its empty offices and to refurbish some older ones in a conservation area; it has decided to reallow speculative office building despite the two million square feet unlet and more in the pipeline; it has built some advance factories including a few 'seedbed' small ones of 500 sq. ft.; sites have been made available to existing firms that needed to move; direct efforts to create jobs and improve training have been made; and planning policies have been re-examined to ensure that they are helpful to industry and employment.

Finally, two rather different actions may be mentioned. A major step was taken by the City in the establishment of the National Exhibition Centre on land just outside Birmingham. This was largely financed and initiated by the City as a catalyst to service employment. Then there is the project 'Self Help', a direct effort to stimulate small, new ventures in the City by bringing together people with ideas and those able to provide finance and management skills.

Thus, Birmingham is involved in industrial planning through its structure planning and its industrial policies. This is also true of most other conurbation districts and their activities are on much the same lines. Wolverhampton is particularly active as it shares many of Birmingham's problems, and Solihull is the least active as industrial and commercial development burgeon there without much effort. Solihull's expansion in a prosperous, middle-class outer suburb with land to spare indicates the obverse side of inner area decline.

C. The Public Examination and the Panel Report

The Panel's Report on the public examination of the six conurbation structure plans brings together the six plans and examines them critically in two respects (Department of the Environment, 1976a). On the one hand, the Report comments on their acceptability as structure plans, rigorously restricting them to land-use policies and thus preventing their use as cohesive industrial plans. On the other hand, the Panel Report tries to draw out of the six plans an overall plan for the County and the policies to implement this in two respects: the control and, where appropriate, relocation of 'bad neighbour' industry and the employment needs of people living in areas suffering from multiple deprivation, elsewhere denoted as the inner areas. The latter has now been overtaken by the surge of activity to help industry in inner areas though this activity has little direct connection or reliance on structure planning as the two are rather different animals and move at a different pace.

The industrial problems of the six plans were seen by the Panel and the six plans as manufacturing decline, industrial structure and performance with the effects concentrated most harmfully in the inner areas. The Panel supported the aims of retaining existing industry and attracting in new industry to diversify the structure. It approved policies to provide land for industrial relocation and expansion and to provide some of this land close-in so that non-mobile firms could take advantage of it. The immobility of much conurbation industry was accepted dramatically by the Panel and the Minister after nearly thirty years of industrial exporting policies and the implication of this view was spelt out in industrial development terms—that the vital need was to find enough land within and in the fringes of the conurbation. Such land then required careful husbanding by giving preference to labour—intensive development, by using small sites and by converting existing premises. But neither the Panel nor the Minister were able to challenge national regional policy; thus policies to admit new firms had to be qualified and only muted complaints against the i.d.c. control were allowed.

Policies on industrial land were, therefore, crucial but not necessarily effective. On the one hand, Dudley's structure plan was 'modified' by the Minister to provide 530 acres of industrial land instead of the 195 acres originally proposed (Department of the Environment, 1976a; and 1977d). This is a huge increase. It suggests that Dudley's already favourable unemployment rate may improve still farther though the intention is to relieve land-hungry industry in Warley and Wolverhampton and to make possible the 'restructuring' of industry in the conurbation. It illustrates the inevitability of treating inner area problems not at their source but where the distribution of potential land permits. However, i.d.c.'s will be needed to develop this land and these may not be forthcoming in Dudley.

On the other hand, while this land in Dudley was identified, less success was obtained with regard to other restructuring sites. The regional strategy (West Midland Regional Study, 1971a) considered that the problems affecting the performance and growth of conurbation industry included inadequate sites and lack of space to introduce modern production methods in existing plants. It conceived of five 'rim' sites to provide relief by relocation of some firms and by provision of improved servicing functions in existing industrial areas. A subsidiary aim was to generate tangential travel-to-work flows.

No specific sites were identified and, as the sites challenged the movement of industry across the green belt to overspill areas, the issue proved to be fraught with political problems (West Midlands Planning Authorities Conference, 1974). At the public examination of the six plans, the rim sites were accepted as crucial to industrial prospects in the six plans' area but none was actually in the plans covered, four being located outside the area and the fifth in theory in Dudley; hence the change in Dudley. Some of the arguments between Wolverhampton and Staffordshire were over the location of the rim site to the north-east of Wolverhampton. With regard to the one relevant to Birmingham, it was not in the Warwickshire structure plan though clearly located there and Birmingham perforce garnered a few acres in several sites as a poor substitute. By the end of the examination, the grave lack of stable, immediately available, undeveloped, sizeable industrial sites anywhere in the conurbation became evident. Few sites seemed positively attractive to industry or at all competitive with greenfield sites available in the new towns and development areas despite the universal desire of the planning authorities to attract fresh industry and to revivify the old.

D. County Structure Plan Activity

The creation of the West Midlands County in 1974 has introduced a new dimension into the structure planning process for the County, and is concerned with the total requirements of the County area and with transport planning. On the other hand, because the County lacks the wider responsibilities of the old County Boroughs, their structure plans have been modified on this account and to leave 'sufficient flexibility' for the preparation of local plans by the new districts (Department of the Environment, 1977d).

Apart from its appearance and the many new documents produced at the public examination, little is known publicly yet of County activity except that work is going along busily. The County is bringing together the eleven structure plans, or parts of structure plans relevant to its area, into a coherent whole, while at the same time bringing them up to date. The County is required to take account of the Minister's draft modifications to the original structure plans. The County has also the opportunity to introduce its own political and planning ideas where these do not conflict with the previous points. The regional strategy review has also been changing the context. In due course, a written statement will be produced and publicly discussed. Subsequent to this, a final written statement will be prepared by the County Council for approval in Autumn 1978 prior to submission to the Secretary of State for the Environment (West Midlands County Council, 1976c).

Considerable new research work has been undertaken within the County through surveys and analysis. During the process, too, the economic situation has worsened while the conservatives have come to power in the County as well as in many of the districts. As the structure plan is a political document, this change of party can be expected to have some effects on policy.

So the County still awaits its first comprehensive structure plan. The districts need this before they can finalize the plans for their own areas. The town maps from the 1950s continue to be used in development control except where specific amendments are recognized. Meanwhile the world has not stood still. The County itself has been pursuing economic planning to which attention is now turned.

(ii) Economic Planning by the County Council

A. Organization and Priorities

Soon after the West Midlands County was set up in 1974, it involved itself in economic planning (*West Midlands Metropolitan County*, 1976; Cordle and Liggins, 1976). There were three reasons for this. Some strategic problems did not involve land-use solutions relevant to the structure planning process; a start was also needed in the short term without awaiting the outcome of the latter; and the politicians in the County were eager to demonstrate that the County had a positive role in a field that did not duplicate the work of the districts. The problem was evident and the Countywide perspective attractive.

Three organizations were introduced in the County to facilitate this economic planning role: first, an Employment, Commerce and Industry Sub-Committee of the County Council's Policy Committee of elected members with Labour in control; and, on the officer side, second a Financial and Economic Planning Division in the County Treasurer's Department with staff that has included half a dozen economists; and third, an Economic Group within the corporate planning system to integrate departments in economic work.

The economic planning operation got underway with the publication in September 1974 of the first version of *A Time for Action* as a discussion document to publicize the alarming trends in many West Midlands indicators (West Midlands County Council, 1974). A second revised edition followed in 1975, endorsed by the districts and extended to include policy proposals to deal with the problems highlighted (West Midlands County Council, 1975a).

The County decided on three priorities for action. The first was to continue to press central government to recognize the need to change regional policy's discrimination against the region and the County. The second priority action was to design a package of policies to assist industry in the County in the short and long term. Included were proposals relating to the industrial development certificate control, training, industrial estates and an industrial information service. While their precise effect was not known, all were felt to point in the right direction. The third priority action was to continue research into longer-term issues and into policies to aid industrial diversification, performance and the attraction of the County to jobs and people to counter decentralization. Major research projects have been looking at industrial structure and performance, growth industries, employment densities, manpower planning and an input–output model for the region. These three met the need for the County to take positive action itself to help its area and to generate responses in the appropriate places. The County demanded meetings with ministers, consulted industrialists, trade unionists and other levels of government and visited the European Economic Community. It gained support from the

West Midlands Economic Planning Council and West Midlands Planning Authorities Conference. And, by 1977, some change of heart in central government was becoming apparent.

The County has tried to get the right balance between research/analysis and action. Because it has had to temper its inclination for action for lack of finance, its advocacy role has been important, absorbing staff time rather than capital sums.

In 1976, the County modestly suggested that:

> the economic planning process at the Metropolitan County level is . . . a marginal process, progress being achieved by a large number of successive smaller steps rather than a small number of major policy initiatives . . . This does not mean, however, that the County Council's thinking should be restricted only to those particular areas in which it can take executive action itself (West Midlands Metropolitan County, 1976).
>
> Efforts to inject this thinking into central government at the policy formulation stage has met with only limited success.

Gradually economic planning has been fitted into the annual routine in the County with an *Annual Economic Review*, *Half Yearly Economic Action Bulletin*, and *County Expenditure Survey*. There have also been many one-off publications on particular topics (West Midlands County Council, 1975–77). While a budget has been agreed for industrial promotion out of locally determined sector funds, all expenditure on industrial development and planning has not been brought together in one place for either co-ordination or evaluation. Early policies were allowed through on grounds of greater comparative expenditure by other metropolitan authorities, expected assistance in relieving economic problems and the promise of appraisal, but the latter has been found to require unjustifiably costly investigation.

B. Particular Policies

Land provision

The County decides land allocations for industry and employment on the basis of forecast supply and demand but relies on the districts being able to find the necessary sites in quantity and quality to attract the envisaged development. There is a shortage of industrial sites and some are derelict, occupied by empty or unsatisfactory buildings or held by firms for their future development. Policies are needed to deal with these issues.

Reclamation of derelict land is a responsibility of both County and districts; 1.7 per cent of County land is derelict or 4.8 per cent including waste land, despite the pressure for development (Gibson and Collins, 1977). A 50 per cent grant towards the cost of reclamation is available only on derelict land in public ownership. Efforts to reclaim land for industrial use have been frustrated by practicalities rather than just money. The hope is to persuade central government to be more generous with its grants.

The Community Land Act could be used to acquire land held by firms for development, but the best hope is for economic growth to generate its use or sale.

Industrial sites zoned for industry in district plans need to be brought forward for development. The County as a new authority owns very little land. The Community Land Act has not proved any help to the County so far for financial reasons and now there are ideological ones as well. The five-year rolling programme became superfluous as decisions came to be taken on a site-by-site basis. In 1976–77, the County purchased no land at all and made no application to do so. Alternative means have to be found of stimulating private activity by County investment in access roads, servicing and land preparation. The 1976–77 capital programme contained £450 000 to strengthen the County economy by purchase and development of industrial sites but proposals remain obstinately in the pipeline dogged by problems of land ownership and finance until external finance can be harnessed.

Industrial estates are recommended in many policy statements at County and district level with no argument to support clustered factories rather than individual, dispersed units, which are an alternative form of development. One suspects many failed to appreciate the distinction. Presumably the estate concept derived from economies of scale in estate services and segregation of uses, and built on a worldwide and unquestioned practice (United Nations, 1966; Bredo, 1960).

Buildings

Policies towards buildings concern both the obsolete and the new. The scale of the former problem is not known, for definitions change with market conditions. Where the buildings are empty and unusable, demolition and replacement can make use of the land; where in use or usable, refurbishment and modernization, either speculatively or by the occupier, is possible. Where the premises are occupied, an industrial improvement scheme is likely to provide a solution shortly (West Yorkshire Metropolitan County Council, 1976; Hargreave, 1976).

An advance factory is one built of standard design ahead of demand (Slowe, 1977). The County programme is designed to encourage private building and to fill gaps in the market in the size and location of units, namely in small units and in inner areas. Its efforts are severely restrained by the i.d.c. control which restricts speculative ventures to under 15,000 sq.ft. even where individual units are smaller.

Many private developers are active and merely await assurance of an adequate return before adventuring ahead of the market or into inner areas. They have moved into building small units too. Some joint schemes are planned. The County has decided on one such scheme. A derelict site in Dudley was chosen to be reclaimed and then used for a pioneer scheme for small premises to encourage entrepreneurs. Nearly £1 million was involved. The Scottish Equitable Assurance Society was to lease the land from the Council and to build 80,000 sq. ft. and then lease the units back to the County to let (*Birmingham Post*, 1977b and 1977c). The scheme harnessed private sector finance in a fruitful way but the application for an industrial development certificate was refused by the Department of Industry as the development was 'inconsistent with the proper distribution of industry'. This was the first refusal in the conurbation for some time and a setback to regeneration proposals. Closer examination suggests refusal was related to the choice of Dudley and that either the building of warehouses or relocation to an inner area site would provide a way forward.

Direct financial assistance to individual firms

Events at British Leyland, BSA-Norton-Villiers-Triumph and elsewhere, caused the County to consider direct assistance to concerns in trouble to preserve jobs. In the event, central government acted in the national interest. The other kind of assistance involved incentives to firms to develop in the County area. Reference has been made to Coventry's activities and to the promise of general powers tied to inner area development. At present, the County considers it lacks such powers (and a bill seeking these was rejected by the Commons) and, even if it had them, it would be limited by funds and regional policy.

Development control

Applications for planning permission are vetted by the development control section of a planning department. Development control represents the interface between planning policies and the firm. Efforts are being made to change from control to positive assistance to industry. Following Circular 71/77 (Department of the Environment, 1977c), the County and districts have accepted this as a useful way in which the local authority can aid industrial development readily and inexpensively.

Priority is being given to industrial cases; flexibility is being introduced in applying the rules on land zoning to permit mixed development; restrictions are being placed on warehouses and superstores developing on industrial land. For instance, planning permission has been given for British Leyland's Research, Design and Development Centre to be built in the green belt in

Solihull. The County also refused all five applications to build retail warehouses and five out of eleven to build warehouses in 1976 (West Midlands County Council, 1977). A proposal for an industrial park beside Fort Dunlop was also refused because too little of the 45 acres was reserved for manufacturing. Doubtless the i.d.c. control encouraged this and now the County is considering approving warehouses as a 'way of getting industry by the back door' through subsequent change of use certificates when industrial tenants present themselves.

Small is beautiful

Both national and local government in England have suddenly swung towards policies that foster small firms. Explanations for this trend include concern at the disproportionate rate of loss of small firms in recent years and about the reduction in local decision-making, the ability of small firms to avoid the i.d.c. control, their happier industrial relations, skill ratios and flexibility and their openness to planners' influence. Support for small firms fits the lack of financial resources and incremental planning mood. It is associated with encouraging indigenous industry, often also in small units, rather than reliance on importing investment from outside. The only problem is the inability of small firm revival to compensate in scale for the job losses in the County.

Industrial promotion and advice and information about sites and premises

The industrial planners in the County (and the districts) identified a gap in the marketing of sites and premises that they have sought to fill with registers of available sites and premises, including those in private hands. The County appointed a full-time industrial promotion officer in February 1977 to run the register and to promote the County as an industrial location through advertising and exhibitions; 35 per cent of metropolitan authorities now have such officers (Handley, 1977). As in the County, not all are given the support that permits them to follow up inquiries and positively seek out others.

Inner area policies for industry

The industrial development policies already mentioned are of general application in the County area. However, because of the concentration of industry and industrial decline in the inner parts of the County, these policies have often operated there and have now been positively rejigged to discriminate in favour of specific inner areas under the central government inner area programme (Department of the Environment, 1977a). In Birmingham, this is the ability to build on community development project and inner area study research (Birmingham Community Development Project, 1977; Department of the Environment, 1977e; Smith, 1974a and 1977a and b).

The programme is in two parts; some initial so-called construction money to be spent before March 1979 and the partnership and other schemes to follow. Birmingham is one of the seven partnership areas and Wolverhampton one of the fifteen second-tier areas while three other districts are to receive smaller funds and powers. A meeting on 13 December 1977 will decide the organization of the partnership between the County, Birmingham City and the Department of the Environment and the precise inner area to be helped. The latter seems likely to be the five inner employment exchanges in Birmingham. New funds (£11 million to March 1979 and £10 million per annum thereafter), new powers (i.d.c. relief and incentives) and the new organization and commitment are concentrated on this area to the disadvantage of others. Industrial development powers are to be provided for local authorities to use in some or all inner areas, notably powers to make loans up to 90 per cent of the cost of new industrial development, to set up industrial improvement areas and to offer two-year rent-free periods. Such incentives, however, will have to be financed by the local authorities. The Department of Industry, for the first time, has been directed to seek industry for the Birmingham inner area—but only from within the region. This area now has second priority to the assisted areas; time will tell how generously this concession is operated.

The County has forced its way into the partnership on the basis of its structure and transport planning responsibilities and its existing activity in economic planning. In 1976, the County published a useful examination of the scale, form and evolution of its inner area economic problem (West Midlands County Council, 1976b). It has set up an Inner Areas Working Party Structure Plan Group to produce a report of survey shortly and an Inner Areas *Ad Hoc* Group to implement its inner area programme. This will be largely responsible for spending the £2½ million out of the £11 million allocated to industry. A few derelict factories are being refurbished, road repairs undertaken, roads and sewers laid to an industrial estate, derelict land reclaimed and two careers offices being improved. In Wolverhampton and elsewhere, the construction money is being spent on building nursery factories on cleared land. These schemes have been prepared locally and approved by the Department of the Environment in record time, indicating the commitment of all parties to the policy. The partnership concept in Birmingham is an attempt to maintain this commitment across all relevant departments in both local and central government and other agencies.

There are problems with area discrimination involving the justice of the boundaries, the wisdom of concentrating effort on what may prove to be unattractive locations to firms and conflict with central government's general industrial strategy. Growth and efficiency may be penalized by concentration on inner areas and on job creation and, if the jobs fail to return to the inner areas, the rehabilitation of the housing and infrastructure there may have been wasted.

Conservative influence on county policy

The Conservatives won the election to the County in 1976, having won many districts in the previous election. Their manifesto announced the reversal of certain Labour policies, notably on consumer protection and economic planning, in an effort to free private choice and reduce public expenditure. In practice, economic planning has survived under a different name and, because of Labour national policies on industry and inner areas, has even begun to expand again. The changes in policy have been fewer than the portents suggested though others, like the refusal to use the Community Land Act, may be largely hidden from public view.

IV. CONCLUSION

Five distinct streams can, thus, be discerned in the industrial planning currently undertaken in the West Midlands County area. These five include the policies mainly at national level concerned with the industrial strategy and inner areas and those largely at local level concerned with local industrial development and performance, structure planning and planning practices helpful to industrial development. The five streams are interwoven and have different and sometimes conflicting objectives though these have not been spelt out. Some diversion of effort has occurred recently towards the first two because of national support and funds.

The two will have different effects; the industrial strategy is likely to cause redundancy through increases in productivity per head while the inner area policy is intended to foster employment by discriminatory policies in designated areas covering only part of the County. Unless the designated areas are the optimal ones for productivity growth, the objectives of the policies will clash with each other and with regional policy. The analogy with regional policy is apt. The key issues are, first, the choice of the areas to be assisted; second, whether there is local and national agreement over these; and, third, the scale and nature of the assistance given; the latter cannot yet be gauged in relation either to the inner area problem or to the disadvantaged areas. As with regional policy, help is being given not because the rest of the County is so prosperous that it needs no encouragement but because of the seriousness of the inner area situation.

Thus, on the one hand, the rest of the County and region will find themselves 'exporting' industry to the inner areas in addition to the assisted areas. Regionwide trends in economic indicators show this to be unwise. On the other hand, the industrial viability of the inner areas has hardly been examined. As with regional policy, the central government is trying relatively feebly to turn the tide of long set-in market trends and past land-use policies at a time of falling manufacturing employment.

The County's industrial planning derives from its statutory land use and transport planning responsibilities and its non-statutory interest in economic planning. Serving both has been its economic analysis work and advocacy role. The latter has been important and has accomplished a good deal, being helped in this by the disastrous economic situation pressed home by the unemployment statistics.

Much of the effort has been concentrated on obtaining a change in the i.d.c. control. This impinges on industrial planning at a number of points. Refusals are a flashpoint but more insidious has been the deterrent to speculative factory-building in new locations and styles and to modernization and replacement schemes and the impetus to warehouse building in an area short of jobs and of industrial land. The recent refusal (see page. 244) shows how the control hinders regeneration proposals in an area where potential industrial land supply has been trebled, and the concession in the inner areas will not prove significant if the assisted area priority remains the determining factor.

The County has undertaken important work on analysing industrial performance. Like central government in its industrial strategy, the County now needs some technique for boosting industrial performance, some method of reaching decision-makers to explain to them ways of improving their plants' performance. Neither central nor County government has the experience or tools for the task. This raises the difficult question of communication with industry on a broader front. Industrial liaison officers, industrial democracy or expensive visits by well-trained personnel rather than just investment subsidies may provide answers.

The districts' industrial planning derives from much the same source as in the County. All have been concerned at local economic decline, backing up the County but also operating their own policies.

Industrial planning has shown up the competitive situation in metropolitan government since 1974 with the County trying to find an identifiable and obvious role in the eyes of the public to avoid elimination in the next round of local government reform. This has been important in shaping County policy. It has encouraged the County to go for the spectacular but also to attempt to be decisive and quick off the mark, even if subsequently the momentum has often been lost.

Far too little attention has been paid to the effectiveness of policies in either influencing industrial investment decisions or being implemented at all or on a significant scale. Few of the long list of policies in section two have been evaluated and, at the local level, schemes galore have been discussed with little outcome. In any case, to take an example, how much extra assistance to industry has the existence of the property register provided at a time when estate agents were touting for work and there were thousands of square feet of property on the market? It has been hard to get policies into action. No one has engineered a way round the difficulties. The County sets its own priorities for its locally determined sector expenditure and action. Therefore, as there have been outcomes in other fields, lack of progress on industrial policies seems to reflect other priorities in a tough financial situation. But, at another level, effectiveness has also been frustrated by the forces mentioned in the model framework (pages 226–235) and the difficulty of influencing the ingredients of economic activity, of reaching enough concerns that are potential developers in the County area and in contacting decision-makers in these firms. This problem is not often confronted openly by planners. It may explain the current enthusiasm for small and indigenous firms, as these are most susceptible to influence. There is a research field here to find out ways in which government, local or national, can influence these ingredients better.

It is possible to see two forces shaping the industrial planning in the metropolitan area. One force comes up from the local economy, indicating the gaps left and the problems created by the market; the other force comes down from central government, indicating another set of gaps and problems. The character of central government activity will be of crucial importance to what local planners need to do and decide to do. Local political choice and economic circumstances will influence the districts and County in deciding how they view what central government is doing and whether they want to work with it or against it or to seek to change it. The County has been seeking to counter and alter central government policies on i.d.c.'s, derelict land grants and regional policy generally. Relations between the County and the districts will be rather similar with the districts identifying gaps or policies they want to counter or change in the County's industrial planning. This may well increase with the inner area policy where some parts of the County are to be treated differently from others.

Industrial planning in the metropolitan area has an important role in overcoming the fundamental problems indicated by the present adverse trends. That view derives more from the seriousness of the problems and the unlikelihood of the market compensating for them than from faith in the success or force of public intervention. New methods are needed to deal effectively with these problems at central and local level. The County has a role in informing central government of how its policies are working out locally, in moderating these policies in their local applications, in co-ordinating the many agencies with a hand in local industrial planning, and in developing communication with the private sector. The problems have been recognized. Needed now are better means for dealing with them, more consensus about means and ends and better co-ordination between the many bodies involved. Of particular importance to success is consensus on objectives between local and central government and between their departments. The inner area programme will provide useful experience in attempting this yet again. The next few years will be important ones in the development of industrial planning.

REFERENCES

Barlow, A. T. and Downing, S. (1976). *Industrial Development Certificates in the West Midlands Region: Projects Abandoned or Not Completed*, Department of Industry, West Midlands Regional Office.

(*Birmingham Post*) (1976). 'Coventry starts drive to reverse exodus'. **20 October**, 3.

(*Birmingham Post*) (1977a). 'Coventry's industrial policy pays dividends'. **28 July**, 11.

(*Birmingham Post*) (1977b). 'IDC refusal wrecks £1m. pilot project'. **3 August**, 1.

(*Birmingham Post*) (1977c). 'Mini-factories pioneer plan'. **19 April**, 4.

Bor, W. (1974). The Town and Country Planning Act, 1968, *The Planner*, **60**, *696–702*.

Bredo, W. (1960). *Industrial Estates. Tools for Industrialization*, London.

Camina, M. M. (1974). Local authorities and the attraction of industry, *Progress in Planning*, **3**, Part 2, 92.

Carter, C. J. (1977). 'Changing patterns of industrial land use 1948–75'. In Frank Joyce (ed.), *Metropolitan Development and Change, the West Midlands: A Policy Review*, Saxon House, Farnborough, 127–147.

Central Statistical Office (1968). *Standard Industrial Classification HMSO, London.*

City of Birmingham (1973a). *A New Plan for the City. First Stage. Report of Survey. Employment and Industry*, Birmingham.

City of Birmingham (1973b). *Structure Plan for Birmingham. Written Statement*, Birmingham.

City of Birmingham (annually). *Birmingham Statistics*, Birmingham.

City of Coventry (1972). *The Promotion of Commercial and Industrial Development. Volume 7. Corporate Planning Survey Report, 1972*, Coventry.

City of Coventry (1973). *Structure Plan 1973. Written Statement*, Coventry.

Confederation of British Industry (1976). *The Road to Recovery*, London.

Confederation of British Industry (1977). *Britain Means Business*, London.

Cordle, P. L. and Liggins, D. (1976). 'Economic planning'. *Public Finance and Accountancy* **January,** 11–15.

Cullingworth, J. B. (1964 and 1974). *Town and Country Planning in England and Wales*, Allen and Unwin, London.

Department of Economic Affairs (1965). *The West Midlands—A Regional Study*, HMSO, London.

Department of Employment (1973). *New Earnings Survey 1972*, HMSO, London.

Department of Employment Gazette (1977). **85**, **June,** 587.

Department of the Environment (1971). *Local Government in England. Government Proposals for Reorganisation*, (Cmnd. 4584), London.

Department of the Environment (1973). *Greater London Development Plan: Report of the Panel Inquiry*, Layfield, Vol. 1, Report, HMSO, London, Chapter 5, 78–80.

Department of the Environment (1976a). *Structure Plan for Birmingham, Dudley, Walsall, Warley, West Bromwich and Wolverhampton. Report of the Panel. Examination in Public*, London.

Department of the Environment (1976b). *British Cities: Urban Population and Employment Trends, 1961–71*, R. Drewett, J. Goddard and N. Spence, Research Report, 10, London.

Department of the Environment (1977a). *Policy for the Inner Cities* (Cmnd. 6845), HMSO, London.

Department of the Environment (1977b). *Circular 55/77. Memorandum on Structure and Local Plans*, London.

Department of the Environment (1977c). *Circular 71/77, Local Government and the Industrial Strategy*, London.

Department of the Environment (1977d). *Statement Relating to the Secretary of State's*

Draft Modifications. Structure Plans of Birmingham, Dudley, Walsall, Warley, West Bromwich and Wolverhampton, undated typescript, London.

Department of the Environment (1977e). *Birmingham Inner Area Study. Unequal City. Final Report*, HMSO, London.

Dudley, N. (1975). 'Industrial productivity—scope for improvement'. *Midlands Tomorrow*, West Midlands Economic Planning Council, No. 8, Birmingham.

Gibson, L. G. and Collins, W. G. (1977). 'Derelict land in the West Midlands'. In Frank Joyce (ed.) *Metropolitan Development and Change, The West Midlands: A Policy Review*, Saxon House, Farnborough.

Grant, W. and Marsh, D. (1977). *The CBI*, Hodder and Stoughton, London.

Hall, P., Thomas R., Gracey, H., and Drewett, R. (1973). *The Containment of Urban England, Vol. 1*, Allen and Unwin, London, Chapter 10.

Handley, I. M. (1977). 'Aspects of industrial development policies in a metropolitan county: the problems of objectives, methods an evaluation'. Unpublished M.Soc.Sc. thesis, Centre for Urban and Regional Studies, Birmingham.

Hargreave, R. (1976). 'An experimental industrial GIA'. *Town and Country Planning*, **44**, 36–38.

House of Commons Expenditure Committee (1973). *Trade and Industry Sub-Committee. Regional Development Incentives. Session 1972–73 and 1973–74 Minutes of Evidence*, 327 and 85–1, HMSO, London.

House of Commons Expenditure Committee (1975). *The Motor Vehicle Industry. Fourteenth Report. Session 1974–75, Minutes of evidence Vol. III, Memoranda*, London.

Howard, R. S. (1968). *The Movement of Manufacturing Industry in the U. K. 1945–65*, Board of Trade, HMSO, London.

Joint Monitoring Steering Group (1975). *A Developing Strategy for The West Midlands. The First Annual Report of the Group*, West Midlands Planning Authorities Conference, Birmingham'.

Joint Monitoring Steering Group (1976a). *A Developing Strategy for The West Midlands. The Second Annual Report of the Group*, West Midlands Planning Authorities Conference, Birmingham'.

Joint Monitoring Steering Group (1976b). *Small Firms in the West Midlands Economy*, (JMSG 76/6), Birmingham.

Liggins, D. (1977). 'Changing role of West Midlands Region in the national economy'. In Frank Joyce (ed.), *Metropolitan Development and Change, The West Midlands: A Policy Review*, Saxon House, Farnborough, pp. 75–96.

Local Government Act 1972 (1972). HMSO, London.

Maton, J. M. (1966). 'Manufacturing output, employment and new buildings. Regional analysis: 1948–58, *Board of Trade Journal*, **190**, i–xvi.

McCrone, G. (1969), *Regional Policy in Britain*, Allen and Unwin, London.

Ministry of Housing and Local Government (1963). *Town and Country Planning: England and Wales. The Town and Country Planning (Uses Classes) Order. Statutory Instruments 1963, No. 708*, London.

Ministry of Housing and Local Government (1965). *The Future of Development Plans: A Report by the Planning Advisory Group*, HMSO, London.

Ministry of Housing and Local Government (1970). *Development Plans. A Manual on Form and Content* HMSO, London.

Ministry of Town and Country Planning (1948). *West Midland Plan* P. Abercrombie and H. Jackson Unpublished, London.

Minns, R. and Thornley, J. (1976). 'Local authorities as shareholders', a paper to the Regional Studies Association Conference on the economic crisis and local manufacturing employment, Birmingham.

Needham, D. B. (1977). 'Employment problems: the public response in Birmingham'. In Frank Joyce (ed.), *Metropolitan Development and Change, The West Midlands: A Policy Review*, Saxon House, Farnborough.

OECD (Organisation for Economic Co-operation and Development) (1977). *Regional Problems and Policies in OECD Countries*, Vol. II, Paris, 7–43.

Palmer, D. J. (1975). *Planning and Forecasting Employment and Economic Development in Structure Planning. Planning Research Applications Group, Technical Paper TP 13*, Centre for Environmental Studies, London.

Prais, S. J. (1976). *The Evolution of Giant Firms in Britain*, NIESR, Cambridge.

Roberts, M. (1974), *An Introduction to Town Planning Techniques*, Hutchinson, London.

Rogers, P. B. and Smith, C. R. (1977). The local authority's role in economic development: the Tyne and Wear Act 1976, *Regional Studies* **11**, 153–63.

Royal Commission on Local Government in England, 1966–69 (1969). *Report* (Cmnd. 4040), HMSO, London.

Saunders, D. (1977). 'The changing planning framework'. In Frank Joyce (ed.) *Metropolitan Development and Change, The West Midlands: A Policy Review*, Saxon House, Farnborough.

Slowe, P. M. (1977). 'Advanced factories in British Region Policy', a paper to the Regional Studies Association Conference. Bristol.

Smith, B. M. D. (1971). Industrial development certificate control: an institutional influence on industrial mobility, *Journal of the Town Planning Institute*, **57**, 65–70.

Smith, B. M. D. (1972). *The Administration of Industrial Overspill: The Institutional Framework Relevant to Industrial Overspill in the West Midlands*, Centre for Urban and Regional Studies, Occasional paper 22, Birmingham.

Smith, B. M. D. (1973). *Black Country Employment, 1959–70*, Centre for Urban and Regional Studies, Research Memorandum 18, Birmingham.

Smith, B. M. D. (1974a). *Employment Opportunities in the Inner Area Study of Small Heath, Birmingham, in 1974. Report for the Llewelyn-Davies, Weeks, Forestier-Walker and Bor Inner Area Study*, Centre for Urban and Regional Studies, Research Memorandum 38, Birmingham.

Smith, B. M. D. (1974b). 'Industry and employment'. In G. E. Cherry (ed.) *Urban Planning Problems*, Leonard Hill, London, pp. 84–112.

Smith, B. M. D. (1975). *Youth Employment in Birmingham in 1972*, Centre for Urban and Regional Studies, Research Memorandum 45, Birmingham.

Smith, B.M.D. (1977a). *The Inner City Economic Problem. A Framework for Analysis and Local Authority Policy*, Centre for Urban and Regional Studies, Research Memorandum 56, Birmingham.

Smith, B. M. D. (1977b) 'Economic problems in the core of the old Birmingham industrial area'. In Frank Joyce (ed.), *Metropolitan Development and Change. The West Midlands: A Policy Review*, Saxon House, Farnborough, pp. 148–163.

Sutcliffe, A. and Smith R. (1974). *A History of Birmingham, Vol. III 1939–70*, Oxford.

Trade and Industry (1976). 27 February, p. 558; 12 November, pp. 410–12; 10 December pp. 715–717.

Trade and Industry (1977). 14 January, pp. 91–94; 11 February, pp. 358–362; 419–423; 488–493.

Trades Union Congress (1974). *Collective Bargaining and the Social Contract*, London.

Treasury (with Department of Industry) (1975). *An Approach to Industrial Strategy* (Cmnd. 6315), HMSO, London.

United Nations (1966). *Industrial Estates: Policies, Plans and Progress, New York*.

West Midland Group for Planning and Post-War Reconstruction (1948). *Conurbation. A Survey of Birmingham and the Black Country*, Architectural Press, London.

West Midland Regional Study (1971a). *A Developing Strategy for The West Midlands. Report of the West Midland Regional study, 1971* (the blue book), Birmingham.

West Midland Regional Study (1971b). *A Developing Strategy for The West Midlands. Report of the West Midlands Regional Study, 1971, Technical Appendix 3. Economic Study 3—Industrial Mobility*, Birmingham.

West Midlands County Council (1974). *A Time for Action. Economic and Social Trends in the West Midlands. A Discussion Document*, Birmingham.

West Midlands County Council (1975a). *A Time for Action. Economic and Social Trends in the West Midlands. Policy Proposals*, Birmingham.

West Midlands County Council (1975b). *Visit to EEC and EIB, September 1975, Research Topics*, Birmingham.

West Midlands County Council (1975c). *The British Motor Car Industry*, Birmingham.

West Midlands County Council (1975d). *Unemployment Measures, Autumn, 1975*, Birmingham.

West Midlands County Council (1975e). *Import Controls*, Birmingham.

West Midlands County Council (1975f). *Annual Statistical Abstract*, Birmingham.

West Midlands County Council (1976a). *The North Sea Oil Industry*, Birmingham.

West Midlands County Council (1976b). *The Economic Problems of Inner Areas in the West Midlands County. A Document Submitted to Government to Stimulate Action*, Birmingham.

West Midlands County Council (1976c). *County Structure Plan. Preliminary Statement*, Birmingham.

West Midlands County Council (1976d). *Annual Economic Review*, Birmingham.

West Midlands County Council (1977). *Annual Economic Review*, Birmingham.

West Midlands Economic Planning Council (1967). *The West Midlands: Patterns of Growth*, HMSO, Birmingham.

West Midlands Economic Planning Council (1971). *The West Midlands: An Economic Appraisal*, HMSO, Birmingham.

West Midlands Metropolitan County (1976). *Economic Planning by the West Midland County, Appendix A2, Chapter 7, International Seminar, Managing the Metropolis, Rotterdam. Papers and Proceedings. 12–15 January*, Coventry.

West Midlands Planning Authorities Conference (1974). *A Developing Strategy for the West Midlands. Report of Conference, Addendum and Letter from the Secretary of State*, Birmingham.

West Midlands Planning Authorities Conference (1975). *Current Developments in the Economy of the West Midland Region*, Birmingham.

West Yorkshire Metropolitan County Council (1976). *Industrial General Improvement Areas. A Report for the Secretary of State for the Environment*, Wakefield.

Wood, P. A. (1976). *Industrial Britain: The West Midlands*, David and Charles, Newton Abbot.

Planning Industrial Development
Edited by David F. Walker

Chapter 11

Developing an Industrial Policy for a Central City: A Case Study of Toronto, Canada

Robert C. Christie

This study is a review and assessment of the newly adopted industrial policy for the City of Toronto. As such, it explores the subject matter of industrial planning of a central city, and illustrates the critical role that planners can play in the industrial development process. Toronto's new industrial policy is the result of an updating in recent years of the city's comprehensive or official plan. In this updating process industry was given special attention, as both planners and city councillors have become concerned about the city's continuing decline in industrial employment. Of course, declining industrial employment is a common phenomenon in central cities and it is presumed that the research undertaken and the measures proposed by Toronto planners regarding the decline of industry in their city will be of interest to many industrial development officers, particularly those engaged in the industrial development of central cities.

Most cities have an industrial policy which is incorporated into their comprehensive plan, a document that provides a generalized long-range strategy of planning and development for the community. The industrial policy section of a comprehensive plan usually indicates in a general way why industry is to be accommodated, to what degree, and in what locations. As such the industrial policy section serves as a guide to planners and city councillors on day-to-day matters related to the planning and development of industry (Black, 1968).

There are four basic steps in the development of a comprehensive plan: (1) undertake preliminary and background research; (2) formulate goals and objectives; (3) develop a strategy to achieve the plan's goals and objectives; and (4) determine appropriate implementation tools such as zoning ordinances to implement the plan (Hunker, 1974, pp. 214–217). The same four steps apply to the development of an industrial policy which, in effect, is but one of several complementary policies that make up a comprehensive plan. These four steps were used in the formulation of Toronto's industrial policy.

The study focuses on a review of two companion reports, *Official Plan Amendments—Industrial Policy and the Central Industrial District* (City of Toronto, 1978b), and *Industrial Zoning—Final Recommendations* (City of Toronto, 1978a). These two reports, referred to in this study simply as *The Industrial Policy Report*, and *The Industrial Zoning Report*, were published by the City of Toronto Planning Board in February, 1978 and their recommendations adopted by City Council in April 1978.

The introductory part of this chapter states the nature of the study, compares Toronto with other central cities in North America and explains the city's loss of industrial employment. The rest of the chapter is divided in to five sections. The first section outlines the work programme undertaken by Toronto planners to determine the social and economic implications of this decline. Section two describes the industrial policy and relates it to the background research on which it is based. The third section presents the land-use measures proposed by the Toronto planners to implement their policy. Section five discusses additional measures proposed to maintain the attractiveness of Toronto for industry. The last section concludes the study by evaluating Toronto's industrial policy in two respects: first, in terms of its appropriateness for the planning and development of Toronto and its metropolitan area; and second, in terms of its relevance for other municipalities.

Toronto as a North American Central City

The City of Toronto is located within what some geographers refer to as the American Manufacturing Belt which extends roughly from Boston and Baltimore on the east to about Milwaukee and St Louis on the west. Like other central cities in the Belt, Toronto has continued to lose industrial employment since the early 1950s. In contrast, most 'younger' central cities located outside the American Manufacturing Belt continued to gain in industrial employment, at least until the early 1950s. These facts are borne out by an examination of data compiled by Andrew Hamer (1973, p. 4). Hamer's data show that between 1947 and 1967 all thirteen central cities of the major metropolitan areas in the American Manufacturing Belt lost industrial employment (that is, manufacturing and wholesale employment), but only San Francisco of the twelve central cities of the major metropolitan areas elsewhere in the United States lost industrial employment during this period.

Although the City of Toronto shares a common trend of declining industrial employment with other central cities in the American Manufacturing Belt, in other ways Toronto is significantly different not only from these 'older' central cities but also from many of the 'younger' ones developed later and located elsewhere in the United States. Toronto differs in three major aspects: (1) it is part of a two-tiered system of municipal government; (2) it has remained relatively free of racially related problems; and (3) it has been able to retain a vital and dynamic downtown core.

The City of Toronto and five suburban municipalities, known as boroughs, constitute the municipality of metropolitan Toronto. In the 1976 Census metropolitan Toronto had a population of approximately 2 125 000, of which approximately 635 000 resided in the City of Toronto. The metropolitan level of government is responsible for such matters as police, public transit, the arterial road system, and social services. The local area municipalities are responsible for fire protection, local roads, zoning, and most public housing.

The contrast between the City of Toronto and many American central cities is most notable in respect to Toronto's relative success in meeting the basic economic needs of its minority population. Toronto does not face the same serious problem of providing employment for a large 'secondary' labour force residing in inner city ghettos; it also has unskilled and functionally unemployable workers, but the relative size of its secondary labour force seems to be considerably smaller than those to the south. Toronto has its own 'minority' neighbourhoods whose adult residents are mostly foreign-born, but by and large these foreign-born immigrants have been absorbed into the regional economy. (In 1971, 44 per cent of the city's population and 37 per cent of metropolitan Toronto's population were foreign-born, according to the Census).

Also, unlike many United States' central cities, Toronto has not experienced serious physical decay in its inner core. To the contrary, in the postwar period Toronto's inner core has undergone dynamic growth and change. The central business district has increased considerably in size and height, best observed by a cluster of high office towers in the King-Bay area. In nearby residential areas high-rise redevelopment and the renovation of existing homes has become common.

As the above remarks indicate, Toronto is not a carbon copy of an American central city, although, as mentioned previously, it has one common characteristic with such central cities as Pittsburgh and St Louis, namely a long-standing continuous decline in its industrial base.

The City's Industrial Decline and Metropolitan's Industrial Expansion

Typical of the postwar trend occurring in other metropolitan areas in the American Manufacturing Belt, industry in metropolitan Toronto has been declining in the central city while expanding in the suburbs. For metropolitan Toronto such a trend has been partly the result of many industrial firms in the city moving to the suburbs to satisfy their need for more space, and partly the result of many newly created firms being established in the suburbs. Relocating firms were usually expanding Canadian-owned firms, whereas new firms were usually in the form of subsidiary plants of large corporations mostly headquartered in the United States. Few cities have as many foreign-owned subsidiary plants as metropolitan Toronto, and it is often characterized as a city of American subsidiary plants.

Within metropolitan Toronto, the central city's loss and the suburbs' gain in industry is well exemplified by the postwar changes in their respective levels of employment in manufacturing. Between 1951 and 1974 manufacturing employment in the city declined from 151 000 to 94 000, compared to an increase in manufacturing employment in the suburbs from 27 000 in 1951 to 178 000 in 1974. The net result of these opposing trends for metropolitan Toronto was an increase in its manufacturing employment of 58 per cent, from 178 000 to 272 000 during this twenty-four-year period.

The central city's decline in manufacturing employment has been most marked in respect to blue-collar jobs. Whereas the city's total manufacturing employment declined by 38 per cent, its number of blue-collar workers fell by 48 per cent during the period 1951 to 1974 (1951 data from city of Toronto, 1978b, p. 17; 1974 data from the Census of Manufacturing). The relatively greater decline in the number of blue-collar workers suggests that automation in manufacturing has eliminated relatively more blue-collar manufacturing jobs than white-collar manufacturing jobs.

The primary feature of the city's reduced industrial employment has been the loss of many industrial firms to the suburbs. Within the city three processes have been in operation that have had the effect of preventing the city from replacing the industrial jobs lost to the suburbs. One such process is the conversion of many industrial sites to other uses, reflecting the strong competition for industrial land for office use and to a lesser degree residential and retail uses. Within the expanding central business district in particular, much industrial space has been lost. Beyond the central business district industrial employment has declined not so much because of a loss of industrial space as its conversion from one industrial use to another. This decline in industrial employment is the result of manufacturing firms leaving the city for more spacious premises in the suburbs and their vacated manufacturing premises often being subsequently occupied by less labour-intensive activities such as wholesaling and warehousing. In combination, these two trends, aided by the employment effects of automation, have resulted in a substantial reduction in the number of industrial workers employed in the city.

I. RESEARCHING TORONTO'S INDUSTRIAL POLICY

Preliminary Investigation into the Consequences of Industrial Decline

City planners became aware of the possible serious consequences of the continuing decline of industry in the city while attempting to identify suitable industrial sites for conversion to residential use to be used for city-owned non-profit housing. In the process the planners became aware that if the city took measures that supported a trend already developed by the market place, then Toronto soon might have only a vestige of the industrial base it once had.

In 1973 the Planning Board established an Industry Work Group. It was composed of both planners who were engaged in general research on industry and those who worked in planning areas with a large amount of industry. Originally the Industry Work Group did not have a representative from the City's Development Department because at that time no one in that department served as an industrial development officer. It was only in 1976, after city planners had publicized their concern about the city's declining industrial base, that a member of the Development Department was designated to work with industry. At that time he joined the Industry Work Group. The city's previous lack of interest in having a liaison officer working with the industrial community in a large part reflects the tremendous growth the city has experienced in the office sector. As a consequence, until recently the city has not concerned itself about the employment and financial implications of its industrial decline. Also, although the city had no one working with existing industry until 1976, it was being served by the Toronto Area Industrial Development Board whose main function is to attract new industries to the Greater Toronto Area. This, however, did not help much as most outside industries are looking for relatively new premises or vacant land to build on, while the city has few modern industrial buildings, no industrial parks, and little vacant industrial land.

In June, 1974, the Industry Work Group completed a discussion paper entitled *A Place for Industry*. This fifty-nine page discussion paper focused on the social and economic implications of the continuing decline of industry in the city. *A Place for Industry* noted that, despite the City's objective in the Official Plan to retain its position as a centre of industry, actual practice has not helped to attain such a goal.

A Place for Industry also indicated that, on the basis of preliminary investigation, there are good reasons for the city attempting to arrest the decline of industry. At the same time the discussion paper stated that it was necessary to validate certain assumptions on the effect of industrial decline and also to determine appropriate implementation measures before a new policy on industry was formulated. Some of the assumptions in *A Place for Industry* were considered to be widely held values of 'what should be' and were not considered in need of validation. An example of such a value is that 'a diversity of socioeconomic groups should have access to central city amenities'. On the other hand, it was felt that statements in *A Place for Industry* on what seemed to be the ill-effects of industrial decline should be validated. Four such statements or assumptions were judged worthy of investigation, each to be the subject of a separate assumption study. The four assumption studies were identified as: (1) a 'hardship study'; (2) a 'linkage study'; (3) an 'assessment study'; and, (4) an 'employment study'.

Background Research Undertaken 1974–78

From the investigations and discussions that followed the publication of *A Place for Industry* it was recognized by the Industry Work Group that some assumption studies could not be done and also that some other studies should be undertaken to determine the possibility of attempting to stem the decline in industry.

Due to data limitations, two of the four assumption studies could not be undertaken. These were 'the assessment study' and the 'employment study'. The two completed studies were the 'hardship study' and the 'linkage study'. Along with these two assumption studies the following were identified as necessary and feasible, and were completed prior to the formulation of the industrial policy: (1) a feasibility study on the economics of constructing a multistorey industrial building in the inner city; (2) a Society of Industrial Realtor's market study on the economic and physical obsolescence of the city's industrial building stock; (3) a feasibility study of relocating some of the city's primary, recycling, and bulk storage establishments; and (4) study on the parking and loading requirements for city industries.

The planners also conducted industrial surveys in all the major industrial areas of the city, and in the process of preparing Part II plans for local areas they assembled and plotted detailed land-use data for all areas containing industry. The five major research studies, supported by the industrial surveys and land-use data, provided the informational base for the planners' industrial policy.

The various studies, whether undertaken or not, were intended to provide the following background information: (a) what are the social needs for stemming the city's decline in industrial employment; (b) what demand is there by industry for buildings and land in the city; (c) how important is the retention of industry for providing tax revenues for the city; (d) where in the city should industry be accommodated and in what manner; and (e) what measures should be adopted by the city to achieve its industrial strategy?

The first three areas of research, namely (a), (b), and (c), were considered for the purpose of determining the appropriate goals and objectives for the city's industrial policy. The research related to these three areas and to the industrial policy's goals and objectives are presented in the next section. The last two areas of research, namely (d) and (e), concern the strategy to be used to achieve the industrial policy's goals and objectives and the tools to be used to implement the strategy. The research regarding these two areas is contained in sections three and four.

II. THE INDUSTRIAL POLICY'S RATIONALE

The Industrial Policy in Brief

In brief, the City of Toronto's newly adopted industrial policy consists primarily of a land-use strategy of retaining and renewing industry in the city's solid industrial areas, and permitting industrial sites outside these solid industrial areas to be gradually converted to non-industrial uses.

Through a number of measures, most notably designating and zoning the solid industrial areas for industrial use only, city planners expect the city will experience no more than a 5 per cent decline in industrial employment in the next ten years (City of Toronto, 1978b, p. 51). Therefore Toronto's industrial policy is intended to slow down but not reverse the industrial decline experienced by the City since the early 1950s.

The Rationale and Related Research

As noted in the previous section, in assessing the need for Toronto to retain and renew industry, city planners concentrated on three areas of research. The three areas were: (a) the social need of retaining industrial employment for the city's resident blue-collar population; (b) the market demand for industrial space in the city; and, (c) the importance to the city of tax revenue from industry. Each of these areas are examined below in respect to its importance in providing the basis for the city's industrial Policy.

A. Social Need

The major thrust of the 1974 discussion paper, *A Place for Industry*, seemed to be that there would be serious social implications for the city, and particularly a certain segment of its population, if its industrial base continued to diminish. These serious implications were reiterated in *The Industrial Policy Report*, and stated as social concerns (City of Toronto, 1978b, p. 5).

The validity of each of these three social concerns is discussed below.

'1. *The continued exodus of industrial firms from the City will result in a serious reduction in blue collar employment opportunities and, consequently, in the diversity of socio-economic groups who are able to use the city as a place of work, a place of residence, and a place of recreation.*'

The continuing decline in industrial employment makes it ever more difficult for city residents of relocating firms to find alternative industrial employment in the city, should they not wish to stay with their firm when it relocates. It also becomes more difficult for the city's younger generation and its new arrivals to acquire industrial employment in the city. However, in evaluating the social need for adopting stronger planning measures to retain and renew industry, it should be noted that, as of 1971, the city had a very favourable ratio of industrial jobs to resident industrial workers.

Reflecting historic locational factors, the city has more industrial jobs than resident industrial workers. As Table 11.1 shows, in 1971 the city had 56 per cent more industrial jobs than resident industrial workers. In 1971 the city employed 32 per cent more blue-collar industrial workers than it had residing there. In respect to all employment sectors, the city had 51 per cent more workers employed in the city than it had workers residing in the city. Therefore, it could be argued that the city should only be concerned about maintaining its 'fair share' of industrial jobs in the Toronto area, such as a number of industrial jobs equal to its number of resident industrial workers.

It would seem that the suburban municipalities of metropolitan Toronto would have greater need for attracting industry, as a source of employment and revenue, than the city would for retaining it since they do not have the same opportunities to attract office employment to their suburban locations. At the very least, the above-mentioned figures indicate that the city has less of a social need for retaining its level of industrial employment than most municipalities in the Toronto area.

'2. *The relocation of industrial firms out of the city results in hardships to some of their city resident employees, particularly low-skilled workers.*' It is true that most city residents are inconvenienced by a longer journey-to-work time when their firm relocates from the city to the suburbs, but only when a firm moves beyond normal commuting distance could it be said that there is widespread hardship among the employees resulting from their firm relocating. In fact, from research evidence, it could be argued that the relocation of industrial firms from the city to the suburbs was a net social benefit since the majority of employees benefited from the relocation even if some employees residing in the city were disadvantaged by the move. This argument could be

TABLE 11.1 Employees and resident workers in the City of Toronto in 1971

Type of employment	Employees (or jobs) in the city	Workers residing in the city	Excess of employees to resident workers
All workers in manufacturing and wholesaling	128 000	83 000	56 per cent
Blue collar workers in manufacturing and wholesaling	71 000	52 000	32 per cent
All employment	506 000	335 000	51 per cent

Source: Special request by City of Toronto Planning Board from Statistics Canada, for 1971 Census of Canada data on employed labour force by place or work, place of residence for the municipalities within the Toronto Census Metropolitan Area.

based on the findings of Assumption Study No. 1, entitled *Industrial Relocation and Its Impact on Employees* (City of Toronto, 1975).

Assumption Study No. 1, identified in *A Place for Industry* as 'the hardship study', was designed 'to test the assumption that relocation of City industries to the suburbs is a problem because, as a result, certain people experience significant social and economic hardships' (City of Toronto, 1974, p. 53). The study was based on interviews with management representatives of eight firms that had recently relocated in the suburbs and on questionnaire responses of employees of five of these firms. For the five firms that agreed to distribute the questionnaire, only employees who had worked with the firm prior to relocation and who were still employed by the firm were asked to participate in the survey.

The study showed that only a minority of the work-force was disadvantaged when their firm moved from the city to the suburbs and that the problem was one of personal inconvenience rather than economic cost. Twenty-four per cent of the employees appear to have been disadvantaged and dissatisfied with their firm's move with the percentage being somewhat higher for the lower income employees and for city residents. This figure consists of an estimated 12 per cent who left the firm when it relocated, presumably because they were dissatisfied with the move, and another 12 per cent who remained with the firm but expressed dissatisfaction with its relocation. On the basis of the responses of the employees that remained with the firm, dissatisfaction almost always stemmed from having a much longer journey to work, which affected a majority of both the lower income employees and city residents.

Although some workers did experience the personal inconvenience of a longer journey to work, there was little evidence to indicate that a firm's relocation caused an economic hardship. Few employees, even among the lower income group, mentioned incurring extra financial costs as result of their firm's relocation. Economic hardship could not be considered a consequence of relocation, even for those with limited resources and living some distance from the firm's new location, because the firm was still within commuting distance and accessible by one-fare public transit.

Equally significant was the finding that, including those who left the firm as well as those who remained when the firm relocated, an overwhelming majority (76 per cent) were generally satisfied with the firm's relocation. That so many were satisfied can be attributed in a large part to the fact that most employees lived in the suburbs and relocation improved their commuting time. Most satisfied employees could be characterized as living outside the city, earning more than $9000 yearly, and commuting to work by private vehicle. Assumption Study No. 1 (p. 53) observed that:

> for these satisfied employees, firm relocation has usually meant a reduction in travel time, a result of these employees now living closer to work and/or

commuting to work on less crowded suburban roadways. Ample free parking, a scarce commodity in most downtown industrial locations, is offered by all firms to employees at the new suburban sites, thereby potentially reducing travel costs. The fact that higher income, skilled industrial workers benefit from suburban relocation was recognized in *A Place for Industry* and is amply demonstrated by this study. What is also clear is that a considerable number of moderate and low income employees are also beneficially affected by relocation, particularly if they have access to automobiles for their journey to work.

It should also be noted that all employees at the new premises received the benefit of working in a more modern and more attractive physical plant.

To these advantages for the employees should be added the benefits to the firm and the regional economy as a consequence of the relocation process. The following are three additional findings in this study:

1. All of the firms in the survey moved to the suburbs in order to accommodate current and future expansion.
2. All of the firms relocated in modern single-storey buildings which, according to management, increased plant efficiency.
3. All but one of the eight firms increased the size of their labour force upon moving, indicating that industrial relocation from the city to the suburbs facilitates industrial employment expansion within the Toronto Metropolitan area.

To the extent that its sample firms are representative of firms relocating from the city to the suburbs, this study shows that only a minority of the employees were inconvenienced by their firm's relocation. Those inconvenienced, usually in low paying and low skilled jobs, decided to either accept a longer journey to work time when the firm relocated (12 per cent), or to find employment elsewhere (12 per cent). Offsetting these problems are the advantages that most employees were satisfied with the move and benefited from it in respect to one or more of the following: (a) a reduction in commuting time; (b) ample free parking; and (c) an opportunity to work in more modern facilities. Also, the study confirmed the expected: that relocation allowed the firms to expand their operations, and in most cases, their employment.

3. '*The relocation of industrial workers outside the city prejudices the stability of old working class residential neighbourhoods.*' In *The Industrial Policy Report* the city planners acknowledge they have not done any research on this point by stating that 'Empirical evidence to validate this concern is difficult to collect, since the future of such neighbourhoods is subject to a variety of forces' (p. 126). Undoubtedly, industrial relocation has had some effect on undermining the city's working-class neighbourhoods, but it may not be sufficiently important

to warrant this being mentioned as a social concern related to industrial decline. The lack of research on this matter also raises the question of what is the social imperative to preserve working-class neighbourhoods. The virtue of retaining ageing working-class neighbourhoods for blue-collar workers was not addressed in *The Industrial Policy Report*.

The Industrial Policy Report makes no mention of what other forces are at work to prejudice working class neighbourhoods. To identify them and discuss their importance would permit a better evaluation of the importance of industrial relocation as a destabilizing force in working-class neighbourhoods. It would seem, for instance that 'white painting' is at least as important as the relocation of industrial firms in undermining working-class neighbourhoods. The growing concentration of white-collar employment in the downtown core has brought about a trend of old houses near the core being bought up and renovated by middle and upper income people. This trend, referred to as 'white painting', has completely transformed the character of some traditional working-class neighbourhoods.

It would also seem that destabilization of working-class neighbourhoods is more a result of people changing residences more frequently than in the past, rather than a result of industrial relocation, although the latter may in part be a cause of the former. An important question to be answered is how stable are inner city residential areas nowadays? It is quite possible that stemming industrial relocation may have no appreciable effect on fostering a low turnover of residents or of maintaining community stability in working-class neighbourhoods.

If city planners consider that the relocation of industrial workers outside the city prejudices the stability of old working-class neighbourhoods, then they should explain the ill-effects of such a destabilizing process. For instance, when white-collar workers move into such neighbourhoods supposedly replacing industrial workers who have moved out as opportunities decline in the city, do the remaining blue-collar residents not like the white-collar workers as neighbours, do they resent white-collar workers renovating their homes and are the services in the area weakened by the influx of white-collar workers into the neighbourhood?

Without a clearer understanding of the importance of preserving the stability of working-class neighbourhoods, not to mention the effect of industrial decline in undermining such areas, it is questionable that this social problem should be cited as a reason for attempting to stem the decline of industry in the city.

B. Market Demand

The rationale for Toronto's industrial policy is related not only to social needs but also to market demand. The latter area is mentioned in the industrial policy in terms of two economic principles which, in effect, are planning guidelines for determining how industrial lands will be zoned given the demand by various uses for industrial sites. The following quotation from *The Industrial Policy Report* (City of Toronto, 1978b, pp. 5–6) indicates the importance of social needs, expressed as social concerns, and of the market demand, expressed as economic principles, in forming the rationale for Toronto's industrial policy. It also defines the nature of the policy's two guiding economic principles.

1. Any City policy to retain industry should recognize the distinction between firms that prefer or require a city location and those that do not. Those that do not will continue to relocate to suburban and ex-urban tracts of land and large, modern single-story facilities. Any City policy to retain industry should not be directed at these firms. On the other hand, there are firms which prefer or require a city location. These types of firms should form the basis for a City policy to retain industry.

   Recognition of this distinction between industrial firms will ensure that a City policy to retain industry is economically realistic and will be consistent with sound economic planning, in terms of productivity and employment generation, for the industrial sector in the larger Toronto area.

2. An efficient allocation of land among residential, commercial and industrial uses should be a fundamental goal of a City policy to retain industry. Such an allocation should take into account both the efficiencies obtained through the operation of market forces and the social objectives that are not accounted for in the normal working of the land market. This economic principle means that industrial activity in the City should be consolidated into areas viable for continued industrial use. Industrial sites outside these viable areas should be allowed to convert, in an orderly manner, to non-industrial uses in accordance with other City policies. Such a consolidation would minimize public and private investment in various facilities necessary to support industrial activity.

In short, the two guiding economic principles are: (1) that the city should attempt to retain and attract industrial firms that prefer or require a central city location; and (2) that an efficient allocation of land among residential, commercial, and industrial uses should be a fundamental goal of a city policy to retain industry. The appropriateness of these two principles are discussed below.

The city should attempt to retain and attract industrial firms that prefer or require a city (*that is*, *central city*) *location*. The research background for this principle was presented in Assumption Study No. 2, *The City's Attractiveness for Industry* (City of Toronto, 1976). This study examined 'the assumption that many industrial firms derive significant advantages from locating their operations in the City' (preface). The study concluded (p. 29) that 'most City firms in the apparel industry, the printing related industries, the jewelry industry, and in wholesaling, auto repair, recycling, and port-oriented activities, derive a significant advantage from a location in the City or a particular part of the City, as opposed to a location in the suburbs'. These findings are essentially the same as those of Raymond Vernon (1969) and Edgar Hoover (1971).

The principle of attempting to retain city-oriented industrial firms has merit both from an economic standpoint and from a social perspective. There is sound economic reasoning in adopting planning measures that will provide some protection for those industrial firms that receive distinct advantages by being located in the central city. Those locational advantages include accessibility to relatively cheap skilled labour (for example, apparel, jewellery, leather, and wholesaling industries), close proximity to buyers or clients (such as in the apparel, jewellery, leather, and printing industries) and the use of cheap industrial space (the apparel, leather, and wholesale industries).

From a social perspective, many city-oriented firms, most notably those in the apparel, leather and textile industries, are reluctant to leave the city because it has the greatest concentration of labour suitable for these industries and the best accessibility by public transit to bring such labour in from the suburbs. Therefore, efforts to retain these labour-intensive industries will help to maintain a source of employment for city residents, many of whom would have difficulty finding alternative employment. Many of the workers in the city's apparel, textile, and leather industries, are foreign-born, are not fluent in the English language, have limited education, and in general lack the skills and qualifications to effectively compete for non-manufacturing jobs. Many also lack the training and experience to compete for better manufacturing jobs available in the metropolitan area.

An efficient allocation of land among residential, commercial and industrial uses should be a fundamental goal of a city policy to retain industry. In practice, this second principle meant that the city planners had to weigh the market pressures by non-industrial uses for industrial land, against the social concerns for industrial employment and the economic concerns for city-oriented industries. On the basis of this weighting exercise, Toronto planners decided to designate less land for industry than the amount in the 1969 Official Plan, but more land than could be retained by industry under open market conditions. Their policy is to encourage industry to remain and renew itself in the solid industrial areas and to permit the market place to gradually convert industrial sites to other uses elsewhere in the city.

Three major sources were used to support the conclusion that the solid industrial areas can remain viable if protected from competition from other uses by appropriate zoning. The three sources were the Planning Board files on industrial floor space data, the SIR study on the marketability of the city's industrial buildings, and finally the local area industrial surveys.

Analysis of changes in industrial floor space in the city showed that the solid industrial areas were not being undermined by other uses. *The Industrial Policy Report* stated (p. 16) that 'the floor space trends indicate that declines in industrial floor space and the accompanying losses in industrial employment have been concentrated, with the exception of a few large sites, in areas outside the City's solid industrial areas. The City's solid industrial areas in many cases have experienced gains in industrial floor space or the levels of floor space have remained relatively stable since 1962'.

The SIR market study concluded that the city's industrial buildings were neither economically nor physically obsolescent. The study was based on a questionnaire drawn up by SIR members and used by them in interviews with representatives of 81 industrial firms located in the city. The results of the questionnaire showed that few firms were dissatisfied with their premises and the vast majority intended to occupy them for some time into the future.

Although some owners and tenants cited problems of insufficient space for expansion, inadequate parking arrangements, and unsatisfactory loading facilities, these problems were mentioned by only a small minority of those interviewed. There were also relatively few complaints about the quality of the industrial structures they occupied and the Toronto planners concluded (p. 16) that 'a policy to retain and renew industry in the City is not likely to be undermined by a predominance of industrial buildings that need redevelopment and massive renovations'.

A demand by industry for the city's industrial buildings is further supported by the local area industrial surveys. They revealed (p. 24) that '85 per cent of existing firms intend to remain at their present location, suggesting that these firms are satisfied with their space'. This finding complements those on the changes in industrial floor space, and the marketability of the city's industrial buildings. Together, this information indicates the demand factor is sufficient to retain industry in areas where it is protected from 'higher uses'.

There is, however, one major negative finding regarding industry's demand for space in the solid industrial areas that should be noted. Between 1962 and 1976 there has been a marked increase in the proportion of the city's industrial floor space, including that located in the solid industrial areas, accounted for by wholesaling. This suggests that land-use controls to protect solid industrial areas for the retention and renewal of industry may result in such areas supporting mostly wholesale activities and providing employment for relatively few blue-collar workers. An analysis of the changing ratio of manufacturing floor space to wholesale floor space is included in the next section.

C. Tax Revenue Requirements

Tax revenue requirements as a reason for retaining and renewing industry were given less discussion than social needs and market demand in *The Industrial*

Policy Report. This was a result of limited information on this subject and an assumption that taxes provided by industry did not form an important factor in determining an appropriate industrial policy.

The tax revenue aspect of the industrial policy's rationale was to be investigated in the assumption study referred to as an 'assessment study'. It was suggested in *A Place for Industry* that an assessment study should be undertaken to consider the role played by industry in supporting the tax base. Difficulty in determining with any accuracy the full cost of the city's services to industry led to a decision to forego this assumption study.

Presumably such a study would indicate that industry should be retained because it provided taxes well in excess of the cost of servicing industry. However, the tax base argument for retaining industry is less relevant for Toronto than for most American central cities. There are three interrelated reasons for this which are outlined below.

First, industry accounts for a small percentage of the city's business and property taxes (only about 10 per cent) and even if the city were to lose much of its existing industrial base, it would not have a significant impact on the city's tax base. Second, as a part of the municipality of metropolitan Toronto, the city as a constituent municipality retains only about 25 per cent of the business and property taxes that it collects, the remaining 75 per cent is transferred to the metropolitan level to cover such major expenditures as policing and education. Therefore, the city only suffers a direct loss in industrial taxes of 25 per cent due to industry vacating a site. Finally, unlike many American central cities that may have difficulty finding alternative uses for industrial sites, Toronto has no such problem. In Toronto there is a strong market demand to convert most underutilized industrial sites to residential or commercial use. In most cases, the conversion would be to medium or high density residential or commercial development which generally would be given a much higher assessment value than its previous industrial use.

In conclusion, since industry plays such a relatively small role in generating revenue for the city it does not seem that the assessment study was of critical importance in setting out a new industrial policy. However, it would have been interesting if the study has been recast into a cost-benefit analysis that compared the municipal taxes paid versus the cost of services rendered for industry, housing and office/retail on industrial sites suitable for conversion. This kind of study might well have shown that the city receives the greatest financial benefit by allowing present trends to continue (in other words, of some industrial buildings being converted to office use and some industrial sites being developed for large residential projects).

Although research indicated that social concerns were not as serious as originally anticipated, Toronto planners recognized that some industrial base has to be maintained to assure job opportunities for the city's present and future resident industrial workers. They also recognized the city's obligation to assure 'that appropriate locations are available to accommodate City-oriented firms that require a city location to optimize the operation of their business' (p. 8). On the other hand, they are aware of the need 'to ensure that land is efficiently allocated among various uses' (p. 31), and the city's concern to accommodate more housing in the city. Therefore, to provide an industrial policy that permits the market place to play an important role in determining land-use patterns, and one that complements other city policies, the city planners proposed giving greater protection and encouragement to industry in the solid industrial areas, while adopting land-use controls that will permit the decline of industry elsewhere in the city.

Considering all the social, economic, and land-use planning aspects involved, this seems to be an appropriate industrial policy for the City of Toronto. It should permit the city to retain most of its remaining industrial base, and in such a way that will minimize conflicts between various uses. It will also permit a greater accommodation of residential uses in mixed use areas previously designated and zoned for industrial (and commercial) uses.

III. THE INDUSTRIAL POLICY'S LAND-USE STRATEGY

Land-use designation is usually the major tool available to planners in influencing the amount and location of industry in their community. For the City of Toronto, planners propose to retain most of the city's existing industry but permit the freeing-up of some industrial sites for other uses by: (1) identifying the solid industrial areas to be protected for industrial use only; (2) having industrial sites in mixed industrial–commercial areas and mixed industrial–residential areas zoned for industrial use but permitting their conversion to retail or office use in designated industrial–commercial areas, or to housing in designated industrial–residential areas; and (3) encouraging industrial sites in predominantly commercial and residential areas to be converted to the dominant use of the areas by zoning such sites as legally non-conforming. The remainder of this section describes the application and evaluates the impact of this land-use strategy.

Identifying Areas for Industrial Protection

Selection Criteria

The City planners recognized that it was a difficult task to determine which areas presently designated for industry should be retained for industry. They considered five criteria: (1) existing concentration of industrial firms; (2) existing stock of industrial buildings; (3) labour accessibility; (4) transportation of goods; and (5) local considerations. Since their concern was to identify the viable industrial areas, the first two criteria were of major importance as the spatial concentration of firms and buildings by themselves defined such areas.

Areas Selected for Industrial Protection

The city planners identified three major solid industrial areas—the *central industrial district*, the *junction*, and *the port*. As Table 11.2 indicates, the central industrial district is by far the most important industrial area in the city, accounting for nearly half of Toronto's estimated industrial employment. Together the three major solid industrial areas support 63 per cent of the city's estimated industrial employment.

The city planners also identified ten minor solid industrial areas which as a group support an estimated 18 000 industrial employees. In combination, the major and minor solid industrial areas have 83 000 industrial employees, or 80 per cent of the industrial employment in the City of Toronto.

Protective Value of 'I' Zoning

It is in the thirteen solid industrial areas that the city planners intend to consolidate industry and encourage its retention and renewal. The major means for doing this is to prevent these areas from being lost to other uses by designating them in the Official Plan as areas of industry, and changing their zoning from their present 'C' zoning that permits both commercial and industrial uses, to 'I' zoning that permits only industrial uses.

In the last ten years a number of industrial sites have been converted to office, retail and residential uses. Most of the conversions have occurred outside the thirteen solid industrial areas, but a few have occurred adjacent to or actually within these areas. The conversion of industrial sites to non-industrial uses has been fostered by both market and regulatory factors. The two major market factors are: (1) an exodus of many industrial firms from the city to

TABLE 11.2. Estimated industrial employment in Toronto, 1977

Type of area	Industrial employment
Major solid industrial areas	65 000
Central industrial district	(47 600)
The junction	(12 000)
The port	(5400)
Minor solid industrial areas	18 000
Total of all solid industrial areas	83 000
Other areas with industry	20 000
Total industrial employment in city	103 000

Source: Information calculated from data presented in Table 6 of City of Toronto (1978b). Industrial surveys were conducted by local area planners. In some areas not all firms were surveyed, so the figures must be considered as estimates only. The surveys included certain industrially related activities as well, such as body shops and construction, not just manufacturing and wholesaling.

the suburbs, resulting in a continuous supply of industrial sites for potential conversion to non-industrial uses; and (2) the ability of non-industrial uses to outbid industrial uses for many industrial sites, indicating a strong demand for these sites by non-industrial uses.

The two regulatory circumstances that have abetted the market forces in the conversion of industrial land to other uses are: (1) zoning regulations that permit commercial uses on all industrial sites and residential uses on some industrial sites, and (2) the practice of the city's Housing Department to purchase industrial sites in areas designated in the Official Plan as areas of industry and for the City Council to redesignate such sites as residential areas.

The demand for industrial sites by office uses has been traditionally limited to the city's central core. In the last twenty-five years a great number of industrial buildings have been converted into office buildings simply by renovating existing buildings located on the edges of the central core and adjacent to the central industrial district.

The conversion of industrial land to residential uses has also become common in recent years. Conversions of industrial sites to residential use have occurred mostly in areas designated in the Official Plan as low density residential, but some have taken place in areas designated for industry. Conversions in designated industrial areas, of course, have required an Official Plan redesignation. This has been done in some areas that were formerly solid industrial areas to permit the city Housing Department to use sites purchased for development of non-profit housing. The largest industrial site acquired by the Housing Department is a 45 acre tract just east of the central core. It is being used to construct a large-scale housing project.

In brief, recent conversion trends show that most solid industrial areas would be eventually undermined unless the city makes a commitment to reserve certain lands for industrial use only. One obvious effect of such conversions is that, by reducing the amount of space available for industrial use, they reduce the city's industrial employment capacity, and in turn, its industrial employment. Also, the intrusion of 'higher uses' into industrial areas usually results in escalating property values and rental rates for industry, and complaints from residents and/or office employees of the new uses about the noise, odour, and traffic congestion associated with most inner city industrial areas.

By reserving certain industrialized areas exclusively for industry the city is preventing the loss of industrial sites in these areas to either residential or commercial uses. However, such a policy will not stop another trend, of older industrial buildings being converted from manufacturing to wholesaling or warehousing uses. City planners are well aware of this trend which is indirectly indicated by the data presented in Table 11.3 showing that between 1962 and 1976 the City experienced a net decline of over 4 million square feet of industrial floor space, but nearly all of this loss is attributable to a decline in manufacturing space, since the amount of wholesale and warehouse space remained virtually unchanged in this time period.

TABLE 11.3. Changes in industrial floor space in Toronto, 1962–76

Type of area	Industrial floor space (1,000 sq. ft.) Manufacturing	Wholesaling/ Warehousing	Total
Major industrial districts	− 1531	+ 1878	+ 347
The central industrial district	(− 533)	(+ 936)	(+ 403)
The junction	(− 1097)	(+ 337)	(− 760)
The port	(+ 99)	(+ 605)	(+ 704)
The downtown area	− 1500	− 2034	− 3534
Other industrial areas	− 829	+ 14	− 815
The entire city	− 3860	− 142	− 4002

Source: Information calculated from data presented in Table 4 of *The Industrial Policy Report* (City of Toronto, 1978b, p. 19)

As Table 11.3 illustrates, since 1962 the downtown area has lost a considerable amount of both manufacturing and wholesale–warehouse space. This loss in industrial space reflects major redevelopment in the last fifteen years, with many new office buildings standing on sites formerly occupied by old industrial buildings. Elsewhere in the city the amount of manufacturing space has also generally declined, but the decline has been more than offset by an increase in the amount of space used by wholesale and warehouse uses. These trends suggested that as manufacturing firms relocate to the suburbs, their premises are often converted from manufacturing to wholesale or warehouse uses. The increase in the amount of wholesale–warehouse space outside the downtown area also suggest that many of the wholesale and warehouse firms that previously occupied buildings in the downtown area have been forced to relocate elsewhere. Presumably many of these firms need a central city location and have relocated adjacent to the downtown area, in the central industrial district.

Therefore, it should be recognized that preserving solid industrial areas for industrial use only may serve the purpose of accommodating the strong demand for industrial space in the city by wholesale and warehouse uses, but it may not be effective in stemming the decline in industrial employment. Manufacturing firms in need of locational conditions that only the suburbs can provide will continue to relocate there and, as in the past, their vacated premises will often become occupied by wholesale and warehouse uses.

Nor can it be expected that there will be much new manufacturing space constructed in the city to counter the conversion of old manufacturing space to less labour-intensive industrial activities. Aside from the odd plant expansion there is little prospect of much new manufacturing space being added in the future. Unlike Detroit and Philadelphia, and many other central cities in the United States, Toronto does not have any industrial parks, or large tracts of land committed for industrial redevelopment. With rare exception, the few vacant industrial sites in the city are too small and too expensive for single-storey operations, and there is a limited demand for new, relatively expensive, multistorey industrial space.

In respect to the economic feasibility of constructing new industrial space, Toronto is similar to Boston in its uncompetitive position *vis-à-vis* its suburbs. Using Boston as a case study, Andrew Hamer (1973, pp. 37–101) discovered that land costs were very high in the central city compared to its suburbs if little vacant land existed in the central city. Through a detailed cost analysis, Hamer pointed out that in land-scarce central cities, such as Boston (and Toronto), it was generally too expensive to build one-storey industrial structures. Also, comparing the cost and efficiency of a multistorey industrial building in a land-scarce central city versus a single-storey industrial structure in the suburbs, Hamer concluded that the single-storey suburban structure was much cheaper and more efficient. He found that the savings in land costs of using less land by constructing a multistorey building in the central city could not offset: (1) the much higher cost of land, per m^2, in the central city; (2) the higher construction cost, per m^2 of usable space, of a multistorey building; and (3) the lesser operating efficiency of a multistorey building.

Both the market and a study commissioned by the Planning Board on the economic feasibility of constructing a ten-storey industrial building in the central industrial district reflect the economic unattractiveness of constructing new industrial buildings in the city.

Although 'I' zoning the city's solid industrial areas is an important means of protecting the city's industrial base, it is questionable if it and other measures adopted by Council to retain and renew industry will be sufficient to limit the decline in industrial employment in the city to 5 per cent or less in the next decade. Despite the application of 'I' zoning to the solid industrial areas, it is probable that industrial employment will still be lost because: (1) industrial sites outside the solid industrial areas, including those that were previously in areas designated for industry, will continue to be converted to other uses; (2) some old manufacturing space will continue to be converted to less labour-intensive activities; (3) little new industrial space will be constructed in the city.

Measures for Improving the Functioning of the Solid Industrial Areas

In *The Industrial Policy Report* and *The Industrial Zoning Report* six major ways are recommended to improve the functioning of the solid industrial areas. The six are: (1) improving land use compatibility in the solid industrial areas through the introduction of a refined industrial zoning system; (2) relaxing the parking standards; and (3) increasing the loading standards for industry; and proposing Official Plan statements that commit the city to provide; (4) good truck transportation to and through the solid industrial areas; (5) good public transit to these areas; and (6) good municipal services in these areas. Each of these measures are discussed below.

1. *Improving land use compatibility in industrial areas.* To reduce the amount of land-use incompatibility between various industrial uses, and between industrial and non-industrial uses, city planners recommended that areas designated for industry in the revised Official Plan be given more specific designations. They recommended five new designations—three of which would apply to the solid industrial areas, and two to mixed-use industrial areas. Each new designation has its own industrial zoning category whose permitted uses list stipulates the uses considered environmentally acceptable for its respective designation. The new designations and their corresponding zoning categories are defined in Table 11.4.

Based largely on its present mix of industrial uses, and the type of uses in neighbouring areas, each of the solid industrial areas have been designated

TABLE 11.4. New industrial categories

Description of area	Official plan designation	Zoning bylaw category	Uses permitted
Industrial areas which are isolated from non-industrial uses	Heavy industrial area	1.4	Most industrial uses, including potentially incompatible uses such as smelters, tanneries, scrapyards, etc.
Mostly industrial areas	General industrial area	1.3	Most industrial uses which are compatible with a wide range of other industrial uses
Those portions of industrial areas which border commercial or residential areas	Restricted industrial area	1.2	Only those industrial uses which are compatible with nearby commercial and residential uses
Areas containing a mixture of industrial and residential uses	Mixed industrial–residential area	1.1	Only those industrial uses which are compatible with neighbouring residential uses and a wide range of residential uses
Areas containing a mixture of commercial and industrial uses or bordering on a commercial area	Mixed industrial–commercial areas	1C	Only those industrial uses which are compatible with neighbouring commercial uses and a wide range of commercial uses

Source: City of Toronto Planning Board, *City Planning* Vol 1 No. 1 (May 1978).

for *restricted industrial use*, *general industrial use*, or *heavy industrial use*. The mixed industrial areas have been designated for *industrial–residential use*, or *industrial–commercial use*, or *general use* which would permit industrial, commercial and residential development.

For zoning, the city planners recommended the introduction of a 'I' zoning system to replace the 'C' zoning that previously applied to industrial areas. The 'I' zoning system excludes nearly all commercial uses in the solid industrial areas and the mixed industrial–residential areas. Also, 'I' zoning varies from the more restrictive I.1, which applies in mixed industrial–residential areas, and I.4 that permits only nuisance industries, to the less restrictive categories of I.2 which applies to solid industrial areas abutting residential areas, and I.3 to solid industrial areas not adjacent to residential areas.

The uses permitted in each industrial zoning category were determined on the basis of their environmental impact. This in turn was assessed in terms of each use's considered characteristics regarding emissions of noise, vibrations, dust, fumes and odours and also generation of truck traffic, parking and loading requirements. For I.1 or mixed industrial–residential areas, the use of night shifts and the general appearance and maintenance of buildings were also taken into consideration in drawing up a permitted uses list.

On the controversial subject of what is the most appropriate method for determining compatible uses for a given zoning category, William Schenkel (1964, pp. 261–262) suggests that 'the list of permitted industries together with performance standards represents a preferred means to select industries . . . (for various types of zoning categories)'. James West (1977, pp. 64–74) agrees but recognizes that administering performance standards can be expensive, and requires sophisticated monitoring and trained personnel. He also mentions that there is a problem of not knowing if the standards will be met until after the industrial facility is built and in operation. For the above-mentioned reasons, plus the fact that it is the Province's responsibility to administer environmental standards, not the municipality, city planners wisely accepted lists of permitted uses rather than performance standards as the basis for determining the industrial activities for each zoning category.

Toronto's new refined system of industrial designation and zoning makes many of the city's industrial firms legally non-conforming. This is especially true in mixed industrial–residential areas where the fewest industrial uses are permitted. However, even in the areas designated for restricted industrial use and general industrial use most recycling activities such as scrapyards will become legally non-conforming. Through the limitations on expansions imposed on the legally non-conforming uses the city planners hope that many such uses will be encouraged to relocate in I.4 areas that they propose be set aside specifically for such uses. Through the relocation of some incompatible firms, the ceasing of operations of others, and the prohibition of new firms considered incompatible, the various industrial areas will become more attractive for industrial uses considered compatible with their local environment.

2. *Relaxing of parking standards and provision of city parking in the central industrial district.* The city previously required that one parking space be provided for every 1,000 square feet of new industrial floor space. Representatives of some industrial firms indicated that this regulation was too stringent, and it was an important deterrent to plant expansions and the construction of new industrial buildings in the central industrial district; most buildings here were built before any parking requirements existed and now what little land is not occupied by buildings is taken up by parking. This makes it very difficult, if not impossible, to expand onto this parking area without violating the present parking requirements.

In addition, it was suggested in *The Industrial Policy Report* that the parking requirements were too high for some industrial firms, such as in the clothing and leather industries, because most of the workers come to work by public transit. As for those industrial firms that can ill afford to reduce their parking spaces the city planners argued that such firms should have the option of providing the space at offsite locations further removed from the firm than was previously permitted by the zoning By-law.

To provide more industrial firms with the opportunity to expand their premises rather than choose the possible alternative of relocating to the suburbs, city planners proposed that the parking standards for manufacturing firms in the central industrial district be changed from one space per 1,000 square feet of manufacturing floor space, to one space per 2,000 square feet of manufacturing floor space. Also, given survey findings that the density of manufacturing employees to industrial floor space is approximately four times higher than the density of wholesale and warehouse employees to industrial floor space within the central industrial district, they recommended that wholesale and warehouse parking requirements in the district be changed from one space per 1,000 square feet to one space per 8,000 square feet. With land costs being much cheaper in other industrial areas of the city, and industrial sites in these areas generally having more space for parking, the city planners did not advocate a change in the parking standards outside the central industrial district. In these areas the standard that previously applied to the entire city will remain, namely, the requirement of one space per 1,000 square feet of industrial floor space.

City planners also recommended that industrial firms who cannot meet the city's parking standards with onsite accommodation should be permitted to provide parking spaces as far away as 2,000 square feet from their property; previously the maximum distance was only 1,000 square feet. In addition, city planners are urging consideration of more parking being provided by the Parking Authority of Toronto which operates a number of city-owned parking lots and garages, most of which are located in commercial areas. The Parking Authority has recently established one parking lot in an industrial area and it is suggested in *The Industrial Zoning Report* that more such parking lots would be very helpful in alleviating both the short-term and long-term parking needs of some industrial firms. The *Report* further suggests that some parking lots could be established through a partnership arrangement between the Parking Authority and interested industrial firms.

The relaxation of parking standards should permit more industrial firms to expand their premises, using land now needed to meet city parking standards; and the establishment of more City-owned parking garages in industrial areas should also facilitate onsite industrial expansions. The provision of more parking by the city should also improve the chances of retaining and attracting industrial firms that cannot adequately supply their own parking needs.

3. *More demanding loading area standards*. In contrast to their recommendation that parking requirements be reduced, the city planners recommended that the loading area standards be increased. As Table 11.5 indicates, the new standards require about twice as much space be set aside for loading as before. In fact, in some cases there is a three-fold increase in the loading area requirement, such as where a larger amount of new space is to be used for warehousing or wholesale activities.

The higher recommended standards are based on comprehensive consultant study on loading requirements for various types of industrial and commercial activities. The study findings and the proposed higher standards reflect the fact that 'industrial loading and unloading processes have changed since the Zoning By-law was written' (City of Toronto, 1978a, p. 49).

The city planners determined the square footage of loading space needed on the basis of the consultant study's estimate of the numbers and types of trucks needed for industrial buildings of various sizes. For example, the consultant study proposed that an 80,000 square foot building used for manufacturing

TABLE 11.5. Loading space requirements for industrial buildings

Manufacturing firm floor area in sq. ft.	Previously required loading area in sq. ft.	New required loading area in sq. ft.
25,000	360	720
100,000	1,080	2,400
400,000	2,160	4,680
Warehouse, wholesale firm floor area in sq. ft.	**Previously required loading area in sq. ft.**	**New required loading area in sq. ft.**
25,000	360	720
100,000	1,080	2,400
400,000	2,160	7,560

Source: City of Toronto (1978a, pp. 5–6).

purposes provided two offstreet loading spaces, one to be 12 feet and the other to be 12 by 40 feet. It is also proposed that there be one 'near street' space (this space would be parallel to the roadway but in the form of a layby or stopping area adjacent to the frontage of the building) which would be 12 feet by 20 feet.

The study, therefore, was recommending that 1,440 square feet be set aside for loading for a manufacturing space of 80,000 square feet. The city planners' reliance on such findings in revising their loading area schedule is illustrated by the fact that city planners recommended about the same amount of loading space as suggested by the consultant study for 80,000 square feet of new manufacturing space. The revised schedule requires a loading area of 1,560 square feet for manufacturing space ranging in size from 50,000 square feet to 85,000 square feet.

The city planners recognize that the number of trucks used by an industrial firm depends on a number of factors, not just the amount of floor space occupied by a firm. They recommended, therefore, that should a firm show 'good cause' for needing less loading space than that required by the new loading area standards; the firm may petition the city's Committee of Adjustment to seek a reduction in its minimum loading requirements. They also recommended that the higher loading standards should apply only to new space and not to all the industrial space on the site when a firm undertakes an expansion.

These qualifications should reduce the number of industrial firms that are seriously affected by higher loading area requirements but their general application should assure a better functioning of the solid industrial areas, and prevent the construction of new industrial buildings with an inappropriate amount of space available for loading.

4. *Good truck transportation to and through the solid industrial area.* The following statements for the Official Plan indicate that the city planners want the city to make a commitment to improve truck transportation to and through the solid industrial areas (City of Toronto, 1978b, p. 55):

> 4.5 It is the policy of Council to ensure that truck access to areas designated for industry is maintained and improved for industrial purposes.
>
> 4.6 It is the policy of Council to seek improvement in industrial traffic flows and access to loading facilities within areas designated for industry, through means such as but not limited to:
>
> (a) adopting measures so that streets or lanes may be efficiently used for activities associated with industrial operations; and
>
> (b) the opening of new streets and lanes, where those new improved routes are to be used predominantly by industrial traffic.

Neither *The Industrial Policy Report* nor its companion document *The Industrial Zoning Report* mention any specific street improvements related to industrial areas. However, the inclusion of the above-mentioned statements in the Official Plan will strengthen the city's commitment to industrial retention and renewal since previously the Official Plan had no specific policy statements of improving truck transportation for industrial purposes.

On the other hand, the city's industrial areas could become much more accessible to other parts of the city and the Greater Toronto Area if expressways were built in certain parts of the city. The extension of Highway 400 and the Spadina Expressway from the northern part of metropolitan Toronto into the central core, and the construction of the long-discussed Scarborough Expressway from the eastern part of metropolitan Toronto into the central core would substantially improve goods movements for the city's industrial firms. However, the prospect of any of these roadways being built is not good since the city is determined to limit road carrying capacity into the central core. This determination is based on the assumption that improved road transportation translates into more use of the private vehicle rather than public transit and more undue concentration of office development in the central core. This position is reflected in the following statements in the proposed Transportation Section of the Official Plan City of Toronto, 1978b, pp. 56–57:

> 7.7 It is the policy of Council that, in order to increase the use of transit and improve the general efficiency of the City's transportation system: (i) no new expressways or extensions to existing expressways be built within the City; (ii) no new arterial roads and major arterial road widenings, which would have the effect of increasing the capacity of these roads for private automobile use, be undertaken within the City; (iii) subject to Section 7.7 (i) and 7.7 (ii), consideration will be given to improvements to arterial roads within the City for the purpose of improving safety and local convenience.

In deference to the proposed industrial policy the Transportation Section adds (p. 57):

> 7.7 (iv) notwithstanding the provisions of Section 7.7 (ii), it is the policy of Council that the construction, extension or widening of roads may be undertaken for the purpose of facilitating truck movement, parking and loading, where such roads or sections thereof are to be used predominantly or exclusively by industrial traffic, and where such action would not result in unacceptable negative environmental impacts on the surrounding areas.

Given the city's dedication to stemming the number of automobiles coming into the city, it is questionable whether any major changes will be made to and through the industrial areas since both city planners and city politicians are likely to interpret such changes, even in industrial areas, as seriously undermining the city's policy of discouraging more automobiles coming into the central core.

City Council's general reluctance to support proposals for improving vehicular movement in the city, and their vehement opposition to having the metropolitan arterial road system expanded within the city seriously undermines the city's position of trying to make its industrial areas more attractive to industry. If central cities are to compete with their suburbs for industry it is very important that they provide their industrial areas with easy and good access to the regional highway network, and that they minimize traffic congestion within their industrial areas.

The importance of these conditions are expressed very well by Paul Shepherd, 1975 President of the National Association of Industrial Parks (AIPR, 1975, p. 35):

> But basically for an industry to be profitable in a core location you need to move materials, so you need transportation. And most of our cities have a real problem with access for movements of goods. That has to be solved.
>
> You have situations where they have stopped bringing the interstate highway system into the city. This has happened in just about every city on the East Coast. 1–95 is stymied at the outskirts of every city including the one we're sitting in (i.e. Washington D.C.). It does not aid the development of the core when you don't allow goods high speed access downtown.

In a similar vein, William Kinnard and Stephen Messner (1974, p. 45) observed that:

> The problems of the city are difficult to classify neatly into broad categories, but it is clear that one aspect of these problems is the economic obsolescence described earlier in the essay. This obsolescence, coupled with another major urban problem—traffic congestion—account to a large extent for the relative (and in some instances, absolute) decline of manufacturing and warehousing employment in the central city.

5. *Good public transit to the solid industrial areas.* The city planners failed to discover any industrial areas that were poorly served by public transit but to encourage the use of public transit in these areas they proposed that the Industrial Section of the Official Plan contain the statement (City of Toronto, 1978b, p. 55):

> 4.7 In order to alleviate congestion and demand for parking in areas designated for industry, Council shall seek to ensure the access to such areas by means of public transit is maintained and improved.

City planners are well aware of the dependence of most blue-collar workers on public transit, especially in such relatively low paying, central city industries as the apparel and textile industries. They also recognize that a major reason for the attractiveness of the city versus the suburbs for low paying industries is its greater concentration of potential workers in these industries and the city's better provision of public transit.

The advantage of central cities in general in offering better public transit service and of having a larger supply of workers for the lower paying industries is well exemplified by the findings of a Chicago study on the locational considerations of 189 industrial firms that had located within the city of Chicago in the period 1959–68. From his analysis of the information, which consisted of ranking a number of locational factors in terms of relative importance, Harry Hartnett (1972, pp. 23–26) noted:

> Of the industrial location factors ranked as vitally important (i.e. most important) labor received the largest number of responses. Four of the first seven vitally important factors concern various types of labor, particularly, the unskilled and female production workers (who are primarily unskilled and semi-skilled), is further enhanced when the rank of public transportation is noted. These workers are compelled out of economic necessity to utilize such means of travel to a much greater extent than the more highly skilled, more affluent workers. In effect, stating that access to public transportation is vitally important is another way of indicating the importance of unskilled and semi-skilled labor.

6. *Good municipal services in the solid industrial areas.* Again the city planners do not cite examples of where municipal services can be improved, but the effect of putting a statement to this effect in the Official Plan should be to strengthen the impression among the city's industrial community that the city is dedicated to the retention and renewal of industry in those areas identified as viable industrial areas.

The proposed Official Plan statement on improving both 'hard' and 'soft services' in the solid industrial areas reads as follows (City of Toronto, 1978b, p. 56):

> 4.11 It is the policy of Council to extend both the range and quality of municipal services provided in *areas designated for industry*.
>
> 4.12 It is the policy of Council to directly provide or to encourage the provision of social services, parks, and recreation facilities in suitable locations in areas designated for industry, which are intended to serve industrial employees and nearby residents.

Summary and Conclusion of Policy's Land-Use Strategy

The adopted industrial policy consists of encouraging industry in thirteen solid industrial areas and permitting industry to remain as conforming uses in the mixed-use areas. To improve the functioning of the solid industrial areas, city planners recommended the application of an 'I' zoning system to these areas, changes in the parking and loading standards, and the inclusion of statements in the Official Plan committing the city to maintaining and improving truck transportation, public transit, and municipal services in the solid industrial areas.

All of the above-mentioned measures will serve to improve the functioning of the solid industrial-areas. Also, the changes in land-use designations and zoning, along with the relaxation of parking requirements will serve to enhance the attractiveness of these areas for industry. The land use designations along with the accompanying Official Plan statements on industry will provide protection for the solid industrial areas from any attempts to redesignate parts of these areas for residential use. The designations will also prevent speculation and inflated values for industrial property. The new zoning system applying to industrial sites will also stop the conversion of such sites to commercial use. Relaxing parking requirements will provide more opportunity for onsite expansion, and more sites will become acceptable to industrial firms presently experiencing a shortage of parking spaces.

The exclusion of commercial uses in the solid industrial areas is consistent with both the city's office development policy and its industrial policy. By preventing commercial uses in industrial areas, the city will stop the present trend of industrial buildings in the central industrial district located close to the central core being converted into office space. Such a trend is contrary to the goal of the city of limiting office development in the City and encouraging its development in subcentres in the suburbs. Of course, preventing industrial sites from being converted to commercial use is also supportive of the industrial policy's objective of retaining and renewing industry in the city's viable industrial areas.

The prospect of retaining and renewing industry in the solid industrial areas should be further improved by the expected stabilization in the cost of property and in the rental rates in the solid industrial areas. Eliminating the possibility of competition from higher uses for space and property in the solid industrial areas should assure the retention for the city of those industries identified as needing a location and often cheap space in the city. Those industries, identified in Assumption No. 2, are the apparel, textile and jewellery industries and many wholesale firms as well. Retaining the port for industrial use only and zoning much of I.4, heavy industry, should also guarantee the retention of most port-related industries and city-oriented recycling activities.

The city planners' strategy of changing the designations of mixed industrial–residential areas from industrial use to industrial–residential use also has logic in terms of responding to market forces and harmonizing the various land-use policies of the city. Such a designation allows the conversion of industrial sites to residential uses in areas where previously such conversions were prohibited. The expected gradual conversion of mixed-use areas to predominantly residential areas will be supportive of the city's housing policy of increasing the amount of housing in the city. The city has adopted a housing policy which sets as a target the production of 40 000 new dwelling units by the end of 1985. On the basis of estimates of residential development potential in areas proposed for residential use in the various Part II, plans, it is apparent that it would be difficult to meet the city's 1985 housing target unless residential redevelopment were permitted in mixed industrial–residential areas that previous to the adoption of the new industrial policy were designated for industrial use only. However, to protect industry that has long existed in these areas, the city planners have wisely proposed that both industry and housing will be permitted in these mixed-use areas.

In conclusion, the land-use strategy identifies the various ways to improve the functioning of the solid industrial areas; it provided the measures for meeting the city's intent of retaining much of its industrial base, and it supports the existing city policies on office development and housing. However, Toronto's industrial policy cannot be considered as strong as those of most American central cities. This is partly reflected in the fact that it is intended to result in a further loss of industrial land, but more so because it does not include any financial incentives for industry or any municipally initiated industrial redevelopment schemes. This general lack of non-land-use measures to encourage the retention and renewal of industry is discussed in the next section.

IV. NON-LAND-USE MEASURES TO RETAIN AND RENEW INDUSTRY

Enhancing Toronto's Industrial Climate

The non-land-use measures to be used by the City of Toronto in achieving its industrial policy are extremely modest compared to the incentives and inducements used by many American central cities in retaining and attracting industry. The only non-land-use measures that Toronto has committed itself to in supporting its industrial land use strategy are: (1) to continue the existence of three already established local area industrial committees; and (2) to continue to employ an industrial officer to liaise with the industrial community.

In 1975 and 1976 Toronto planners were responsible for setting up three Industrial Co-ordinating Committees and at the same time the city appointed an Industrial Officer to work with these Committees. Each Committee consists of the two ward aldermen and representatives of industry in the area. These

Committees, aided by the city's Industrial Officer, have been able to work out satisfactorily a number of municipally related problems experienced by some industrial firms. Through these Committees the industrial community's views are being heard and generally supported by City Council. The city's policy to relax the parking requirements for industrial buildings, and to construct a city-owned parking lot in an industrial district are but two examples of how these Committees have helped shape the city's new industrial policy and contributed to an improvement in the functioning of the city's industrial areas.

The work of the Industrial Co-ordinating Committees and the city's Industrial Officer supplement the land-use measures, in indicating to the industrial community that Toronto is committed to retaining and renewing its industrial base. As to the fact that the city does not intend to offer industry the types of incentives and inducements provided by American central cities, this is partly attributable to legal constraints and partly due to the city's evaluation that additional inducements are not needed to meet its goal of retaining and renewing industry.

An Industrial Policy Without Prospecting, Land Banking and Financial Incentives

The City of Toronto does not intend to engage in industrial prospecting since this function is already being performed in the Greater Toronto Area by the Toronto Area Industrial Development Board. Also, since the city has few vacant industrial sites and no industrial parks, prospecting would rarely yield returns. As mentioned above, most industrial firms interested in locating in to the Toronto area wish to operate in modern premises and usually this need can only be provided in the suburbs.

The city has also decided not to engage in land banking, preferring to let underutilized industrial areas be converted to other uses, and allowing the private sector to maintain the viability of the industrial buildings in the city's solid industrial areas.

In regard to financial incentives, such as tax abatements or low interest loans, the province of Ontario does not permit the use of such measures except in designated underdeveloped parts of the province, namely eastern and northern Ontario. In these areas the provincial and federal governments offer grants and loans to municipalities and industrial firms for the purpose of directing industrial development away from wealthier and economically more diversified southern Ontario. With rare exception, the province does not allow such locational incentives in southern Ontario since it considers it unnecessary and counterproductive. It results in undermining the municipality's tax base and provides preferential tax treatment for some industrial firms at the expense of others.

The provincial government need not concern itself about Ontario losing industry to other parts of Canada due to a lack of provincial and municipal subsidies for industrial development in southern Ontario. The spatial distribution of Canadian industry and Canadian markets dictate that most industrial growth in Canada, at least in the secondary manufacturing sector, will occur in southern Ontario. That southern Ontario is the most favoured location for the expansion and location of manufacturing in Canada, is an advantage that no one state can claim regarding the best location for industrial development in the United States. In the United States many states are usually viable candidates for acquiring an industrial firm interested in relocating or estabilishing a new plant. This much stronger interstate competition undoubtedly accounts for the common use of financial inducements at both the state and municipal levels, compared to their illegal use in Toronto and the rest of southern Ontario.

Financial Inducements in American Central Cities

Several American central cities, such as Cleveland and Detroit, like Toronto, have established successful local area industrial committees, and presumably all allocate considerably greater manpower than the City of Toronto to industrial development. In addition, most American central cities offer financial inducements to retain and renew industry and many have municipally owned industrial properties for sale, often at rates well below cost.

Unlike Toronto, with its favourable industrial location in southern Ontario, American central cities face competition not only from their suburbs and the surrounding region, but also from other metropolitan areas, and most seriously, from communities in the South. The South (which Southerners like to remind northern industrial prospects is part of the Sun Belt) has distinct locational advantages over the North (which Southerners like to refer to as the Snow Belt) in respect to labour rates, heating costs, certain natural resources, and, of course, a more benign climate.

The type of financial inducements used by American central cities to encourage industrial development are exemplified by those offered by the City of Philadelphia. In Philadelphia industrial development is the responsibility of the Philadelphia Industrial Development Corporation (PIDC), a quasi-public agency established in 1958. On behalf of the City, PIDC offers tax-exempt, long-term, low-interest loans up to 100 per cent of the total development cost of a project–including land, building and related capital equipment (PIDC, 1976). PIDC also markets several hundred acres of industrial properties in city-owned industrial parks located throughout the city. Philadelphia is selling this fully improved industrial park land for as little as one-tenth the normal rate (Verespej, 1978). Unlike some central cities, such as Detroit, which offers a twelve-year tax freeze on business expansion, Philadelphia does not advertise special tax concessions to industry but it does claim that its real estate taxes are lower than the surrounding suburbs and other major cities in the East.

Financial inducements for industry are usually considered secondary locational factors (Hunker, 1974, pp. 157), but most central city industrial development agencies can cite several instances where they were critical in keeping or getting an industrial firm (Verespej, 1978, pp. 49–51; Pryor, 1978, pp. 70–71; PIDC, 1976). In fact, for older central cities inducements and incentives seem a necessity to offset the inherent locational advantages and/or financial inducements offered by their suburbs and communities in the South.

V. CONCLUSION

The planners for the City of Toronto have engaged in a very comprehensive research process in their attempt to discover the social need for retaining industry and the demand by industry for space in the city. The research has proved fruitful for it has allowed the city planners to develop a land-use strategy based on the realistic need and demand for industrial land by the various competing uses. Although *The Industrial Policy Report* does not explicitly acknowledge the fact, the background research has indicated that the city's social need for retaining and increasing its present industrial employment is not as compelling as it is for most communities in the Toronto area, and presumably in the country as a whole. Nevertheless, the fact that the city has an above-average amount of employment in general, and industrial employment in particular, is recognized in the land-use strategy whereby a considerable amount of land previously zoned exclusively for industry has now been zoned for mixed-use development.

The research also permitted the city planners to recognize the type of industries it should attempt to retain and this was taken into consideration in the changes to the land-use designations. Their research also revealed that it was a viable proposition to protect the solid industrial areas from higher uses, that a demand existed for the city's industrial buildings and that they were suitable for continued industrial use.

The comprehensive research also permitted the city planners to marshal a strong argument for changing the attitude of City Council from one of apathy to one of strong commitment to retain in industrial base in the city, and to improve the functioning of the solid industrial areas.

The keystone to Toronto's industrial policy is its land-use strategy of designating and zoning all solid industrial areas for industrial use only. This strategy has merit for it prevents a further loss of industrial land in such areas, and prevents the intrusion of incompatible uses into these areas. It also produces land-use stability for the local industrial community and encourages them to remain and maintain their premises.

Toronto's industrial policy is also interesting in its application of mixed-use designations and zoning. Whereas 'I' zoning attempts to assure an industrial base for the city, the use of mixed-use zoning allows some consideration for the strong market demand to convert industrial sites to other uses, most notably residential use.

It is questionable if the city's industrial policy, based essentially on a land-use strategy, can limit the city's industrial employment decline to 5 per cent or less in the next decade, but the land-use measures themselves should have a positive effect on slowing down the city's industrial decline of some twenty-five years. The extent that any slowdown occurs must to a large degree be attributable to the efforts of the city planning staff that formulated Toronto's new industrial policy.

Toronto's industrial policy is not only appropriate for the city, but it is also complementary to the industrial development needs of the rest of metropolitan Toronto. The intent of the policy is to retain most of the industrial firms that wish to stay in the city, accepting the fact that industrial firms needing large modern premises will locate in the suburbs.

Toronto is a real latecomer, compared to American central cities, in making a determined effort to retain and attract industry. Even its new industrial policy offers much fewer resources for encouraging industrial retention and development than those used by American central cities. Yet, despite these circumstances, Toronto's experience in developing an industrial policy should have some relevance and value for industrial planning in other central cities and other metropolitan areas. For instance, research background in the preparation of Toronto's industrial policy provides some interesting findings on such industrial development subjects as the effect on employees of their industrial firm relocating from the central city to the suburbs, and the economic and physical obsolescence of industrial buildings in a central city. Toronto's land-use policy for industry also provides an interesting basis of comparison with the land-use policies employed by other central cities. Finally, Toronto's industrial policy also indicates the important role that planners can play in encouraging industrial development.

In respect to Toronto's industrial policy, city planners alone were responsible for identifying the need to retain an industrial base, for determining the methods to do it, and assuring proper imput from the industrial community through the establishment of local area industrial committees. In most other communities such responsibilities would be shared with the community's industrial development officers. The Toronto example simply highlights the important role that planners can play in determining the framework for industrial development (see Sparks, 1974).

REFERENCES

AIPR (1975). 'Let's Recycle Our Cities'. *American Industrial Properties Report*, **June**, 29–59.

Black, A. (1968). *The Comprehensive Plan: Principles and Practise of Urban Planning.* International City Managers' Association, Washington, D.C.

City of Toronto (1974). *A Place for Industry*, City of Toronto Planning Board, Toronto.

City of Toronto (1975). *Assumption Study No. 1. Industrial Relocation and Its Impact on Employees*, City of Toronto Planning Board, Toronto.

City of Toronto (1976). *Assumption Study No. 2. The City's Attractiveness for Industry*, City of Toronto Planning Board, Toronto.

City of Toronto (1978a). *Industrial Zoning Final Recommendations*, City of Toronto Planning Board, Toronto.

City of Toronto (1978b). *Official Plan Amendments—Industrial Policy and the Central, Industrial District*, City of Toronto Planning Board, Toronto.

Hamer, A. (1973). *Industrial Exodus from the Central City*, Lexington Press, Lexington, Mass.

Hartnett, H. D. (1972). *Industrial Climate of Central Cities, AIDC Journal*, **7**, 19–35.

Hoover, E. M. (1971). *An Introduction to Regional Economics*, Alfred A. Knopf, New York.

Hunker, H. L. (1974). *Industrial Development*, Lexington Press, Lexington, Mass.

Kinnard, W. N. and Messner, S. D. (1974). *Inner City Industrial Development: Employment and Industrial Development Opportunities in the Inner City*, University of Connecticut, Center for Real Estate and Urban Economic Studies, Storrs, Conn.

PIDC (1976). *The New Philadelphia Story*, Philadelphia Industrial Development Corporation, Philadelphia.

Pryor, J. (1978). 'The rehabilitation of industrial corridors: a procedure for central city economic development'. *AIDC Journal*, **12**, 47–80.

Schenkel, W. (1964). 'The economic consequences of industrial zoning'. *Land Economics*, **40**, 255–265.

Sparks, R. W. (1974). 'The role of planning in the development process'. *AIDC Journal* **9**, 89–96.

Verespej, M. A. (1978). 'Innovation slows exodus of inner-city plants'. *Industry Week*, **January 23**, 47–51.

Vernon, R. (1959). *The Changing Economic Function of the Central City*, Committee for Economic Development, New York.

West, J. (1977). 'Industrial zoning: evaluation of multiple and single classifications'. *AIDC Journal*, **12**, 59–82.

Planning Industrial Development
Edited by David F. Walker

Chapter 12

The Industrial Park

William P. Buck

The phenomenon of real estate development commonly known in North America as the 'industrial park' is largely instrumental in providing the contemporary environment for industrial expansion. The industrial park is as much a philosophy as it is a name ascribed to an industrial real estate development and this philosophy will be explored further in this essay.

The development of new industrial and business communities in a planned setting is responding effectively to a variety of needs of modern industry. Such an attractive working environment has greater social acceptability both to the community in which it is located and to the employees themselves. There is a also great economy in concentrating services to an industrial area and this economy of service is maintained in the concept of an industrial park. The total effect however, is to integrate economy and function with pleasing aesthetics and controlled environment to the long-term benefit of both industry and the community.

EVOLUTION AND BACKGROUND

The industrial park is essentially a form of development arising since the Second World to meet postwar industrial expansion. It is reported that during the period 1940–59, over 1000 planned industrial districts were developed in the United States compared to thirty-three prior to that time. More recently, the character of development has changed due to the increasing awareness of community compatibility and aesthetic appeal.

Some of the important factors behind the spetacular growth and popularity of the industrial park are:

1. The expansion of industrial activity since the Second World War due to increased consumer demands for goods and services reflected by a higher standard of living.
2. The ageing and increasing inefficiency of the older industrial areas; in particular, those located downtown. Many manufacturing operations

were conducted on several floor levels, but with increased mechanization and production volume demand, these buildings were no longer suitable.

3. Lack of space in the urban core made it virtually impossible to expand in existing premises. This resulted in a move to the suburban areas where land was available for longer-term expansion programmes. This trend also initiated a concentrated concern for redevelopment of many core areas and an attempt to encourage existing industries to remain. Unfortunately, the high cost of land in the centre is limiting this effort.
4. The increased use of automobile commuting and truck transportation has permitted a greater flexibility in the location of industrial parks. The majority of these are still to be found within the periphery of large urban centres while some are clustered at major highway intersections or near commercial airports.
5. There has been increased emphasis by industry on the provision of a pleasant and convenient working environment. The mixed-use industrial park is a prime example of this.
6. The increased sophistication of the industrial developer in providing services other than land development to industry. Examples of this are the design–build services and the ability of developers to provide a complete 'package'. Often this is on a net lease basis which requires less capital investment by industry into lands and buildings.

We find then that the industrial park developed out of the needs of industry and the increased mobility of workers that accompanied the massive postwar industrial expansion.

WHAT IS AN INDUSTRIAL PARK?

The concept of a more highly restricted type of planned industrial district or area has resulted in a number of definitions advanced by such organizations as the Urban Land Institute (1952 Definition), National Industrial Zoning Committee's (Definition of an Industrial Park 1966), United States' Department of Commerce (1954), and the Dartmouth Conference on Industrial Parks which produced a widely accepted definition in 1958, as follows (Baldwin, 1958, p. 27; Boley, 1958, pp. 3–6):

> An INDUSTRIAL PARK is a planned or organized industrial district with a comprehensive plan which is designed to ensure compatibility between the industrial operations therein and the existing activities and character of the community in which the park is located. The plan must provide for streets designed to facilitate truck and other traffic, proper setbacks, lot size minimums, land use ratio minimums, architectural provisions, landscaping requirements, and specific use requirements, all for

the purpose of promoting the degrees of openness and park-like character which are appropriate to harmonious integration into the neighbourhood.

"The industrial park must be of sufficient size and suitably zoned to protect the areas surrounding it from being devoted to lower uses. The management is charged with the continuing responsibility of preserving compatibility between the park and the community as well as protecting the investments of the developer and tenants."

From the foregoing definition it is apparent that the main elements of a well conceived industrial park include:

1. Comprehensive plans.
2. Compatibility between land uses within the park.
3. Compatibility between the total development and the character of the community.
4. Compatibility between the total development and the neighbourhood.
5. Zoning to protect surrounding areas.
6. Design standards such as:
   access and movement of traffic;
   building setbacks;
   lot size minimum;
   minimum land to building area ratios;
   aesthetic control;
   landscaping.
7. Parklike character.
8. Continuing management to preserve compatibility with the community.
9. Protection of the investment of the developer and tenants.

In summary, an industrial park could be described as that area of suitably zoned industrial land which is or has the potential of generating its own distinctive environment both functionally and aesthetically. It is to be expected that within the terms of these definitions, there is a broad range of examples of industrial parks. Each will produce its own character for a variety of reasons not the least of which will be a reflection of the community within which it is located.

One factor is the size of the park itself. This may range from a small tract of approximately 20 acres to over 1000 acres at the other extreme. Those larger tracts may be better described as 'industrial districts' and may incorporate a number of phases each having the characteristics of an industrial park.

A well-planned industrial district may, for example, include areas devoted to heavier industrial uses, research and development or commercial office buildings. These subareas are often described as 'heavy industrial', 'R and D park' and 'office park' respectively. The most common, and one that best suits the small community, is the 'mixed-use industrial park' which provides for a wide range of compatible uses. This park will cater to both the needs of industry and the employees. Such ancillary facilities as banks, restaurants and recreation are commonplace.

Another factor affecting the character of an industrial park is ownership. This can be examined further by identifying the types of ownership. In broad terms, these are:

1. Public
2. Professional industrial developer
3. Industrial subdivider.

Public ownership is usually at the municipal level and is the result of a positive effort by the municipality to encourage industrial development in the absence of private initiative. There are many examples of successful parks which are a credit to the foresight and dedication of the municipalities.

The objectives of public ownership are in many ways similar to the private sector with the major exception being the profit motive. However, each strives to attract industry, promote higher quality investment in lands and buildings and ensure that those employed in the industrial park will be relatively content. The municipality receives the benefits of tax revenue and employment, the latter of which, when expressed in payroll generated, can be seen to contribute in great measure to the economic strength of the community. Public ownership does not usually result in outstanding industrial park development, since it is often hampered by lack of expertise, frequent administrative and political changes and the absence of commitment to development management over the long term. This may result in deterioration in the appearance and use within the park.

The most successful parks have been those owned and managed by professional industrial developers who retain ownership of a majority of buildings and seek to attract tenants. These developers may erect speculative buildings in anticipation of a tenant and will also build to suit the custom requirements of a prospective industry. The result is that the lands and buildings are maintained in a way attractive to prospects.

The industrial subdivider is, on the other hand, the least desirable owner as his objective is usually that of selling off land for a profit without too much concern or commitment to the performance or final outcome of the development. It is questionable whether many such developments do qualify as industrial parks.

NAIOP Industrial Parl Criteria and Standards (1971)

The National Association of Industrial and Commercial Parks (NAIOP), an organization representing private industrial developers in the United

States and Canada, has further expanded the definition of an industrial park to form a code of standards to which members are asked to adhere. This code of standards is as follows:

Criteria

An *industrial park* is the assembly of land, under one continuing control, to provide facilities for business and industry consistent with a master plan and restrictions, resulting in the creation of a physical environment achieving the following objectives:

1. Consistency with community goals.
2. Efficient business and industrial operations, human scale values.
3. Compatibility with natural environments, achieving and sustaining highest land values.

Standards—physical

1. Paved streets.
2. Adequate utility systems for multiple industrial users.
3. Setback or percentage coverage requirements (that is, distance from lot lines and maximum building-land ratios).
4. Landscaping.
5. Offstreet parking.
6. Architectural control through the approval of
   appearance;
   siting;
   building materials;
   signs.

Standards—operational

1. One management.
2. Master plan.
3. Design review process.
4. Enforcement process.
5. Restrictions.
6. Legal representation.
7. Effective supervision of environmental conditions.

It is apparent therefore, that the common element found in good industrial parks is the management directed at both the short-term promotion and development and the long-term profit arising from successful sales and satisfied tenants and owners.

LAND USES AND CONTROLS

The creation of an industrial park provides the planner with a fresh opportunity to respond to the anticipated final use, both in the designation of areas for general categories and the description of each category itself. Thus a given master plan may include both 'heavy' and 'light' industrial permitted uses, as well as certain commercial uses. The designation of these areas will have a significant influence on the types of industry or enterprise that will eventually operate within the park, and the acceptability of the park to new industry. The zoning designation is therefore an important step in the plan and must relate to the type of industry contemplated.

Each municipality or region will have some idea of its potential to attract certain types of industry that are compatible to its location and resources, both material and human. There are a number of techniques which can be applied to identity potential industry, such as:

1. Industrial linkage study:
   This measures the forward (market), backward (raw materials) and service requirements for existing industry and will assist in identifying opportunities for new industry.
2. Forecasting ouput:
   This will identify changes in gross production which may indicate an industrial opportunity arising from growth in a particular sector.
3. Import substitutions:
   The identification of local markets presently supplied by importing goods and services. This can be used to demonstrate the need to substitute for imports through the establishment of new industry.
4. Valued added:
   If raw materials are available for potential production of finished or semi-finished goods, further industrial development opportunity may be identified.

A well-conducted forecast of potential industrial development will include the review of the availability of serviced industrial land, with adequate and correct zoning designation.

In the smaller municipality, the mixed-use industrial park is most favoured where, as a typical example, the following uses are permitted:

1. 'Medium' industrial including controlled outside storage.
2. 'Light' industrial—no outside storage.
3. 'Light' warehousing—no outside storage.
4. Office commercial.
5. Multiple industrial and warehousing

6. Service stations.
7. Banks—restaurants—recreational uses.

Zoning can often become too detailed and name specific uses (e.g. manufacture of canvas, cellophane and cord) but the list could be simplified and possible omissions might be corrected by some comprehensive definition, for example 'light manufacturing carried on in a wholly enclosed building'. The mix of 'light' versus 'heavy' and provision for outside storage should be determined through the identification process previously described.

In the larger urban areas, the various uses will become more clustered into industrial districts which are of greater area and homogeneity. Rail transport or access to deep-water port facilities may dictate a particular theme. The identification study will be less relevant to the determination of land use within an industrial park.

As defined, the industrial park requires more control than can normally be provided by zoning. Insistence on professional architectural designs, use of quality construction materials, the provision for suitably landscaped sites, are all 'extra' controls usually 'custom tailored' for each particular industrial park and are implemented through 'protective covenants', which are registered on title for each property and form part of each offer to purchase or lease.

Every prospective customer is made aware of the existence of these covenants at an early stage in negotiations. Past experience indicates that genuine purchasers or tenants will readily realize that these have been created for their own protection and will co-operate in enforcing them.

The following is a brief list of some protective convenants used:

1. Stipulate construction of a specified number of square feet of building within a specified period of time after closing of the sale.
2. Control siting of buildings, vehicular access points, parking layout, lighting and screening of parking areas, landscaping and fencing, storage and garbage disposal facilities.
3. Reserve the right to repurchase for the original purchase price (plus expenses) any property on which sales conditions have not been met.
4. Reserve the right to repurchase any portion of lands declared surplus by any purchaser at original purchase price (plus expenses) for a period of twenty years or so.
5. Stipulate that all architectural landscaping and drainage plans be prepared by qualified professionals and be subject also to municipal approval.
6. Control and/or prohibit the incorrect use of certain building materials.
7. Control signs, billboards, shipping and receiving areas. (Generally no shipping or receiving area should face the street.)
8. Stipulate that all ravines shall be maintained in their natural state during and after construction and no dumping be allowed.

General Layout

The planning of the physical layout, zoning and protective covenants for a particular industrial development will depend upon a number of variables such as:

1. The objective of the developer.
2. The types of industry the project is expected to attract.
3. The location, size and topography of the tract.
4. The availability of rail, utilities and other services.

One of the key rules is to provide as much flexibility as possible in the layout plan. A considerable degree of this can be achieved through: (a) block planning and (b) phased development.

Block Planning

Through this method, the roadways are established by taking into consideration various depths of lots which may be critical to the expected size of industrial buildings and operations. An overall size of block may be determined but individual side lot lines within the block are established later to meet the user's exact requirements. Figure 12.1 illustrates a typical arrangement of creating a variety of block sizes and depths for a small industrial park. The cul-de-sac roads need not form part of the initial construction and are only used to break up the larger parcels if so warranted.

It is important to fully appreciate the need for the proper selection of block depth, which is the distance from the street line measured perpendicular to the rear lot line. A building size range will be compatible to a given block depth. For example, assuming no outside storage and normal setbacks, normal parking requirements and the need for 50 per cent future expansion of the building, the lot depths in Table 12.1 would be acceptable.

It follows, therefore, that a variety of block depths will accommodate a range of building size more efficiently than one standard depth. It is preferable to maintain a larger proportion of available lots in the 200 to 500 feet range due to the predominance of this size range of buildings.

Phased Development

Directly related to block planning is phased development, wherein the entire park is planned as a comprehensive unit but is developed in economically feasible stages. This approach saves capital and allows for future layout modifications and development alternatives. As shown in Figure 12.1, a 61.1 acre industrial park has been divided into three separate phases of approximately

TABLE 12.1. Optimum lot depths for various sizes of buildings

Initial building size (sq. ft.)	Optimum block depths* (ft.)	Corresponding lot area (acres)
10 000	200	1.0
20 000	270	1.5
30 000	320	2.0
40 000	360	2.8
50 000	390	3.4
80 000	480	5.5
100 000	530	7.0
200 000	730	14.0
500 000	1 100	35.0

*Allows 50 per cent future building expansion.

twenty acres each. The exact limits of each particular phase may be revised at a later date depending upon market conditions.

The most appropriate location within the development for marketing the first phase of land should be thoroughly studied. Marketing considerations may dictate that early construction phases be located near an existing major offsite roadway. Such location would provide the shortest initial roadway construction but perhaps result in a substantial amount of storm and sanitary sewer or water-main construction.

Considerations will vary with each project depending upon a number of physical and marketing factors. The introduction of a cul-de-sac to break up a larger lot may also be considered a part of the phasing strategy.

SITE TOPOGRAPHY AND SOIL CONDITIONS

Aerial photography provides an excellent tool for the planning and layout of the industrial park. The availability of an aerial photograph series which extends beyond the limits of the actual site may be used in the planning process to study offsite influences including access, vehicular circulation and recent construction in adjacent areas. From the aerial photography a topographical map can be produced quickly, economically and accurately so that road profiles of existing ground elevations may be analysed for each alternative layout to eliminate major cuts or fills.

It should be noted that there is a direct relationship between gradient and optimum size of building. The larger buildings require relatively flat terrain in order to avoid excessive earth moving costs and associated deep-fill sections which can produce serious differential settlements under floors, and require deeper foundations in order to be founded on undisturbed soil. While there are some general guidelines to be used in layout, it is important that a detailed

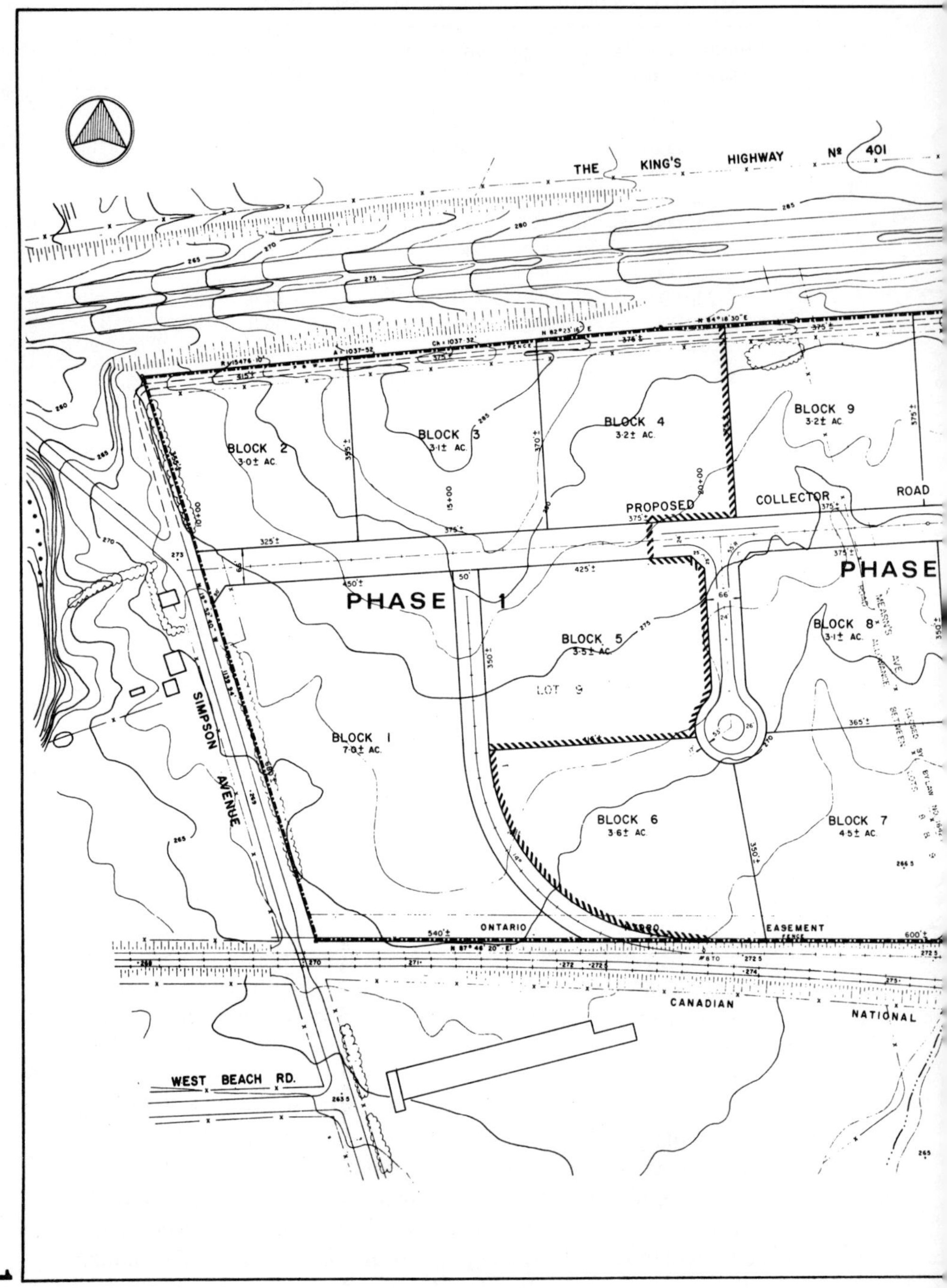

FIGURE 12.1. Park layout and servicing

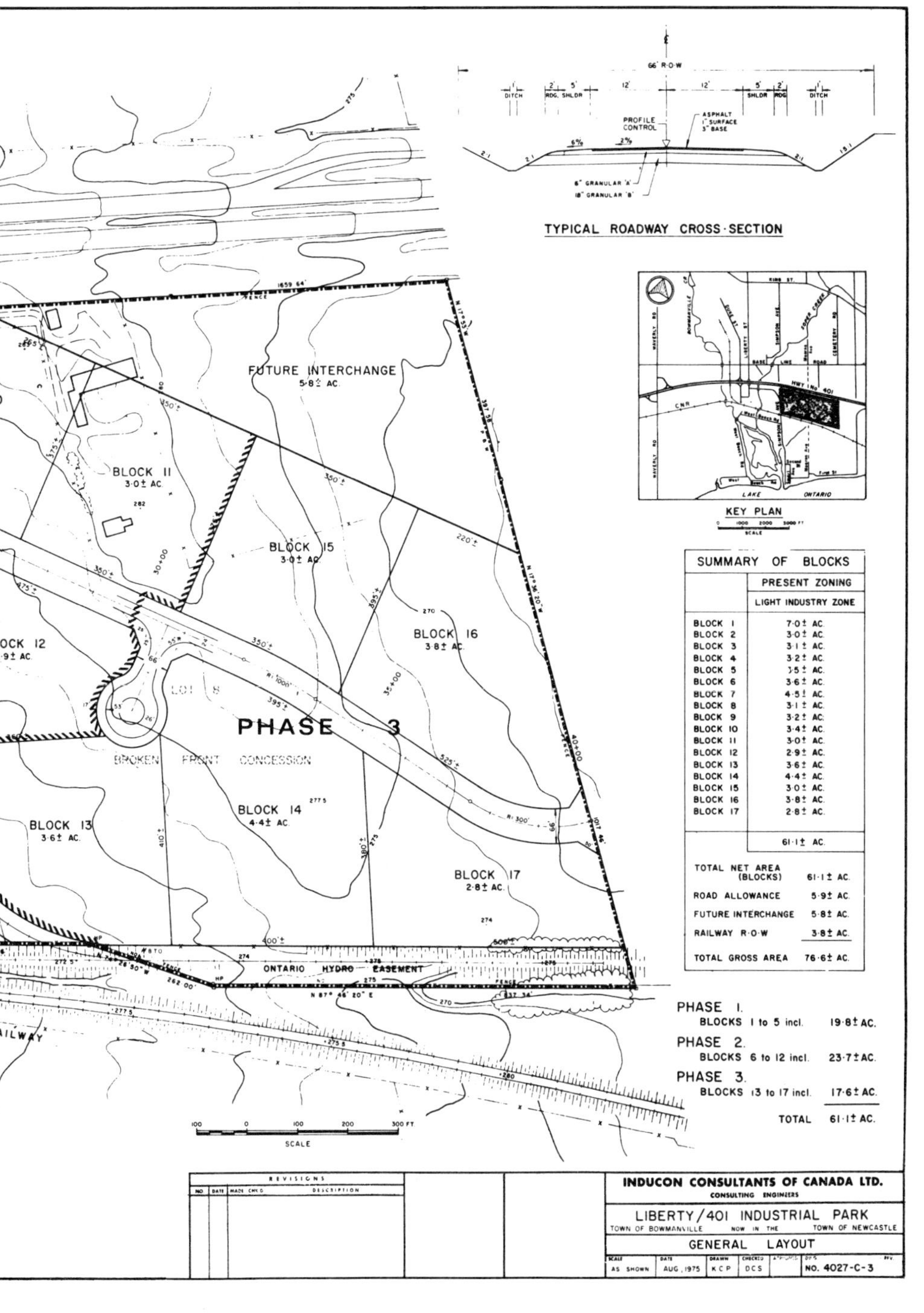
TYPICAL ROADWAY CROSS-SECTION
66' R.O.W
DITCH
RDG. SHLDR
SHLDR RDG
PROFILE CONTROL
ASPHALT 1" SURFACE 3" BASE
6" GRANULAR 'A'
18" GRANULAR 'B'
KEY PLAN
KING ST.
BASE LINE ROAD
HWY No 401
CNR
LAKE ONTARIO
WAVERLY RD
LIBERTY ST
SIMPSON AVE
CEMETERY RD
SUMMARY OF BLOCKS
PRESENT ZONING
LIGHT INDUSTRY ZONE
BLOCK 1 7·0± AC.
BLOCK 2 3·0± AC.
BLOCK 3 3·1± AC.
BLOCK 4 3·2± AC.
BLOCK 5 3·5± AC.
BLOCK 6 3·6± AC.
BLOCK 7 4·5± AC.
BLOCK 8 3·1± AC.
BLOCK 9 3·2± AC.
BLOCK 10 3·4± AC.
BLOCK 11 3·0± AC.
BLOCK 12 2·9± AC.
BLOCK 13 3·6± AC.
BLOCK 14 4·4± AC.
BLOCK 15 3·0± AC.
BLOCK 16 3·8± AC.
BLOCK 17 2·8± AC.
61·1± AC.
TOTAL NET AREA (BLOCKS) 61·1± AC.
ROAD ALLOWANCE 5·9± AC.
FUTURE INTERCHANGE 5·8± AC.
RAILWAY R.O.W 3·8± AC.
TOTAL GROSS AREA 76·6± AC.
PHASE 1. BLOCKS 1 to 5 incl. 19·8± AC.
PHASE 2. BLOCKS 6 to 12 incl. 23·7± AC.
PHASE 3. BLOCKS 13 to 17 incl. 17·6± AC.
TOTAL 61·1± AC.
FUTURE INTERCHANGE 5·8± AC.
BLOCK 11 3·0± AC.
BLOCK 15 3·0± AC.
BLOCK 16 3·8± AC.
BLOCK 12 2·9± AC.
PHASE 3
BROKEN FRONT CONCESSION
BLOCK 14 4·4± AC.
BLOCK 13 3·6± AC.
BLOCK 17 2·8± AC.
ONTARIO HYDRO EASEMENT
RAILWAY
SCALE
REVISIONS
INDUCON CONSULTANTS OF CANADA LTD.
CONSULTING ENGINEERS
LIBERTY/401 INDUSTRIAL PARK
TOWN OF BOWMANVILLE NOW IN THE TOWN OF NEWCASTLE
GENERAL LAYOUT
SCALE AS SHOWN
DATE AUG. 1975
DRAWN KCP
CHECKED DCS
NO. 4027-C-3

analysis be undertaken by a professional engineer at the time the layout is made.

Where steeper gradients exist, roads should be run perpendicular to the contours; this enables the siting of each building with its own balanced cut and fill. Furthermore, by judiciously locating the shipping and receiving dock on the downhill side, one can take advantage of the natural gradient. Gradients steeper than 3 per cent will dictate smaller buildings in the 10 000 to 30 000 square foot range.

Extreme caution must be exercised in choosing sites which have areas with marsh or swampy conditions requiring drainage, frequently at prohibitive cost. Clay-loam, sand, gravel or porous materials afford good soil drainage and economical construction. Sites that once served as dumps or have otherwise been filled, and those with underlying rock close to the surface or high groundwater, are more expensive to develop. Test boring should be made in various parts of the property and conditions carefully noted.

Soil-boring programmes normally involve subsurface investigations with a truck mounted rotary drilling rig. The soil report will show a profile and log of each borehole, describing material encountered. The soil profiles may then be shown superimposed on the final engineering road profiles in preparation for construction tendering by qualified roadbuilding and utility contractors. A contractor will be in a much better position to bid fair unit prices with a good knowledge of subsurface conditions.

Where natural watercourses exist on the site, block property lines may be laid out in such a way that rear or adjoining lines are centred on the watercourse. This method eliminates expensive watercourse realignment or filling of the building sites prior to construction.

ROAD LAYOUT

General requirements of design principles for streets are in accordance with traffic volume ranges. Design traffic is expressed as 'design hourly volume' (DHV) or 'average daily traffic' (ADT). The average daily traffic is the most suitable for use in design of industrial streets.

Road right-of-way (ROW) widths are usually established by the municipality. A typical chart of industrial road classification and respective number of traffic lanes, pavement widths, ROW and ADT is shown in Table 12.2.

An example of two typical industrial road cross sections are shown in Figures 12.2 and 12.3.

Utilization of industrial park streets for parking and loading should be prohibited. The industrial park developer should establish offstreet parking and loading standards which will be accommodated in an adequate and satisfactory manner by every tenant or owner in the development.

Industrial sites which have frontage on an existing freeway or expressway

TABLE 12.2. Roadway design data

Type	Lanes	Asphalt pavement width	ROW	ADT
Local industrial	2	28 ft.	66 ft.	2500 vehicles
Minor industrial collector	2	38 ft.	86 ft.	2500/5000 vehicles
Arterial	4	44 ft.	100 ft.	5000/10 000 vehicles

have a tendency to create a double frontage condition. Industrial building sites would have frontage on a local industrial road as well as on the existing multilane highway. This presents a predicament to industry in that it must provide a favourable façade in two directions, while having to solve the problem of future expansion and the location of the shipping and receiving areas. No shipping area should face a roadway. As shown in Figure 12.4, this situation can be eliminated by including a service road between the abutting industrial blocks and the freeway. By avoiding a double frontage layout, optimum architectural control and cost savings can be realized by the ultimate industrial user.

Pregrading requirements for the industrial site are considered at the time of layout as a result of storm drainage requirements. Where possible, filling of industrial blocks should be avoided until the actual industrial user is well established.

A common mistake associated with the preparation of industrial land for marketing is the presumption that a level site is a prerequisite. This leads to unnecessary earth moving and, in particular, to dumping with fill over large areas and in substantial depths. As mentioned before, this will create problems and additional building construction cost to the end user. Should filling be required, it is imperative that the topsoil first be removed from the area to be filled and then the fill material be placed under professional supervision so that the desirable compaction is attained. This will ensure that floors later placed on this ground will not crack due to differential settlement.

A good drainage plan is one that will assure economical development of individual sites for purchasers as well as economical site development costs for the developer.

Proper street layout and design is most important in industrial development, as the principal means of access for abutting property. Streets, frontage roads and intersections must be designed to the standards and specifications of the local municipality. This ensures that the municipality will assume responsibility for all roadworks and services upon satisfactory completion of all construction work.

Location of streets is determined by optimum block sizes, existing facilities, future expansion, grading and alignment relating to topography, rail service,

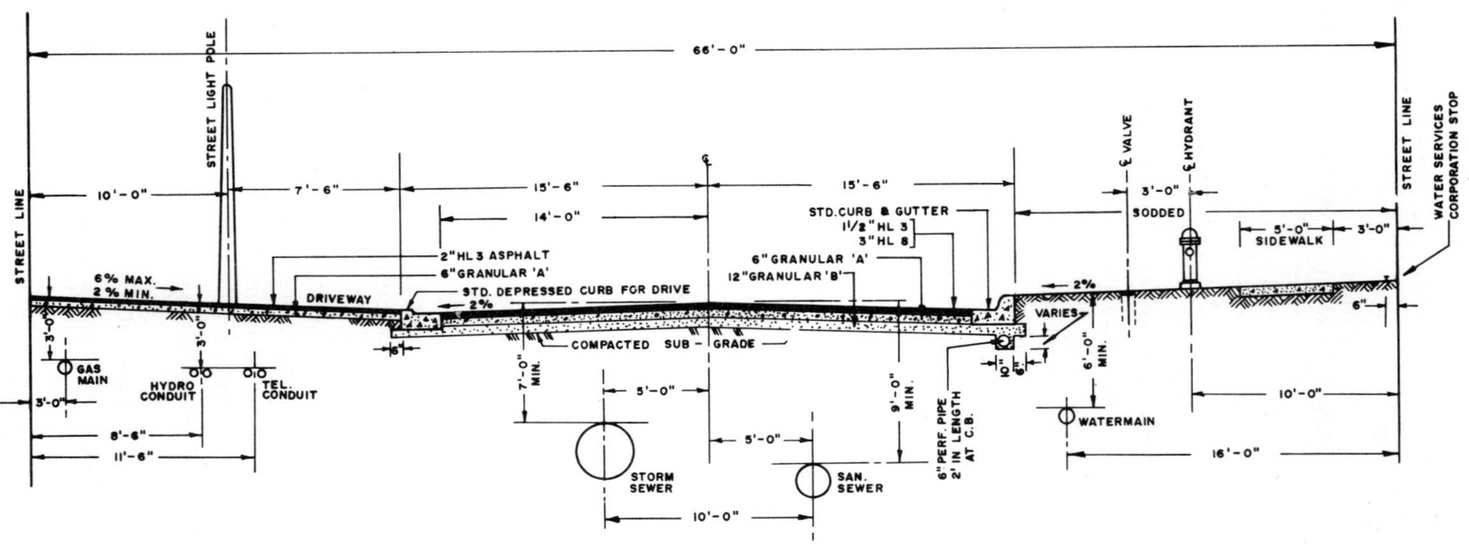

TYPICAL LOCAL INDUSTRIAL ROAD (66' R.O.W)

TWO LANE, CURB & GUTTER WITH UNDERGROUND STORM DRAINAGE

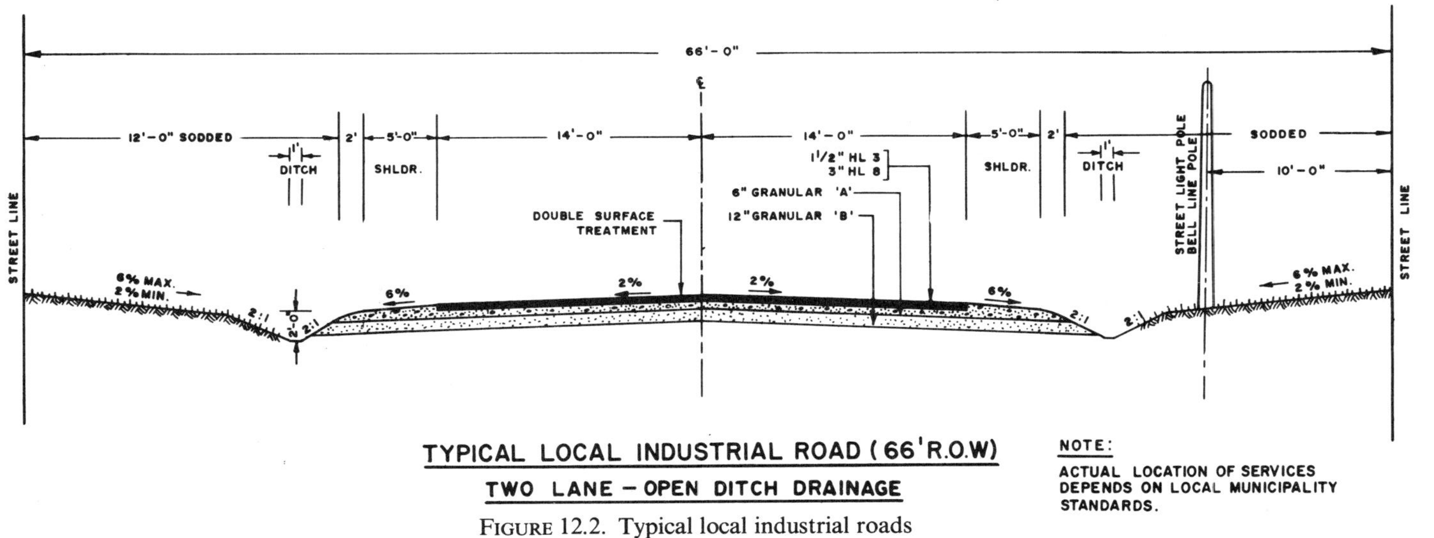

FIGURE 12.2. Typical local industrial roads

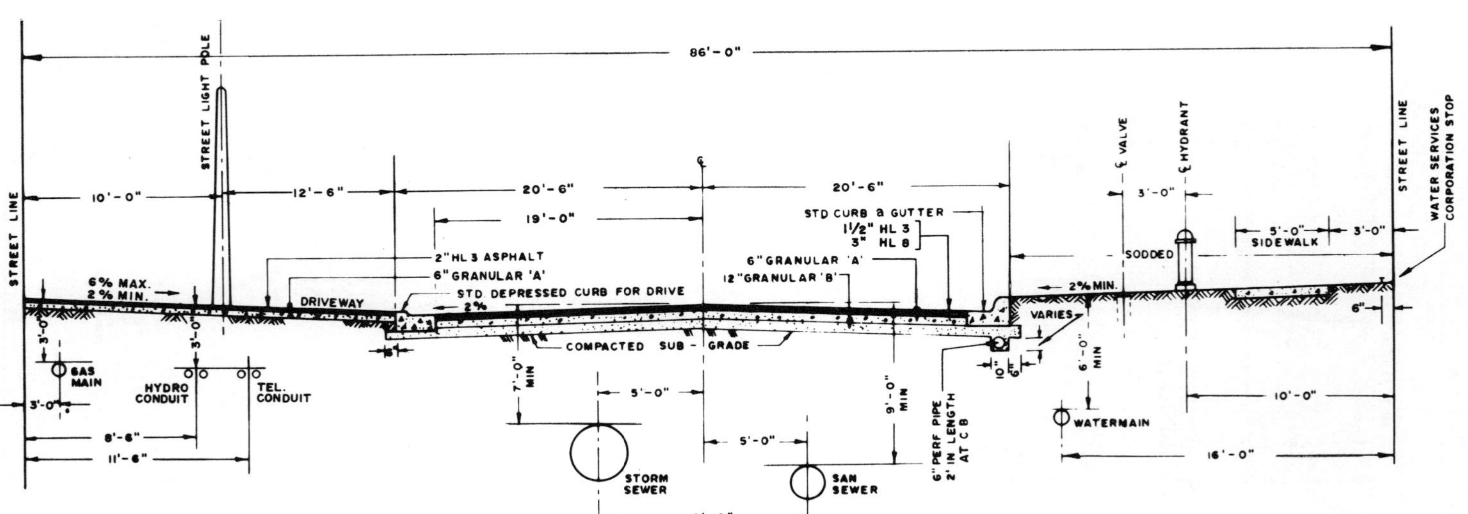

TYPICAL INDUSTRIAL COLLECTOR ROAD (86' R.O.W.)

TWO LANE WITH PARKING, CURB & GUTTER, UNDERGROUND STORM DRAINAGE

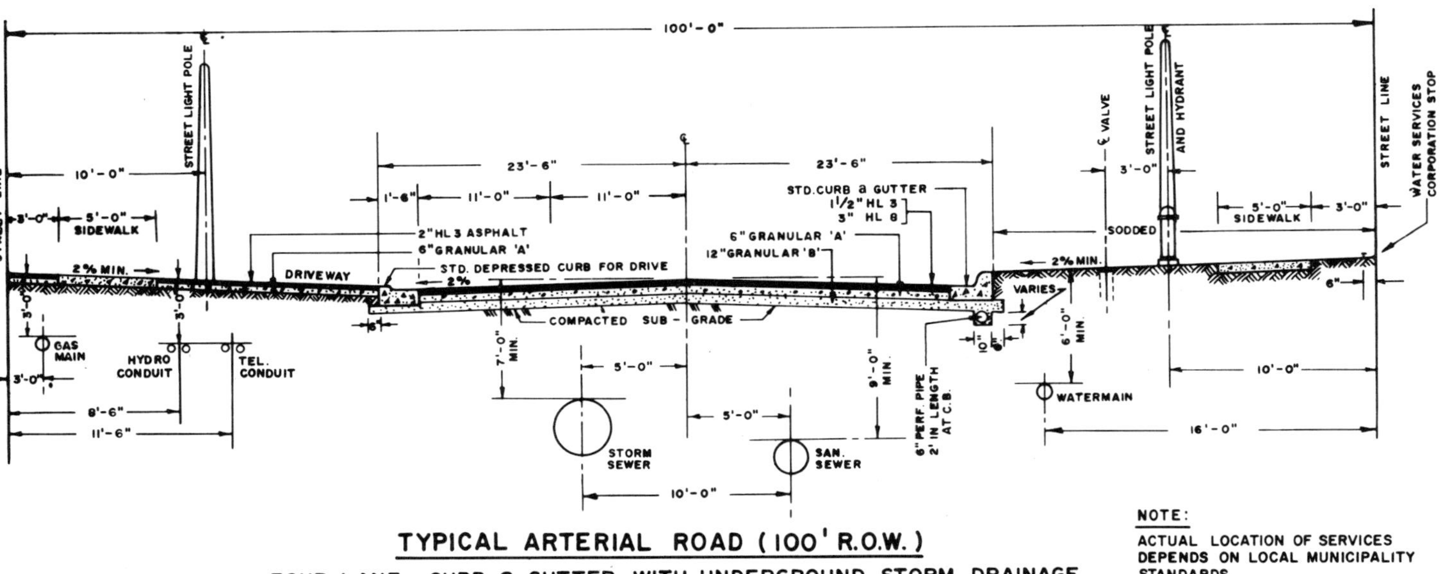

FIGURE 12.3. Arterial and collector roads

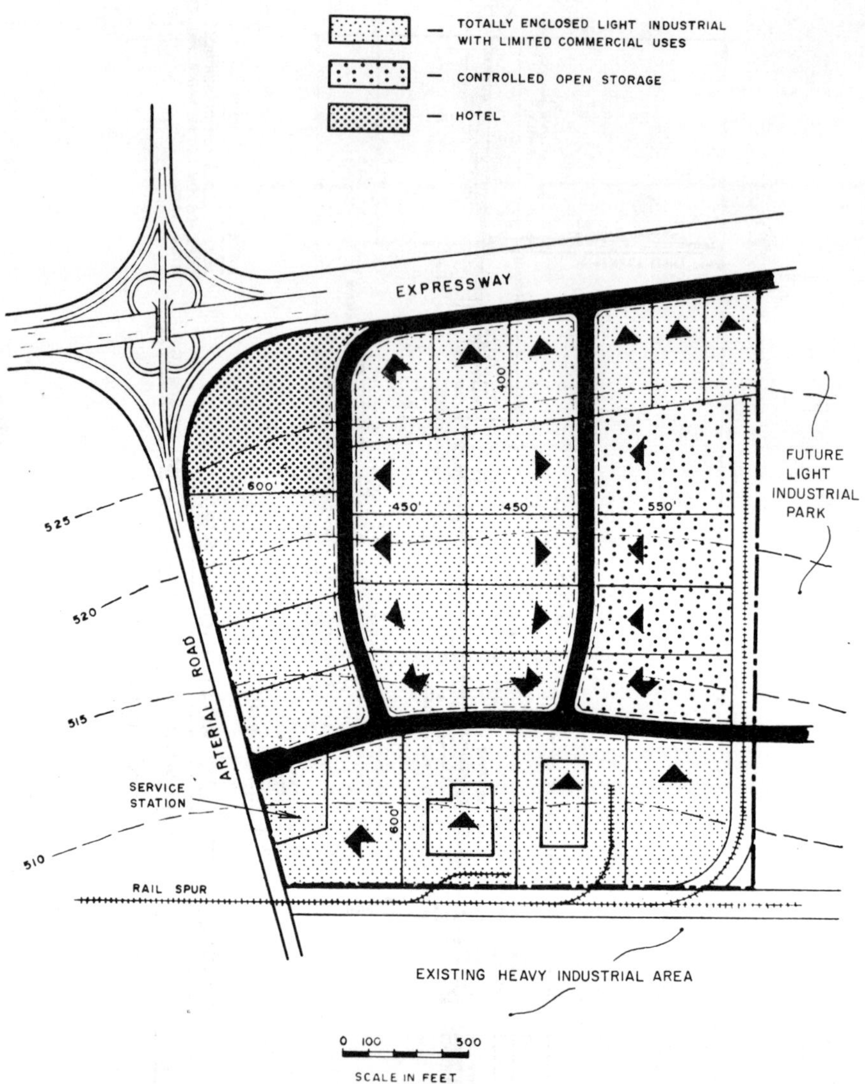

FIGURE 12.4. Typical industrial park

soils and drainage. Clearing and grubbing requirements and tree preservation are also considered in selecting the location of roads.

'Gridiron' street patterns which are straight and extend for several blocks within an industrial area tend to attract fastmoving traffic. Gently curving road alignment is recommended, as it produces a better aesthetic appeal in the development.

Cul-de-sac streets are preferred under steeper topographical conditions where length of the street is limited to a maximum of 600 feet. In such an instance the cul-de-sac streets should end in a paved turn around of approximately 80 to 100 feet in diameter. This diameter will accommodate larger trucks, including 45-foot trailers, and will allow a full turn without backing. A cul-de-sac street can offer good flexibility in future phases of the development inasmuch as large lots—from 500 to 700 feet depth—may be broken into two medium-depth parcels.

A good industrial street plan will creat the maximum number of desirable building sites with a minimum of grading, and at the same time provide adequate local access and discourage through traffic.

UTILITIES

In general, utility capacities for an industrial park will be larger than those associated with residential and commercial uses. In planning for utilities, five basic factors should be considered: adequacy, efficiency, maintenance, flexibility and economy. Planning will have to be done for easements which are generally placed within street or railroad rights-of-way or to the rear of lots. Water pressure in an industrial area must be high and steady enough to operate sprinkler systems so as to maintain favourable fire insurance ratings. The capacities of sanitary and storm sewers, electric power and gas (if available) plus telephone service must be adequate to handle needs of anticipated industrial operations.

Watermains

Water supply in industrial development is determined from the domestic and process water requirements and/or the fire protection. It is imperative that the modern industrial park can provide full sprinkler fire flow protection to its occupants. Accordingly, it is normally the fire flow that determines the water supply.

A 200 000 square foot building of non-combustible construction and low hazard occupancy may require 3000 gallons per minute for a duration of three hours. A 50 000 square foot building on the other hand, would require 1800 gallons per minute for a duration of two hours. It is important, therefore, that a clear understanding of the limitations of a given water supply are understood in order that marketing will be compatible. For a sprinklered building, the line pressure should not be less than 60 p.s.i. static pressure but on the other hand should not exceed 75 p.s.i., as plumbing fixtures in a building would be subjected to undue stress and create maintenance problems. It is necessary, therefore, to size distribution lines large enough to minimize pressure drop under full flow conditions. Thus pipe sizes in the 8 to 12 inch diameter are commonly found, whereas 6 inch diameter would not be adequate.

In laying out the system, the water-mains should be looped to provide continuous service to users. Individual water service connections are not installed during the mainline installation until the actual industrial building is located on each site.

Fire hydrants are installed along the street within a radius of about 300 feet from one another. Flow tests are made at hydrants within the system from time to time in co-operation with the fire department to substantiate the fire protection classification of the local area for insurance purposes.

Sanitary Sewers

A complete system of sanitary sewers must be provided to serve each lot in the industrial development. Sewer pipes are designed to maintain a self-cleaning velocity of sewage of about 2.5 feet/sec. When it comes to designing sanitary sewers within an industrial park, gently undulating topography is preferred as pipes may be designed to flow under gravity thus eliminating the need of costly pumping stations.

Sanitary sewer sizes of no less than 10 inches in diameter are recommended. Treatment of wastewater discharges from the development will usually be done by the municipality under the operating authority of the appropriate environmental protection agency. Most industrial wastes are similar to residential sewage and no problems should arise at the treatment plant. However, some industrial wastes may be corrosive or volatile and require pretreatment at some other location.

'Wet' versus 'Dry' Industry

There are many cases where the municipal waste treatment facility is limited and its immediate expansion will require substantial capital expenditure. Here it would be advantageous to consider the effect of limiting the industrial park to so-called 'dry' industries until such time as the problem is rectified. These are the industries that do not require water for process or cooling purposes. We are, then, concerned only with the domestic requirements of the employes working in those firms.

Using the example of a 100 acre industrial park which generates an employee density of 10 per acre, we have a potential connected population of 1000 persons. Using the standard of 40 gallons per person per day per eight-hour shift, the resulting daily flow would be in the order of 40 000 gallons per day per eight-hour shift, plus an allowance for infiltration of ground-water into the collection system.

The 'wet' industries will require a wide range of water quantities depending on the size of plant and the particular process.

Gas, Electricity, Telephone

Utilities such as natural gas, electricity and telephone may be installed within the industrial development by the utility company. It is preferable to install these services underground so that a more attractive environment for commercial and office occupants may be obtained. In addition, underground services are not as exposed to damage by winter conditions as overhead wiring. Utility easements are usually located along street rights-of-way. Easement widths of 20 to 30 feet are also common along side and rear lot lines.

A suggested rule of thumb for estimating the initial electricity requirements for an industrial subdivision is 70 kilowatts per acre. The preferred utilization voltage is 347/600 volt, 3 phase, 4 wire, 60 cycles. Normally any one industrial consumer is given by the utility company up to a 500 kva (kilovolt-amps) substation at utilization voltage. Power in excess of 500 kva is provided only at higher voltage. In that case the consumer must provide his own substation.

If preference were given to the available alternatives for electrical installation, the order would be: (1) complete underground distribution using direct burial cable with pad mounted transformers, (2) overhead distribution with pad mounted transformers, and (3) complete overhead and pad mounted transformers as the last resort.

Street Lighting

The subdivision ordinance of the municipality or Public Utilities Commission (PUC) will usually establish the requirements for street lighting within the industrial development. Evenly spaced street lights are needed in areas of high pedestrain activity, but are not necessary where most movements are by private automobile or by various modes of public transportation. Complementary to street lighting is the highlighting of building façades and parking lot lighting. The use of concrete spun light poles greatly enhance the appearance of an industrial street. Where it is feasible, street lighting located within a landscaped median offers an attractive diversity from the standard pole locations near the street line.

DRAINAGE

Final elevations of streets should be depressed sufficiently to provide drainage for the adjoining property. The streets may then be used as carriers of runoff water, which is dumped into catch basins that lead either into underground drainage pipes or into open ditches, according to the location and the volume of water to be handled. It is usually the developer's responsibility to take care of all general area drainage; the purchaser is responsible for the drainage within his own site. Underground storm sewers are aesthetically desirable and such add value to the land. An underground system also frees the above-ground space for parking or other uses.

In some other cases, the value of the land will not support the cost of an underground system and a decision will have to be made to excavate open channels or roadside ditches. In most cases the local municipality will have knowledge of the local storm history and will recommend either an open ditch or underground storm drainage system.

Through the use of special hardware in industrial roof design, such as 'low-flow' hoppers, retention times of storm water may be prolonged to reduce the impact on the storm sewers during times of heavy precipitation. The rational method of storm water design ($Q = AIR$) is still the most popular means of design, where Q is flow in cubic feet/sec, A is area in acres, I is the rainfall intensity in inches/hour and R is the coefficient of runoff.

POLICE AND SECURITY PROTECTION

Local municipal police forces usually carry out periodic spotchecks throughout the industrial park during the night hours of 11.00 pm to 6.00 am. Building with good exterior lighting afford extra protection by acting as a deterrent to unwanted intruders. Some industrial users require additional part-time security guards during inactive periods. Costs of the extra building security would be at the expense of each particular industry.

GARBAGE REMOVAL

Most industrial users make provisions for a large industrial waste container to be located at the rear of the building. The local municipality may empty this container on a weekly basis and deposit waste material in a local landfill site or transfer station, or this service may be provided by a private disposal carrier. Industries which generate process wastes will be required to dispose of the material at their own costs. Industries of this type will be subject to all of the odour and emission controls stipulated by the relevant environmental protection agency.

SNOW-PLOUGHING

Where climate dictates, the local municipalities should snow-plough the industrial roads throughout the winter months, and it is important that these be placed high on the priority list for snow removal. However, each industrial user is normally responsible for the snow removal on all private driveways or parking lots. To have this work carried out, in an industrial multiple building each tenant pays a portion of the cost to the developer under the terms of lease.

RAIL SERVICE

Where rail trackage is to be provided, key considerations include location and widths of rights-of-way, curvature standards, gradients, clearance, payment arrangements for lead-track installation and spur trackage, etc.

A minimum radius of 420 feet is standard for rail lead curves. Lesser curves for spurs are possible only in places where diesel switching engines are used. Spur tracks are depressed 3 feet 6 inches to bring the level of the freight-car door even with the building floor slab. The topography of the land tract must be adapted to the requirements of 2 per cent as the maximum grade for all trackage (see Figure 12.5).

The curve of rail leads and the space required for spur track turnouts will inevitably result in some irregularly shaped building sites. Developers have made every effort to minimize the site area needed for turnout curves. Private spur tracks to a plant start curving from the rear of the adjoining site so that the spur enters the plant parallel to the lead (see Figure 12.6).

The right-of-way for industrial lead tracks are normally dedicated to the railroad, with the provision, however, that if the rails are removed, title reverts to owners of the abutting land.

AESTHETICS AND LANDSCAPING

Aesthetics factors form an important consideration in good design practice, particularly within the development. For example, the alignment of the road should compliment existing physical features and blend into the terrain. Visual or physical obstruction near the roadway should be minimized. Underground in lieu of overhead electrical distribution lines is a significant contribution to aesthetics.

Landscaping of the strips between the street pavement and the property lines of sites is customary. The developer provides the basic planting as an encouragement for the landscaping required as part of the site treatment. Where the developer also supervises or constructs the buildings, landscaping is included in the site planning. Where purchasers build their own plants, it is customary for the developer to review site and building plans to see that landscaping is included in the design.

Properly designed earth slopes for roadways in cut or fill will enhance the industrial park aesthetically. Slopes steeper than 3:1 should be avoided as they cannot be maintained easily with mowing equipment. Excavated material considered unsuitable as foundation soils may frequently be used as earth

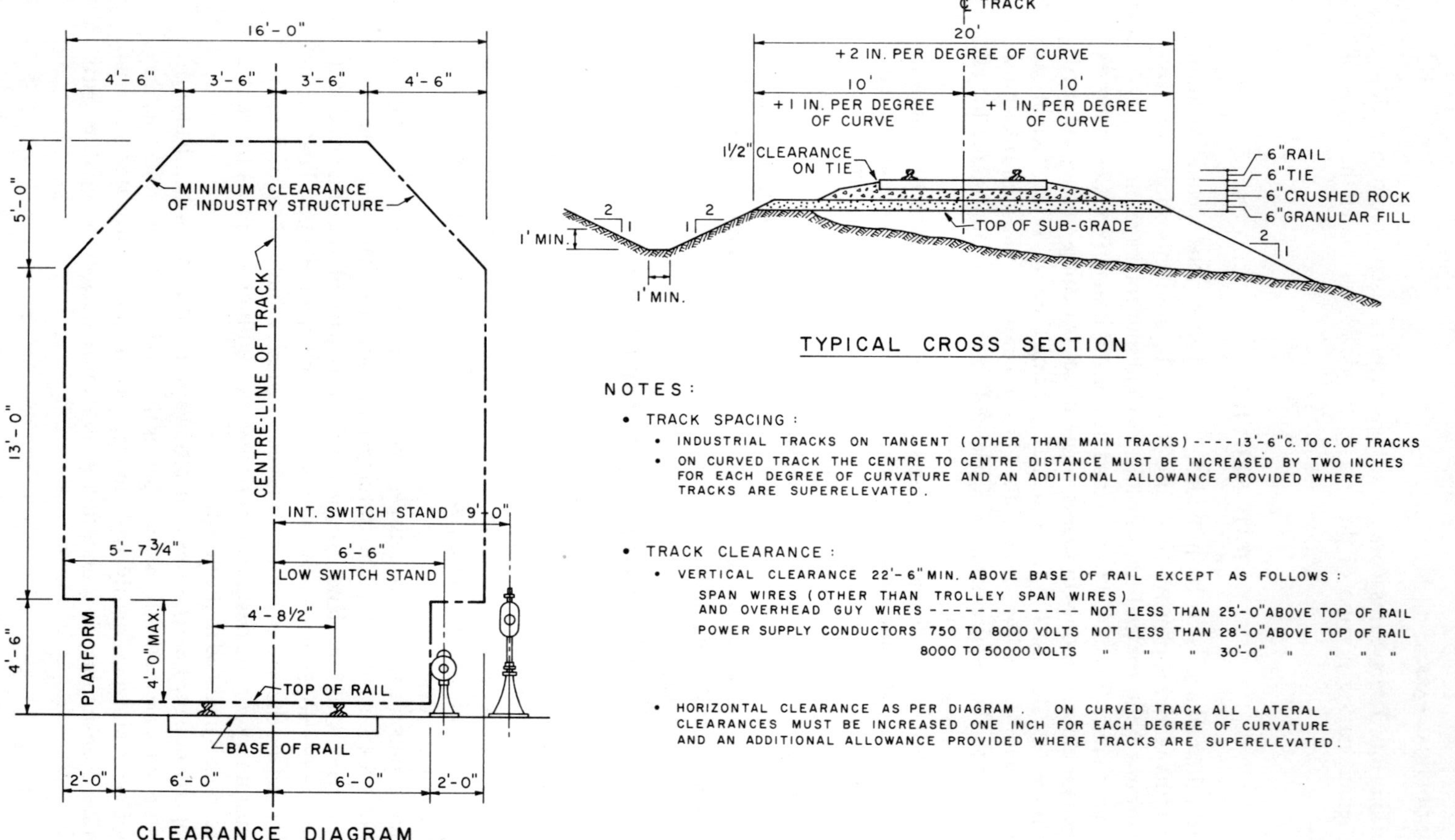

FIGURE 12.5. Typical industrial siding cross-sections

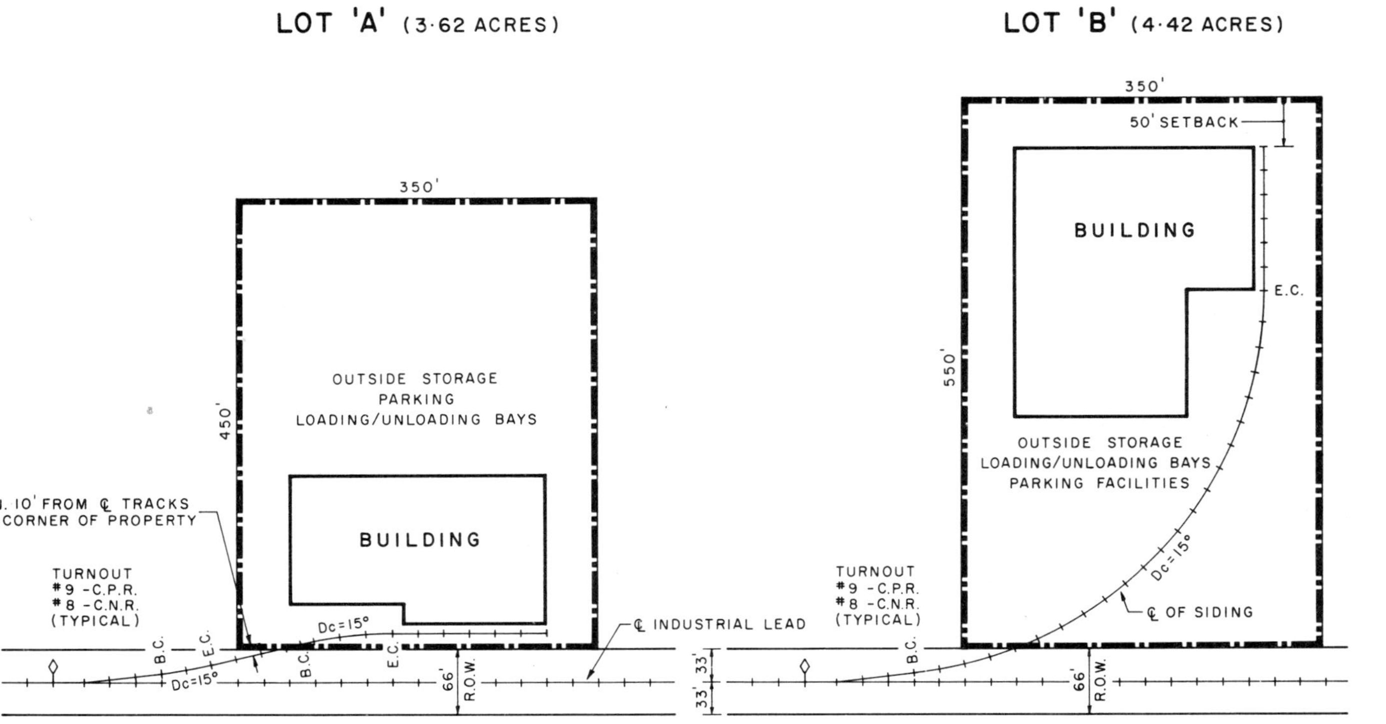

FIGURE 12.6. Typical industrial siding layouts

berms. These become attractive landscaped site features with functional value as screens for parking lots and building maintenance areas.

Siting of buildings in most developments require setbacks of a certain distance from the front and side lot lines. New parks usually require front yard setbacks of 30 to 100 feet and side yard setbacks of 20 to 30 feet. Setbacks help to assure ample landscaping areas, permit easier building identification and encourage better and safer traffic flow.

The importance of creating an attractive appearance within the industrial park through landscaping and proper maintenance cannot be overstressed.

ESTIMATED DEVELOPMENT COSTS

A vital factor to determination of project feasibility is the development cost estimate. The site layout plan will be worked out with the objective of maximizing marketing potential while minimizing the cost of site development. Typical 'unit cost' estimating sheets for roads and services are shown in Figures 12.7 and 12.8 for two lanes with and without curbs respectively. Net saleable acreage should be calculated for the project so that development costs per net saleable acre are determined by deducting the proposed dedicated rights-of-way and otherwise unsaleable from the gross acreage of the site.

A breakdown of development costs should be made for each phase of the development. This will be necessary to properly evaluate costs in the financial planning of the project. The cost per acre for developing the area included in the first phase of a project may be found to be substantially higher than the average cost per acre for the entire project. This frequently occurs due to the need for constructing complete storm and sanitary sewerage and outlet facilities during the first phase, which will ultimately serve the total project. Cost analysis should begin early in the development and continue through to development completion.

BUILDINGS

The definition of an industrial park implies the provision of facilities including buildings for the purpose of sale or lease to an end user. These can be categorized in the following manner:

1. *Custom built* to fit a specific industry's requirements. This can be further subdivided into two classifications describing ownership.

   (a) *Industry as owner*
   This is the most common situation and implies that industry will purchase land and contract to have the building erected. Most industries would prefer to own their own real estate for both control and long-term realization of profit on the sale of the facility.

JOB No. ....
Prepared ....
Date ....

PRELIMINARY UNIT COSTS
FOR ROADS AND SERVICES
2 LANES

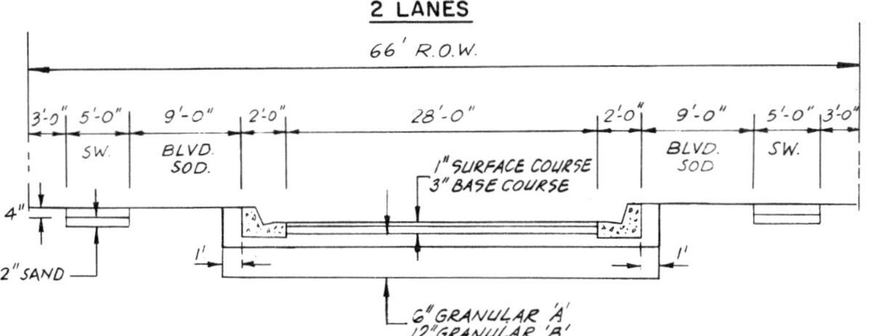

CODE	ITEM	QTY/LF	UNIT PRICE (1)	COST PER LF.	NOTES
212	Sanitary Sewer Pipe (18"Øav.)	1 LF	1.2 x		
	Sanitary Sewer Manholes	1/300 Ea	1.2 x		
213	Storm Sewer Pipe (36"Ø av.)	1 LF	1.2 x		
	Storm Sewer MH and CB	3/300 Ea	1.2 x		
215	Watermain Pipe (12" Ø)	1 LF	1.2 x		
	Hydrants with Valves	1/300 Ea	1.2 x		
220	Road Excavation (3' deep)	3.78 CY	1.2 x		
222	Granular B	2.39 T	1.2 x		
223	Granular A	1.48 T	1.2 x		
224	Curbs	2 LF	1.2 x		
225	Paving, Base Course	0.525 T	1.2 x		
226	Paving, Surface Course	0.175 T	1.2 x		
227	Sidewalks	2 LF	1.2 x		
228	Sodding (Blvds.)	2.67 SY	1.2 x		
229	Street Lights	1/120 Ea	1.2 x		
241	Clearing, building removals	allowance	1.2 x		
256	Underground hydro distrib.	1 LF	1.2 x		
	Sub-Total				
	Engineering 15%				
	Development Mgmt. 5%				
	TOTAL (2)				

(1) Includes 20% contingencies
(2) Culverts, retaining walls, fences, lot grading not included

INDUCON 730 FEB.'75

FIGURE 12.7. Preliminary unit costs for roads and services: two lanes

(b) *Industry as tenant*

In many cases, corporations prefer to lease facilities and will enter into an Agreement to Lease with an industrial park owner who, in turn, will arrange financing and proceed to erect a building to suit the tenant's requirements. The term of lease will vary from five to

JOB No. ....
Prepared ....
Date ....

PRELIMINARY UNIT COSTS FOR ROADS AND SERVICES

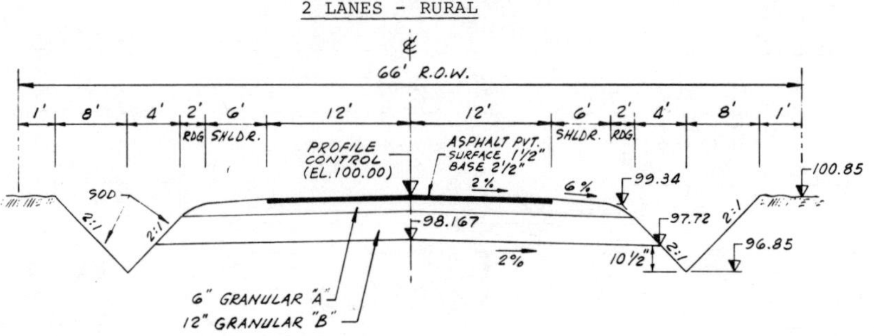

CODE	ITEM	QTY/LF	UNIT PRICE (1)	COST PER LF.	NOTES
212	Sanitary Sewer Pipe (10"Ø av)	1 LF	1.15 x 12.00	13.80	
	Sanitary Sewer Manholes	1/300 Ea	1.15 x 1100.00	4.22	
215	Watermain Pipe (12"Ø)	1 LF	1.15 x 22.00	25.30	
	Valves in Chambers	1/500 Ea	1.15 x 2200.00	5.06	
	Hydrants with Valves	1/300 Ea	1.15 x 1200.00	4.60	
220	Road Excavation (3' deep)	6.40 CY	1.15 x 1.25	9.20	
222	Granular B	3.00 T	1.15 x 3.00	10.35	
223	Granular A	1.65 T	1.15 x 3.50	6.64	
225	Paving, Base Course	0.375 T	1.15 x 17.00	7.33	
225a	Paving, Padding (if work in stages)	0.120 T	1.15 x 20.00	2.76	
226	Paving, Surface Course	0.225 T	1.15 x 20.00	5.18	
228	Sodding	3.0 SY	1.15 x 1.10	3.80	
229	Street Lights	1/150 Ea	1.15 x 1000.00	7.67	
241	Clearing, removals	allowance	1.15 x 1.00	1.15	
	Sub-Total			107.06	
	Engineering 15%			16.06	
	Planning, Admin., Management 5%			5.35	
	TOTAL (2)			128.47	

(1) Includes 15% contingencies

(2) Culverts, retaining walls, fences, lot grading, U/G Hydro not included.

Inducon Dec. 77

FIGURE 12.8. Preliminary unit costs for roads and services: two lanes rural

twenty years. This reflects the desire to avoid tying up capital in an investment not directly related to the business of the corporation. A capital-intensive industry, however, will be less likely to seek leased premises since the leases are relatively short term and substantial structural and mechanical design may be required.

A variation of this is the so-called 'lease-back' which occurs when an industry no longer wishes to own the building. The industry will seek an investor who will purchase the facility and lease it back to the industry for a period of years.

2. *Speculative buildings* are those that are erected in anticipation of an owner or tenant. These generally fall into two categories:
   (a) Single occupancy larger space (usually greater than 20 000 sq. ft). This will be a general-purpose type of building that will accommodate light manufacturing, warehousing or assembly activities with minor modification. Office space will be provided of approximately 10 per cent of of the total.
   (b) Multiple occupancy (industrial centre or industrial mall). The design of this type of building is one which developed in the early 1960s from a need for small space for a variety of uses. The building is usually long and rectangular and provides office on one side and shipping and receiving facilities on the opposite side. This enables an efficient 'sectioning off' of units during occupancy. The building is usually in the range of 25 000 sq. ft. to 100 000 sq. ft. in gross floor space and provides unit space in multiples of 2000 to 5000 sq. ft.

   Generally, the building is owned by a developer who provides space on a net lease basis. This means, in effect, that the tenant pays a basic rent to the developer to cover the provision of space only and is responsible for paying all other charges, with the exception of realty tax, in addition to the rent.

   It is well accepted that this type of building is complementary to an industrial park since it attracts service firms, sales and distribution companies and can often provide an effective 'incubator' for small manufacturing enterprises within the community. It is not uncommon to find banks and restaurants located in industrial malls as well.

   A well-executed design will provide a prestige location, well landscaped and maintained, with good access and identification. The developer will benefit from these provisions in attracting tenants for an optimum initial rental rate and the escalation potential inherent in such a project over its lifetime. The terms of these normally range from three to five years allowing the developer an opportunity to review the rate at at frequent intervals.

   The tenant will be attracted by the flexibility and variety of choices and can easily establish the cost of overhead for his space requirements. Full services including fire sprinkler protection enables the firm to optimize on operating efficiencies and insurance rates.

   A typical unit in a multiple will provide approximately 10 per cent of the total area in finished office space, frequently air-conditioned. The remaining space will be devoted to manufacturing or warehousing with direct access to a shipping and receiving area behind the building.

> Each unit will be separated from adjoining units by means of concrete block demising walls. These finishes and demising walls are installed to suit each tenant in the process of 'leasing up' the building. Subsequently, re-leasing will be largely confined to the original space configuration within the building.

A successful multiple industrial building requires the following prerequisites:

1. A satisfactory market.
2. A select location.
3. An effective, flexible design.
4. Low maintenance design features.
5. An owner with equity capital.
6. A mortgage fixed rate preferred.
7. Property management.

Suitable sites for these buildings can be preplanned in an industrial park such that an orderly programme can be generated.

CONCLUSION

The industrial park in North America has been a post-Second World War phenomenon. It developed in response to industry's needs for greatly expanded light manufacturing and warehousing facilities. At that time, many industrial activities were carried on in old, multistorey buildings situated in the city's core. But the satisfying of people's pent-up demand for consumer goods quickly proved these facilities to be inadequate. As well, these older structures almost invariably had no provision for expansion and, because of their multistorey design, did not suit the modern concept of production and assembly flows. For these reasons, coupled with the scarcity and high cost of downtown land, the industrial park came into being.

In place of crowded, dingy, aesthetically incompatible structures, the industrial park was pleasantly situated on suburban land. It featured well-separated, modern, single-storey buildings whose architectural and engineering designs provided clean, uncluttered façades and bright, airy working areas. These pleasant surroundings in turn attracted the best and most productive workers. The greatly expanded use of truck transportation made the industrial park possible, as did workers' increasing ownership of automobiles. Public transportation, although often available, was no longer essential for employees to get to and from work.

Although industrial parks have been built by a variety of different interests, such as municipalities and industrial subdividers, the most successful parks have been designed and built by professional industrial developers. The reasons for this include the developer's skilled and experienced staff who are continually involved in the many aspects of land assembly, planning, layout, drainage, roadway, services, architectural and engineering design, and marketing demands of a successful industrial park. In addition, the industrial developer, because of a variety of leasing arrangements and because of the value he places on his reputation, has an ongoing interest in the marketability of each of his industrial parks.

With his staff and facilities, the industrial developer is able to provide a great many essential features others would find difficult, if not impossible. For instance, the overall layout and siting plan provides good surface drainage and landscaping. Each structure within the park is compatible with its neighbour. A sense of spaciousness prevails. Gently curving roadways and cul-de-sacs discourage through traffic. Modern street lighting standards, underground electrical service, and large-capacity water and sewerage services are invariably provided.

In total, the developer's industrial park is aesthetically pleasing and a credit to its neighbourhood. This harmonious integration within the community is another important feature of an industrial park produced by a reputable industrial developer, for it encourages acceptance by governments, employers, neighbours and employees alike.

At the present time, the industrial park appears to be a very successful answer to the needs of industry, business, governments and workers. Its popularity attests to this. Also, because it provides a large and stable base, the industrial park is encouraged, even sought after, by the majority of municipalities. In summary, industrial parks were the right idea at the right time immediately following the Second World War. Since the 1940s they have continually satisfied industry's growing needs. Their ability to do this for the foreseeable future is readily apparent. For the longer term, their basic flexibility of concept and design holds their continuing acceptance in good stead.

REFERENCES

Baldwin, W. L. (1958). *A Report on the Dartmouth College Conference*, Arthur D. Little, Cambridge, Mass.

Boley, R. E. (1958). 'Effects of industrial parks on the community'. Urban Land, **17**, 10, 3–6.

Planning Industrial Development
Edited by David F. Walker

Chapter 13

Regional Policy and the Geography of Welfare: Theory and Practice

Morgan Sant

> The shift from high mass-consumption to the search for quality is a real discontinuity in the life of man in industrial society—in one sense the first major discontinuity since take-off (Rostow, 1971, 203).

Whether or not the process of economic change falls into discrete stages, there can be little doubt that fundamental structural change requires the resolution of deeply conflicting forces. Stresses arise not only between groups pursuing different ambitions, but also within individuals being forced to assign priorities among the many roles they must perform. Most important of all are conflicts of philosophy or ideology upon whose resolution depends the social behaviour of a people.

Of course, Rostow (in the above quotation as elsewhere) severely exaggerates the division of stages. The 'search for quality' is not new. One need not go further back in history than the utopian movements of the early nineteenth century and hence to the more modern architects of civic reform to realize that the 'search for quality' has been an essential antithesis to the drive towards high mass-consumption. And yet, if the work of these early seers and practitioners denies the sequence of clearcut stages it does not represent an even balance of forces. Utopians and reformers, for all their importance, have done no more than temper the worst barbarities of the economic machine. Except for sporadic and localized occurrences, they have never dominated the form or functioning of a developed western civic culture, let alone a national one. If this were to happen, we would then experience a real discontinuity.

But what is this search for quality that Rostow and others have identified? What are its characteristics and what distinguishes it from similar movements in earlier times? Clearly, it is not about the quality of life of a privileged few: that is the traditional motivation of the competing participants in the mainstream of economic development. Nor is it *necessarily* about revolutionary change and the substitution of political systems and élites (though that may be a precondition in some instances). Rather, it is about matters that are much more mundane: security, environments for living and working, the right to participate in making decisions that affect these things and, above all, a more equitable access to the goods (and bads) that are the measure of the quality of life. The list (and no doubt it can be lengthened) is a familar one. Indeed, it is indistinguishable from the goals set by the utopians and reformers mentioned previously. What, then, is different between the present and the past? It would be facile to argue that problems are any more severe or urgent. That may be true, in so far as economies are now divided into larger, more powerful industrial organizations—and possibly more amoral ones (Bower, 1974)—consuming vastly more resources and spewing out vastly more non-biodegradable pollutants. But that, by itself, does not constitute the crux of the difference. The crucial point, we would assert, lies in the evolution of social and economic thought: the acceptance that money income is a poor surrogate for quality of life (though that can be a dangerously patronizing statement if used to justify someone's exploitation); that not all goods are private goods but some are public or merit goods;[1] that left to itself the process of economic change may bring about conditions that satisfy no one or, at best, very few.

But these are generalities. Though they pervade contemporary social and economic debate, our interest here must be more narrowly focused. Primary concern is with urban and regional issues, the distribution of economic activities, and the nature of policies related to these. Emphasis, insofar as it can be directed at all, is directed towards the last—the formulation, content and implementation of policy. This is justified because the role of policy is not just a reactive one. Policy is much more than a response to issues. It is, simultaneously, the source of much of the observation which leads to the recognition of issues and the pivot on which is balanced the continuing debate about the character and quality of urban and regional environments. If the world was once so simple that we could conjure up entirely novel policies to deal with newly discovered ills, it is certainly not so today when we have the twin spectres of interdependence and opportunity cost always hovering over us.

In a stimulating evaluation of location theory, Michael Chisholm (1971) posed the questions of what sort of theory was required, and at what scale it should apply. Asserting the need for normative theory, he then proposed that this was more likely to be derived from ideas contained in welfare theory than from micro-economic theory. With this we would concur. But at the same time we should see Chisholm's conclusion as no more than an initial foray into the little-charted territory of welfare geography. Better location theory may be a necessary condition for better locational planning, but it is not a sufficient one. The viewpoint presented here is that the fundamental factors in relating industrial distributions to the geography of welfare are found in the political and institutional environments in which locational actions occur. Closer consideration of these is essential if progress is to be made towards using the distribution of economic activity more effectively and more sensitively to achieve greater equality and better environmental conditions. This may sound like 'applied pragmatics' rather than locational economics, but this approach contains two advantages. It helps to identify limits within which location theory is able to contribute to questions of welfare: and it identifies what else is needed apart from faith in the efficacy of location theory.

The remainder of this essay is divided into four sections. The first is a brief discussion of the components of welfare geography, in which attention is drawn not only to economic disparities but also to questions of accessibility and negative externalities. This is followed by a statement of the criteria by which urban and regional policies might be judged. Next is a description of what we have termed the policy-making environment, which is treated within the framework of welfare geography only. Lastly, there is a short review of regional policy and its impact on one of the welfare components, regional disparities.

WELFARE GEOGRAPHY AND THE DISTRIBUTION OF ECONOMIC ACTIVITY

The content of urban and regional studies in recent years has been distinguished by two important characteristics. One has been the growing recognition that an interdisciplinary challenge is posed by urban and regional problems. The other is the assertion of a value judgement that, at its mildest, seeks a more equitable distribution of the benefits of economic activity and a reduction of its disbenefits. At the radical extreme there are some who have imposed a Marxian framework on their theory and analysis, but the majority, no less committed, have opted for the immediate task of seeking improvement within the system rather than waiting for its destruction before building the new utopia. It is this group (and it must be emphasized that it is very heterogeneous) that has created the corpus of what has come to be known as 'welfare geography'. Much of the work has been summarized in David Smith's *Human Geography: a Welfare Approach* published in 1977.

Questions of distribution, in Smith's words '. . . who gets what, where . . .', dominate welfare geography. However, it is clear that the distribution of goods (and bads) has three geographical components; economic disparities, spatial accessibility and negative externalities.

1. Conventionally, attention has focused on those direct indicators of economic health at the regional level that are paralleled in national economic accounts: per capita income, unemployment, productivity, expenditure on private and public goods and services. Although this component will undoubtedly continue to play a major role in regional studies increasing attention is likely to be directed towards the other two.

2. Secondly, in the attempt to define 'real income' or welfare, close account has been taken of variations in accessibility, particularly to public goods and services (such as hospitals and clinics, schools and libraries) but also to private services. Access is related to a number of criteria of which income is only one. The location of activities, the times of their opening and closing, the distribution of population, the quality, price and coverage of public transport and the availability of private transport to individual members of the household, are all important factors. Hagerstrand's (1977) concept of time–space budgets, taken up by several researchers (such as Moseley *et al.*, 1977) has provided a new way of extending and operationalizing Pahl's (1971) dichotomous classification of the rich–poor, amenity–tyranny reaction to geographical space.
3. The third component in the distribution of welfare is the incidence of negative externalities—the costs of an act that do not fall upon the perpetrators of that act but are incurred by other people. There is a tendency to oversimplify these, presenting them under the blanket heading of 'social costs'. This ignores the characteristic that negative externalities are essentially geographical; the costs usually fall most heavily on people closest to the origin of the externality. Pollution, the most obvious of negative externalities —whether in the form of atmospheric or water contamination, noise or visual intrusion—has marked spatial relationships (Starkie, 1976). It is likely, too, that the broad spatial distribution of these externalities affects the quality of neighbourhoods at the micro-level. Given appropriate conditions the 'good neighbourhood' emerges from reciprocal investment in externality-creating improvements. Everyone benefits from the maintenance and upgrading of surrounding properties. Conversely the 'bad neighbourhood' lacks this reciprocity not, be it noted, through the general bloody-mindedness of the occupants, but because environmental (and, possibly, institutional) constraints make reciprocity difficult or unrewarding (Cox, 1973).

Listing these components of welfare enables at least a description of the inequalities that inevitably occur in the human landscape. To complete the picture, however, requires an examination of the links between these components and the distribution of economic activity.

A useful starting point in identifying the potential conflict between locational strategies and the distribution of welfare or consumer surplus is Hotelling's (1929) model of monopolistic competition between two icecream vendors on a beach. Given the assumptions of the model, the outcome (concentration of both vendors at the centre of the beach) imposes a loss of consumer surplus at the more remote ends of the market. Even with more than two suppliers there is likely to be some loss of consumer surplus which would be exacerbated if, perchance, there were agglomeration economies in the supply of icecream.

But what if we were to extend Hotelling's idea, such that there is a small group of people who do not like icecream but do enjoy being on the beach. If they arrived at the same time as the vendors, they could do no better than locate themselves as far as possible from them—either at the extremities of the beach or right at its centre. Of course, if they were perspicacious and predicted the eventual location of the vendors after their jockeying for position they would choose the extremities. But in their innocence they choose the centre. Eventually, the vendors get there too. In pursuit of the market they advertise by loudly playing their merry jingles and, having got their market, they cut down costs by deliberately not providing garbage receptacles. We now have a second group of disadvantaged (and powerless) people: non-consumers of icecream—by now they probably have a vitriolic hatred for it!—who have to absorb a reduction in welfare whether they stay and endure the inconvenience or whether they decide to incur the 'cost' of moving to the most remote corner of the beach.

This takes care of two of the welfare components—accessibility and negative externalities. To build in a picture of economic disparities we should need to extend the assumptions of the model so far as to make it unrecognizable. Our beach would become a set of regions, we should have to introduce more activities with different levels of productivity and different rates of growth, and our sybarites would become employers and workers. From there it is a simple step to Myrdal's (1957) model of cumulative causation and centre–periphery disparities.

Hotelling's case is little more than an allegory: short-run locational adjustments of the kind required are barely possible even in the most trivial examples of the street vendor type. Indeed it makes more sense to treat the linear market as a metaphor of the spectrum of possible price adjustments open to firms competing for imperfectly informed, heterogeneous markets. Nevertheless, the lessons from the model are clear enough. Locational patterns are fundamentally influenced by their institutional environments. When, as in the above instance, institutions are marked by their absence, the permissiveness of the system and the limited rationality of location decision-makers creates an equilibrium that is optimal neither for suppliers nor consumers: it is neither efficient nor is it equitable.

This simplistic discussion needs to be replaced by something more realistic, but first it is appropriate to raise one further issue. When we describe a distribution as 'suboptimal' we are making a welfare statement. We imply that by doing things differently someone (or some group) may benefit without causing a reduction in someone else's utility. But—and this is crucial to the whole of welfare theory—the fact that a distribution is suboptimal almost certainly means that the institutional environment is suboptimal too. Usually this is taken to mean that institutions are too permissive in allowing negative externalities to be imposed on one group, or surplus value to be appropriated by another.

It seems these days to be a normal reaction against liberal utilitarianism to argue for greater controls and less permissive institutions. However, inefficiency and inequity can also arise from over-restrictive conditions. A legal monopoly, where entry to an industry is deliberately restricted, provides the most obvious example.

In asserting the importance of institutions we add another dimension to the concept of *bounded rationality*. Hitherto we have tended to think of bounds arising from imperfect knowledge and satisficing motives on the part of locational decision-makers. The evidence is sufficient to show that this is true in the private sector (Townroe, 1971). Weak information systems and poor ability to use information, however, provide only one side of the picture. Even in the unrealistic situation of perfect knowledge and impeccable judgement, the decision-making process serves only the rationality imposed by the firm or individual within the bounds set by the institutional environment. The power of policy to shape the distribution of economic activity is clearly exhibited in British experience since 1945, to which we will return later. That policy there has been so effective is chiefly due to the relative power of central agencies capable of channelling resources along decided paths rather than to inherent locational advantages and disadvantages.

WELFARE CRITERIA FOR SPATIAL POLICIES

To begin with a metaphor: the economic environment of an individual is an imperfect combination of the games of chess and snakes and ladders. Lateral movements are constrained by rules, routes and barriers. Vertical movements are facilitated by access to ladders and proximity to snakes. As in the combination of games, a mixture of skill and luck determines the outcome, but these attributes are not equally or randomly distributed. Pawns, being more restricted by the laws of mobility, are more dependent on luck (so, presumably, are kings who are only slightly more mobile) but the other pieces are much more free to range over their 'environment'.

Games, of course, are no more than a parody of the real thing. Yet in this case there is something suggestive in the metaphor. As Donnison (1974, p. 191) has asserted in the context of regional economic policy 'we must beware of *discontinuities*, where the rungs of a ladder are missing or lead nowhere and *disjunctions*, where neighbouring ladders are not available to provide mutually supporting opportunities'. Writing of British experience he continues, 'the poorer regions appear to have more than their share of these discontinuities and disjunctions. Some are the result of long term changes in the pace and direction of their economic development. Some have been exacerbated by clumsy public intervention in the region's affairs.' As an example of clumsiness he cites the location of showpiece investment—an aluminium smelter—in a less densely populated assisted area, an action which does little to reduce the discontinuities of job opportunities and may actually be detrimental to the development of alternative activities.

If the above metaphor and Donnison's comments are translated to the conditions of urban and regional *welfare* policies a number of criteria can be distinguished by which these policies could be evaluated. The *first* and most pressing demand is that such policies should be sensitive to specific needs. Places do not all share the same problems with the same intensity and even where the symptoms are similar the prescription may properly be different. *Secondly*, policy should act directly upon those conditions that give rise to the deprivation of individuals. This is far from simple or straightforward in practice since all policies have external effects. However, the principle is unambiguous; disjunctions and discontinuities in the ladders of opportunity are experienced by individuals. It may be that many, or even most, of the individuals in a place suffer similarly from some problem, and that the appropriate policy is one that works generally, but this does not detract from the principle. The *third* requirement is for long-term perpectives. It is much simpler, of course, to offer subsidies or divert resources or pass laws that offer immediate amelioration and this is an important test of the effectiveness of governments and bureaucracies. The ability to meet immediate needs is also a precondition for successful long-term policy. Nevertheless, when we talk of discontinuities and disjunctions we are concerned with structural conditions that require a long view. *Lastly*, and in this case we acknowledge some idealism, the welfare approach demands the ultimate removal of *all* discontinuities and disjunctions. This is not to state that the goal is totally equality—that has never been a definable, let alone a practicable, objective. What is practicable is that impediments hindering a more equitable distribution should be removed progressively.

Donnison's comments relate to a broad regional scale and chiefly to economic disparities but they are also relevant to the other two welfare issues. The connection is most obvious in the case of access to public goods and services where inequalities can be greatly affected by location and allocation policies, by decisions on the size of units for service delivery, and by supporting policies for transportation.

Criteria for *spatial* policies on negative externalities are far more difficult to specify. To date the only confident intervention in the location of noxious activities has been in the most obvious cases where absolute standards can be applied in order to protect health and property. These are isolated instances, such as lead smelters. A partial exception in Britain was the location of nuclear power stations, where a minimum distance from settlements was imposed in the 1950s, but later relaxed. As a general criterion the slogan 'Let the polluter pay'—by applying emission controls, by compensating sufferers or by incurring the costs of relocation—provides a reasonable principle, but is not a guide to a practicable spatial policy. Identifying the real costs (net of benefits that the offending activity might provide) are difficult enough. Distributing these costs among heterogeneous and geographically dispersed populations makes the problem virtually insuperable. Moreover, variability in the distribution of costs through time results in the total impracticability of a general spatial policy. This means that, in the absence of universal criteria, spatial policies towards negative externalities need to be (a) flexible with respect to time and place and to the nature of the activity, and (b) powerful enough to impose the cost back on the perpetrator of the externality.

These, then, are idealistic criteria by which to judge the expected impact of policies. What actually happens when policies are formulated and implemented depends upon the combination of elements in the institutional environment.

Locational Planning and the Institutional Environment

All planning has its foundations in some conception of an ideal state. The ideal may not be socially just, nor need to be economically efficient. It may be as trivial as a desire for a quiet life, or it may stem from an ideological demand for a fundamental social change. Whatever the motivation, the essence of planning is to convert ideals, or goals (the words are used synonymously) into policies and thence to find or create the resources to implement them. Here the problems begin.

In the 1960s several authors put forward schematic versions of their view of the planning process (Hall, 1974). Common elements ran through them all: the process was regarded as linearly directed and emphasis was on the modelling and projection of systems and the generation and evaluation of alternative simulations. They tended to ignore essential features both of the planning process and of the planning environment. Their simplicity gave them an air of unreality. That is a danger to be faced by all such schema, and it is one that can never be totally overcome. Nevertheless, at the risk of similar criticism an alternative has been devised and is illustrated in Figure 13.1. The intention here is to emphasize the elements that compromise the planning environment and thereby to set a framework for considering the ways by which intervention in the structure, distribution and development of economic activity is actually carried out.

At the centre of the figure is the planning process itself: in essence it differs little from those schemes referred to above. Surrounding this are four boxes describing the environmental elements; ideals, institutions, resources and information systems. Each of these interacts with the others and with some or all of the steps in the planning process. A brief discussion of these elements and steps follows, but there is insufficient space here to examine all of their ramifications or to trace the interaction between the elements in the planning environment. These remain as potentially very fruitful areas for future studies.

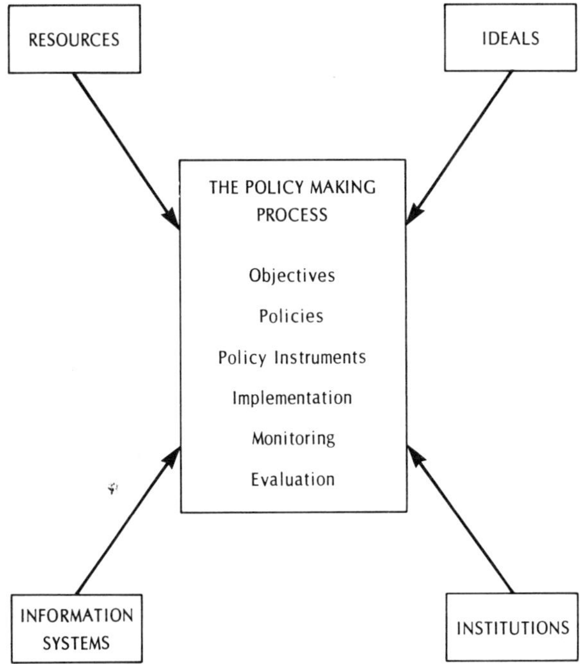

FIGURE 13.1. A schematic view of the components and environment of the policy-making process

Ideals

National economic goals—growth in total and per capita GNP, stability in monetary values and employment, equitable distributions of earning and wealth, and so on—are all reflected at the urban and regional scales. Moreover, there, as at the national level, these goals are surrounded by conflicting debates about their relative importance and what they imply for industrial and spatial planning.

Two sets of ideals have traditionally influenced attitudes, official and unofficial, towards distributions of economic activity.

(a) *Utilitarianism.* The distribution should be such that the sum total of individual utilities should be maximized. In the sense used here this sum is manifest in indicators of aggregate growth in GNP. Clearly, as Figure 13.2a indicates, interregional and interpersonal distributions are irrelevant, at least in the short term. (It is sometimes argued, especially by more conservative political parties, that inequality inspires incentive and hence economic growth, which in turn allows redistribution. Such statements deserve the scepticism they usually get.) The pursuit of efficiency and productivity has severe implica-

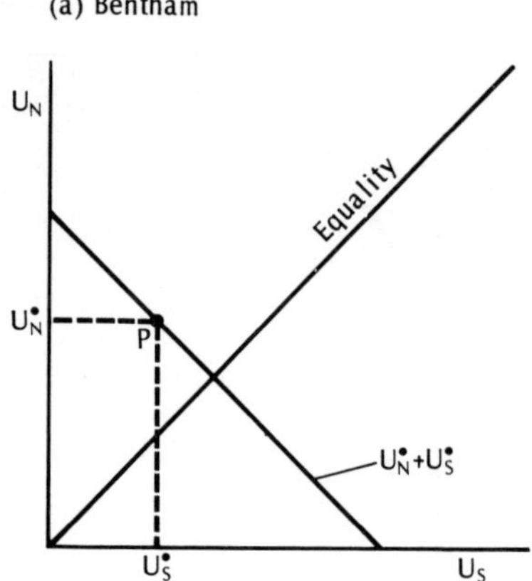

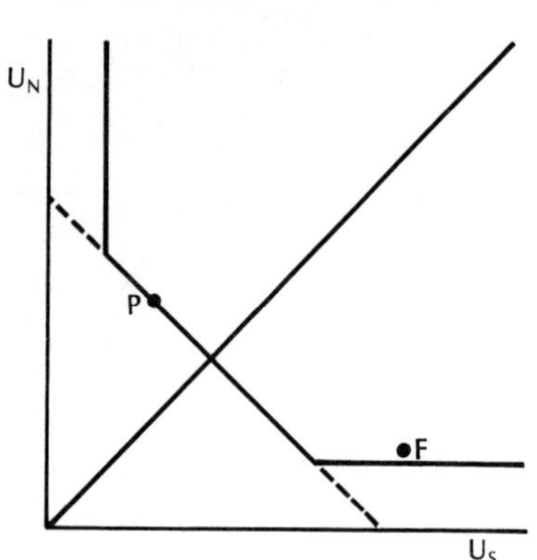

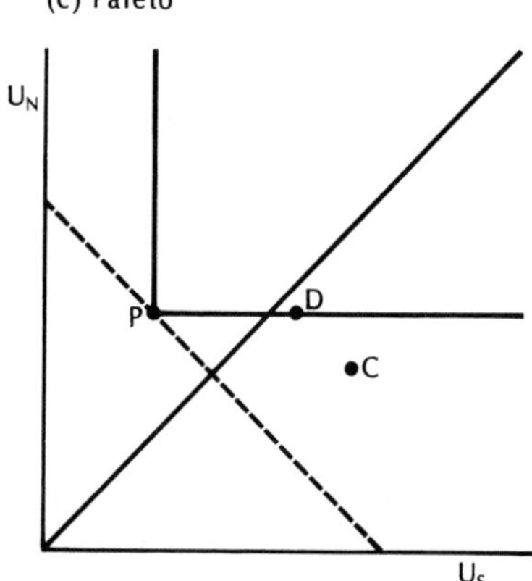

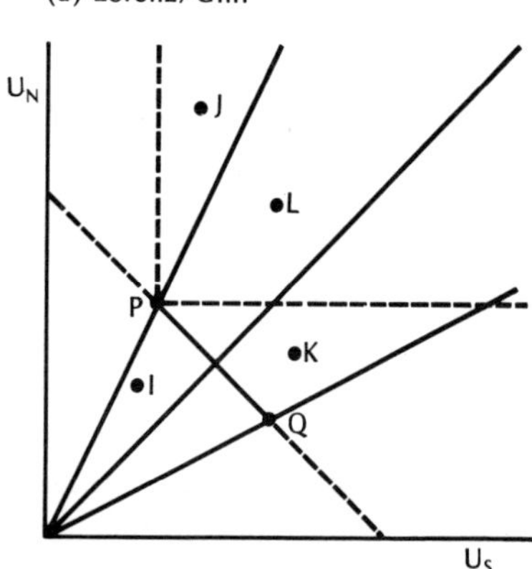

FIGURE 13.2. Alternative criteria for judging improvements in distribution among regions. The diagrams describe the distribution of utility (or welfare) between two regions, or two persons. In each case it is assumed that the initial distribution is defined by point *P*, where U_N is twice the value of U_S. In the classical utilitarion (Benthamite) case any position to the right of the welfare transformation line is an improvement. In the remaining cases 'improvement' is progressively more narrowly defined. Type (d), the Lorenz/Gini distribution, contains a paradox in that a shift from *P* to *T* signifies an improvement in the distribution despite a reduction in the welfare of both regions. Source: D. M. Smith (1977), p. 152

tions for locational and allocational policies, especially in the supply of public goods and services. Scale economies can only be achieved at the cost of accessibility—a cost which is likely to be passed on to consumers. Also, the definition of public goods and merit goods is likely to be very stringently made. They need the characteristic that their efficient operation will raise GNP: their welfare potential is irrelevant. Technical education fits this requirement; access to public open space does not. Negative externalities, because they are transfer payments not included in the national accounting matrix, do not affect aggregate utility, though they do alter its distribution. They are unlikely to occur at random in the population and in fact one would expect, in a utilitarian system, that the power of political and economic élites would be sufficient to ensure that negative externalities fell on others rather than themselves. Of course, appropriation of total output by one region or group is impossible, and Figure 13.2a is totally unrealistic. Utilitarianism, however, may be expressed in a constrained form which allows the weaker group no more than a minimum subsistence level (Figure 13.2b). Statutory unemployment benefits and minimum wage laws are manifestations of this.

(b) *Egalitarianism.* Regardless of place of residence, every member of the population should have equal access to economic opportunities and public services, and none should incur any greater negative externalities than any other. Also, using Paretian criteria, none should be adversely affected by the actions of another. More far-reaching conditions of equality move the concept of egalitarianism towards utopian socialist ideals of total equality in the distribution of resources and income as well as the more limited notion of 'opportunity'. Figures 13.2c and 13.2d describe the progression through increasingly strict definitions of equity in the distribution of welfare. The implications of egalitarianism for urban and regional economies are far-reaching indeed. Balanced development becomes an important goal. Since much inequality in incomes and unemployment can be explained by differences in regional industrial structure, including differences induced through corporate concentration (Westaway, 1974), a case exists for more even distributions within the limits of factor endowments. Importance is also attached to the defining of public goods and merit goods, and in manipulating them to achieve locational patterns that are more equitable, if less efficient, than the utilitarian approach would produce. Similarly, egalitarian ideals embrace a broader definition of social costs, and a greater willingness to take account of the distributional effects of environmental deterioration. As we have described them, these two idealistic standpoints appear as polar opposites. In reality, of course, most of us—in the name of pragmatism or expediency—compromise most of the time. Moreover, there is now an argument, concerning regional economic policy, that the regional redistribution of industry facilitates growth and stability in the national economy by relieving inflationary pressures in areas of high labour demand and diverting growth to areas of excess capacity. If this is valid it is a case of an egalitarian act for utilitarian motives (or vice versa). However, the argument is not totally proven (Chisholm, 1976), and, in any case, relates only to one of the three welfare issues. It is not relevant to the questions of accessibility and environmental quality.

Institutions

Simultaneously, institutions define the power relationships and the locus of responsibility for urban and regional planning. This is not to say that institutions are immutable. As Blondel (1969) has remarked, sometimes the most important aspects of political institutions are the unwritten ones, and these, emerging from custom and usage, depend on continued tacit acceptance. Many of the relationships between local governments and between local and central government are of this nature. For present purposes three characteristics of institutions are particularly interesting.

(a) *Centralization:* the degree to which power and responsibility are vested in a single authority, hence allowing policies for economic activity to be pursued in a unitary manner. The antitheses, regionalism and localism, acknowledge a geographical separation of powers which, in turn, may encourage diversity in attitudes and practices towards economic structure and development. There is, however, a wide spectrum of arrangements between complete centrality and pure federalism; two examples are regional budgeting and administrative delegation. In practice both regional separation of powers and centrality can be ambivalent in their effects. Where there is separation, for example, there may be duplication and waste of resources: Linge (1967) describes how this has occurred in the interstate distribution of secondary industry in Australia. In the delivery of public goods and services, on the other hand, the separation of powers may be conducive to more equitable accessibility.

(b) *Interdependence:* the extent to which different responsible bodies (central and local government and their agencies) are able or required to co-ordinate their actions. Administrative articulation poses a major challenge to policy-makers who may find their activities less effective than anticipated because other ministries or departments are independently pursuing their own policies. The creation of superministries with responsibility over wide-ranging functions may go some way towards alleviating this, but total co-ordination is unlikely ever to occur in urban and regional planning.

(c) *Permissiveness:* the degree to which the private sector is free to decide upon its own actions and to which the public sector is required to recognize and impose established standards of service delivery and environmental quality. The *ability* of governments to intervene is a crucial attribute in urban and regional planning, and requires their having a battery of controls and incentives at their disposal.

Resources

Intervention in the distribution of economic activity may, as Moore and Rhodes (1974) have argued, be resource-creating in the long run. However, over any shorter period intervention imposes budgetary demands (and inevitable opportunity costs) such that the nature of the intervention is crucially affected. The size and stability of public finance and the flexibility with which it can be diverted between uses and geographical areas influence the ability to commit resources to long-term policies or programmes.

Information Systems

In a world where decision-making is constrained by knowledge (and the lack of it) and behaviour is characterized by its 'bounded rationality', the quality of information is a vital influence on the nature of policy-making. Again, several features can be listed.

(a) *Accessibility*. The question of access to information is important in so far as it helps to balance the powers of actual or potential competitors and influences the quality of public participation in policy-making. That accurate and up-to-date information is also important to government goes without saying, but collecting, monitoring and evaluating the social and economic statistics that are necessary even in terms of national aggregates has tested the capacity of most states. A further issue under this heading is the quality of the information received by the private sector concerning policies that directly affect it: as Green (1977) has shown, the quality of businessmen's perceptions of the value and geographical incidence of regional assistance is far from perfect.

(b) *Aggregation*. Earlier it was asserted that one welfare criterion for policy is a sensitivity to discontinuities and disjunctions in the distribution of opportunities, and that these are experienced by individuals (albeit in association with other individuals). This must pose problems for information systems. Although the basic information unit for statistical purposes is an individual person or household or industrial establishment, the local government area or region of industry tends to be used as the basis for analysis and prescription. The institutional reasons for this are easy enough to understand. Aggregation simplifies the analytical process; local government areas are planning and budgetary units; and, in the context of regional economic policy, it is less complicated to designate whole areas for assistance on the basis of standardized criteria and to bring blanket controls and incentives to bear on firms than it is to identify precisely where problems fall. In this respect administrators have been supported by some students of urban and regional issues, whose concern with social and economic indicators have reified averages and aggregates.

For example, Knox (1975) states that, ideally, indicators should be comprehensive, aggregative, available as time series and for geographical areas, refer to outputs of the system and relate to public policy goals. By itself this statement is not sufficient to serve the criteria discussed earlier. It provides us with choropleth maps when what we may need are point distributions When those maps are derived from factor analyses the irrelevance is compounded.

(c) *Evaluation*. Techniques of plan and project evaluation have proliferated in recent years (Litchfield, 1970), but none has proved universally acceptable chiefly because there are no natural guidelines to the items that should be contained in a cost-benefit balance sheet. There are also well-documented difficulties involved in measuring costs and benefits and in attributing weights to different items. The choice of evaluation technique clearly influences the estimated advantages of different courses of action.

(d) *The state of theory*. Planning and policy is greatly influenced by prevailing theory. It also tends to adopt fashions: the conventional wisdom of one decade may be radically different in the next. Perhaps the most dramatic example has been the adoption, and international diffusion, of growth centre theory despite the disturbing lack of consensus either on the ramifications of the theory or a clear understanding of how to apply it (Moseley, 1974). However, it would be both unfair and dangerous to ignore the positive contributions that have come from advances in theory. Examples include: the shift from classical models of equilibrating adjustments to cumulative causation models of unbalanced change; the development of the theory of public goods and its implications for normative modelling; and the replacement of deterministic models by probabilistic ones that take account of ignorance and uncertainty. East of these has entered the thinking of researchers and planners and influenced the content of policy. Predicting the next paradigm is difficult, but if it is true that every action generates its own reaction, it may be that the present predilic-tion for large-scale mathematical modelling within the framework of systems theory will be countered by a Schumacher-style concern for micro-environments. These, then, are the elements of the planning environment. We could go on to describe their interrelationships; for example, the influence of ideology on the distribution and use of resources, or the link between institutions and information systems. Instead these, and the relationships between the environment and the planning process at the core of the scheme are left to the individual reader to reconstruct.

There is, however, one further point that should be made. This is the need to impose a distinction between objectives, policies and policy instruments. If this is ignored it can have serious consequences. In our scheme, policy instruments exist to serve policies and, in turn, policies serve objectives. Now, first, it is obvious that instruments can be extremely effective, serving the policy very well but, at the same time, for various reasons (one of which may be that the magnitude of the original problem is greater than anticipated) the policy may fail to meet the needs of the objective. This is illustrated below, using British regional policy as an example. Secondly, the dilemma also occurs in reverse. Given a problem and the specification of an objective, what policy should be adopted and what instruments are needed to meet the needs of the policy? The answers are not always obvious.

LOCATIONAL POLICIES FOR ECONOMIC DISPARITIES

Few countries now lack some form of intervention in the location of economic activity. The degree of control that they exercise varies widely, as do the resources they commit to regional policy. Differences also occur in the manner of intervention, due largely to their institutional conditions. Yet, despite the dissimilarities there remains a remarkable conformity in the broad conduct of regional policy and in its questionable effectiveness.

The conventional response to regional disparities among developed western countries has been, almost without exception, one that lies firmly within the framework of Myrdal's cumulative causation model. Correctly, the view has been accepted that, in dynamic equilibrium, regional disparities will be perpetuated by factor movements responding to unequal demand. With this diagnosis the Myrdallian prescription is an attractive one: that to reduce or remove disparities requires intervention in the distribution of economic activity, thus inducing a stronger 'spread' effect. The concept has some elegance and, of course, fulfils whatever regionalist demands might exist (not unimportant in democracies where regional assistance enhances electoral chances. No aspiring politician can afford to tell a constituency that it should decline or be poorer than others). Yet there is a massive gulf between the concept and the practice of regional policy, as is discussed below. In particular, attention must be given to two questions: *first*, the extent to which adequate resources are available and can be diverted between regions ('resources' here includes the supply of mobile industry); and *second*, the degree to which the conduct of policies apparently aimed at a more equal distribution of welfare actually adopt and apply measures that act *directly* upon that objective.

Two approaches, often used in combination, have been embodied in regional policies: a broad designation of areas for general assistance, and a more selective specification of places (sometimes referred to as growth centres) for concentrated development. Backing up these are provisions for moving resources through inducing relocation in the private sector and by diverting public expenditure on infrastructure and services. Stated cryptically, the *objective* is the removal of disparities, *policy* is the relocation of activity, and *instruments* of policy comprise the designation of areas for assistance and the battery of controls and incentives.

Evaluation of regional policy in Britain, where it has been pursued with a vigour not exceeded elsewhere, indicates a rather mixed picture (Sant, 1975), but helps to illuminate the questions posed above. It has been concluded, first, that the instruments of policy have been remarkably powerful in influencing both the volume of industrial movement from year to year and its redistribution from the richer regions to the assisted areas. By the mid 1960s policy-induced movement of manufacturing industry into the assisted areas amounted to about 100 establishments per annum, leading to an employment increment of 15 000 to 20 000. However, the second conclusion is that the evidence for a reduction of disparities is very weak. Some indicators show a slow improvement in the assisted areas (for example, female activities rates, manufacturing employment); others point to no significant change (such as per capita earnings, unemployment, migration) which may, of course, mean that assistance prevented things from getting worse in the poorer regions. Thirdly, it was becoming apparent by the early 1970s, after more than two decades of fairly heavy industrial movement to the assisted areas and the new towns, that the supply of potentially mobile industry is not inexhaustible. Depletion was setting in, and the main source areas, London and the West Midlands, were beginning to show concern at the erosion of the more dynamic elements of their manufacturing bases. The cost of inducing an additional job in an assisted area was steadily increasing, yet the demand for jobs was barely diminishing. At current values, and excluding investment grants and the regional employment premium (in other words, labour subsidy), the Exchequer cost per job arising from assisted projects rose by 150 per cent between 1965 and 1973. So the answer to the first question posed above—the availability of resources for effective regional policy—is, as far as British evidence provides a lesson, that regional disparities tend to be of such a magnitude and so entrenched that the conventional sources implied in Myrdal's model are almost certain to be inadequate. Using Britain as an example for the rest of the world is a dangerous procedure, but it should be recalled that Britain's manufacturing sector is large and tends to be concentrated in large organizations amenable to having branch plants diverted to assisted areas, and that the Westminster system is relatively unconstrained in the powers available to pursue a regional policy. It also has relatively small regional disparities compared with most other countries. Thus it might justifiably be asked whether others, less well able to mobilize and divert resources and perhaps also less committed to doing so, have any more chance of successfully combating their disparities using similar techniques.

Part of the problem is that regional policy in its conventional form is an *indirect* way of tackling inequality. This has become evident as studies have begun to identify the beneficiaries of policy. Most revealing have been analyses of the impact upon employment. The tendency has been for labour, excluding that brought from outside, to transfer from other jobs within the assisted area. Demand is especially great for skilled workers. Meanwhile, those who constitute the basis for a regional welfare policy—the poor and the unemployed—are probably the least likely to benefit: the poor remain poor, the unemployed are the least likely to get the new jobs. Nor are they likely to be easily absorbed in the older firms in the region. These too may be hit by the specific labour demands of new firms coming into the region. On the other hand, apart from a few notable exceptions, it is clear that industry does not suffer by being relocated. Employer's organizations, especially those dominated by larger companies, have tended to show only one major concern, namely that the policy instruments should be held stable (Stewart, 1974). One presumes, therefore, that they are not unhappy with the level of inducements to invest in the assisted areas.

These comments are not a condemnation of conventional regional policy. Rather they are a statement that, in the pursuit of equity, industrial decentralization, by itself, is almost certain to be insufficient. Decentralization may still be justified for other reasons, such as relieving metropolitan congestion and managing the national labour market, so it is sensible also to use it as part of a package of welfare policy instruments. The issue then becomes one of defining the other instruments that might be included in the package.

When one reaches the dilemma that is now being faced in many countries trying to deal with regional inequalities, the sensible step would seem to be to look again at the nature of the regional problem. It is not insignificant in this respect to note that in Britain the crucial document from which modern regional policy has flowed was the Barlow Report (Royal Commission on the Distribution of the Industrial Population) published in 1940. Subsequent documents have done little to alter the basic conduct of regional policy embodied in the legislation following Barlow. Retracing one's steps is difficult and not recommended as too frequent an exercise, but if it leads to better policies it will have been worthwhile. Arguably, there are several countries (for example, Italy, Britain, Canada) where serious regionalist issues demand a reconsideration of regional policy. Perhaps more complex, but no less critical, is the future of regional economic policy in the European Economic Community. If that organization of states is to realize the full potential seen by its founders it will require a strong approach to protect the welfare of inhabitants of the peripheral regions. Otherwise they will be forced to rely on their one powerful resource—their votes—to force their national governments to be more protective than their long-term interests justify.

Reassessment of the regional problem can take several forms. One is simple: the application of arithmetic just to find out the magnitude of the problem. The conclusion might result in pessimism if, as in the British case discussed by Cameron (1974), it appears that certain welfare objectives are beyond the limits of achievement. In that instance it was considered that to bring regional labour demand approximately into parity would require about one million jobs to be created in the assisted areas within a decade—or about three times the rate of job creation achieved during the previous decade when policy had been vigorous. This leads to the second possibility—the reassessment of objectives. Given the limitation imposed by resources, where should priority lie? In the United States, where this limitation was recognized, a 'worst-first' approach was proposed. This method no doubt appealed on social welfare grounds, though it was also justified on the basis of efficient resource management; the return on public investment was expected to be greater in these areas (Cameron, 1971).

Although these two approaches to reassessment are valuable they stop short of fundamental questions. It may seem iconoclastic to suggest that the idea of *regional* welfare is ill-served by present policies, but to justify this view we would return to earlier sections of the paper—to the description of the elements of welfare geography and to the criteria for policies. Against those lists it is clear that the conventional approach occupies a very narrow part of the spectrum of possibilities. Future developments in the planning of industrial distributions will need to broaden the vision. But, to give effect to a new concept of regional welfare will also need much greater attention than hitherto given by regional analysts to the institutional environment that sets the limits on planning and policy-making.

CONCLUSION

Poverty, deprivation and inequity are issues that, rightly, are dominated by national policies. But evidence is abundant that they also have a geographical dimension and that spatial policies are able to usefully supplement general ones. However, since all intervention has an opportunity cost it is essential to ensure that spatial policies are effective. It will never be possible to examine opportunity-costs exhaustively; too many dimensions would always be involved. It is however, desirable that policies should continuously be subjected to far greater critical evaluation than is generally the case—and this includes policies of 'doing nothing'.

In recent years we have witnessed a shift towards an advocacy of regional policies that are more sensitive to the current and projected needs of urban systems rather than approaches based on blanket designation of assistance and controls (Goddard, 1974; Chisholm, 1976). The basis for this argument has been that such an approach would be more flexible in the face of the major cyclical and structural changes such as those being experienced in the 1970s. We would go further, however, and assert that policies based on the needs of individual towns and cities, as well as the needs of whole systems of towns and cities, permits all of the different welfare criteria to be pursued more satisfactorily than at present.

The institutional demands posed by this shift in opinion are, of course, much greater than those posed by the conventional approach to regional policy. Not least it would pose problems of administrative articulation among activities that are generally the responsibility of quite separate government departments and agencies. This is, however, a problem being tackled by local governments through the adoption of corporate management techniques and there may be significant lessons in this for higher levels of government.

In any event, re-evaluation of regional policy is not something that can be overlooked. Otherwise 'legislating against geography' becomes a matter of faith rather than an act of confidence.

NOTE

1. The term 'public goods' is generally taken to mean goods for which there is 'joint supply' and from whose consumption no person is excluded by pricing policies. 'Merit goods', though not hitherto given much attention by economists, are, nevertheless of crucial importance in debates on public finance and resource allocation policy. They are defined as those goods (and services) whose consumption is considered so meritorious that they are provided in excess of the rate of consumption chosen voluntarily by individuals in the market place. A corollary exists in the form of 'merit bads'—excessive consumption of detrimental goods (Musgrave and Musgrave, 1976). Two points arise from these definitions. First, and especially in the case of merit goods and 'bads', there may be very few goods that fall unequivocally into these categories. Working definitions ultimately will reflect political value-judgements. Secondly, the dividing lines between merit goods, public goods and private goods are not always clearcut. In addition, it is likely that merit goods will also be public goods, though the reverse is not necessarily true.

REFERENCES

Blondel, J. (1969). *An Introduction To Comparative Government*, London, Weidenfeld & Nicholson.

Bower, J. (1974). 'On the amoral organization'. In R. Marris (ed.) *The Corporate Society*, (Macmillan, London, pp. 178–213.

Cameron, G. (1971). *Regional Economic Development: The Federal Role*, Johns Hopkins University Press, London.

Cameron, G. (1974). 'Regional economic policy in the United Kingdom'. In M. E. C. Sant (ed.) *Regional Policy and Planning for Europe*, Saxon House, Farnborough, pp. 1–41.

Chisholm, M. J. (1971). 'In search of a basis for location theory: micro-economics or welfare economics'. *Progress in Geography*, **3**, 111–133.

Chisholm, M. J. (1976). 'Regional policies in an era of slow population growth and higher unemployment'. *Regional Studies*, **10**, 2, 201–213.

Cox, K. (1973). *Conflict, Power and Politics in the City*, McGraw-Hill, New York.

Donnison, D. V. (1974). 'Regional policies and regional government'. In M. E. C. Sant (ed.) *Regional Policy and Planning for Europe*, Saxon House, Farnborough, pp. 187–199.

Goddard, J. B. (1974). 'The national system of cities as a framework for urban and regional policy'. In M. E. C. Sant (ed.) *Regional Policy and Planning for Europe*, Saxon House, Farnborough, pp. 101–127.

Green, D. H. (1977). 'Industrialists information levels of regional incentives'. *Regional Studies*, **11**, 1, 7–18.

Hagerstrand, T. (1977). 'The impact of social organisation and environment upon the time-use of individuals and households'. In A. Kuklinski (ed.) *Social Issues in Regional Policy and Regional Planning*, Mouton, The Hague, pp. 59–67.

Hall, P. G. (1974). *Urban and Regional Planning*, Penguin, London.

Hotelling, H. (1929). 'Stability in competition'. *Economic Journal*, **39**, 41–57.
Knox, P. L. (1975). *Social Well-Being: A Spatial Perspective*, Oxford University, London.
Linge, G. (1967). 'Governments and the location of secondary industry in Australia'. *Economic Geography*, **43**, 43–63.
Litchfield, N. (1970). 'Evaluation methodology of urban and regional plans: a review'. *Regional Studies*, **4**, 2, 151–165.
Moore, B. and Rhodes, J. (1974). 'The effects of regional economic policy in the United Kingdom'. In M. E. C. Sant (ed.) *Regional Policy and Planning for Europe*, Saxon House, Farnborough, pp. 43–69.
Moseley, M. J. (1974). *Growth Centres in Spatial Planning*, Pergamon, Oxford.
Moseley, M. J. *et al.* (1977). *Rural Transport and Accessibility*, Centre of East Anglian Studies, University of East Anglia. Norwich.
Musgrave, R. A. and Musgrave, P. B. (1976). *Public Finance in Theory and Practice* McGraw-Hill, New York.
Myrdal, G. (1957). *Economic Theory and Underdevelopment*, Duckworth, London.
Pahl, R. (1971). 'Poverty and the urban system'. In M. J. Chisholm and G. Manners (eds.) *Spatial Policy Problems of the British Economy*, Cambridge University Press, Cambridge, pp. 126–145.
Rostow, W. W. (1971). *Politics and the Stages of Growth*, Cambridge University Press, Cambridge.
Royal Commission on the Distribution of the Industrial Population (1940). *Report* (Cmnd 6153), HMSO, London.
Sant, M. E. C. (1975). *Industrial Movement and Regional Development: The British Case*, Pergamon, Oxford.
Smith, D. M. (1977). *Human Geography: A Welfare Approach*, Edward Arnold, London.
Starkie, D. N. M. (1976). 'The spatial dimensions of pollution policy'. In J. T. Coppock and W. R. D. Sewell (eds.) *Spatial Dimensions of Public Policy*, Pergamon, Oxford, pp. 148–163.
Stewart, A. (1974). 'Objectives for regional policy—the view from industry'. In M. E. C. Sant (ed.), *Regional Policy and Planning for Europe*, Saxon House, Farnborough, pp. 225–234.
Townroe, P. M. (1971). *Industrial Location Decisions: A Study in Management Behaviour*, Centre for Urban and Regional Studies, University of Birmingham, Occasional Paper No. 15.
Westaway, J. (1974). 'The spatial hierarchy of business organisations and its implications for the British urban system'. *Regional Studies*, **8**, 2, 145–155.

Author Index

Subject Index